The Jesuits

Other books by the same author:

Catholic Recusancy in the West Riding of Yorkshire, 1558-1791
Northern Catholics
Catholic Recusancy in York, 1558-1791
The Handle and the Axe
Post-Reformation Catholicism in East Yorkshire
St. Peter's, Yaxley: the History of a Parish

The Jesuits

J. C. H. Aveling

DORSET PRESS

New York

First published in the United States of America
in 1982 by Stein & Day Publishers Inc.

This edition published by Dorset Press,
a division of Marboro Books Corporation,
by arrangement with
Stein & Day Publishers Inc.
1987 Dorset Press

ISBN 0-88029-133-8

Printed in the United States of America

M   9   8   7   6   5   4   3   2

Contents

Introduction

'. . . the Padre Eterno sniffed and said, 'a Jesuit! and what,
in the name of goodness, is that?'

(Frederick Rolfe, *About the Heresy of Fra Serafico*, in *Stories
Toto Told Me*, London, 1969.)

In early August 1945, full of expectation and fright, I rang the
front doorbell of the Jesuit house of studies in Oxford, Campion
Hall. I was an Anglo-Catholic priest, until recently a novice in the
Anglican Community of the Resurrection at Mirfield, seeking
reception into the Roman Catholic Church, and had been invited
to stay at Campion Hall.

I had never before that day met a Jesuit in the flesh but had
long had a strong image in my mind of what to expect. Academic
history studies at school and at Cambridge had given the image
a solid, if dull and uninspiring, outline. According to my teachers
and the best textbooks the Society of Jesus was the spearhead of
the aggressive Catholic Counter-Reformation of the 16th and
17th centuries. In the 18th century it had suffered a mysterious
eclipse. But in the 19th and early 20th centuries it had revived
to become the main dynamic force in modern Roman Catholicism.
Its record of success was uniquely remarkable. Jesuits had rolled
back the powerful tide of 16th-century Protestantism. They had
brought back France, Austria, Czechoslovakia, South Germany
and Poland to Catholicism. They had planted vigorous 'underground' Catholic communities in solidly Protestant countries
like England and Holland and had narrowly failed to do the same
in Sweden and Russia. But that was only a small part of the
immense Jesuit achievement in early modern times. Simultaneously they had become the chosen confessors and advisers
of almost every Pope, most of the Cardinals, many bishops and
noblemen, and every Catholic sovereign. They had established a
huge network of secondary schools — Colleges — the organisation
and teaching in which was deeply admired by even their toughest
Protestant enemies. The Jesuits educated almost every Catholic

man of real consequence from St. John of the Cross, Cervantes and Galileo to Descartes, Molière, Corneille and Voltaire. As if that were not enough, the Jesuits had at the same time invented modern foreign missions. It was they who nearly converted Japan, established thriving missions in Peking and Delhi, and were to be found among the Canadian Hurons, in California, Mexico, Brazil, Chile and Peru, in the Philippines, Malacca and Macao, in West Africa and Damascus. Jesuits were brilliantly prominent in other fields, often unlikely ones. Their astronomers discreetly supported Galileo and taught his system to the Imperial Court of China. A good many features of the moon's surface still bear latinised forms of the names of the Jesuits who first discovered them. It was Jesuit missionaries who first introduced Europe to quinine, ipecacuanha and sasparilla, the use of umbrellas, and the delights of *Chinoiserie*. No respectable history of architecture can neglect the influence of Jesuit Baroque, or history of the theatre the influence of Jesuit drama and ballet.

And all this achievement, said the textbooks, was due to the unique character given to the Society by its founder, Ignatius Loyola. He discovered — where others merely tinkered with the problem or failed — a daring and effective way to conserve medieval Catholicism in very hostile environments by adopting the methods of its enemies. This required an extremely delicate balance of rigidity over essentials of tradition combined with extreme flexibility in adapting inessentials. For individual Jesuits it also meant an equally delicate balance between monastic contemplation and a life of great activity. The textbooks accounted just as easily and coolly for the extraordinary amount of violent abuse piled on the Society down its history by a great variety of enemies, Catholic as well as Protestant. No Catholic religious Order has ever endured so many martyrdoms and imprisonments and so many forcible expulsions from whole countries as the Jesuits. Obviously, rootedly conservative Catholics and anti-religious liberals would both regard the Jesuit balance as a cheat. Strong Protestants would inevitably judge Jesuits as far more insidious opponents than straightforward Catholics. Lax or ambitious Catholics would abhor and fear the great influence of the Society in high places.

The writers of textbooks on 19th and early 20th century history paid relatively little attention to Church matters. Manifestly at this period neither the Catholic Church as a whole nor the Jesuits in particular achieved obvious and glittering public successes. The writers were therefore distinctly at a loss to account for the undoubted fact that violent abuse and maltreatment of Jesuits mounted to a record level between the 1830s and 1880s. They could only suggest that the Society was now exercising great power and influence in hidden and unspectacular ways.

I was a product of the inter-war years. By that time old-fashioned liberal and Protestant hatred of the Jesuits had lost most of its original force and reality. I could, no more than my textbook writers, understand properly, or share in, that old feeling. I had not been brought up a Catholic, so I did not even have that basis for understanding the old Catholic tradition of hostility toward the Jesuits. (But by the 1930s that old tradition was dying fast.) So I was innocent of any prejudice against Jesuits. Moreover the atmosphere of undergraduate life in Cambridge in 1935-8 inevitably drew me into the prevailing anti-liberal political and religious mood. I readily rediscovered a traditionalist Christianity for myself, and then a reactionary form of Anglo-Catholicism. For me and others like me, the very dry bones of textbook Church history burst into life. My new ideal of a 'Catholicism' both reactionary and in a sort of revolutionary revolt against modern thought and living dictated my reading. This ideal and my romantic imagination gave my image of Catholicism, and my textbook image of the Jesuits, colour and glamour. Francis Thompson's *Life of St. Ignatius Loyola* and Evelyn Waugh's *Edmund Campion* helped, eked out by copies of the spiritual writings of the Jesuits Grou and de Caussade which I bought, but never read through. Books on modern Jesuit life were much harder to come by. The works of Martin Darcy, Cyril Martindale and Archbishop Goodier seemed to bear out fully my predisposition to believe that Jesuits still had a sort of effortless superiority in the fields of learning and spirituality. But O'Rahilly's *Life of Father Willie Doyle SJ* pulled me up short. Doyle was a Dublin Jesuit with none of the polish of Darcy and Martindale. His type of Jesuit piety was like that of St. Patrick, St. Cuthbert or the Fathers of the desert: it was committed, with a shattering roughness and directness. I was fascinated by his endless counting of acts of penance (on a bicycle meter hidden in his pocket), by his sacrificial missions to gaol-birds, condemned murderers, prostitutes and, finally, to Irish troops in the trenches in France in 1915-16, where Doyle met his death. By this time my own personal preferences were for Catholic monastic Orders — seen in an equally romantic, bookish way. But I certainly reserved the place of honour in my image of Catholicism in general for the Jesuits: they were the quintessence of the Church.

All this accounts for my mixture of expectation and alarm on the doorstep of Campion Hall. Three weeks later, I left the Hall and Oxford as a Catholic. My short stay had not destroyed or even dinted my home-made image of the Jesuits. Indeed I retained it for some years more, but rather as one keeps something valuable on a shelf without adverting to it much. But the impressions of the Jesuits I gathered at Oxford had puzzled me: they forced me to realise that the Jesuit reality was somehow related to the image but unrelated to it also. The reality seemed at once more earthy and yet more mysterious than my image. I began to realise how little I knew about the Jesuits.

A first impression I gained was of ordinariness. My original undergraduate image of the life of clergy and religious Orders had been tempered and weathered already by periods of residence in Anglican religious institutions, ending up with Mirfield. Yet, as I first entered Campion Hall, I did expect something very extraordinary. In fact I found the physical set-up astonishingly like that of Mirfield: the same rather slovenly fittings, institution atmosphere, brown paint, smell of floor-polish, many clear evidences that it was an all-male 'bachelor' household. It had the physical atmosphere of an old-fashioned Temperance hotel. In other ways the house was very like a boarding school or army barracks. The inmates had long ago been drilled in the many rules: they were second nature. In general they kept them automatically. In practice they had long ago slipped into cutting corners, disregarding rules on occasion. Duties tended to be got over with remarkable expedition and matter-of-factness. The Latin Mass (to which I was still unaccustomed) was said by most priests with a speed and efficiency I found astonishing. The evening Litany or Rosary was said like machine-gun fire. The Jesuits themselves, like the Mirfield Fathers, came in all sorts — except that the Jesuit spectrum of types seemed a good deal wider. There were the usual old men put out to grass, infirm and sometimes distinctly eccentric. Such was a Fr. Cuthbert, who had been engaged for years in writing a book on Machiavelli. The floor of his room, the table tops and the chair seats seemed permanently covered with typewritten sheets, yellowing and dusty. He swept papers on to the floor so that we could sit on his bed. Piles of books, newspapers and file boxes lay everywhere. Then there were donnish young Jesuits, preoccupied and distraught about completing their degree theses. There were student Jesuits on holiday from other houses. They were clearly not all nicely standardised products of Society training: as I first entered the Hall, one of them was regaling others with a mildly blue story. There were American Jesuits, wearing a some-what different gown from their English colleagues. There was a rather strained-looking Dutch student Jesuit, who, though his English was good, kept apart from the general conversations. Eventually I talked with him a good deal. He said bluntly that English members of all religious Orders were peculiar, easy-going and slack. English Jesuits, he thought were regarded on the Continent as 'not quite members of the Society'. Lastly there were administrators. The Procurator had been told off to give me my formal instruction and supervise my reception into the Church. He was, or pretended to be, much overworked and fixed the time for our daily session at eleven o'clock at night. At that time, for three or four nights, as we both nodded with sleep, he droned through the Penny Catechism, periodically interjecting that it was a waste of time since I must know it all. Finally he broke off the course and cheerfully committed himself to 'the formality' of assuring the Archbishop of Birmingham that I had received thirty-six hours of instruction. Thus all in all I had plenty of evidence that the Society consisted largely of ordinary mortals reacting in very ordinary ways.

My other impression was more confused and hesitant. It was that, in spite of the human fallibility, there was a strong element of difference between Jesuits and other religious and secular priests. My friend the Dutch Jesuit complained at length that in Holland (and, he gathered, everywhere, even in England) out-siders always treated Jesuits with caution, suspiciously. 'Why', he said plaintively, 'are we different?' He felt that there was a very old and deep-seated gulf which neither side felt able, or disposed to bridge. The result was, he felt, the Society's very strong habit of exclusiveness and secrecy about its affairs. The same evening I received some sort of confirmation of what he said. Hugh Montgomery was the only other non-Jesuit staying in the Hall. He was a Catholic convert of years standing, an aristocrat and recently retired from the Diplomatic Service. He was a very large man, short-sighted and extremely physically clumsy. After 1945 he made an abortive effort to become a Benedictine, and died some years ago as a secular priest. He told me that he would never become a Jesuit. Yet he was obviously fascinated by the Society. 'If I were in a real jam,' he boomed, 'I would never go to confession to anyone except a Jesuit.' He spoke, he assured me, from long experience of confessors of all kinds. I was impressed. I told myself that it was absurd for me, a green outsider, to expect to make any valid judgement on Jesuits on the strength of three weeks at Campion Hall. No doubt the mere humanness and 'Englishry' so evident there was on the surface only and, hidden underneath it, was that marvellous and unique spiritual mastery. The books said it was there. The Society's past record must mean something. Hugh Montgomery must be right.

* * *

Almost thirty-five years have passed since my first introduction to 'the Jesuit problem'. In the claustrophobic world of Catholicism (and the Society of Jesus) they have been exciting and unsettling years. Their events and movements are far too recent, far too tied up with the reputations of great institutions and persons still alive for their history to be sketched in more than broad outlines. From 1945 to the early 1960s to all outward appearances the Catholic Church suddenly became healthier, more dynamic and more meaningful to the outside world than at any time since the later 17th century. The religious Orders reported their biggest influx of vocations ever recorded. The Society of Jesus profited more than any other Order: its numbers swelled to a record level of well over 36,000. It had become by far the largest of the Orders. Again, to all outward appearances, this boom reflected a widespread post-war disillusionment with modern society and a strengthening of the pre-war religious traditionalism. A handful of discerning Catholic thinkers asserted that the boom was a fragile, superficial affair, that, like the hard crust over the top of a temporarily quiescent volcano, it concealed a pent-up mass of molten lava — of liberal reaction and angry dissent. These thinkers were largely disregarded. Hence when the Catholic volcano erupted in the mid-1960s, during and after the second Vatican Council (1962-5), the sheer violence of the eruption of criticism, change, unsettlement and plain disorder shocked even the liberal Catholic leaders. There began a massive flow out of the religious Orders and secular priesthood into lay life or even out of the Church. Even worse, there was a mounting, almost hysterical loss of confidence in their institutions and in their future among clergy. The Jesuits were naturally very hard-hit. By 1977 their numbers were down to 24,000 and they were, significantly, closing down noviciate and student houses. The Campion Hall which I had visited knew great vicissitudes between my departure thence and the 1970s. In the 1950s it was uncomfortably crowded and on the crest of a wave: in the later 1960s it was finding difficulties in keeping going. At one stage almost the entire student body *en masse* left the Society.

Not surprisingly in recent years the public image of the Society has tended to grow pale and indistinct. It now seems to arouse astonishingly little reaction — of admiration, dislike or real interest — in any quarter. That now unfashionable group, the anti-Popery Protestants still thunder against the Pope and the Church of Rome but never mention the Jesuits. The columns of Catholic periodicals still contain vigorous, even ill-tempered, criticisms. Occasionally the target is individual Jesuits, charged with either radicalism or traditionalism, both of which are represented in the ranks of the Society. But the Society as a whole is never attacked or defended. Secular newspapers still have sharp noses for hints of extremism, intrigue or scandal in any religious group. Their references to the Society are rare and brief: for instance departures from the Society of well-known priests, Jesuit statistics and the Chinese Government's invitation to the Society to return to Shanghai. It is a long time since journalists gave up bothering to speculate about Jesuit influences at papal conclaves. The only recent exception to this disinterest was the extensive reporting of the strange circumstances surrounding the death in Paris of an eminent Jesuit theologian, Jean Daniélou. But even here there was little stress on his admittedly then thin (he had been made a Cardinal) connection with the Society.

Meanwhile the Jesuits themselves seem to have slipped into a grey indistinctness of character. To the eye of a casual outsider they appear, in dress, mannerisms and occupations not very markedly different from the modern-minded clergy of any Order, or, indeed, of any denomination. Except perhaps in some more rootedly conservative areas of the Society, the training of novices and students has become a good deal less stereotyped, regimental and monastic. Jesuit student life is less confined than it was. An intelligent student is set to do a large part of his studies in houses containing non-Jesuit teachers and students, even on the campus of a state university. An able Jesuit teacher may well be a university lecturer drawing a state salary. Jesuit secondary schools, once so famous and numerous, are today, at least in Europe and America, relatively few. In them lay teachers (even women) outnumber Jesuits. The schools have a much less intensely pious, shut-in atmosphere. The same is true of Jesuit parish churches and missions. They are no longer museums of Jesuit Baroque, cluttered with statues, relics, side-altars, much-frequented confessional boxes, frequent Benedictions and elaborate Devotions and parish sodalities. The modern Catholic 'liturgical revolution' and a very sharp decline in the practice of Confession — and a change of taste — have effected a transformation here almost as great as that which has (due to the post-war death of colonialism and rise of indigenous Churches) happened to Jesuit foreign missions.

Today, as in all great Catholic Orders and the major Christian denominations, a large slice of the tightly stretched Jesuit manpower is swallowed in the maw of modernised administration, paperwork and 'committee government'. Thus an able American Jesuit may find employment as, say, full-time Vice-Provincial for Formation, or as Counsellor to Father General in Rome. A Basque Jesuit (long an exile from Spain) could be Director of Inter-Provincial Work in the South-East Asian Assistancy. A still larger slice of manpower gets entangled in those modern inventions now favoured by all Christian institutions, 'work-teams'. They research into religious sociology and statistics, advise on policy, research into (and train others in) a multiplicity of experimental ventures. There are catechetics, social work, psychiatry and counselling, marriage guidance, encounter groups, the direction of prayer groups, charismatic and pente-costalist groups. A sizeable new class of Jesuits commutes round these operations while taking retraining courses and post-graduate degrees. Thus an American Jesuit may, say, be a team-worker in Tertianship, in the Institute of Jesuit Sources at St. Louis or the Institute of Jesuit Spirituality in Rome, or be Apostolic Coordinator of charismatic groups in San Francisco. A French colleague may lecture in the Institut Catholique in Paris, work in an editorial team for *Etudes* or *Action Populaire*, join the Centre Culturel at Chantilly or be seconded to the Jesuit Biblical Institute in Rome. Everywhere he is nowadays liable to find laymen and laywomen increasingly sharing in the teamwork.

Of recent years the Society has, to some degree, significantly modified its traditional rules of rigid secrecy about its internal affairs. The Jesuit *Constitutions*, for centuries printed (like the Society's other books of rules) privately and for limited circulation among members, are now on sale to the public. Today the shelving of all major public libraries contains the fifty large volumes of the continuing series of the *Monumenta Historica Societatis Jesu*. This is a vast compendium of published private records of the early, formative days of the Society. An increasing number of Jesuit archives in Rome and elsewhere have recently been opened to outsiders: hitherto they were shut even to the generality of Jesuits.

This new attitude of openness, and the effects of the training of some Jesuit historians in the spirit and techniques of modern research, has started to produce marked changes in Jesuit historical writing. In the past, with few exceptions, their historians, were untrained and had very little access to archives. The superiors had what then seemed to be excellent reasons for a distinct distrust of history. The calls on their manpower were so great that historical writing came very low on the official list of priorities. Archives were primitive, dirty, uncatalogued store-rooms. Their contents were frequently scattered or lost when persecution of the Society led to confiscation of its houses and expulsion of the inmates. Moreover the old Society had long been accustomed to, even trained to, a posture of defensiveness. Ordinary prudence seemed to dictate locking up archives and using Jesuit historians largely as defenders of the good name of the Society from calumnies. Hence Jesuit historians automatically worked within the narrow bounds of officially-approved traditions. Today they are emerging from the old catacomb. It is not surprising that some still shrink from the unaccustomed glare of the light of day, and others are inebriated by it and launch out into radical reassessments of Jesuit history, treating tradition as so much legend.

The Jesuit 'new historical writing' is still thin in quantity. But it is contributing to the demolition of the old tradition of the Society's uniqueness and separateness. Today all fields of Church history are being radically reassessed: the history of New Testament times, of the early Church, of the early Papacy and episcopate, of the ancient monastic Orders, and of the formative years of the great Protestant denominations. It is becoming clear that the Jesuits are common clay: they are not alone exempt from the process of demythologisation. The new historical writing has also undoubtedly increased the modern sense of insecurity within the Society. Its 'structures' which, for so long, appeared inevitable and unquestionable, are now seen as products of past situations long gone, 'museum-pieces' ripe for abolition or extensive change.

Similarly modern tensions and quarrels within the Society are no longer systematically, as a matter of policy, concealed or played down. This change of attitude has, like the 'historical revolution', not come easily to Jesuits (especially administrators) bred another way. There always were 'apostates' — ex-Jesuits or ex-pupils — who published startling 'revelations' about the Society's inner life. Before the early 19th century these inspired little confidence, since they lacked objectivity and knowledge. James Joyce's *Portrait of the Artist as a Young Man* and George Tyrrell's autobiography and letters, however, had both, even if they did no more than cast thin torchlight beams into a vast, dark, mysterious cavern. With the traumatic 1960s came broader beams of light cast by serving Jesuits. Cyril Martindale SJ, in his memoirs of his colleagues Bernard Vaughan and R.H.J. Steuart, was frankly critical of some features of the Society. The letters of the French Jesuit, Teilhard de Chardin (published well after his death in 1955 and not by his colleagues), were still more sharply critical. Nowadays Jesuit biographers of dead colleagues increasingly breach the Society's old canons of discretion. On occasion the editors of Jesuit magazines like *America, The Month, Etudes* and *Stimmen der Zeit* have recently revealed clashes of view within the Society. In the old days rebellious-minded Jesuits furtively circulated duplicated radical articles among trustworthy friends. They had no hope of getting official permission for publication and their secret operations sooner or later led to delation to the General, exposure and their expulsion from the Society. Nowadays things are rather different. Eminent Jesuits with a proven record of loyalty can get permission to publish their lectures to colleagues on 'the Jesuit dilemma': the lectures can be brutally frank. The English Province's magazine of piety, *The Way*, recently published intimate documents of the 1974-5 Jesuit General Congregation in Rome. These included frank, if generalised, admissions of low morale and disorders and a stinging rebuke from Pope Paul VI. The Pope said he had sent similar rebukes to the General privately in earlier years. *The Way* then published supplements full of Jesuit contributions to the internal debate on reform: some were anodyne, but some blunt.

This new Jesuit openness has limits. Some are due to ingrained habit, others to the natural instinct for self-preservation of an old and great institution. But enough light has been cast for outsiders to realise that the Society is fighting to find a sense of identity, and, indeed, for its very life. In 1974-6 an American Catholic journalist reported a saying in Rome that once the Society saved the Church, now it seemed that the Church must save the Society. Paul VI certainly thought so. What he called 'the insecurity', the lack of balance and grip, of the modern

Society frightened him. From 1966 to his death he insisted that the old image and function in the Church of the Jesuits was unchangeable. They were 'born to be' the essential agents of an autocratic Papacy, helping the barque of Peter to ride intact through 20th-century storms which he thought no worse than their 16th-century counterparts. So, like Caesar's wife, Jesuits must be utterly disciplined, supremely orthodox, supremely able and obviously holy. Like the Papacy and Church at large the Society must weather the storm by giving itself a new look: but it must not transform itself into something else. Hence in December 1974 and again in 1975 he lectured the General Congregation on its history. His view of it was strongly traditionalist. He flatly refused to allow even the modest reforms proposed by the Congregation.

The Pope was addressing, not the Society's rank and file, but its upper echelons. They were obviously soldiering on, putting on as brave a face as they could, and assuming that the Society could display its legendary ability to surmount crises and balance successfully on the tight-rope between tradition and change. One of them admitted in print in 1967 that, of the four most common views on the Jesuit dilemma current in the Society, one was that 'in the process of historical evolution the Society is due to disintegrate and decay and may well come to be regarded as useless'. He did not agree. Others frankly doubted the Pope's tactics. They felt the Society would never have a chance to fulfil its old vocation in the long term unless, here and now (and for many years to come) its superiors were allowed much more room for manoeuvre. Bernard Lonergan, the Society's most prestigious academic thinker since the 1950s, has diagnosed the crisis as something much deeper than a new assault of the old liberalism on an obsolete Society. The trouble, he thinks, is a massive 'cultural change', 'alienation', of a universality, scale and completeness never before seen in Church history. It has rendered meaningless and irrelevant to human concerns the great systems of thought relied on alike by Christians, Humanists and Communists. All are suffering a crisis of credibility and faith. The building up of new systems meaningful in the new developing culture will take many years. Meanwhile Jesuits, like everyone else, must flounder and be content with provisional hypotheses. But here, Lonergan concludes, is the supreme justification for, and test of, the traditional Jesuit vocation. Here — even if the proportions of change are novel and disconcertingly huge — is just that sort of emergency the Society was designed to cope with — and it only.

Meanwhile Karl Rahner, the Society's most respected thinker bred in earlier times, had floundered outside the lecture-rooms. In the traumatic crisis years of the 1950s and 1960s he toured groups of anxious German Jesuits trying to explain what was happening to them and put some spirit into them. He had to urge superiors to be thankful if their few remaining students had not rejected Catholic dogmas outright, while asserting that they were simply 'Christians' and found Catholic dogma meaningless. He had pleaded with Jesuit hard-line traditionalists (especially numerous then in Spain) not to separate themselves from the main body of the Society. He had pleaded with colleagues about to quit the Society to think again. The crisis, he said, was so universal that it was an illusion to imagine that 'reality' could only be found outside the Society and traditional Catholic institutions, in novel secular Institutes, in Catholic lay life, or outside the Church. One year Rahner was insisting that formal Jesuit praying would have to give way to experimental prayer: the next year he pleaded for the retention of at least some of 'the old solidity' of formal prayer. By 1973 he was broadcasting his anxieties in the pages of a national newspaper, the *Frankfurter Allgemeine Zeitung*. The occasion was the bicentenary of the papal suppression of the Society in 1773. The resurrected Society after 1814, he wrote, had never recovered its old dynamism and sense of purpose. The present crisis might well prove the final blow to a long-failing Church and Society. By the 1990s he fore-saw the Church as a *diaspora* of small, linked congregations, stripped to the bone of ceremonies, structures and material resources, pluralistic in thought and very humble. The Society, Rahner thought, would survive as one congregation among many, since it did produce true Christians. In 1978 he published what he regarded as his last word on the Jesuit dilemma: imagining what Ignatius Loyola would say to the Society today. The concluding passage is a quotation from Ignatius's own writings, that if he heard that the Society was dead, he would know it was no longer needed and would, after ten minutes of prayer, dismiss the matter from his mind. Rahner's view of the Society's future contrasts with both Paul VI's desperate plea for 'business as usual' by the 1980s and Lonergan's hopes of spectacular triumphs for Jesuit creativity and tactical skill in the 21st century.

Today the senior members of the Society are nearing the twentieth year of their crisis. They must find it hard to cast a balance of their assets and liabilities. The crisis has revealed that they have, in every Province, a hard core of the unwavering — of the temperamental conformists, of last-ditch traditionalists and of simple-minded pious souls. But few of these are really sensitive to the depths of the crisis. Again, the Society has gained by the loss of much of its human and institutional dead wood: in 1978 Rahner insisted bluntly that it could, with profit, afford to lose still more. But it has also lost far too many of its ablest and most original minds. Even the Jesuits could not keep their nerves extended at crisis-pitch for two decades on end: inevitably the years of strain have had a case-hardening and anaesthetic effect which is psychologically merciful but soporific for the mind.

Perhaps the most saddening feature of the crisis for older Jesuits must have been the wilting under pressure of so many of their students and novices. This has produced an overdue reassessment of training methods. But it will be a long time before the 'experiments in formation' prove their efficacy. They may not, in the end, prove better than the old methods which, in some Provinces at least, oddly combined extreme formalism with a pragmatic liberalism. (Witness Dennis Meadows who, as an English Jesuit student in the early 1900s, was instructed to avoid formal 'manifestations of conscience' and to substitute active work for formal meditation.) Early in the century George Tyrrell complained that the Jesuits 'press-ganged' raw adolescents from their schools into the noviciate. The decline of the schools has removed much of this danger. At the end of 1978 the Society was able to report a decided up-swing in recruitment. But even this development, though ostensibly heartening, has its drawbacks. The new novices must come into an insecure Society from an even more insecure world outside. They come too late, and in very insufficient numbers, to prevent a further drastic reduction in the size of the Society over the next decades. The clergy, like all professional men, are nowadays at grave risk in middle age from the diseases of stress. The sizeable body of ageing Jesuits recruited during the halcyon post-war years cannot find adequate replacement in the very small number recruited between 1962 and 1977. Meanwhile the general crisis is no nearer resolution. It certainly will not be resolved by the traditionalist reaction now growing in the Church. That is likely to be no more than a temporary lull in the storm. The history of the Church and the Society since the 16th century has seen a long succession of crises, followed by reactions, and then by renewed and deeper periods of crisis. The reactions have invariably been accompanied by upsurges in recruitment to the Orders. The identity and future of the Society still hangs, and will long hang, in the balance.

*   *   *

When I left Campion Hall in 1945 I was still generally disposed to regard the Jesuits as an essential, central feature of real Catholicism and its most dynamic element. I also had the beginnings of an impression that the relationship between the public image (and professed ideals) of a religious Order and its realities could be very complex. But during the next twenty years my interest in the Society faded away. I became a Benedictine. Ostensibly this, in itself, should have accounted for my loss of interest. The Catholic religious Orders are rather like regiments in an army. They have their own traditional loyalties and family life and hence many inducements to be exclusive and the rivals of other Orders. The English Benedictine Congregation had special traditional reasons for disliking the Jesuits. It was founded in the early 17th century from men who were either hostile to the Society or ex-pupils of it in violent revolt against their mentors. In later years the Benedictines fought a good many brisk actions with Jesuits over mission areas in England. Even in the 1950s these old battles were fresh in the minds of the older monks. But by my time the younger monks felt no such hostility. Our contacts with Jesuits were fairly frequent and cordial. From our house of studies in Oxford we hob-nobbed with Jesuit students at Campion Hall: on Saturday nights most of us went regularly to Confession at the neighbourhood church of St. Aloysius, which happened to be staffed by Jesuits. Jesuits visited our monastery fairly regularly as guests or retreat-givers. Some members of our community had Jesuit relations or had been educated in Jesuit schools. As I became increasingly involved in historical research, teaching and writing, these pursuits led me to visit a number of Jesuit houses including Stonyhurst, Farm Street and Richmond. As a retreat-giver I often visited convents closely connected with the Society. In all these Jesuit contacts I encounteed numerous oddities. A proletarian Jesuit acquaintance introduced me to the sharp distinction in the Society between 'old Stonyhurst Boys' and lesser breeds. I came across a rustic Jesuit mission used to house priests who were mentally or physically handicapped. Farm Street seemed bleak and institutional and its occupants, mostly then well-publicised

Jesuit 'stars', supremely ordinary. Stonyhurst was in every way a museum piece. The blind devotion of some older nuns to 'the Fathers' seemed eerie and unhealthy. But, at the time, none of these oddities caused me any other feeling than mild surprise: I had met all these sorts of human eccentricity abundantly among Benedictines.

My distinct lack of interest in, and curiosity about, the Jesuits during these years was due to my absorption partly in studies and teaching, and partly in what then seemed to be a peculiar and private dilemma of the Benedictines. The 'Benedictine image' is a double one. Its 'low life' form is of a Pharisee, a religious hypocrite, who, while making a great show of austerity, is at best an overeating idler and at worst a libertine. I am reminded of a Victorian monastery in which the monks asked their abbot for real work: he replied, 'You have the choir and the refectory. What more do you want?' This 'low life' Benedictine image has lasted well. Partridge's *Dictionary of Historical Slang* has the entry: '*monk* — a term of contempt: low: from *c.* 1860.' On the other hand the 'good image' of a Benedictine for the monks themselves and their supporters is of an enclosed contemplative prolonging into the alien modern world a primitive and medieval way of life. This romantic image is thought of as either a spiritual absolute utterly detached from the ever-changing course of social and economic progress, or as the absolute indissolubly united to a primitive, agricultural form of society. Since at least the later Middle Ages most monks have been obsessed by this 'good image'. There have been countless monastic 'reforms' seeking to 'return to primitive observance'. Also, repeatedly, the consciences of monks have secretly condemned their own common sense modernisations. What we called P.O. tendencies drove some monks away to unashamedly medievalist monastic Congregations, and others (including the historian David Knowles) to a kind of eremitical existence. Some insisted on monastic forms: others were barely willing to think of themselves as monks. Some thought privately that our life was play-acting: some pragmatists were content; and some hankered after turning the monastery into a charismatic commune. But we all thought of our dilemma as a kind of family weakness, a discreditable secret not to be aired in public. It was this habit of mind which prevented us realising at first that the general Church crisis of the 1960s was our dilemma writ large right across all the structures, material and doctrinal, of the whole Church. Indeed, when I left the Benedictines in 1967 I still did not realise this fact clearly.

Meanwhile my Church history research and writing had confronted me with another local form of the general dilemma. If monks were haunted, confused and upset by clinging to a false image of monasticism, clerical historians were just as deluded by their image of Church history. This regarded Church history as the passage through a chronically changeable, inconstant world of its one unchanging focus, the Catholic Church, a perfect society, the vehicle of the Spirit. From this point of view the wounds the world inflicted on the Church and apparent changes in Church structures were superficial 'crosses to the main chance'. It followed that the only true interpreters of Church history must be the ministers of the Spirit, priests. 'Materialistic' secular historians were to be avoided. The influence of social and economic factors in Church history could safely be ignored or soft-pedalled. Historical research almost seemed unnecessary — unless it could help to dot the 'i's and cross the 't's of the official interpretation. I began my Church history research in this spirit. But I gradually began to doubt the validity of the whole 'image'. By 1967 I was unable to avoid feeling that Bayle, the 18th-century French thinker, was right when he wrote:

> 'Writing history is no suitable function for a priest; it is a function that requires objectivity in everything, and a priest can be objective about nothing . . .'

My Church history research therefore was beginning to make me realise the full dimensions of the Church's crisis.

Simultaneously my researches and teaching directed my attention back to Jesuit history. The textbooks and Church history tradition gave the Society pride of place (after the Papacy) in modern history. In what sense, if at all, was this really true? On the one hand this appeared to be 'a good Jesuit image'. For the last two hundred years the Society had certainly not occupied a dominant position in the Church. But on the other hand the evidence I had available to me suggested that, whatever the shortcomings of the Society itself, its influence on others by action and hostile reaction against it did seem a constant and dominant feature: 'Jesuitism' was something far bigger than the Society. Almost every historical field I happened to look into had 'Jesuitism' squarely across it. This was true of Church history but also true of modern secular European history and English political history. I had to admit that English Benedictine history owed much more than I had realised to Jesuit influences and Benedictine counter-action. Read a modern study of 19th-century

European literature and you will be astonished at the impact of the Jesuits, their 'image' and 'Jesuitism'. Jesuit characters (idealised or caricatured) appear in profusion in novels and plays. 'Jesuitism' is treated very seriously by most major writers.

Naturally I then looked for some published full historical treatment of 'the Jesuit phenomenon' — and was gravely disappointed. Jesuit historians, until very recently indeed, have limited themselves to research into minor details and into writing pious apologies for the Society's past. Non-Jesuit historians with exceedingly few exceptions have fought shy of poaching on clerical ground where, until recently, printed sources were rare, archive sources unavailable to students, and the ground heavily defended by the 'flak' of Jesuit defenders of the 'good image' of the Society. The exceptional non-Jesuit historians, Boehmer and Fülop-Miller, were brave and competent but had to rely greatly on intelligent guesses. My consuming interest in the Society's history is as great as theirs — probably greater, since I feel a personal involvement. If my historical ability does not equal theirs at least I now have more source material available to me than they had in their day.

1
The Jesuit Image in Literature

'It quite astonishes me how little the Jesuits are understood
or estimated generally . . .'

(J.H. Newman, 25 July 1847 to his sister)

At first sight it seems that the Jesuits and their activities have
made a deep and lasting impact on world languages. A little
research into this subject is an enlightening experience. The first
surprise is that the word jesuit occurs in the dictionaries of most
developed languages, even in Russian, Finnish, Norwegian,
Chinese and Japanese. A bigger surprise is the size of the crop
of derivatives coined from jesuit: for instance jesuitic, jesuitical,
jesuited, jesuitish, jesuitism, jesuitees, jesuitocracy. In English
dictionaries the crop contains almost twenty words, in French
nearly thirty. Then there are, scattered widely elsewhere in the
dictionaries, upward of a hundred other words connected with the
Society. In English there are Loyola (a name and also an adjective
coined by James Joyce in *Ulysses*), Ignatian, Exercises, Society,
College (for a secondary school) and a string of esoteric, private
Jesuit terms mostly used by Joyce in his *Portrait of the Artist
as a Young Man*: for instance rector, director, sodality, sodalist,
minister, prefect of studies, themes, and pandybat. French has
its equivalent terms like *décurion, examen, répétiteur, théologat,
salles des actions* and *battalions*.

The literary dictionaries give clues which have to be followed
up in more technical manuals. Medical dictionaries have jesuit's
bark, jesuit's nut, jesuit's powder, jesuit's drops, jesuit's tea,
jesuiting, to jesuit a patient, cinchona, ipecacuanha, mate and
tobacco. The first eight of these expressions have to do with
quinine and the legend that its medicinal use was first detected
by Jesuit missionaries in Peru when they dosed the Countess
of Cinchona. Oliver Cromwell was one of the scrupulous Protestants who preferred to let his fevers run their course rather
than be jesuited with quinine. Perhaps this religious prejudice
prevented apothecaries dubbing ipecacuanha jesuit's purge and

tobacco jesuit's weed. Both, according to legend, were first used medicinally by Jesuits in Paraguay and Brazil. The dictionaries of architecture and interior decoration yield another small crop of 'Jesuit words': *jésuitière* (the barracks-style adopted for large French and German Jesuit Colleges), *fenêtre jésuitique* (a one-way glass), *chinoiserie* (a fashion owing something to Jesuit missionaries in Peking, and to jesuit a church (transform its inner appearance from gothic to baroque). Histories of everyday things and costume add some more 'Jesuit words'. The umbrella just possibly owed its first vogue to the Peking missionaries. A *soprabito* (or *soprano*) was the 'winged' indoor gown worn once by all Jesuits in cold houses, and replaced by the wingless *roupe* everwhere except in conservative Provinces like England. Jesuit gowns were ladies' morning indoor coats copying the shape (if not the colour) of a Jesuit *soutane* and briefly fashionable just after the suppression of the Society in France in 1767. French peasants, brought up on Jesuit missionary tales, tended to call anything imported from other continents *jésuite*, including partridges (*poules jésuites*). In England literary people dubbed *rime brisée* jesuitical writing. Even the dictionaries of vulgar, low-life expressions add their modest quota of 'Jesuit words'. In English taverns a jesuit was a homosexual, the jesuits' fraternity the 'gay' underworld, and the expression to box the jesuit meant to masturbate.

A really exhaustive search of the dictionaries would, in all likelihood, raise the total count of 'Jesuit words and phrases' to two or three hundred. But this fact is no proof either that the Jesuits made a deep impression on society, or that there was much general understanding of them.

In the first place comparatively few of the words were coined by Jesuits, and none of these entered into wide general use. Of course like schoolboys, soldiers and civil servants, Jesuits have always been great coiners of private jargon and slang. As is normal, some of this was universal, quasi-official and lasting: much was severely local, unofficial and impermanent. As is normal also, Jesuit private terms gained almost no currency outside the restricted circle of the Society and those brought up under its guidance. Few outsiders have ever made real sense of terms like scholastics, spiritual coadjutors or particular examen. Recent generations of English Jesuits are probably ignorant of the meaning of slang terms used by their 19th-century predecessors like Cur Vals and Rings. On the whole the public store of 'Jesuit words' represented the outside world's view of the

Society. It was part caricature, part abusive and part legendary. The Jesuits themselves rejected much of it and accepted the rest either as a matter of convenience or because they approved of the more complimentary of the legends. The oddest example of Jesuit acceptance is that root-word jesuit. It was not coined by the Society. It appeared in the Netherlands and Rhineland at least a century before the Society was born. *Jésuita (jesuista)* was one of several abusive terms applied by exasperated people to devout busybodies who practised novel devotions and spoke censoriously of the clergy, religious Orders and ordinary Catholics. Such busybodies often practised an emotional devotion to the name and person of Jesus, contrasting themselves with conventional 'Christians'. The cap fitted the infant Society of Jesus and the abusive name was hurled at it. The Society for decades indignantly rejected *jesuitae*. Then, well after the death of their founder, they gradually and quietly tolerated its use. It replaced the original official term, 'companions'. Their motive was partly practical convenience, and partly a sense that it would be fitting if they wore 'a badge of shame' as a 'badge of glory'. Even today, though the term is used constantly by the Society, it is semi-official and used with a certain self-consciousness. After all the dictionaries still speak with one voice round the world:

> jesuit: (i) a member of the Society of Jesus (ii) (pejorative or figurative) a hypocrite or sly person . . .

The 'Jesuit terms' to be found in technical dictionaries have been frequently quoted in the Society's works of apologetic as proof positive of its versatility and the world's grudging acknowledgement. In reality the terms are few, out-of-date and relate to peripheral things or matters of legend. Their fewness is due, to a small degree, to anti-Jesuit prejudice, but far more to the slightness of the Jesuit impact in technical fields. There never was a distinctively Jesuit style of architecture or church decoration: not even confessional boxes owed their (surprisingly late) vogue to the Society. The Jesuits contributed nothing to dress. Those Victorian Protestant humourists who published 'Catholic Bestiaries' with caricatures of all the Catholic Orders' official plumage had difficulty in giving the Jesuit picture much distinctness. The dictionaries of arts, sciences and literature contain, without prejudice, exceedingly few references to Jesuit influence.

Again dictionaries of current usage of words reject the vast majority of the old 'Jesuit terms' as obsolete. The terms were mostly the products of a strange, violent, emotional obsession which gripped the Society's enemies at particular periods of history. That obsession has long ago run almost entirely out of steam and the terms have faded with it. Thus, for instance, the English terms are vintage crops, produced in the heat of 'Jesuit scares' between 1580 and 1900: by far the largest crop appeared in the mid-19th century. The terms expressed a deeply super-stitious terror of the Satanic power of Popery in general and Jesuitry in particular as its spearhead. This enemy bore all 'the marks of the Beast' for generations bred in an imaginative vision of Satan and Hell. Satan (and so his sworn emissaries, the Jesuits) was an angel of light and charm in outward appearance, but within a dark, impenetrable mystery of nightmare horrors, lies and deceit. He operated by capturing souls and depriving them of their liberty. Perhaps our age keeps this fantasy-world alive tenuously in our interest in the occult and space-fiction. Such language tells us far more about the mentality of its adepts than about their subject: in a real sense they do not want to plumb its realities. Some words never really took hold, for instance jesuitocracy and jesuitish. And one strange word, jesuitess, had two lives. It was coined by Catholic opponents of a Jesuit-sponsored Order of active nun auxiliaries in the mid-17th century. Rome, alarmed by the scandal, suppressed the Order and jesuitess lost popularity. Two centuries later a far larger outburst of Jesuit foundations of active women's Orders produced in France a best-selling anti-Jesuit novel which had a sinister aristo-cratic lay jesuitess as an important minor character. The idea and the word regained life in England. For decades few Pro-testant novelists who had an eye on the market dared to avoid making use of absurdly sinister jesuitesses.

Finally these 'Jesuit terms' should be put in the right per-spective. They were the natural products of centuries when religious books had to figure prominently on most publishers' lists, and religious themes and controversy were a major interest even for sceptics. The Jesuits however did not, because of this atmosphere, automatically and easily command a position of influence. In reality they always had to struggle to get their voices heard in the clamour of battle between many large competing religious groups inside and outside the Catholic Church. All of these groups fought to gain the ear of the educated public: all had striking successes; all left their mark on our languages. In the background existed always the great, apparently inert, unintellectual mass of parochial clergy. They most probably had more influence on the minds and language of their parishioners than all the elite religious groups put together. Moreover these groups, the Jesuits included, all suffered another restriction on the spread of their influence. In our anxiety to do justice to (us moderns) the extraordinary religiosity of past ages, we habitually oversimplify and exaggerate their susceptibility to the influence of the clergy and religion. Even in the Middle Ages the ordinary person's daily preoccupations were mostly secular. The dictionaries make this clear. A glossary of bawdy in Shakespeare's plays has (even when we make allowances for censorship) startlingly few references to the clergy and religion, and those often conventional. The dictionaries of vulgar, low-life terms contain the language natural to people uninhibited by censorship. Their stock of words was huge, but their references to the clergy and religion scanty and, in the 17th and 18th centuries, positively antiquarian. Any very idle lay-about was a monk, a pimp an abbot, a brothel madame an abbess, a brothel a nunnery. The only 'modern' clerical references were to Jesuits, a subject which preoccupied the vulgarians' betters. In the taverns two classes of unfortunates, the 'gay' and sailors, were called jesuits. Perhaps the vulgarians imagined that Jesuits lacked (because of their special discipline, loneliness and mobility) the opportunities enjoyed by heterosexual landsmen and clerics for the pleasures of straightforward vice.

* * *

It is wise not to make easy presuppositions about the impact of the Jesuits on literature. Thus it does not necessarily follow that this must have been small because their impact on language was relatively slight. A few poets, playwrights and novelists were fascinated by the Society and could not help writing about it. Because they had been bred in its schools (or had even been Jesuits for a time) they were well-acquainted with its ways and private language. They used this profusely since even the most trivial Jesuit family term sufficed to rouse intense emotions in them. This was true of James Joyce, of an obscure French novelist whose work he admired, Octave Mirbeau, of Voltaire and Diderot. These writers had a peculiar, private love-hate relationship with the Society. In 1923 Joyce wrote part flippantly, part seriously, to a French acquaintance:

> 'How I write in present circumstances I don't know — influence of ad majorem dei gloriam perhaps . . .'

But these writers were very exceptional. There were a great many others who referred to the Society or created Jesuit characters in their plays or novels, yet did so with an extraordinary economical use of 'Jesuit terms'. The fashion was probably started by Eugene Sue who, in the 1840s and 1850s, was Europe's top best-selling novelist. The first printing of his bitterly anti-Jesuit novel, *Le Juif Errant*, in 1845 ran to 120,000 copies. The book had numerous reprints, was translated into English, German, Italian and Spanish, and several times adapted for the stage in Paris and London. George Lander's English adaptation was still being reprinted in the 1880s. Sue made some half-hearted efforts to indicate that he had researched his subject: he several times quoted the Jesuit *Constitutions* in footnotes. But in the text he used only three 'Jesuit terms', jesuit, jesuitess and General, each no more than three or four times in a novel of five volumes. His aim was to portray the accepted popular image of the Society using all the tricks of romantic melodrama. In that image the Jesuits hid behind a dark veil of mystery and secrecy: it was their natural habitat and their source of power. Sue builds up the image by suggestion and implication, avoiding outright statements. So, for instance, a hundred pages after we are introduced to the wicked Rodin and his master, the Marquis d'Aigrigny, we are still left wondering whether they are Jesuits or not. This literary trick was widely used by 19th-century English novelists. Even the respectable Thackeray used it lightly in *Henry Esmond*. His Jesuit character, Father Holt, is, unlike Sue's comic opera Jesuits, an English gentleman capable of generous impulses and rather pathetic human failings. But the usual veil of mystery surrounds him and the unseen organisation he represents. So Thackeray excuses himself from research into, and much use of, 'Jesuit terms'.

The field of literature by, or about, Jesuits is enormous. The Society has patiently amassed some seventy volumes of published catalogues of Jesuit writings. They admit the work is very incomplete and still in progress. No single person or organisation has yet attempted to chart the field of writings about Jesuits by outsiders. There have been interesting forays into limited sections of the field to take samples. In the last century the Paris Province of the Society collected hundreds of anti-Jesuit publications and cartoons and made a museum of them at their College in the Rue des Postes. Jesuit periodicals have, until recently, made it their practice to review a few of the more popular anti-Jesuit novels. The field of 'wicked Jesuits' in English

19th-century fiction has been surveyed, if not thoroughly explored. Jesuit apologists have acquired, over many years, a stock sample of compliments paid to the Society by writers generally hostile to Catholicism — for instance from Voltaire, Lamartine, Goethe, Robert Louis Stevenson and Brecht. So we have to be content with rather speculative feelings.

A first impression is that the huge literary output of the Jesuits has been very narrowly clerical and professional in character. The great majority of Jesuit writers have stuck rigidly to well-worn, traditional clerical paths and genres of literature. They have shied away from anything that could be regarded as 'secular modes of writing'. They have concentrated on the defence and extension of the Society and the Catholic Church. Almost all the writing has been severely practical: practical scholarship, practical theology, practical schoolbooks, practical spirituality, practical history and apologetics. Literary experiment, specu- lation and self-revelation have been in extremely short supply. The Jesuits were reluctant to venture into vernacular verse, drama, fiction, autobiography or critical biography of their members. Gerard Manley Hopkins, something of a rarity, a Jesuit major poet, attempted to account for this reluctance:

> 'Show and brilliancy do not suit us . . . we cultivate the commonplace outwardly and wish the beauty of the king's daughter to be all from within . . . Our Society values and has contributed to literature, to culture, but only as a means to an end . . .'

Elsewhere he added bitterly (thinking of poetry):

> 'Our Society cannot be blamed for not valuing what it never knew of . . .'

His own sources of inspiration derived from influences outside the Jesuits, from his formative years as an undergraduate romantic at Oxford, from private, rather surreptitious, reading of books far outside the courses prescribed within the Society. He did his best to channel his inspiration within the narrow limits of orthodox Jesuit piety, not always with success. He tried valiantly to accept the puritanical literary standards he felt were required by his vocation: to dismiss the Romantics as frivolous worldlings, to find Latin classical literature lacking in a proper 'high seriousness', to give even Dante bad marks for 'farce'. All this was Jesuit tradition. The most popular textbook on verse composition used in Jesuit schools and scholasticates throughout the 17th century put the ebullience and literary ambitions of bright pupils firmly in their place. Poetry, said the Czech Jesuit author, is, like all the arts, not an end in itself but to serve 'virtue and the glory of God'. It is a sort of jam to cover the bitter medicine of truth. In an ideal world without original sin, the arts would be unnecessary. Robert Southwell, an Elizabethan Jesuit minor poet, suffered much as Hopkins was to do three centuries later. He was bored by Jesuit scholastic discipline and teaching. He too covertly experimented with verse forms remembered from pre-Jesuit days or picked up from illicit reading matter. He too did his best to stick to the official line: he wrote that poetry has always been a bad, wordly influence. So Jesuits might have a true vocation 'to weave a new web with their loom', using the seductive romanticism of verse to teach the hardnesses of virtue and Catholic doctrine. The case of Friedrich von Spee, a German Jesuit poet of the mid-17th century, contained the same features of tension perhaps more painfully and harshly. He was out of sympathy with the aggressive militancy of his Province, deeply engaged in the religious wars in Germany and the forcible conversion of captured Protestant areas. Von Spee petitioned his Provincial in vain for permission to go to Italy. He wrote fine lyrical poetry in the midst of carnage and horrors. He never hoped to see it published. He even had printed, without permission of his superiors, an indictment of the involvement of many of his brethren in hunts for witches.

It would be unfair to the Society to dismiss this evidence of clerical narrowness as peculiarly Jesuit and monochrome. Until quite recently all clerical organisations, Catholic and Protestant, adopted much the same official attitude toward 'worldly literature'. The inner tensions suffered by Hopkins, Southwell and von Spee were not unlike those felt, for instance, by Donne, Herbert, Vaughan and Newman. Newman offered advice to Gallwey and Coleridge, the Jesuits who founded *The Month* in 1865. He was inclined to believe that English Catholics needed *The Month* to be Catholic in tone, but also written in an idiom which would appeal to educated Protestants. Its influence would then, he said, serve to break down the cultural isolation of Catholics. *The Month* ought to put itself into the mainstream of non-Catholic thought and literature. Like *The Cornhill Magazine* it should be genuinely interested in everything: it should print novels in instalments, some 'ethical' (as Thackeray's or Trollope's), some 'sensational'. After the first flush of his enthusiasm Newman began to have misgivings which were

shared by his Jesuit friends. There were subjects which it would
not be wise or fitting for Catholic clergy to touch on. 'Sensational
novels' were hardly for Catholics (though Newman unbent so far
as to beg *The Month* to review one written by a deserving and
poor convert lady). 'Ethical' novels also simply could not be
written by real Catholics: 'theology' must creep in, even if 'in
undress'. But Newman's real inhibitions were these:

> '. . . I know what a difficulty a Priest has in writing or editing
> literature which is not theological. I feel it very much myself. I
> have been too long in the groove, to say nothing else, to write
> any thing which has no theological meaning . . .'

As for verse, Newman confessed a guilty secret. He had caught
himself actually enjoying writing it. He had, he admitted, a
'facility' for it which he lacked for prose. Hence he held his gift
in leash, limiting it mostly to hymn-writing.

Jesuit writing has certainly tended to be monochrome. The
mainstream of it has been, as Voltaire complained in his *Account
of the Sickness, Confession, Death and Apparition of the Jesuit
Berthier*, solid, pious, and unexciting. His story's principal
character, the editor of a Jesuit review of literature, dies of sheer
boredom. But, alongside the Jesuit mainstream there has always
been a small counter-stream, a Jesuit 'literature of dissent'.
The first generations of the Society tended to be busy, sturdy
evangelists. Their attitude to learning and the arts was pragmatic, utilitarian and sometimes outright Philistine. By the 17th
century force of circumstances, not deliberate Jesuit choice, made
the Society's main work schoolmastering. This remained true
until recently. Hence the average modern Jesuit is distinctly
better-educated than his forebears. Schoolteaching is a laborious,
exhausting task which eventually deprives most teachers of
mental energy. They become creatures of mental habit and
routine. A small minority, by reaction, are stimulated to attack
routine and seek adventurous outlets. The impact of these forces
is evident in the Society's history. Quite apart from the inhibitions
imposed on them by what Newman called 'the groove', very many
Jesuits while trained to write, had no taste for that occupation.
If the orders of superiors or practical necessities impelled them
to write, they did so as a duty and a chore. The dissident and
adventurous minority found writing an essential way of blowing
off steam, a therapy. The Jesuit superiors were, with some exceptions in every age, not Prussian disciplinarians nor rigid
reactionaries. They had, somehow, to keep a balance: to keep the

Society from ossifying, to keep it stable and not to offend powerful outside interests. On the whole, therefore, official Jesuit policy about writing fluctuated between two poles, the fairly permissive and the reactionary. The stream of Jesuit 'counter-literature' always flowed. Sometimes it received a measure of encouragement from above: sometimes it was repressed and its leaders disciplined or even summarily expelled from the Society.

In times of official approval, the dissidents surfaced. Their writing achieved publication, chiefly in Jesuit magazines. Most of these owed their existence to dissident groups. When the official sun shone on the groups, the magazines tended to show real literary vitality. When the sun went behind a cloud, the magazines passed into the hands of conformists and became what Voltaire called 'boring'. So, for instance, the most famous Jesuit periodical, *Civilta Cattolica*, began its life in 1850 in Naples as the brain-child of a group of ardent young liberal Jesuits anxious to reconcile the Italian Church with political Liberalism. It was only gradually over the course of the next fifteen years that *Civilta* became a reactionary periodical, though still using the unstuffy literary style of the liberal founders. The chief German Jesuit periodical as *Stimmen aus Maria Laach* was at first liberal and adventurous and then long reactionary. Later, it became *Stimmen der Zeit* and regained something of its pristine vigour.

In times of official disapproval, Jesuit dissidents went underground. They continued to write, but could find an outlet only by passing their work privately in manuscript form round trusted friends. This was a procedure which did not begin with George Tyrell or Teilhard de Chardin: it was traditional in the Society from the later 16th century. On occasion these secret manifestos were published, usually anonymously and at presses which had no connection with the Society. It was not even a peculiarly Jesuit procedure. Every Catholic clerical grouping has always had its dissidents fighting censorship.

Undoubtedly a great deal of Jesuit dissident writing has perished or survives only in manuscript in archives. Much that did get published is of historical, but not much literary, interest today. If there were dissident Jesuits with real poetical gifts, very little of their work has seen the light of day. As Newman discovered for himself, a disciplined training in Latin versification could produce a pleasure and facility in vernacular versification which stifled a poetic gift or provided a third-rate substitute for it. The career of Jean-Baptiste Gresset shows this. He was a French Jesuit dissident schoolmaster who, in 1734, at a time when the official sun was shining on men of his metal, got permission to publish a satirical decasyllabic French satire *Ver-vert*. It was charming and facile. It also was intellectual dynamite. His story was of a convent's pet parrot. Like a good child, for rewards of sweetmeats, it acquired a vast repertoire of highly pious remarks. The nuns were enchanted and passed the parrot round other convents to edify their sisters. On its travels the parrot picked up many swear-words and obscenities. Undeterred, its mistresses re-educated it in lush piety, but killed it with an overdose of its usual rewards. The following year Gresset published an altogether more ambitious — and bitter — verse satire, *La Chartreuse*. This caused so much annoyance in high places that Gresset was dismissed from the Society. On the strength of his facility in verse, his liberal convictions and freedom from Jesuit censorship, he hoped for a profitable career in writing librettos for musical comedies. But he never fulfilled his ambition, partly because of his limited talents, and partly because he retained for life the pious inhibitions implanted in him by his Jesuit training.

Perhaps also the ranks of the Jesuit dissidents contained men with real gifts as novelists or playwrights. In his novel, *The Laodicean*, Thomas Hardy makes use of quotations from the published *Maxims* of a mid-17th-century Spanish Jesuit, Balthasar Gracian. Hardy was puzzled. Some of the *Maxims* were what he expected from a Spanish Jesuit: but many of them were definitely not. They seem worldly and *picaresque*, almost like a notebook kept by a natural novelist. There were plenty of other dissident Jesuit versifiers, pamphleteers and controversialists who displayed considerable natural skill in creating imaginary characters and situations caught from life. Yet only one such Jesuit of real ability wrote a full-length novel and had it published — and it was published after he had left the Society. This was Prévost, the author of *Manon Lescaut*. Ironically the Society's authorities did, for a time in the mid-19th century, encourage novel-writing. They employed Jesuits who were safe conservatives, skilled in the arts of *pastiche* (in this case copying the artifices of secular romantic novelists) and dedicated to attacking liberalism in politics and religion. The most famous example by far of this race of Jesuit pseudo-novelists was Antonio Bresciani of the editorial team of *Civilta Cattolica*. He was violently opposed to all liberalism and detested literary romanticism. Yet, round 1850, he set out deliberately to use the Liberal romantic Devil's weapons against him. Bresciani's answer to

Eugene Sue's anti-Jesuit melodramatic novel, *Le Juif Errant*, was the romance *L'Ebreo di Verona*. It first appeared in fortnightly parts in *Civilta Cattolica* and created a great sensation. Bresciani followed it with a string of other *romanzi* with titles like: *Lionello; Ubaldo and Irene; Edmondo; Olderico, the Papal Zouave; Don Giovanni; Matilda of Canossa;* and *Lorenzo*. He died suddenly in 1862 leaving his current novel in the *Civilta Cattolica, The Defence of Ancona*, unfinished.

It is customary nowadays for histories of the theatre to treat what they call 'the Jesuit theatre' with respect. From the mid-17th to the mid-18th century when Jesuit Colleges were numerous and often well-endowed and largely frequented, plays performed in class or in public on prize-days were taken very seriously. The type of Latinity which was taught involved training in Latin oratory: this made Latin plays a natural class-exercise. The Jesuits were competing vigorously with the schools of other Orders for the attention and patronage of well-to-do people who often had a passion for the public theatres and private theatricals. Elaborate stage-sets including ingenious mechanical devices were the fashion. Jesuit schoolmasters therefore often had to turn their hands to set-designing, choreography, stage engineering, producing and sometimes acting. Above all they had to breed in their ranks competent playwrights. The Jesuit 'groove' demanded Latin and piety in school plays. The Jesuit dissidents daringly experimented with the vernacular and with satirical themes. Generals and Provincials watched all this from afar with a mixture of approval and alarm. They constantly issued, or reissued, stringent codes of procedure, to which the dissidents paid no more than lip-service.

Not a single one of these Jesuit playwrights has an important individual place in histories of the theatre. A few left the Society and gained a modest living by writing for the public stage. It is possible that Corneille and Molière, both of whom were educated at Jesuit Colleges, owed some of their dramatic skill to their schoolmasters. But it would be hard to prove it. The 'Jesuit theatre' occupied only a small patch of European drama at an early stage in its modern expansion. College plays returned with the 19th-century revival of the Society, but, for a variety of practical reasons, were unambitious, domestic affairs. Perhaps this modest theatrical activity had some effect on Jesuit evangelisation, but the evidence is slight. Jesuit missionaries in America used dramatic processions and pictures to impress Indian converts. But they were copying methods used more extensively by Franciscan missionaries who preceded them in America. The Jesuit tradition in preaching was not dramatic. The Fathers were taught to avoid intellectualism and high-flown language and stick to plain, direct exposition. There is one striking example of a Jesuit preacher who over-stepped the mark, partly due to his own histrionic gifts and partly to his experience in producing College plays. This was Bernard Vaughan. His sensitive Jesuit brethren winced at the high and vulgar drama of his courses of sermons up and down Edwardian England. They could not deny his burning sincerity or his phenomenal success. His sermons (especially a Farm Street series on 'The Sins of Society') packed churches and confessional queues and (or so legend asserted) led to startlingly sudden conversions to Catholicism of aristocratic ladies. All this had some connection with his early years teaching at Stonyhurst College, where private theatricals were his forte.

Very little of the published Jesuit 'counter-literature' casts much light on the realities of life within the Society. There were more or less dissident writers who had a gift for biography. In some ways Jesuit training encouraged use of the gift: in other ways it was strongly discouraged. From the later 16th century to at least the early part of this century, novices were required to write out for the records a succinct account of their lives, background, education and reasons for wishing to enter the Society. But, for both practical and spiritual reasons, the accounts had to be brief, bald and piously stereotyped. As novices and students, Jesuits were encouraged to keep spiritual diaries. These were frequently used as material for published biographies of eminent Jesuits after their deaths. On the other hand the diaries, though private and individual efforts, almost invariably followed a pious, uniform pattern, a reflection of the traditional shape of the training. The surviving diaries of Teilhard de Chardin bear witness to this. The official biographies were written to edify the rising generation in the Society, its pupils and its lay supporters. Thackeray, in his *Henry Esmond*, catches the flavour of these biographies without much exaggeration. In the novel Father Holt instructs little Henry and tells him of:

'. . . the glories of his order, of its martyrs and heroes, of its Brethren converting the heathen by myriads, traversing the desert, facing the stake, ruling the courts and councils or braving the tortures of kings; so that Harry Esmond thought that to belong to the Jesuits was the greatest prize of life and bravest end of ambition; the greatest career here, and in heaven the surest reward . . .'

But the 16th and 17th century Jesuit dissidents broke out of this narrow tradition. Some wrote of their superiors in unflattering terms in manifestos which were unlikely ever to be published. Thus we are told that, of the first generations of the Society's leaders, Ignatius was an ill-educated autocrat, Bobadilla an insubordinate braggart, Laynez a tactless bully, and Francis Borgia a grossly fat man full of whims and strange pieties. Later generations of exasperated dissidents have carried on this tradition of hostile character sketches. The private correspondence and memoirs of, for instance, Leonard du Cros and George Tyrrell in the early years of this century, and Teilhard de Chardin after 1945, abound in them.

Another, odder class of dissidents specialised in collecting as holy relics the autobiographical jottings of their 'martyred' leaders. These were the 'Spirituals', a peculiar breed. They flourished persistently in the Spanish Provinces in the 16th century and in the French ones in the 17th century. Their passionately-held view was that the Society had been mortally corrupted by military activism. Salvation could only come from the cells of 'Spirituals', men of contemplative prayer, dedicated to war on Satanism and witchcraft. Their leaders, men like Rigoleuc, Surin and Crasset, and some remarkable women disciples, had suffered a 'white martyrdom' at the hands of superiors and the Devil in person. A collection of 'Spiritual' biographies actually achieved publication in the 1680s. It remained unnoticed on library shelves until unearthed by Henri Brémond, an ex-Jesuit writer, in the 1920s. Aldous Huxley, in his *The Devils of Loudoun*, made use of some of the more sensational detail in these naive biographies, at once grotesque and moving. The 'Spiritual' strand remained a part of the Society's life in the 19th century. It then produced more odd biographical material which lies hidden, partly in the official histories of 19th-century foundresses of some Orders of nuns, and partly in manuscript in archives.

This century has seen the timid beginnings of yet a third type of Jesuit biography belonging to the dissident wing of the Society. It is the product of a conviction that the Society has lost credibility and will only regain it if its biographies and histories give frank coverage to Jesuits' eccentricities, doubts and struggles. In the field of history before the 1890s non-Jesuit scholars had to rely on a very few official versions commissioned hesitantly by past Generals. These versions were gallant efforts made by Jesuit historians who worked under every kind of restriction. The gradual opening of Jesuit archives and official publication of part of their contents made possible, by the 1920s and 1930s and mostly in Germany, a series of markedly less inhibited studies of the Society's early history. In England after 1950 Bernard Basset's *English Jesuits* and James Brodrick's studies of Jesuit origins, of Ignatius Loyola, Xavier, Canisius and Bellarmine followed suit rather gingerly. In Germany Schurhammer and Hugo Rahner took the same path with the same rather exaggerated caution. In the field of individual Jesuit biographies Karl Rahner's recent brief memoir of his dead brother, Hugo Rahner, was a brave and moving acceptance of modern openness. In England Cyril Martindale was the brave pioneer with his life of Bernard Vaughan (1923) and short memoir of Robert Steuart (1952).

Thus Jesuit self-revelation in print, both official and 'dissident', has been large enough to occupy a good many shelves in libraries. It is, advertently and inadvertently, informative. But, to an outsider, it remains disappointing material, for two reasons. It covers only patches of Jesuit history and it is overwhelmingly 'domestic': that is to say it was written by men so deeply involved in Jesuit family life and tradition and so immersed in the internal struggles of the Society that they take for granted and do not explain to outsiders great tracts of 'Jesuitry'. Their non-Jesuit readers inevitably feel a mixture of sympathy and suspicion. The curtain has, here and there, been parted sufficiently to make us glimpse the ecclesiastical 'ordinariness' and earthiness of Jesuit life and history: that arouses warm sympathy — it seems they bleed as we do, suffer as we do, are weak and incapable as we often are. But the curtain is still kept drawn across large areas. We cannot help feeling that the emperor retains most of his clothes and regalia, because he still wishes to keep his royal *mystique*. Without that he is an ordinary man and the empire is at an end.

*　　*　　*

The literature of straightforward polemic about the Jesuits and written by outsiders has been enormous. The field is broad. It ranges from a recorded speech by Sir Walter Mildmay M.P. in the House of Commons in the 1580s through library rooms packed with calf-bound volumes of Protestant sermons and controversial writings to speeches in the 19th century House of Commons, Reichstag and Chambre de Deputés. The ideological and literary value of most of this spate of words was very low, and lowest perhaps in 17th-century Germany. Here and there they were more profound and measured, the more memorable sentences, usually culled by Jesuit apologists. *A Decacordon of Ten Quodlibeticall Questions Concerning Religion and State* (1602) by an English secular priest, William Watson, is worth remembering for some fine phrases:

> '(the Religious Orders) . . . in the World's Theater represent a mournfull tragedie of mans miseries: how like to flowers, they have now one then another order, companie or societie, burgeoned, blossomed, bloomed and flourished, and yet subject to the fates of freewill in all human wights . . . the Jesuits tampering, temporizing and statizing like martiall men . . .'

Vincenzo Gioberti's *Il Gesuita Moderno* (1846-7, five large volumes) was a block-buster of invective which caused a deep sensation in the Italy of his day. It has received scant attention from historians of Italian literature, but is worth remembering for some passionate rhetoric:

> 'Jesuitism, a human institution, born in time and destined to die in time, is already morally dead . . . a vain shadow and a corpse . . . A terrible battleground, I repeat, is the Jesuit noviciate: terrible in the omnipotent strength the institution and the discipline have on human nature . . .'

There are the *Memoirs* of Prinz Chlodwig von Hohenlohe-Schillingfuerst, a solid but conventional Catholic and briefly Chancellor of the German Empire. In the Reichstag in 1872 he said:

> 'The Jesuits and their friends wonder why the modern State abhors them. And yet their Society has taken upon itself to make war on the modern State . . .'

In 1875 he wrote to a friend:

> 'Mendes Leal, the Portuguese ambassador, has the keenest nose for the Jesuits that I have ever seen. He asserts that international relations are under the lead of the Jesuits, and the Jesuits will place Don Carlos on the French throne, and the

whole of the fancy goods business in Paris is in their hands, also the guano trade &c.'

Lord Acton was an eminent Victorian Catholic and an unrepentant liberal. His views on Jesuits are worth remembering for both fine rhetoric and stern Puritan analysis. A good example of his rhetoric is this, from his first *Quirinus Letter* (1869):

'. . . that great ecclesiastical polypus, with its thousand feelers and arms, the Jesuit Order, works . . . under the earth and on the earth . . .'

And a typical analysis of Jesuitry is given in one of his letters to Mary Drew in March 1882:

'It is this combination of an eager sense of duty, zeal for sacrifice, and love of virtue, with the deadly taint of a conscience perverted by authority, that makes them so odious to touch and so curious to study . . . The Jesuit goes wrong for the worthiest motive: that the disinterested spirit of religion, which to other men is a safeguard, is as fatal to him as vulgar passions to other men. The true Jesuit falls better than that. His decay begins at the top . . .'

It is strange to find in the same series of Acton's letters a scornful rejection of Macaulay's most famous treatment of the Jesuits in his review of Ranke's history of the Popes (1840). Acton calls it 'flashy and superficial', incompetent history, and a compendium of popular prejudices. In fact Macaulay's review is a wonderfully Dickensian piece of prose. In it he sees Ignatius Loyola and the Society as typical extreme religious fanatics, to be classed with Teresa of Avila, John Wesley, the Countess of Huntingdon, Mrs. Fry and Joanna Southcote. Had the Jesuits been born Anglicans they would have been cast out by the Church of England as it cast out all other 'enthusiasts'. But Rome's policy is much more daring and unscrupulous. She welcomes fanatics of every shade, dresses them in the habits of new religious Orders and assigns them:

'. . . some forlorn hope, in which intrepidity and impetuosity are more wanted than judgement and self-control . . .'

Finally, in a very amusing passage, Macaulay imagines what Rome would have made of Wesley ('the first General of a new Society . . .') or Joanna Southcote ('she founds an order of barefooted Carmelites . . .'). We may wonder whether Macaulay had ever read the passages in Wesley's *Journals* where he expresses a vague sneaking admiration for Jesuit organisation and devotion.

John Henry Newman was undoubtedly the most measured and profound of this class of writers about the Society. Shortly after his conversion to Catholicism in 1845 he went to Rome for theological studies and lodged in a Jesuit house. His confessor in Rome was a Jesuit, Giuseppe Repetti, whom he always remembered fondly as 'one of the holiest, most prudent men I ever knew'. At first Newman very seriously considered joining the Society. His decision not to do so was based on careful thought and typically English pragmatism. He retained for the rest of his long life a dislike of the Society which his frequent dealings with Jesuits only served to deepen. However, his ecclesiastical position after 1850 made it impossible for him to write in print or even in private letters with the frankness possible to a Macaulay, an Acton, a von Hohenlohe or even a Jesuit 'dissident'. We have to rely on his frank letters written as a layman from Rome in 1846-7, some indiscretions in his later correspondence, and his memoirs, kept under lock and key by him at the Birmingham Oratory.

In public he steadily maintained that the Society was an admirable body for whose marvellous services to religion the Church must ever be profoundly grateful. He extolled Jesuit devotion to hard work (greater than that of any other Catholic clerical group), and the holiness of a good many individual Jesuits. When the young Gerard Manley Hopkins wrote to him saying he had decided to enter the Society but dreaded 'hard Jesuit discipline', Newman drily remarked that it was a way to heaven.

In private he wrote of the Society as a disaster for the Church, albeit one which God in his inscrutable Providence seemed, for the time being at least, to tolerate. In a wildly indiscreet letter to his one close Jesuit friend, Henry John Coleridge, in 1869 he wrote:

'(God) . . . has once interfered and thrown you back, and, if you get too powerful, He will do so a second time . . .'

But the letter was never posted. The reasons for the 'Jesuit disaster', Newman thought, stemmed from the fact that their founder was a soldier:

'. . . and they are, in a certain sense, a military body. They are the Knights Templar of modern history. They have the excellence and the fault of soldiers: they are perfect as an organised body, but, as individuals, they are often little more than mechanical instruments, and are, least of all men, able to deal with strangers, or with enemies, not to say with friends . . .'

Twenty years earlier Newman had been even blunter:

'The Jesuit does not know what tact is, cannot enter into the minds of others, and is apt to blunder in most important matters from this habit of mechanical obedience to a Superior and a system . . .'

Newman was very insular and very much an Oxford college man. The contemporary continental style of religious education struck him as disastrously misguided. The life of the religious Orders, which were truly international and centralised like the Jesuits, equally repelled him. (He excluded from this blanket condemnation many English religious groups because they were incurably insular, and 'local bodies' rather than Order men.) He therefore thought the average run of Catholic religious, men and women alike, ill-educated and boorish. They had not the benefits of English gentry breeding, so did not know what to do with proper freedom and had no genuine community life.

'They conform, they obey, because they are under a *vow* . . . they obey, not for the sake of obedience, but from a past act which binds them . . .'

Newman felt that he could never have endured being 'tethered' by a vow of obedience, least of all that severest version, the Society's. No one would ever have known whether what he said was his own genuine view or that imposed by authority. When asked to go to the first Vatican Council as a theological adviser, he drew up a list of reasons for refusing. High among his real reasons (not included in his brief official letter of refusal) was:

'I have never got on intimately with ecclesiastical superiors. It arises from my shyness and a sort of nervous continual recollection that I am bound to obey them, which keeps me from being easy with them, speaking my mind without effort and lucidly and calmly arguing with them . . .'

All this might be dismissed as Newman's 'Macaulayism', the personal prejudices of an insular-Anglican kind remaining in an otherwise 'High Church Catholic' mind. But Newman had other more general reasons for regarding the Jesuits coolly.

They were, he thought, because of their militant temper, incapable of 'live and let live' with other Catholic bodies: they wanted to dominate. Hence as the Society's influence increased, dissension was sown and the Church endangered. Again, he rejected the popular view that the Society was flexible. He thought them past-masters at going through the outward motions of modernisation while remaining grimly antiquarian. The world was also wrong, he believed, in thinking Jesuits the most insinuating, tactful and worldly-wise of men. In his experience they were almost wholly devoid of these talents. True, they attracted to themselves clever men: but he saw these as a familiar type, the Oxford '1st class men', good examinees but intellectually unbalanced, lacking in judgement and sagacity.

It is ironic that Newman, as seen in his letters, displayed most of the characteristics popularly attributed only to Jesuits. Thus in 1879-80 he used a Jesuit as his amanuensis, congratulating him baldly on the publication of a book of scholastic philosophy (which Newman abhorred). When another Jesuit wrote from Rome on behalf of the General, congratulating Newman fulsomely on his cardinalate, he answered drily:

'I have always admired and honoured your Society, though I have felt its grandeur and force of action were so much above me . . .'

A lay supporter of the Society wrote complaining of mounting attacks on it. Newman answered sharply that the Society could look after itself: the attacks were caused by its growing strength and refusal to 'live and let live'. Then, to take the sharp edge away, he added:

'When penitents and converts leave me, I always ask them, "Are Jesuits near your new home? Go to the Jesuits if you can" . . .'

*   *   *

The writers of polemics displayed a wide spectrum of attitudes towards the Society. The same spectrum was reflected in that section of popular literature which contained Jesuit characters. Hunting through this for them can be an absorbing task, especially because the 'bag' turns out to be surprisingly large. Initially we expect to find Jesuit characters or references in plays and novels by, say, bitter French and Spanish anticlericals,

James Joyce, Baron Corvo, Aldous Huxley and Evelyn Waugh. We are startled to find them also in, say, works by Charlotte Bronte, Thackeray, Dickens, Disraeli, Dumas, Zola, Balzac, Dostoievsky, Mrs. Humphrey Ward, Wilkie Collins, Sheridan Le Fanu, Thomas Mann, Berchtold Brecht, Kingsley Amis, Somerset Maugham, Muriel Spark and even in the latest spy story by Jack Higgins. We are then inclined to fall into the trap of imagining that 'Jesuitry' must be a major theme of modern popular literature. The truth is more modest. For a few very brief periods in history in certain countries 'the Jesuit issue' appeared to be of major political and social importance. Public debate created, or appeared to create a demand which popular novelists and playwrights were eager to supply. Outside these short periods, literary interest in the Society sank to a low ebb generally. But even then there remained some types of writers who were willing to touch, even if only lightly, on the unfashionable 'Jesuit theme'. Some were writers who had been personally involved with the Society and felt that they must either get their revenge on it, or get its influence out of their system: it was their private nightmare. Others were writers of what Newman called 'theological' or 'ethical' novels. Their minds were exercised by ideas. Their characters tended to be representative figures voicing separate ideological systems. Dialogue tended to be lengthy academic debate. In this scheme of writing it often seemed necessary to include a character who could speak for Catholicism. Who better than a clever Jesuit? A third kind of writer, at a loss to find some unusual and exotic character as a foil to the main action, sometimes plumped for a Jesuit (rather than a wise old Jew or an inscrutable Oriental).

Most of the Jesuits of fiction were therefore very shadowy, unconvincing characters. Eugène Sue's vastly successful potboiler, *Le Juif Errant*, was built to standard, well-tried specifications. The ingredients of the elaborate plot were ancient. A French Jew dies in 1682, the victim of a Jesuit design to delate him as an insincere convert to Christianity. He is, in some deeply mysterious way, a descendant or reincarnation of the legendary Wandering Jew. To save his fortune from the hands of the Jesuits, he places it in trust, walled up until 1832 in a mansion in Paris. The Jewish guardians of the fortune invest it at compound interest so that by 1832 the sum will be a huge one. The heroes and heroines of the book are all lineal descendants of the unfortunate Jew. They possess talismans which entitle them, if they can arrive at the sealed house on a fixed day in 1832, to joint-ownership of the fortune. The baffled Society of Jesus bides its time. As 1832 approaches it tries every possible subtle villainy to get the fortune for itself to restore its failing influence. The 'goodies' in the novel are a strange collection including a handsome innocent youth, Gabriel, seduced by the Jesuits into joining the Society, an Indian prince, an old Napoleonic Marshal and two beautiful, innocent Polish girls. The 'baddies' are an even odder lot of mysterious Jesuits and their sworn assistants, a hideously cadaverous villain called Rodin, a French Marquis, the Princesse de St. Dizier, a Siberian convert ex-Jew and animal-trainer who hawks crucifixes and rosaries on the side, a thug brought over from India, and a monstrously ugly giant of a 'hit-man' called Goliath. The novel grinds on, fortnightly part after part, each bound to end in a cliff-hanger situation to be resolved marvellously at the start of the next part. The ranks of the two parties are thinned by agonising deaths. In the end Rodin bribes his way to become General of the Society but is poisoned by the highly confused thug. Rodin dies screaming in a burial vault full of his victims' coffins. His sole surviving assistant, the Princesse-jesuitess finds his body and goes raving mad. The set-up of the novel was so stock that Sue could easily have made the 'baddies' Jews, Turks or any international gang of criminals without major changes in the plot.

The 'penny dreadful Jesuit' of fiction enjoyed a long innings stretching from the Gothic horror romances of the later 18th century (at least in southern Europe) to as late as the 1930s. The English crop was relatively small, and, as befitted writers who were mostly churchgoing maiden ladies in reduced circumstances, fairly restrained. One exception, *Hawkstone* (1845), written by William Sewell, the English Sue, piles on the horrors and ends with the agonising death of the Jesuit villain in a dank cellar eaten alive by huge rats. The French, German, Italian and Spanish selections were larger and not infrequently pornographic. Some writers for this continental market were distinguished novelists and their works classics. Diderot's *The Nun* (1770) was a highly sophisticated novel which took as its target the whole scene of clerical obscurantism, until recently dominated by the influence of the Jesuits. They are in the wings of the action, but never appear on the stage in person. Ramon Perez de Ayala's play *A.M.D.G.* (1932) was an almost surrealist vision of the horrors of a Spanish Jesuit College where an innocent pupil is surrounded by violent, greasy, repulsive Fathers including Padre Olano, a seducer of women, and Padre Atienza, a scholar bent on escape from the Society. The memoirs of ex-pupils of the Jesuits (for instance the Belgian Rexist leader, Léon Degrelle, and the Spanish author, Arturo Barea) describe how anxious their masters were to protect pupils from the flood of cheap anti-Jesuit paperbacks. No doubt the paperbacks contributed something to the physical violence of attacks on the Jesuits in Republican Spain, and to Rosenberg's scurrility against them in Nazi Germany.

Then there were the 'comic Jesuits' of fiction, still villains but ridiculous and ineffective ones. The literature in which such characters appeared also ranged in quality from real artistry to bathos. John Donne, a Jacobean Dean of St. Paul's and major poet, had been brought up as a Catholic recusant and probably tutored by a Jesuit. In *Ignatius his Conclave* (1610) he imagines a debate in hell to decide who is to find a place at Lucifer's right hand, Machiavelli, Ignatius Loyola, Philip Neri, Copernicus or Paracelsus. Ignatius is the clear victor. But Lucifer is so worried at the prospect of falling under Jesuit influence that he despatches Ignatius to the moon to found a 'Lunatique Church' there, confident that 'after the Jesuits have been there a little while, there will soon grow naturally there a hell also'. Blaise Pascal, a pious French mathematician, wrote his anonymous series of tracts, *The Provincial Letters* (1656-8), to expose to the world what he regarded as a vast Jesuit plot to dominate it and pervert Catholic truth. The series ended as a passionate but academic diatribe. They began (Letters I to IX) as an amusing comic dialogue with a bumbling Jesuit who is vastly stupid and complacent and quite unaware of the gross absurdity of his views. But as a satirist of the Jesuits Pascal was a child compared with Voltaire. Voltaire was educated at a Jesuit College and retained contacts with some Jesuits for the rest of his life. In later life he provided house-room for a mild and rather stupid ex-Jesuit priest, left destitute when the Society was suppressed. Voltaire's anti-Jesuit satires are brilliant slapstick comedy informed with wit and a deadly serious purpose. In *Ingenuous: a True Story* (1767) the hero is a naive, well-meaning Huron Indian who visits Louis XIV's France and runs into what he, and the reader, find a crazy situation where Père La Chaise and the Jesuits dominate French Society. In *Berthier* (1759-60) we meet the Jesuit editor of the *Journal de Trévoux* dying of sheer boredom because of the volume of dull publications by the Fathers which he is bound to read word for word and review at length. *Candide* (1759) was incomparably the most effective anti-Jesuit satire ever produced.

It abounds with human stupidity of every kind. But the limelight always returns to comic Jesuits strutting self-importantly about Europe and drilling their Indian troops in the Paraguayan Reductions.

Candide set a standard for the future. Its influence crops up in unexpected places. In John Buchan's romance, *Castle Gay*, Jaikie, a Gorbals die-hard transformed into a Cambridge undergraduate and rugby international, sets out to prick the balloon of the pious complacency of Mr. Craw, the pompous newspaper magnate:

> "Personal experience is not the decisive factor", said Mr. Craw. "You have the testimony of the ages to support your faith."
> "Did you ever read *Candide*?" Jaikie asked . . ."

Elsewhere in modern English literature traces of *Candide* show up, amidst a lot of native slapstick which owes more to the music halls. Thackeray had a comic Jesuit, Fr. Holt, in *Henry Esmond*. Dickens, alas, never got further than a sentence in *Pictures from Italy*:

> 'The Jesuits too, muster strong in the streets, and go slinking noiselessly about, in pairs, like black cats . . .'

Disraeli's *Lothair* owes something to *Candide*. The novels of Emma Worboise (*Fr. Fabian: the Monk of Malham Tower*), Jemima Luke (*The Female Jesuit*) and Trollope's mother's *Father Eustace* are bad music-hall stuff. In this century 'comic Jesuits' have had more skilful treatment. Joseph Hocking, a Methodist, started off with a series of novels in which there was a running battle in the Buchan or *Boys Own Paper* tradition between gallant Protestant guerillas and a band of wicked Jesuits. The guerillas sought to rescue poor souls trapped by Rome. The Jesuits defended Rome's bastions, the monasteries and convents in which the poor souls were imprisoned. As in Buchan, the Jesuits were apparently foreigners, led by a Dutchman, Fr. Fitzroom. They wore disguises, bowler hats and tweeds, and tried every unpleasant trick. Frederick Rolfe was a satirist more in the style of Oscar Wilde. He was a convert, a 'spoiled priest', and a writer determined to get his own back in print on the haughty clerical institutions which had rejected him. These included the Society, since Rolfe claimed to have suffered much humiliation from Fr. Beauclerk, an English Jesuit. In his novel *Hadrian VII* (1904), he imagines himself suddenly promoted to the papal throne. As

Pope he summons the major superiors of the religious Orders and gives each a stern dressing-down. To the Jesuit General he says:

> 'Three fourths of you trade upon the reputation of your Company for cunning and learning. One fourth of you is the Christians of the world . . . Your erudition is showy enough . . . but it is superficial. Your machinations are sly enough . . . but they are so silly. Ye are not monsters either of vice or of virtue: but only ridiculous mediocrities, always painfully burrowing like assiduous moles, always seeing your pains mis-spent, your elaborate schemes wrecked, except sometimes when, quite by accident, ye chance to kill a king . . .'

Rolfe's *Stories Toto Told Me* (1901) is written in a mock-Italian anticlerical idiom. He includes in the collection four stories about Jesuits. Ignatius Loyola, a morose and unpopular inhabitant of heaven, broods over the degeneration of the Society. By mistake he gives it as a cure something which in fact turns many Jesuits' hearts to stone. There are two worthy Jesuits, both punished by the General for their adherence to the rules. For their sake alone, God decides to spare the Society and overlook the venality and stupidity of their brethren.

It may be significant that Rolfe and English creators of comic Jesuit characters who came after him were all, with one exception, Catholics. The exception is Kingsley Amis, whose *The Alteration* (1976) portrays a modern Europe which went totally Catholic from the 17th century. Its culture is static and near-medieval. Sartre is a French Jesuit philosopher and Ayer a professor of dogmatic theology. The Pope's secretary, Gregory Satterthwaite, is a 'pale, thin-lipped' English Jesuit, who raises no objections to any vagary of papal policy. Evelyn Waugh's *Vile Bodies* (1930) was written as a youthful extravaganza when he was on his way to conversion to Catholicism. One of the book's main characters, Fr. Rothschild SJ is an odd cross between a comic opera Jesuit villain and a profoundly wise man. Bruce Marshall and Muriel Spark, both Catholics, have not treated their Jesuit characters with any particular tenderness. Muriel Spark, in her *The Abbess of Crewe* (1974) has a Voltairean satire on the Jesuit approach to the modern Catholic crisis. A convent of Benedictine nuns, secretly advised by Jesuits, sets out to preserve its antique way of life in the teeth of modern papal directives for reform. Liberal-minded nuns, Felicity and Gertrude, are given much freedom as a cover to impress the outside world and Rome. Electronic bugging devices are fitted throughout the convent to enable two successive abbesses to stamp on any liberal rebellion in the community. The whole elaborate scheme falls apart, largely because of the indiscipline and inefficiency of the Jesuit advisers. Felicity is seduced by a liberal Jesuit, Thomas, goes off with him and tells her story to the press. A plot engineered by Maximilian and Baudouin, the two Jesuit advisers, to use Jesuit novices as burglars of the convent to get incriminating counter-evidence against Felicity misfires badly. The novices are expelled from the Society and blackmail the abbess. The advisers find it prudent to leave for the United States to give seminars in 'ecclesiastical stage management and demonology'.

On the continent few anti-Jesuit writers have felt able to satirise the Society with real wit and humour. Perhaps 19th- and 20th-century circumstances there have created a new kind of bitterness. Stendhal and Zola caricatured the Jesuits without either wit or humour. Neither Balzac, nor Dumas, nor the Realist novelists, nor the Catholic convert writers of the early 20th century were in the mood for elegant satire. François Mauriac, for instance, in *The Nest of Vipers* and elsewhere, limited himself to acid references to Jesuit College education. But the Voltairean tradition is not quite dead in France. It came alive again recently in Roger Peyrefitte's novel, *The Keys of St. Peter* (1968). He creates two fine comic Jesuits. One is Fr. Capello, a professor of canon law at the Jesuit Gregorian University in Rome, a dry academic. Much to his disgust, the *beatas* of Rome have come to swear by him as a great oracle and wonder-worker. He slips away from the university daily furtively to the confessionals at the Gesu to endure crowds of penitents who kiss his hand and pull buttons from his *soutane*. The other is Fr. de Trennes, a strange mixture of a man, allowed to live apart in Rome and drag out his existence writing ephemeral pieties which, he believes, are of immense importance.

Literary classifications are never completely satisfactory. Not all the writers just classified as creators of Jesuit melodramatic villains were without sympathy for their victims. Even Eugene Sue was careful to write that the Society began as an admirable institution, and that, though now perverted, it contains many holy and humble men. Not all the satirists of the Society were without human sympathy for many Jesuits. Voltaire himself is a good example of this. Nevertheless it is possible to see a third, distinct class of Jesuit characters in fiction. Here the authors' intention was to see them as human beings compounded strangely of virtues and faults, and not as mere villains or comic characters. In England Grace Kennedy's *Father Clement* (1823), while sternly opposed to the Society in principle, attempted to portray various types of Jesuit, some bad, some well-meaning but pathetic. Early in his career Disraeli had a romantic attachment to Catholicism. Hence in his first novels he treats the Jesuit minor characters with a kind of distant sympathy. Joseph Shorthouse's extraordinary novel, *John Inglesant* (1880), was basically an Anglican tract. Shorthouse attempted to show that the mystique and glamour surrounding Catholicism in the minds of many educated Anglicans were illusory. The all-too-familiar and unglamorous Anglicanism in which they had been bred contained all that was good in Catholicism without its vices. The hero, John Inglesant, is planted by Shorthouse in the mid-17th century and in the curious position of being an Anglican, closely instructed in Popery by an able Jesuit, taken to Rome to meet the General, but allowed to stay in Anglicanism as a stalking-horse to bring about an avalanche of conversions to Rome. The subtle Jesuit plan, of course, misfires. But, if only to make the ploy plausible, Shorthouse has to portray Inglesant's tutor as a good man of the utmost sincerity. In 1898 Mrs. Humphrey Ward's novel, *Helbeck of Bannisdale*, caused a great sensation. The hero was a country landowner, a devout Catholic, and educated by the Jesuits. Mrs. Ward earnestly explores relations between Protestants and Catholics. Her Jesuit character, Helbeck's chaplain, is shown as someone who is both alien and yet more genuinely friendly towards Protestants than they are to him.

It is usual to emphasise the bitterness and dislike of the Jesuits expressed in James Joyce's *A Portrait of the Artist as a Young Man* (1924). The bitterness and dislike are there in abundance, ending in a piled-up indictment of the Society which, surely, has never been expressed with such force and artistic integrity. Stephen Daedalus, the hero, looks at the Jesuit Dean of his university:

'. . . the silent soul of a jesuit looking out at him from the pale, loveless eyes. Like Ignatius he was lame, but in his eyes burned no spark of Ignatius' enthusiasm. Even the legendary craft of the company, a craft subtler and more secret than its fabled books of secret, subtle wisdom, had not fired his soul with the energy of apostleship. It seemed as if he used the shifts, and lore and cunning of the world as bidden to do, for the greater glory of God, without joy in their handling or hatred of that in them that was evil, but turning them, with a firm gesture of obedience, back upon themselves: and for all this silent service it seemed as if he loved not at all the master, and little if at all the ends that he served . . .'

But that devastating passage ends with pity and affection:

'. . . for this faithful servingman of the knightly Loyola, for this half-brother of the clergy, more venal than they in speech, more steadfast of soul than they . . . how this man and his companions had earned the name of worldly also for having pleaded, during all their history, at the bar of God's justice, for the souls of the lax and the lukewarm and the prudent . . .'

Since Joyce's day two great English writers, both without definite religious affiliations, have written of the Society with sympathetic interest. In his novels (for instance *After Many a Summer*) Aldous Huxley writes of Jesuits as if they were aliens from decent, humane society. But in his close studies of 17th-century religious history, particularly in *The Devils of Loudoun*, he displayed an intense and not altogether morbid interest in the mentality of Jesuit missioners. Somerset Maugham also mostly steered clear of religious themes in his novels. Yet his travel book, *Don Fernando*, is a genuine effort to explore the mind of 16th-century Spanish Jesuitry. He even took the trouble to attempt to take Ignatius Loyola's *Spiritual Exercises*. His description of the experience shows that he realised, better than his Jesuit critics, what was antique, strange and almost savage about the original form of the *Exercises*.

Continental literature about the Jesuits, perhaps understandably, contains few examples of efforts to probe clinically into their humanity. Goethe, in his *Italian Journey*, seems conscious of his own daring broadmindedness when he suggests, tentatively, that the producers of a play he saw at the Jesuit College at Regensburg felt a simple artistic pleasure in their achievement. Thomas Mann's novel *The Magic Mountain* has a Jesuit character, Leo Naphta. He is a convert from Judaism whose health, physical and mental, has been broken by three years of Jesuit training. He is a pathetic creature who has received, from Judaism and Jesuitry, a shattering double dose of Messianism and alienation from modern society. The reader is not surprised when he challenges a Liberal to a duel and shoots himself when his opponent, true to his principles, fires wide. Berthold Brecht had no brief for the Jesuits, or, indeed, for any form of

Christianity. There seems to be no hard evidence to support Orson Welles's view that he came under Jesuit influence in Augsburg when young. Nevertheless in Brecht's play *Galileo* Christopher Clavius, a Jesuit astronomer, is shown as an honest but genuinely puzzled man, and Cardinal Bellarmine, his colleague, as a mixture of wiliness and bluff practicality.

In Latin countries novelists have been even less given to mixing abuse and sympathy when portraying Jesuit characters. A favourite theme has been the terrible power of the Society over women and boys, filling them with deep inhibitions. The theme, as developed passionately by, for instance, Octave Mirbeau (in *Sebastien Roch*), Manzoni, Vincente Ibanez and Ramon Perez de Ayala, seems to exclude sympathy for the Jesuit seducers. But sometimes artistic integrity does triumph momentarily over moral indignation. Mirbeau's seducer of the young, Father de Kern, is both vile and pathetic. A Jesuit colleague is honestly shattered when he learns of his wickedness, even if he fails to denounce him for fear of sullying the Society's good name. In Ibanez' *El Intruso* the heroine's Jesuit confessor, Padre Pauli, combines a voracious desire to control her life with a sensible attitude toward her devotional excesses. He orders her to replace her hairshirt with silk underwear so as to improve relations with her husband. Marco Bellochio, in his film, *In the Name of the Father* (1971), imagines a Jesuit St. Trinian's where the corruptness of the masters and juvenile delinquency of the pupils are alike attributed far more to the system than to individual badness.

The moral dilemmas of Jesuits have fascinated some non-European novelists. Dostoievsky hated the system of Jesuitry which he thought a perversion of the Gospel. But he puts into the mouth of Ivan Karamazov a curious apologia for the Society. Karamazov rejects the opinion that they are atheists seeking power: no one, he thinks, could be as totally evil as that. The Jesuits are atheists, but kindly ones. They have abandoned the love of God and replaced it by a vast love of miserable humanity. They judge that, in a world without the Gospel, the people desperately need a 'pretend-religion' which will relieve them of the burden of moral choice and be infinitely indulgent toward their failings. In Japan, Shusaku Endo, possibly inspired by Graham Greene, has dealt (in his novel, *Silence*) very frankly with the moral struggles and apostasy of a 17th-century Jesuit Provincial of the mission there.

Lastly there is a fourth class of Jesuit characters in fiction, the heroes. These are relatively few. In most cases they are more devotional tributes to the Society than living figures compacted of light and shade. Perhaps Gerard Manley Hopkins was right when he suggested that his colleagues could rarely produce, or inspire others to produce, dramatic art because 'we cultivate the commonplace outwardly'. Calderon, in his *Great Prince of Fez*, makes the hero become a Jesuit and celebrates the event with a hymn to Ignatius Loyola. Calderon was a secular priest with Jesuit friends. Mrs. Elizabeth Inchbald's *A Simple Story* (1791) was written in very different circumstances. Brought up a Catholic, she went on the stage and her life then fluctuated between Bohemianism and respectability. Hazlitt, who advised her on the writing of the novel and who was much in love with her, re-read it constantly in floods of tears. Although the Society had been suppressed and discredited years before Mrs. Inchbald set pen to paper, her romantic hero is a Jesuit, Mr. Dorriforth, the heir to a peerage. Her sentiments were liberal, and clearly the Jesuits appeared admirable. Dorriforth holds to the 'philosophical' part of Catholicism and firmly rejects the 'superstitious'. His Jesuit training has taught him never 'to shelter himself by the walls of a cloister', and made him a master of the art of drawing all hearts, especially of women, toward himself. He succeeds to the Earldom of Elmwood, and is dispensed from his vows by Rome so that he can marry and continue the noble family. At the end of the book he has the best of both worlds, a Jesuit training and a comfortable family life.

Victorian English Catholic families had available to them for Sunday evening reading aloud quite an array of popular romantic fiction by Catholic authors and with Jesuit heroes. There were aristocratic Jesuits, tall, dark, handsome and good (Agnes Stewart's *Father Cleveland, or the Jesuit*, 1868), juvenile delinquents transformed into positively angelic Jesuit novices (F.M. Oxenham's *Edith Sydney*, 1867) and gentlemanly Jesuits labouring in East End slums (Lady Georgina Fullerton's *Mrs. Gerald's Niece*, 1869). There were Jesuits martyred in Japan (Lady Fullerton's *Laurentia*, 1861), going bravely to the scaffold in Elizabethan England (Thomas de Longueville, *The Romance of the Recusants*, 1858) or saving Catholics' sanity by giving them the Spiritual Exercises (as in Canon Barry's *The Two Standards*, 1898).

Since the turn of the century a few Catholic novelists have continued this romantic tradition, for instance, in England, Jane Lane and Hugh Ross Williamson, in France Paul Claudel (in

Le Soulier de Satin), and in Spain Jose Maria Peman. But tastes have changed. The very modern Jesuit hero of fiction has to be a tormented, chain-smoking proletarian (as in William Blatty's best-seller, *The Exorcist*), a quixotic prophet (as in Miguel de Unamuno's *Life of Don Quixote and Sancho Panza*) or a volunteer to suffer with the Jews in Auschwitz (as in Hochhuth's *The Deputy*). He may be an anguished 18th-century missioner in Paraguay taking up arms to defend exploited Indians (as in Hochwalder's *The Strong are Lonely*) or an apostle of human freedom held by the K.G.B. for torture (as in Jack Higgins's *Day of Judgment*.)

*   *   *

Thus the Jesuit image in language and literature is blurred and multiform. Depending on the prejudice of the writer a typical Jesuit may be a revolutionary or a stiff conformist. He may be an infinitely dangerous immoralist, a danger to society, a wrecker of homes and perverter of the young: or he may be the gentlest, most scrupulous and permissive of spiritual advisers and mentors. The anonymous author of a pornographic novel on sale in the Strand in the 1840s, *Venus in the Cloisters, or the Jesuit and the Nun* and respectable Spanish anticlerical novelists saw him as salacious and lustful. Others saw him as the most angelically pure of men. Thomas Mann imagined that Jesuit obedience produced zombies, their personalities 'completely atrophied', their minds reduced to 'a state of insensibility in which the individual becomes a lifeless tool' with a 'blank, staring face'. Even Cardinal Newman found Jesuit obedience sinister. Yet other writers imagined their Jesuits as constantly in revolt against their superiors. In the end all these contradictory views have one common denominator: all agree that the Jesuits are in some way extraordinary.

2
Ignatius Loyola's Early Life
1491-1537

'Surely one of the greatest men that ever engaged in the
support of so bad a cause . . .'

(John Wesley, *Journal*, 16 August 1742 on Ignatius Loyola.)

An outside observer might easily be pardoned for thinking that
the Jesuits regard their founder, Ignatius Loyola, not as an
ordinary saint but as a massive cosmic phenomenon, a great and
unique sign from God to the modern world. To this way of
thinking God revealed to Ignatius alone a deep insight into the
meaning of Christianity, an insight without which the Church
cannot survive. God inspired him to create an entirely new kind
of religious Order to propagate this insight and save the Church.
The Society is thus a peculiar, wholly unique institution and in
every essential detail the brain-child of Ignatius, the intimate
friend of God. Moreover he did not merely plant the Society and
then leave its future in the hands of his successors. By divine
appointment he remains, and will always remain, the very direct
and living source of its spiritual power. Without constant
reference back to his words and spirit the Society would lose
inspiration, wither and die. Then the whole Catholic Church
would be in mortal danger.

The evidence to show that this is Jesuit tradition appears over-
whelming. As recently as 1978 the present General of the Society,
Pedro Arrupe, addressed a meeting of his colleagues in Rome.
He said:

'In the Gesu the statue of the saint above his tomb shows us
Ignatius the priest radiating forth all the energy of the Society
across time and space . . .'

He was referring to the highly dramatic early 18th-century
sculptured reredos behind Ignatius's tomb in the Society's
mother church in Rome. Ignatius is shown hovering as if in flight

in the vaults of heaven high over the world. He is preaching to it and stretching out his arms widely and energetically to embrace it all. Over his head the Trinity hover to inspire him. Down below, at each side of the altar, moved on by Ignatius, two figures representing Catholic faith convert unbelievers and tread down heretics. Fr. Arrupe went on to refer to an even more famous and striking Jesuit artefact, the great painting covering the ceiling of the church of S. Ignazio also in Rome. It is the work of Andrea Pozzo, a Jesuit laybrother, in the 1680s on the detailed instructions of his General. Pozzo used all the tricks of *trompe l'oeil* of contemporary theatrical scenery painting to make us imagine that we are gazing upwards into the heights of heaven. They are dominated by three figures: God the Father in the far distance, Christ carrying his cross in the middle distance, and Ignatius in the foreground, kneeling on a cloud borne by angels. A beam of intense divine light pours down from the Father, through the heart of Christ to the breast of Ignatius who is utterly rapt in ecstasy. From his heart in turn the same beam pours down the firmament to the four corners of the earth beneath, America, Asia, Europe and Africa. There it enters the hearts of Jesuits labouring amongst the people. Fr. Arrupe explained the picture's meaning:

> 'This is Ignatius the mystic . . . (he) assures his Society of a lasting dynamism — the breath of the Spirit, which drives it along in constant search, without binding itself to any one situation or concrete form . . . it is no museum-piece . . . it is in a state of constant creativity . . .

The highest authority in the Church appears to have endorsed this tradition. In a solemn pronouncement in 1814 Pope Pius VII called Ignatius and his Society 'the glory of the Church' and (using an oddly antiquated metaphor deriving from Mediterranean galleys) 'those strong and experienced rowers' of 'the Barque of Peter' through the tempests of modern life. And in 1974 Pope Paul VI told the Society that it must for ever cling without wavering to the inspired rules of 'your father and lawgiver Ignatius'. Then he used an even odder metaphor, calling the Society:

> '. . . a sort of hinge by means of which the whole Church has moved through its significant efforts and initiatives so that it can turn events to a true and perennial advantage . . .'

The Society he added:

> '. . . has been across the centuries an indication of the Church's vitality . . .'

The evidence provided by Jesuit everyday practice seems to bear out this impression abundantly. It seems so full of reminiscences of, and references to, Ignatius that his physical presence appears to brood over the Society. Its churches and houses contain pictures and statues of him in every pose and in every event of his life. The names of the places connected with his life, Loyola, Manresa, Cardoner, Montserrat and Montmartre constantly recur in the names of Jesuit establishments and even rooms in Jesuit Colleges. Dr. Ignaz von Döllinger and Dr. Joseph-Ignace Guillotin are just two random, famous examples of the practice of families devoted to the Society and habitually naming their sons after the saint. The womenfolk of these families sometimes carried the devotion further. The 17th-century English Mary Ward and early 19th-century Belgian Emilie d'Oultremont were brought up under Jesuit direction. For years they were haunted by visions of Christ accompanied by Ignatius bearing the open book of his *Constitutions*. In every detail the imagery of the visions reproduced that of the most widespread mass-produced statue of the saint. Emilie could not escape the vision and Ignatius's constant prophecy:

> 'You will take and live by my rule . . .'

It pursued her from her oratory into the family drawing room, to meal-times, to balls and to her box in the theatre.

But is all this a true interpretation of the Jesuit view of Ignatius? In reality the average Jesuit, like the average member of most large institutions with a remarkable past, has never shown a close interest in his Society's history. He has been too tied up in the day-to-day routine and problems of life to do more than accept, always incuriously and sometimes rather sceptically, the brief, officially-inspired summaries of the Society's origins. Again, like most other religious Orders, the Jesuits had a long, stiff battle to get their Constitutions finally approved by Rome, Ignatius canonised and the Society assured of a place at the forefront of Catholicism. It took the best part of a century to achieve this, in the teeth of furious opposition, especially from the older Orders. But holding great power and prestige had its own dangers and in 1773 the Society was discredited and officially disbanded. It was, indeed, restored in 1814 but then had to face another century of battle to recover its lost position. Hence during most of the Society's history its superiors have, perforce, had to be ecclesiastical politicians, deeply concerned about their public image. It was always vital for the Society's credit that Ignatius should be seen as a very great saint and creative personality. Jesuit historians, artists and sculptors tended to have their work officially tailored to fit this aim. There was no conscious hypocrisy in all this. Since early Church history every ecclesiastical institution had had to defend its interests vigorously. In the Middle Ages the foundation documents of Orders and the deeds of property of Church corporations were often 'improved' or outrightly forged. Superiors and the forgers believed innocently that spiritual truth was on their side and the good of souls, so they were justified in manufacturing or clarifying evidence where, by merely material chance, it happened not to exist.

The Jesuits' opponents, the older Orders, had, in reality, far more uncertain origins than the Society. In most cases the ancient saints whom they claimed as founders and lawgivers had only a vague and tenuous connection with the Orders and their Rules. The Franciscans, the biggest Order, claimed as their founder Francis of Assisi, who persistently refused to be responsible for the creation of a conventional Order of any kind. Yet it was these older Orders who, in the course of the 17th century, had their mother-churches expensively and lavishly adorned with paintings and statuary designed to convey an over-simplified or distorted view of the Orders' origins. In 1646 a Jesuit General Congregation complained that Ignatius's tomb and the Society's greatest churches were still meanly adorned, while Benedict was glorified at Monte Cassino, Francis at Assisi and Dominic at Bologna. Belatedly, and in sheer self-defence, the Society spent money it could ill afford in following suit. The overall result was odd: four sets of impressive baroque paintings, each claiming forcefully that one particular saint-founder was, by God's will, the Church's only hope.

There is yet another reason for interpreting the documents and artefacts of Jesuit tradition about Ignatius with care. Spiritual teaching in words, painting or sculpture, is, of its nature, rather akin to poetry. It tends to use deliberately startling flights of imagination and imagery to move and to convey the ultimately mysterious and incomprehensible. We are often left in doubt whether the writer, preacher or artist really intended these flights and images to be taken seriously. In Catholic theology there have been schools of theologians who have been maximists in this matter and others who have been very critical minimisers. Hence among Jesuits themselves both tendencies have been represented.

There is another confusing factor. Imagery is dated. Even great and conservative ecclesiastical corporations have eventually, however unwillingly and slowly, to accept these changes or cease to be able to communicate with the world and their own younger members. The very earliest writing about, and portraiture of, Ignatius were the work of men who had known him far too intimately for them to be able, after his death, to put their impressions into conventional hagiographical forms. He was still too close to them for a view in perspective. Their feelings about him were often mixed. In any case his Society was small, struggling, and still very much in the melting pot and the *Constitutions* were under fire and as yet unenforced in the Society. This was not the time for 'triumphalism'. The paintings of Ignatius of this period were domestic and factual. Twenty or thirty years later that generation of Jesuits had mostly died out and the Society was governed by men to whom Ignatius was beginning to be a part of history, a legend. It was now therefore that many strange legends about him proliferated. Most were slavishly copied, stock 'wonders' of a kind attributed to every medieval saint. Thus, for instance, Ribadeneira, the first official writer of a *Life* of Ignatius, padded its first editions with unlikely wonders. For example, Ignatius's first religious conversion on his sickbed at Loyola was accompanied by this:

'. . . the house rocked with a great crash and the stout stone wall split through its entire thickness . . .'

Ribadeneira should have known better, since he was one of the few survivors who had met the saint in the flesh — but when he was very young. A slightly later official *Life* is illustrated with engravings. They and the text run through a whole gamut of conventional wonders. In them Ignatius, like Moses on his return to ground-level from intimacy with God on the mountain, wore a halo or nimbus of supernatural glory. Philip Neri, himself haloed, often saw it. At every turn in his life divine light, holy voices and special divine interventions direct Ignatius and ward off shipwreck and the daggers of murderers. Though exceedingly unlearned, he is filled with divine wisdom and writes the *Constitutions* and *Spiritual Exercises* by the light of heaven and in obedience to divine dictation. After death he still performs miracles from his tomb.

These publications were, for the most part, official evidence assembled to forward the cause for the canonisation of Ignatius by Rome. However fanciful and conventional the portraiture was, it did also convey something of Ignatius's mentality. As we shall see, he personally expected to have constant divine lights and visions, and thought that he received them every day. At least some of the highly coloured biographical detail was real reminiscence of his sermon style. He was given to startling extreme flights of fancy. He did compare the obedient Jesuit to a corpse and a walking-stick. He did once say that he would lose no sleep if the Pope disbanded the Society. Alphonsus Rodriguez, an early Jesuit novicemaster, relayed a saying which bears all the hallmarks of being genuinely Ignatian:

> 'Ignatius said . . . that if the Holy Father were to order him to set sail in the first boat that he might find in the port of Ostia . . . and to abandon himself to the sea without a mast, sails, oars or rudder or any of those things which are needed for navigation and subsistence, he would obey not only with alacrity but without anxiety or repugnance, and even with great internal satisfaction . . .'

In these early years the Society lacked the patrons, money and artistic skill needed to forward its own and Ignatius's cause by lavish church decoration. Its only two efforts in this direction were large mural paintings in two Roman churches used by its novices and students, S. Stefan Rotondo and S. Vitale. The subjects chosen were not Ignatian but early Christian martyrs. They were painted in a crude, *farouche* and 'clinical' style meant to shake, inspire and edify the young. The surviving remnants of these early paintings, in S. Stefan Rotondo, are nowadays locked away from public view as too horrifying.

By the mid-17th century fashions in Church art and hagiography were changing. Conservative minds, well represented inside the Society, revelled in miracles and supernaturalist extremism, and even in blood: they detested, as irreligious, the new, unsuperstitious, humanistic styles. Ignatius was now safely canonised: the Society was large and powerful. The minds of many Jesuits seem to have been torn between loyalty to the old styles and attraction toward the new baroque which seemed to express admirably their feeling that Providence had given Ignatius and the Society a central place in the Church and a unique, cosmic vocation. At this period Surin, a French Jesuit 'spiritual' of distinctively conservative tastes, wrote confidently that if the New Testament had never been composed, Ignatius's *Spiritual Exercises* would have been enough Holy Writ for Christians. Meanwhile the old, crude biographies of Ignatius were quietly withdrawn from print. More sophisticated and better documented ones replaced them. Patronage and money became available for the building of large, splendid Jesuit churches over much of Europe and their decoration in the new baroque style. Br. Pozzo and other technically competent Jesuits were set to work to do the decorations. The theme was to be the glory of Ignatius and his Society rolling back the tides of Protestantism and unbelief throughout the world. Progress was slow and the resistance of conservative Jesuits dogged. Even Pozzo himself, though competent in the new style, was, in private, more conservative in his tastes. Over the next half-century Rome became Europe's greatest attraction for Protestant tourists. With a weather eye to their conversion, the Generals extended the local display of baroque artefacts. At long last the tomb of Ignatius in the Gesu, thronged with worshippers but artistically mean and primitive, was turned expensively into a scenic representation of the triumph of Ignatius and the Society over unbelief: the statue of the saint was of solid silver. Tourists were admitted to an upstairs room in the Roman noviciate. It became one of the sights of Rome, a strange, grisly mock-up in painted stone of the death-bed of the young Jesuit saint, Stanislas Kostka.

During most of the 19th century the stock Jesuit image of Ignatius remained a superficially updated version of that in the 18th century. Its style was influenced by several currents of contemporary Catholic thought and feeling. During much of the century Jesuits inclined to the idea that an exact, literal and rather wooden observance of old traditions was essential. During the long periods when they lived in makeshift premises, deprived of their old houses and churches (including the Gesu and S. Ignazio), a strong emphasis on continuity with the glorious 17th-century past helped morale. Many Jesuits sympathised warmly with the Catholic traditionalists who regarded 'modern civilisation and progress' as empty and godless. Another influence was early 19th-century romanticism, the force of which was still evident in Francis Thompson's *Life of S. Ignatius* late in the century. Yet another influence was the cult of apocalyptic, mysticism and 'reparation' for the sins of society. These found outlets in the building of the Sacré Coeur church at Montmartre, the rise of numerous Orders of nuns devoted to reparation, and a passionate belief in the genuineness of heavenly signs and apparitions manifested to simple souls at La Salette, Pontmain, Banneux, Lourdes, Fatima and elsewhere. Jesuits were involved in all these matters. They found that an extreme, mystical and apocalyptic interpretation of the old image of Ignatius fitted admirably into this scheme of ideas. The meeting of ideas is reflected in the entries for 1898 in Teilhard de Chardin's school-boy diary when he was a sodalist contemplating entry into the Jesuit noviciate.

But the traditionalist-mystic reaction produced its counter-reaction, a mounting groundswell of Jesuit criticism. Dissidents like George Tyrrell were only echoing the views of a long succession of earlier sceptics within the Society when they insisted that the stock image of Ignatius was largely a 17th-century fabrication: the real Ignatius had been a far more human, fallible person, tentative, sometimes modest and sometimes cocksure, sometimes authoritarian, sometimes very libertarian. This view steadily gained ground, especially after 1945. In 1974 Paul VI, in aligning himself with the Jesuit traditionalists, was supporting a fading concept. The same year the General Congregation, never renowned for radicalism, abandoned the idea that the Society's foundation documents were Holy Writ. In his pronouncement in 1978 Fr. Arrupe tried to be kind to the feelings of his traditionalist colleagues. No doubt he was also mindful of that sentence dictated by Ignatius in his *Rules for Thinking with the Church*:

'We should praise church decoration and architecture, as well as statues, which we should venerate in view of what they portray.'

Nevertheless he interpreted the old images of Ignatius in the Gesu and S. Ignazio in a modern sense which was far from that intended by their creators.

* * *

What kind of man was Ignatius Loyola? Hagiographers in the 19th century did their best to find colour, drama and romance in the material details of his life-story. His own rather bald account of the details, dictated in his office in later life in instalments to an amanuensis, is flat and matter-of-fact. He thought that the drama lay elsewhere, in God's dealing with his soul. He was right. The material facts of his life are almost entirely lacking in the obvious warmth, colour and daring action so evident in those of, say, Francis Xavier.

The sixty-five years of Ignatius's life (1491-1556) can be divided into three distinct periods. The first thirty years, his secular period, were mostly spent obscurely in the commonplace duties of a feed retainer of noblemen. The next twenty years, his academic period, were almost entirely spent in universities as a mature student uncertain of his future. The last fifteen years, the period of his Jesuit Generalate, saw him confined to the desk-bound existence in Rome of superior of the small and struggling Society of Jesus.

Jesuit historians have sought, with much labour and ingenuity, to penetrate the veil of obscurity which hangs over his first thirty years. They have had relatively little success. Legend credited him with an aristocratic family. In reality he belonged to what we today call the middle class, a large, very variegated social stratum which was neither noble nor peasant. This stratum in the 16th century provided society's functionaries (civil servants, the upper servants of the nobility, lawyers, doctors and Church officials) and business men. They depended very largely on royal or noble patronage for advancement. They were very numerous: altogether too numerous to fit into the limited supply of available jobs. In this highly competitive atmosphere, the successful had to be ambitious and pushing. The most successful of all achieved legal status as noblemen, with all the social and financial privileges then attached by law and custom to high rank. These groups 'of the middling sort' always included university students or the temporarily unemployed searching for jobs, and a host of unsuccessful people, down-and-outs living by their wits or practically as peasants. The great European price-rise, which began in Ignatius's teens, provided a very sharp spur to all this middle class effort. The great majority of eminent people in 16th-century Europe — for instance Luther, Calvin, Erasmus, Zwingli, Columbus, Cortes, Cranmer, Thomas More, Thomas Cromwell, Teresa of Avila, John of the Cross and Cervantes — came from this rather vague background.

Ignatius's name had about it some of the indeterminacy of his social status. In his time personal and family names did not have the permanence they have today. Persons of his class not infrequently changed their personal names in middle life. Their baptismal names were formal, religious tokens mostly taken by the baptising priest from the Church Kalendar. The owners were quite capable of preferring nicknames, alternative names they chose themselves, or names imposed on them by registrars or monastic superiors on their entry into a university or religious house. Ignatius was baptised 'Inigo' ('Eneco' in Castilian Spanish) after a local Benedictine saint. Yet in later life he used 'Ignatius', the name of an early Eastern saint, apparently accepting a mistake made by the registrar at the University of Paris. The new name, Latin in form, no doubt was convenient when it had to figure in Roman official documents written in Latin. Contemporary surnames were quite often equally indeterminate. Some were really names of properties and were changed when the properties were sold or new ones acquired. New names could be adopted because of an inheritance or benefaction, or (as in the case of Spaniards who were of Jewish descent) to conceal a family's past. Ignatius's original surname was Lopez de Recalde. He adopted 'Loyola' (the name of his father's main property) sometime in middle age. His reasons for the change are unknown. At least one of his brothers called himself Pero Lopez. Yet a youth called Milian Loyola became a Jesuit in 1549. He came from Azpeitia, Ignatius's home town and the place where Pero held a chaplaincy: it is likely that Pero had four illegitimate children, of whom Milian was one. Ignatius was far from being the only prominent early Jesuit who suffered a name-change. Eberhard Reiter, a native of Marcour in Luxembourg, entered the Society in Italy in the 1560s. The novicemaster hastily Latinised his name as Eduardus Aritirus Mercurianus. In later life in the Society, and as its General from 1573 to 1580, Eberhard for some reason found it convenient to call himself Everard Mercurian. There were other prominent victims of Latinisation, such as Piet Kanis (Peter Canisius) and Kristoph Klau (Christophe Clavius).

Ignatius, of course, had his own 'nation' and 'country'. Every European state was then really a federation of small minority groups, each strongly attached to its own homeland, dialect and distinct laws and customs. When outside their own 'country' such people, Catalans, Basques, Sicilians, Gascons, Normans, Welsh and Saxons alike relied heavily on their countrymen established in their place of exile. As they received patronage from them, so, when themselves in office, they bestowed much of their patronage as a sacred duty on their countrymen, especially their relations. When they were sick they made the journey home to die. To all who were caught up in such networks of 'country', clan, family loyalties and duties, words like 'honour' and 'service' had an emotive force. Inevitably it was the middle classes of these 'nations' who travelled furthest abroad in largest numbers and so felt most the tug of these loyalties — as well as the duty of excelling or at least succeeding in some activity. The tug varied in force from man to man and also from nation to nation. The Basques were generally acknowledged in the 16th century to be the most narrowly nationalistic people in the Spanish peninsula. This had something to do with the fact that they are a people apart, neither Latin nor Germanic nor Celtic. Their language is neither a dialect of Castilian Spanish nor French but a separate language. They had played off their overwhelmingly powerful neighbours, the crowns of Castile and France, against each other to good effect. The Basque province of Guipuzcoa had elected to accept the ultimate overlordship of Castile. In return it had gained exceptional privileges throughout Castile and its American empire. All Guipuzcoan Basques, rich or poor, rated as nobles with the precedence of nobles, and had nobles' rights to certain top posts in the Church and State and to crucial tax exemptions. They were also allowed to maintain their old exclusion from Guipuzcoa of *conversos*, persons descended from families which had originally been Moors or Jews. The Basques, like the Swiss, had no real nobility. Their Government was a curious oligarchy of the heads of the twenty-four chief families. In a real sense the Basques were all 'of the middling sort', possessed, as Ignatius said by '. . . an immense desire to acquire vain honour . . .' They had, for their own sake and that of their families and nation, to get on and succeed in the hostile outside world of foreigners. In Ignatius's lifetime the Basques were generally disliked throughout Spain and South America for their arrogance, drive and clannishness. With some exaggeration, but much truth, Spaniards maintained that a relatively small number of pushing Basques shared with aliens (Netherlanders, Italians and Germans) and *conversos* all the crucial top offices in Church and State in Castile, Aragon, Italy and South America: They shared a monopoly of foreign trade while the Basques also dominated Spanish Atlantic shipping and the mining industry. In every Iberian centre of economic life, it was said, a tiny number of powerful Basques resided, behaving like a secret society. They had their own exclusive clubs, religious confraternities and platoons in the city militias. And they never ceased to trumpet that they were the only Iberians to have 'pure blood', unmixed with Moslem or Jewish taints.

Now Ignatius was a Basque of Guipuzcoa and a member of one of the Twenty-Four families. His father, a doctor of canon and civil law of the University of Bologna, seems to have had a career as a retainer of the crowns of both Castile and Aragon and established useful contacts at both Courts. Presumably therefore his influence had secured for two of Ignatius's brothers good Church benefices, for a third a post as retainer to the Aragonese Viceroy of Naples, for a fourth a similar post with the Emperor in Hungary, and for a fifth royal permission to be a gentleman-volunteer and shareholder with Cortes in the enterprise of Mexico. Ignatius rarely talked about his family. He revealed these details in an unusually uninhibited conversation with his Jesuit secretary, Polanco. But, characteristically at that late stage in Ignatius's life, he passed over the issue of his family's network of Court influence, and stressed that his brothers in Mexico, Naples and Hungary had ended their lives there fighting the heathen, rebels and Moslems.

Naturally Ignatius, the youngest son, when pushed out of the family nest at the age of seven was tonsured as a cleric and provided by influence with the post of a page in the household of the Treasurer of Castile: thence he passed, his way smoothed by recommendations, to the post of gentleman-retainer to the Viceroy of Navarre. The Basques, like the more prudent gentry of every 'nation', believed in keeping open as many options as possible for their children's careers. It seems possible, reading between the lines of statements made by Ignatius and passed on to one of his biographers, Nadal, that Ignatius was considered to be without ability for a trade or the law. The law would mean a very long and tough university course for which he cannot have shown the least aptitude. The options left were the clerical state and a gentleman-retainership. By securing Ignatius the position of a page in a household containing notably pious ladies, his father must have acted shrewdly. If the boy showed a real aptitude for clerical life, the household would form it, and the ladies might secure him a good benefice or entry into a good monastery. It is quite likely that one of his (much older) sisters had preceded him into service in the same household, and that its ladies had eased her financially into a reformed Franciscan convent to which they were devoted. But, in the event, Ignatius developed into a very unclerical young man. So only one option remained, the ill-paid trade of a gentleman-retainer in a more military household.

His Basque nationality coloured his outlook and career in other ways. He admits this drily and briefly in his dictated auto-biography. His 'immense' desire to succeed in all he undertook, to gain honour, to excel foreigners, was, he recognised, though reinforced by his reading of romantic novels, part of his family breeding. So also were his Basque *punctilio* about proper behaviour. Those of his colleagues who came from backgrounds which were peasant or slatternly middle class marvelled at his primness and naively imagined that it came from aristocratic ancestry or his long sojourn in noble households. He had an obsessive interest in 'a proper order' in Jesuit houses especially at meal-times, and about cleanliness and good turn-out. His middle class origins made him shrink from servile work in the kitchen and stables. He clearly regarded ordinary parochial clerical work like visiting and catechising children as just as servile, fit for peasant, uneducated Mass-mongering clergy. He had a violently physical aversion from ugly men and did his best to keep them out of the Society. His aversion from heretics, Moslems and Jews was still more instinctive. His family background and lay training accustomed him to an automatic reverence for aristocrats and rank, and made him expert in lobbying the great. His biographers went further. They tended to attribute his habitual detachment and difficulty in communicating with his colleagues to his nationality. They never went so far as to suggest that he, more especially in his later years in Rome, thought in Basque and so had great difficulty in expressing himself in other languages. His linguistic ability was notoriously limited: his preaching in French was treated with levity, and his efforts to preach in Italian a farrago of Italian, Latin and Castilian words. In spite of his immensely long university career his command of written Latin was so uncertain that he used skilled Latinists to translate his Castilian into something which would pass muster with the Roman bureaucrats. There is some evidence that his command of Castilian Spanish was imperfect. The one and only surviving specimen in that language in his own hand is a fragment of his private spiritual diary for 1544-5. It is full of smudges and alterations and shows little regard for punctuation or syntax. But this is inconclusive evidence. Diary entries written for no eye but the writer's and in a tense and highly emotional state are not literary compositions. The original text of the Jesuit *Constitutions* was in Castilian, not written by Ignatius but by his secretary, Polanco, a much better-educated man. Bobadilla, an independent-minded Spanish Jesuit who knew both men, complained that the text was an unreadable jungle of words full of interminably long sentences packed with restrictive clauses. No doubt its literary shortcomings were the result of a combination of factors: Ignatius's Basque mind, the fact that he was tortured with scruples about the wording of many crucial passages, and the fact that Castilian may not be a language well-fitted for legislative texts. The Emperor Charles V, a contemporary and a good judge of languages, remarked that German was good for controlling horses, French for statesmen, English for calling birds, and 'Spanish' for addressing kings and God.

In Ignatius's time and for almost a century afterwards the Society was gravely troubled by the competing nationalisms of its members. The Castilians, Aragonese and Portuguese complained bitterly that the Generalate in Rome was dominated by men not of their nations. In 16th-century Europe and in religious Orders dominated by the middle classes it was practically impossible to exclude national and family loyalties. The earliest members of the Society often seem to have regarded themselves as recruiting sergeants. Some inevitably recruited their brothers, nephews and cousins. Among these foundation members were Codure, Canisius, Laynez and Salmeron. It is noticeable in an early list of Jesuits received into the Society in Italy that there are two men named Codure, two named Canisius, three named Laynez and two named Salmeron. Did Ignatius himself recruit Basques and give them important posts in the Society? Two of his nephews, Milian Loyola and Antonio Araoz, certainly became Jesuits in his time. Milian was soon sent home to Guipuzcoa to die young. Antonio was made Provincial of Castile. Ignatius's first secretary was Francis Xavier, a Guipuzcoan Basque: later he was Ignatius's commissary in charge of all Far Eastern Jesuit missions. Otherwise the admittedly incomplete lists of early Jesuits contain extremely few who can be identified as Basques: none of them attained any eminence in the Society. No doubt Ignatius realised that Basque dominance of the very insecure infant Society would be fatal to its chances of survival and growth. So he confined himself to favouring enough relatives and other Basques to give the lie to any charge at home that he was lacking in 'proper' loyalties.

It has sometimes been argued that Ignatius's character in his Jesuit days owed far more to his military training, ascetic ideals and purely personal idiosyncrasies than to his national origins. The idea that he was, before all else, a soldier, and so made the Society a 16th-century equivalent of the Salvation Army dies hard. It is even possible, with some stretch of the imagination, to think that his portraits bear a resemblance to those of General Montgomery. But hard evidence for this view is lacking. Ignatius did certainly say of himself:

'. . . above all he loved exercises in the use of arms, drawn by an immense desire to acquire vain honour . . .'

His training as a page and gentleman-retainer must have included exercises in horsemanship and the use of a sword, fowling piece and boar-spear. But, as Cervantes noted, the days of the armoured fighting retainers who peopled the pages of Ignatius's favourite light reading were practically over. Like all men of some station in society, Ignatius the retainer habitually wore a sword and practised with it since he had 'affairs of honour'. But he was not a trained professional soldier. Like the 'gentleman' minor characters in Shakespeare's plays his working life mainly consisted of running errands and endless, boring waiting in anterooms.

His ascetic ideals certainly led him to impose upon himself and upon all Jesuit novices a limited but dramatic measure of acceptance of things which he naturally hated. During one short period during his thirties he deliberately behaved 'improperly', becoming dirty, unshaven and frowsty. Some years later, again temporarily and with self-conscious effort, he undertook 'servile works' as a hospital porter and washer-up in kitchens. Normally he travelled sensibly on a horse or mule, abandoning the roads for boats wherever it was possible. Travelling long distances on foot was immensely wasteful of time and energy, particularly for Ignatius who had a permanently damaged leg. However, he does seem a few times to have gone on foot as a penitential exercise. His *Autobiography* and *Constitutions* show that, to his way of thinking, 'proper' conduct and common sense must normally prevail: ascetic practices are rare exceptions which prove that rule.

He had his share of personal idiosyncrasies about which his colleagues groused. He could be wildly inconsistent in his behaviour. Jesuits who worked for years in close contact with him seemed, as Laynez complained, constantly to be the butts of his harshness and ill-humour. 'He never', wrote Ribadeneira, 'spoke a kind word to Polanco.' Yet Polanco was his secretary for years and practically the co-author of the *Constitutions*. On the other hand Ignatius treated some of the Society's most tiresome prima donnas — for instance Simon Rodriguez and Francis Borgia, Duke of Gandia in his early days as a Jesuit — with extreme indulgence. His behaviour over admissions to, and dismissals from, the Society was, as he himself later admitted, totally illogical. He was given to very contradictory rhetorical statements. On some occasions he ruled out almost any justification for disobeying a superior's order, above all if the superior were the Pope. Yet he himself several times did his best, by lobbying the influential, to secure papal decisions of the sort he wanted, or to bring about the repeal of decisions he thought wrong. On at least one occasion he urged a Jesuit to ignore the Society's rules and do what he thought best. Sometimes Ignatius attacked the anti-Semitism of most Spanish Jesuits. He received *conversos* into the Society in Italy and harboured Laynez and Polanco though he knew well they were 'New Christians' of Jewish descent. Yet, in an uninhibited moment, he could boast that Guipuzcoa contained no *conversos* or agree with Simon Rodriguez' view that an Inquisition should be set up in Portugal to harass Spanish *conversos* fleeing there from the severities of the Spanish Inquisition. At one time Ignatius could direct Jesuits in Germany to treat Protestants kindly: in 1554 he instructed them to press for penal sanctions against them and regretted that politics prevented the setting up of a German Inquisition.

Hagiographers have found a variety of excuses for his harshness and inconsistency. Ribadeneira suggested piously that, as a saint with supernatural vision into the needs of particular Jesuits' souls, he treated the weak kindly and braced the strong. Recently it has been suggested that the inconsistencies were part of a deliberate policy of extreme flexibility. There is a small modicum of truth in both explanations. But no amount of explanation can smooth away Ignatius's real native roughness of character. Pope Paul IV was not exaggerating greatly when, after Ignatius's death, he called him 'the old tyrant'.

Ignatius's anti-intellectualism was probably the result of both his nationality and his personal taste. Basque parents in the 16th century had a keen eye to the main chance and a utilitarian attitude toward academic learning. Ignatius shared this attitude. The sections on Jesuit studies in the *Constitutions* treat learning bluntly as something essential, as clerical society was then organised, to set Jesuits free from the servile chores performed by a host of uneducated clergy, and to give the Society prestige. The content of the Society's education must be utterly orthodox. The methods used must therefore be authoritarian: lectures by masters drawn *verbatim* from 'approved authors', dictated notes to be memorised by the pupils: no reading of books other than approved texts. Ignatius's own mental limitations and painfully long academic experience fitted in here with his breeding.

The few surviving pages of his spiritual diary show us at least a part of his mind with its defences down. His entries show how very little his years of academic theology at university had changed the primitive, peasant way in which he regarded the ultimate truths of his faith. In the last resort whatever the theology lecturers said, Ignatius was sure that 'the eternal Father' is like a distant, all-powerful monarch: the 'Son' and 'the Mother' are, like earthly aristocratic patrons, the ordinary person's necessary 'Mediators' with 'the divine Majesty', and, as such, are treated as if of equal importance. The imagery is drawn from Court life and also from the pictures and statues round Ignatius's oratory. Very occasionally it occurs to him that he is thinking untheologically, and he makes an effort to put the record straight. Thus on 8 February 1544 he wrote:

> 'This I willed to offer to the Father with the mediation and prayer of the Mother and the Son. And when I had addressed myself in the first prayer to her to aid me with her Son and with the Father, then I did so to the Son that he would aid me with the Mother before the Father . . .'

Or, more clearly, on 18 February:

> '. . . there came into my mind to address myself to all the saints through whom I could get our Lady and her Son to intercede for me to the most Holy Trinity . . . I presented and confirmed the completed oblation to the most Holy Trinity before all its heavenly Court, thanking with a very intense love the Divine Persons, then our Lady and her Son, then the angels, the holy Fathers, the apostles, the disciples and all the saints who had helped me. Then I vested and prepared the altar and there came to me to say: Eternal Father, I confirm; Eternal Son, I confirm; Holy Eternal Spirit, I confirm . . .'

He was much concerned about using the proper channels of approach to the divine Majesty. On at least one occasion he was very upset because he felt that he had offended the Mother by concentrating his attention too exclusively on the Son as Mediator.

It was quite natural that a man whose mind moved on this plane, should have instructed Jesuit students to endure cheerfully a pemmicanised form of the highly intellectual theology of Thomas Aquinas. This was exactly what he himself had endured. All the experts agreed that Aquinas's theology was currently highly approved by Rome: study of it was essential for any Order seeking Roman approbation. But the Jesuit students need have no fears. Ignatius's piety had passed unscathed through the academic fire, and so therefore could theirs.

Ignatius had a last idiosyncrasy which was perhaps his most curious one and, for that reason, not much remarked on by Jesuit historians until recently. This was his attitude to, and relations with, women. He belonged to a European society in which females were officially regarded, and customarily treated, as minors and moral weaklings. In Spain, as Teresa of Avila noted, the menfolk monopolised the chairs while the womenfolk squatted apart on the floor, ladies sitting on cushions. Women who appeared in public places unchaperoned and unveiled were presumed to be of bad character. Respectable women were expected to pass their whole lives under male tutelage. Their fathers committed them to the power of their husbands (or, if they became nuns, to the power of the bishop). Widows were expected to remarry or be 'veiled' by a bishop and enter a semi-nunnish existence at home under his guardianship. Ignatius's general attitude to women was inevitably conventional. In the *Spiritual Exercises* he remarks that the Devil behaves like a woman: if treated firmly he gives no trouble: if treated gently he will soon become the master. No doubt Ignatius agreed with Francis Xavier's comment that it was a waste of time to evangelise women: convert the husbands and fathers and they would automatically see to the conversion of their womenfolk.

In real life, however, as Ignatius's comment shows, the situation of women did not correspond with theory. Many wives had the whiphand over their husbands and households. There were many wealthy and aristocratic widows who were a law unto themselves. Isabella the Catholic Queen of Castile was a very effective ruler of her own kingdom and, though conforming to convention in public with her husband, King Ferdinand of Aragon, very much the mistress in her own house. There were abbesses, prioresses and many aristocratic communities of nuns who paid scant lip-service to their subjugation to episcopal authority. Also, of course, especially in large towns, there were many women, especially domestic servants and prostitutes, who were in no way respectable or conventional.

Ignatius lived in a Catholic society where virginity, celibacy and the sanctity of the marriage bond were held in high honour. A large proportion of the population was unmarried. It included priests, monks, friars and nuns who were very numerous: a town like Seville had forty religious houses and at least as many churches, each served by a multiplicity of curates and chaplains. Then there were the universities. Since they were still regarded as Church seminaries, the teachers and students were all officially celibate. Lay life also contained a great many men and women who never married for a variety of mostly economic reasons. In families like Ignatius's, younger sons were discouraged from marrying so that the family property might be saved from division. Had Ignatius remained a layman and retainer, it is unlikely that he would have been able to marry. Many women were kept at home as spinsters to help support their ageing parents.

But the sexual practice of society was very often at variance with the ideal. Ignatius's own family contained at least one example of a repeated breach of clerical celibacy. Such breaches were so frequent in Spain that the bishops and the Inquisition often treated them leniently. Ignatius's contemporary and correspondent, the Englishman Reginald Pole, became Cardinal Legate for England and Ireland. His Legatine Register contains numerous dispensations to the illegitimate sons of priests in Ireland to be admitted to Holy Orders. When Ignatius was General of the Jesuits he was faced with the problem of admitting bastards to the Society. In some cases, where, it seems, the bastardy was particularly notorious or the circumstances unnusually bad, he accepted men semi-officially as 'oblates'.

In his *Autobiography* he admitted that, before his first religious conversion at the age of thirty, he was 'a man of the world absorbed in vanity'. He makes it clear that he was unchaste, like all other gentlemen-retainers, and was 'obsessed' with women. Some hagiographers have blamed him for pious exaggeration on this point. Others, concerned to show how remarkable his conversion was, have suggested that he was a Don Juan. But Ignatius was being drily matter-of-fact: his sexual behaviour and standards had been those normal in the circles in which he had moved and quite unremarkable. He therefore regarded it as positive proof of the divine origin of his very first vision ('an Image of our Lady with the Holy Child Jesus') that it brought with it a miracle:

> 'It was followed by a great disgust of his past life especially carnal things. From that moment to August 1553 when he wrote this memory, he never gave the slightest consent to sensual solicitations . . .'

We can hardly interpret this sweeping statement as meaning that, from the moment of the vision Ignatius became incapable of sexual feelings and fantasies. The *Autobiography* and, still more, the *Diary*, show that his external habit of gravity and reserve coexisted uneasily with a very volatile and emotional temperament. Though he certainly tried to sort out (and even analyse) his moods and feelings and not remain merely a prey to them, his inner life was often turbulent to the end. Moods of exaltation and depression alternated in his mind: he was tortured by temptations or suspected temptations and by scruples. His instructions, in the *Spiritual Exercises*, on how a Jesuit director should deal with penitents' temperaments and scuples in order to guide their storm-tossed minds into the haven of 'holy indifference' are no indication that he himself attained that haven permanently and securely. In Paris, before the start of the Society of Jesus, he seems to have confided to a much-tempted colleague, Pierre Favre, that he himself was tormented by scruples about his past confessions and also by temptations of the flesh and to vainglory. A few months after the crucial first vision, Ignatius only narrowly prevented himself from assaulting and killing a Moslem with whom he argued about religion. His action, not long· afterwards, in leaving his weapons hung up in in a shrine of our Lady was probably an act which was at once pious, symbolic and prudential. The extraordinary physical penances which he then undertook, with little regard for his health or discretion, were undoubtedly meant, in part, to help in his struggle to overcome carnality. In later life in Rome, even when much sickness, a sedentary life and a settled habit of piety had weakened his impulsiveness he could still alarm his colleagues with fits of blazing anger.

Considering these facts, it is therefore remarkable that, from immediately after the first vision until about 1547, he displayed a marked interest in women. After the vision his first stay of any real length of time was at Manresa. There a group of aristocratic women took a great deal of interest in him, sought his advice freely, and supported him with alms. They were so much with him that the locals sardonically nicknamed them 'Inigas': 'Inigo's women'. When he moved on from Manresa it was usually women who offered him alms, and, if he stayed any length of time, formed a group to whom he gave spiritual instruction. At Barcelona he was succoured by the widow Pascual and Isabella Roser, whose spiritual direction he undertook and who provided for his keep and his tuition. From this point onwards in his changes of residence through university towns, his lady friends remained loyal to him after his departure, sending on bankers' drafts to him. At university he was repeatedly drawn, as if by

a magnet, to the direction of women of every kind, idle aristocrats, widows, workmen's wives, unmarried working girls,
women of doubtful virtue and 'beatas' (those females in black
veils who have always haunted churches and presbyteries.) His
talks to groups (sometimes up to forty at a time) of these produced
some strange effects: black depressions, visions of the devil as
a savage black dog, fainting fits and ecstasies. His dogged
perseverance in these activities as a lay student aroused hostile
comment, prosecution by the Inquisition and two spells in gaol.
He was forbidden by the Church authorities to continue his
teaching of women. His enthusiasm for the activity was cooled
but not destroyed. In Paris he had new groups of women. A short
begging trip to Flanders provided him with yet another enthusiastic group of female supporters and correspondents. When he
finally settled in Rome and was caught up in the toil of establishing the Society, he actually extended the scope of his work
with women. He undertook on a considerable scale the highly
delicate and thorny job of 'reforming' unruly convents. He undertook the guidance of groups of aristocratic women, putting
them through spiritual exercises. It is true that the rather bleak
and terse official text of his *Spiritual Exercises* speaks of the
exercitants as male. But the 16th-century Castilian and Latin in
which it was written were languages with a strong male bias. The
text was doctored for the consumption of critical Roman bureaucrats. Neither Ignatius nor any other Jesuit before the 19th
century dreamed of using it as it stood in print with exercitants.
He certainly used some sort of exercises constantly with women
from his Manresa days. Also he started homes for repentant
whores and girls without visible means of support, insisting on
undertaking the chaplaincies himself. His principal woman
friend, Isabella Roser of Barcelona, with whom he had long
corresponded, now joined him in Rome. In 1545, by arrangement
with him and the Pope, she and two friends formed a Congregation, the nucleus of what was meant to be a disciplined body
of female auxiliaries.

The experiences of a host of highly ascetic clergy from Paul of
Tarsus to Jerome and Basil, the Celtic and Anglo-Saxon monks,
the toughly male Cistercian founders, Francis of Assisi and
Dominic had showed that spiritual leaders attracted women in
large numbers. Europe and the Near East always contained a
huge, largely untapped and uncontrolled fund of feminine
enthusiasm, organising power and religiosity. The average
clerical leader boggled at the discovery, showed acute embarrass-

ment, tried to escape involvement, and ended by compromise. An effort was usually made to fend off the wilder majority of females and to herd the apparently more docile and useful minority into convents straitly dependent on the authority of the Orders. The real result was rarely so tidy and seemly. So, for instance, the grimly austere Cistercians had, for many years, to endure an embattled array of militant aristocratic Cistercian abbesses of huge convents. They bullied the Popes into allowing them to ordain (personally) their own chaplains: they picketed the Geneal Chapter of Cistercian abbots and refused to accept its rulings. The moves made by Isabella and Ignatius in 1545 led to a very severe Jesuit crisis. Its ramifications, made obscure by the burning of almost all Ignatius's private papers, on his orders, after his death, have only recently been gingerly investigated by a Jesuit historian. There were powerful enemies of the Society who were, or professed to be, very scandalised by the intense interest Ignatius showed in women. Prominent Jesuits resented the intimacy he gave to women (and some laymen) and denied to his colleagues. They felt that he would wreck the Society. It would collapse under a load of scandal and the great weight of feminine influences. Ignatius seems to have been caught unawares by the violence of the storm, although it had been brewing for years, at Manresa, at Barcelona, at the Spanish university towns, and when the 'Homes of Rescue' in Rome were opened.

The outcome was a curious compromise. Isabella and her companions were, no doubt with great difficulty, persuaded to leave Rome for Spain, where they mostly entered conventional nunneries. With papal approval an odd clause was put into the Jesuit *Constitutions* forbidding them:

'to take charge of religious women or any other women whatsoever to be their confessors regularly or to direct them ...'

This, fairly effectively, demonstrated to the critics that the Society would never have any formally organised, disciplined 'Jesuitess' auxiliaries either kept in convents or under vows but in lay life. It most probably also was meant to fend off female enthusiasts who might use their influence in the corridors of ecclesiastical power to infiltrate the Society and swamp it. No woman, however highly-placed, now had any right to demand Jesuit direction. But, on the other hand, Ignatius and the Society were allowed a great deal of latitude. The clause in the *Constitutions* goes on to say that the prohibition in no way bound them to refuse to hear the confessions of nuns, even whole convents of them, provided the arrangement was not contractual. Ignatius and the Society since his day interpreted all this to mean that they could undertake whatever work among women they chose, without being in any way bound to it, legally or spiritually, the moment they decided its continuance would cramp their style or lead them into danger. Ignatius, after a discreet pause, resumed his female friendships and correspondence, perhaps with a shade more caution.

In his case, as in those of a great many austere spiritual leaders who have had close association with women, the real nature of the relationship will always remain obscure. He very probably found, without acknowledging it to himself, an ease and comfort in the relationship which was lacking in the rather stark, all-male atmosphere of the Society. Without knowing it, he was possibly a little in love with Isabella Roser. He does seem to have been in love with our Lady as she appeared in his frequent visions and in her 'loquelae' (words) spoken to him in the intimacies of his mind. His *Diary* for 1544-5 — just before the Roser crisis — records the agonies of remorse that he felt when he began to imagine that he had offended our Lady by neglecting her. Her face and voice no longer came to him. When they did return he was blinded with sobs and floods of tears. Still, he was a man of intense emotions which could surge out ungovernably in all directions. The *Diary* is all blotted with his tears. We might find this intolerably at variance with his rigidly traditional and conventional opinions about womankind in general, marriage and love. He was the man who wrote in the *Exercises*:

'In a quarrel with a man, it is natural for a woman to lose heart and run away when he faces up to her; on the other hand, if the man begins to be afraid and to give ground, her rage, vindictiveness and fury overflow and know no limit . . .'

Almost every phrase in that can be found in the works of standard medieval and early 16th-century spiritual writers. We are not wrong in detecting in Ignatius's statement and other passages in the *Exercises* and his letters an assumption that a man and a woman cannot meet as equals: the relation must be that of master and servant or parent and child. The section on making a decision in the *Exercises* presumes that it is a man who marries: the bride submits. Marriage, he writes, should be undertaken objectively for the service of God, not for merely human and carnal reasons. Marriage is a very poor second best to virginity and celibacy.

The glaring contrast between these opinions and Ignatius's affection for women cannot be piously smoothed away. But the contrast can be found all over the pages of Church history.

*   *   *

During most of the second period of his life, from his thirty-first to his forty-eighth year, Ignatius's life-style was that of an itinerant student. He was badly wounded during military operations at Pamplona in Navarre in May 1521 and carried to his family home at Loyola, where he remained as a sick man for nine months. During that time his religious conversion began. In February 1522 he set out on a series of pilgrimages, first to a Basque shrine at Aranzazu, and then across to Catalonia to a famous shrine at Montserrat. Here he dramatically laid aside his role as a gentleman-retainer, collected his arrears of pay and began to cast round for a new role. He experimented with several. First he toured monasteries of Carthusians, Benedictines and friars, staying in their guest-houses and sampling their ways of life. Then followed spells as a hospital attendant and a 'holy tramp'. Finally he set up as a hermit in a cave by the River Cardoner, not far from the town of Manresa. There was nothing particularly original about any of these experiments. He, like most of his contemporaries, was much affected by images of the saints in churches. He had often seen the saints following these ways of life, represented in statues, wall-paintings, altar-pieces and stained glass. At Loyola he had had the time to read a book of colourful *Lives of the Saints.* Anyway contemporary Spain, to judge from its police-court records and *picaresque* novels, contains plenty of pious eccentrics. Like them Ignatius was treated with a mixture of derision and respect. Other devout or eccentric persons flocked to visit him and bring him food. This pleased him because he was trying to embark on a proper 'life of devotion'. He was anxious to pick up tips on devotional technique and by no means averse to trying out his methods on others.

Then in February 1523 he abandoned his hermitage. His attempts to copy the hints on penance culled from hearsay and the *Lives of the Saints* had made him thoroughly ill. He cut his hair, beard and nails, washed and set out on the greatest of all pilgrimages, to Jerusalem. To many medieval and 16th-century devout people this was the peak of their spiritual aspirations. He was probably pleased at first to discover that the pilgrimage route was so heavily frequented and well-organised that ample provision was made for poor pilgrims like himself. He was less pleased when he got to Palestine to find that the roads were patrolled by armed Moslems and the Holy Places straitly controlled by authoritarian Franciscan Guardians. His typically brash effort to evade their regulations led to his deportation not long after his arrival. Back in Spain after a year's absence, he was in a quandary. His feelings and his devotional exercises provided no clear answer to what he was coming to see as his absolute need for a divinely guaranteed vocation.

In the event he plumped, possibly persuaded by Isabella Roser, for what was then an increasingly popular standby occupation for youths and young men of some ability but no prospective niche in life — university studies. Isabella provided him with a tutor to give him an intensive pre-university course in elementary Latin grammar. The course, which went on for two years, did him little good. Part of the reason for this was his constant preoccupation with 'devotion' and the affairs of his devout acquaintances. Then he left Barcelona and embarked on a course of university studies which was to drag on for more than twelve years and carry him to Alcala and Salamanca in Spain, to Paris, and then to Venice.

He found himself in yet another very unfamiliar environment. In some ways it suited his purpose: it provided a convenient haven or base while he continued his spiritual search; in university towns he could hope to find devout persons and spiritual instruction and stimulus. But in a good many other ways a university environment did not suit him. To start with, early 16th-century universities were not islands of tranquillity in a turbulent Europe. Indeed they did have an element of discipline and tradition. But they had to coexist with turbulence and disorder among both masters and students. Ignatius's Europe was, if anything, over-provided with universities, a good many of which had been founded in the recent past largely to gratify the desire of princes, archbishops and town councils for prestige and economic gain. The overall student population was steadily increasing, but not large enough to fill all the universities which therefore competed hotly with each other. Masters and students were constantly moving from university to university and were rarely refused entry. The academic world was not insulated against the pressures of society and governments: in fact it was ultra-sensitive to them. A university could be hard-hit by war and the dismissal of alien students: and wars were frequent. It could be emptied by an epidemic of plague: and plague was endemic in much of Europe. Its population could be drastically reduced by famines and bouts of inflation. Ignatius's academic career coincided with the severe onset of the great 16th-century price-rise. Just as surely, the student population could be decimated by bouts of official repression caused by evidence of heretical teaching and practices, or even by disorderly academic wrangles. Ignatius's university years also coincided with a series of unpleasant official persecutions. His stay at Alcala and Salamanca coincided with attacks by the Inquisition on groups of 'the Illuminated', of followers of the Dutch critic of the Catholic establishment, Desiderius Erasmus, and of secret Protestants. Ignatius's efforts at Alcala to launch among undergraduates and women of the town what would today perhaps be called 'charismatic groups' of an extremist kind led to his arrest and imprisonment. Like a good many others at the time he left for Salamanca. There, with great disregard for common sense and authority, he tried to start more 'charismatic groups', was again arrested and lucky to escape severe punishment. He left, with other suspect persons, for Paris.

The University of Paris was not exempt from the general academic malaise. There was tension between traditionalists and 'Erasmians', and a good deal of covert Protestantism. Ignatius secured entry to the College of Sainte Barbe which had a reputation for moderate Erasmianism. But he now behaved more circumspectly. He was fortunate because while he was in the College in 1534 the Protestant groups staged a brave 'demonstration'. They plastered the main buildings in the university and city with provocative posters stuck up at dead of night. This led to a violent purge from the university of all suspects. Ignatius this time escaped attention. By 1535 he had moved on to study in Venice. The usual storms in academic life were raging in Italy and the highly sophisticated city had a reputation as a great centre of Erasmianism and Protestantism. Ignatius's acquaintances there included both Erasmians and ecclesiastical reactionaries. By this time he had learned by hard experience that he and his friends, as itinerant students, were certain to be cross-questioned and watched by the Church authorities everywhere they went. His streak of brashness had brought him into dangerous conflict with them; his other, very native, streak of hard-headed prudence had narrowly got him out of trouble. Now both tendencies in him combined oddly. He and his friends had agreed in Paris to remove themselves to Jerusalem and so escape the broils in Europe. At Venice they discovered that war in the Mediterranean made this expedient impracticable. Now Ignatius supported a proposition that they should go boldly straight to the top, to the Pope, the supreme Church authority, and ask to be received under the shelter of his patronage. It was a daring scheme which appealed to both his brashness and his prudence. Pending the execution of the plan, and during the negotiations in Rome which were bound to be protracted and difficult, hard prudence dictated that he and his companions should behave with the utmost circumspection and live down their reputation for radicalism. This decision is surely reflected in the extraordinary language of Ignatius's *Rules for Thinking with the Church* incorporated into his *Spiritual Exercises*. Their extreme Catholic conformism reads almost like a radical's recantation. It has all the atmosphere of those turbulent and confused 1530s and 1540s when strong criticism of the Church establishment was rife, and panic-stricken conservatives saw Protestantism lurking behind the mildest Catholic critics:

'We should put away completely our own opinion and keep our minds ready and eager to give our entire obedience to our holy Mother the hierarchical Church . . . We should speak with approval of confession to a priest . . . we should openly approve of the frequent hearing of Mass . . . and of all the canonical hours . . . We should speak with particular approval of religious Orders . . . we should express approval of the vows of religion . . . we should approve of the relics of saints . . . visits to Station churches, pilgrimages, jubilees, Crusade bulls, the lighting of candles in churches . . . the laws of fasting . . . we should praise church decoration and architecture . . . Finally all the Church's commandments should be spoken of favourably, our minds being always eager to find arguments in her defence, never in criticism . . .'

Ignatius also soon discovered that the universities were far from being centres of deep piety and other-worldliness. Most of the students and young masters he met were consumed with anxiety about money and their chances of getting a good livelihood when they left university. The sharpest and financially best-provided students headed straight for universities with faculties of civil and canon law; graduating in those disciplines almost guaranteed them lucrative posts in Church or royal administration. Those rather less intelligent, but with funds and stamina, steeled themselves for the very long haul to a doctorate in theology. That would open doors to teaching posts in universities, to canonries in cathedrals, and, patrons and luck providing, possibly to the episcopate. The dullards or the lazy who could not attain to these heights or afford financially to stay at university so long, hoped only for a bachelorship or mastership in arts. Then, with luck and patronage, they might attain a good Church benefice, the mastership of a school, or a post as a secretary. If all else failed, they could enter a religious Order. If they were careful to chose a religious Order or house ill-endowed with graduates, they might end their lives as superiors. And lastly there were numerous dropouts who left the university without graduating at all or as mere bachelors of arts, defeated by lack of money and stamina. Some of these ended as poor curates. Others entered religious Orders: the infant Society of Jesus was to suffer from a surfeit of applicants of this type. Others went into business or drifted off to America. Ignatius's first four intimate student-friends all became drop-outs. One, Calixto de Sa, was pious: he went on a pilgrimage to Jerusalem and then escorted a group of Ignatius's 'spiritual women and beatas' to America, ostensibly to enter convents there. Calixto went into business on the American frontier and became a rich man. Juan de Arteaga also drifted off to Amerca, took Orders there and became the bishop of a frontier diocese. Lope de Caceres lived a not very edifying life as a layman at home in Segovia. Jean de Reynalde, a Frenchman, went back to France and joined a religious Order.

In the first flush of his conversion Ignatius gave away his money and expected to live as God provided: that was how *The Lives of the Saints* seemed to indicate that saints lived. He never abandoned the idea that this was the proper way for the really devout. But hard experience taught him that compromise was essential, especially for poor university students. At Manresa and Barcelona he acquiesced in the arrangements made by his hard-headed women friends. He lived on their regular remittances, only resorting to door-to-door begging in times of necessity. Common sense taught him that begging was time-consuming and brought him a reputation for idleness and sponging. At Alcala and Salamanca he found that the fortunate few lived on regular remittances from relatives or patrons or on the proceeds of benefices. The average student struggled on, living from hand-to-mouth on occasional remittances from home (usually in food), begging from door to door on feast days, and on touting for free or cut-price lectures. In Spanish universities bursaries and charitable university Colleges were few and over-subscribed.

In fact Ignatius's steady income from remittances, his mature age, and knowledge of the world made him popular and something of a 'student counsellor'.

In Paris he found the money situation worse than in Spain. His lady friends had difficulty in finding merchants able to remit cash over the frontier. Ignatius was no linguist. Spanish students were often treated almost as enemy aliens in France. He was refused employment as a servitor to rich undergraduates and dons. The only lodging he could get was in a hospital, in exchange for menial tasks. The Montaigu, a very Spartan charitable hostel which normally accepted Netherlanders and Spaniards, was full up. In desperation Ignatius took off on begging tours to Flanders and England, sensibly choosing countries allied to Spain. 'Begging' for a man so mute in French, Flemish and English, inevitably meant applying to Spanish expatriates, friends of friends. The proceeds of the tours tided him over further searches for cheap lodgings and tuition. He was driven to strange expedients. He did his grammar and philosophy courses in Sainte-Barbe, a privately owned pre-university cramming establishment for young boys run by a Basque. Ignatius and a few friends shared a free chamber there in exchange for teaching boys. In their spare time they touted for needy bachelors and masters of arts, finding them paying pupils and, in return, getting free or cheap tuition. Food was not provided in Sainte-Barbe, so the friends messed together and shared a common purse as many of their contemporaries did. The theology course provided special difficulties. Sainte-Barbe only dealt with arts. The lecture fees at the great theology Colleges, the Sorbonne and the Navarre, were beyond the friends' means. Ignatius made do with free lectures at the Dominican house of studies of St. Jacques (probably recommended for charity by Spanish friends in the Order) and from friends who were bachelors of theology. The arrangements would be the usual private ones: Ignatius got free or cut-price tuition in return for finding paying pupils for his teachers. Then his health broke down badly and his course and residence at Paris came to an abrupt end. He had to return home to Guipuzcoa to recuperate. He undoubtedly made use of the opportunity to solicit donations and remittances. Then he set out for Venice to rendezvous with his Paris friends. Venice, like most Italian universities outside Rome, had no proper faculty of theology: anyway Ignatius could not afford faculty lecture fees. As usual he made do with a private coaching in theology, mostly from Paris friends who had attained their bachelorate.

His hard experiences of student finances left their mark on the Jesuit *Constitutions*. In these Ignatius rejected any idea that Jesuit students should try to live by begging or soliciting remittances. They must live in Jesuit hostels which had adequate endowment funds. Begging was only allowed if the endowment arrangements broke down, due to the superior's lack of financial sense or fraud on the part of the patrons or trustees.

Careerism, money cares and fecklessness were not the only features of university life experienced and deplored by Ignatius. As a mature student with an unacademic cast of mind, he had no hope of passing examinations unless his studies were directed by authority, his courses were cut to the bare minimum, and his tuition contained careful drilling in basic elements. In theory university regulations provided admirably for such cases. In practice there were islands of system and direction in an academic sea of near chaos. Ignatius floundered hopelessly for years. At Alcala, his first university, he found himself in a strange environment. The university was dominated by academic 'Modernists' who based their courses on revolutionary new principles. Traditional university teaching was at a discount. Ignatius fell between two stools. He lacked the linguistic and literary ability and training needed for the new courses. The old courses were badly covered and required in beginners a training in technical dog-Latin and logic which his intensive course at Barcelona had hardly given him. As he later admitted he wandered blindly round the available free lectures in any and every subject. Most of them were far over his head. Salamanca, his second university, was mainly 'Traditionalist', but his stay there was too troubled and brief for his studies to take shape. By the time he got to Paris, his third university, he realised that he would get nowhere unless he could get that necessary and effective pre-university course in Latin grammar and logic which Barcelona had failed to give him. After two more years of financial anxiety and floundering he at last got the course he wanted, at Sainte-Barbe. Enormous and painful efforts by Ignatius, his friends and his tutors hoisted him up through the examinations for the bachelorate and mastership in arts. Laynez, one of the private tutors, frankly wrote later that he was lucky to scrape a pass. At this stage Ignatius's difficulty was that his friends had already embarked on courses for the post-graduate degrees in theology. If he did not follow suit he would have to leave them and the university while he was still quite unsure of his vocation. Consequently, he was forced to attempt the theology course, though he and his tutors knew well that it was beyond his capability. By this time the theology syllabus was divided into two parts, 'Scholastic' and 'Positive'. 'Positive Theology' had been admitted very recently as a grudging concession to the strength of that 'Modernist' movement in learning which Ignatius had encountered first at Alcala. It involved a close literary study of Scripture and the Church Fathers. For this beginners had to have a good grounding in classical Latin and the ability to learn some Hebrew and Greek. Ignatius was a non-starter at 'Positive'. 'Scholastic' was the old traditional core of the subject. Its approach and manner of exposition were abstract, rational and philosophical. It abounded in technical jargon, complexities and subtle distinctions. No student could stay the course or pass the examinations unless he had gained a good pass in arts, but Ignatius had barely scraped through arts. He was weary of study, feeling old, and losing his good health. He missed out 'Positive' and tackled 'Scholastic' resolutely without acquiring any more than a certain familiarity with the outlines of the subject or coming within measurable distance of pass standard in 'Scholastic' for the bachelorate of theology.

All this bitter experience comes out in his *Constitutions*. He regarded academic success with a mixture of scorn and respect. His experience inclined him to believe that university courses were ill-regulated and far too long-winded. Jesuit students must, as much as possible, be taught in separate Colleges only appearing before university dons for degree examinations. Their courses must be abbreviated. Ignatius often echoed the words of his favourite book, *The Imitation of Christ*, that it is far better to know real faith, hope and charity, than to be able to define them with scholastic exactitude. Yet, on the other hand, conventionality, hard common sense, spiritual judgement and an academic habit of mind all inclined him to agree with Teresa of Avila that, if you have to choose between judgement and learning in a priest, you should, on balance, prefer learning. It did seem in the early 16th century that the religiosity of the ignorant all too often turned to fanaticism and was unteachable: the learned, if devoid of piety, were unlikely to be fanatics and could perhaps be taught better. So Ignatius insisted that full membership of the Society of Jesus should be limited normally to men who, unlike himself, were capable of a full theology course, both 'Positive' and 'Scholastic'. The 'unlearned' or 'insufficiently learned' (like himself) should normally only be admitted sparingly as coadjutors or auxiliaries of 'the Fathers'. Every literate entrant into the

Society must, as a main priority, be given a thorough grounding in Latin of the sort which Ignatius himself had never received.

But his greatest complaint against the universities was their ignorance of, and resistance to, 'the life of devotion'. Etienne Pasquier, a distinguished graduate of Paris University after Ignatius's day, reported that in the early decades of the century students often lived in a disorderly way, gaming, drinking, playing violent pranks and whoring. It was not uncommon in the crowded conditions of city life for one building to have rooms for students and rooms for prostitutes side by side. Hostels like the Montaigu and Sainte-Barbe did stand as islands of discipline amidst licence. In such an atmosphere hostel discipline had to be draconic. Ignatius himself, despite his mature age and his position in Sainte-Barbe as both a student and graduate teacher of the boys, was repeatedly reprimanded severely by the principal for interfering with his disciplinary .arrangements. Once he was seriously threatened with a public flogging. As he later said, no amount of penalties, imprisonments in the hostel or floggings could prevent many boys and students from idleness and keeping bad company. Compulsory attendance at Mass in the hostel chapel and 'exercises' — the recital of set forms of prayer in common — had no better effect.

Ignatius's *Autobiography* casts light on the social and religious conditions which produced this feckless behaviour among men and boys who were almost all supposed to be tonsured clerics destined for the service of the Church. Many of them were no more religious than the ordinary women of the town. In fact Ignatius had found numbers of such women who were more quickly responsive to 'real devotion' than intelligent and well-meaning masters of arts like his friends Pierre Favre and Francis Xavier. They had all grown up in a society where the Catholic religion was taken for granted as a natural fact of life, an inevitability like the soil and the weather. It was also, as in Moslem countries today, a communal inheritance in which all shared by birth. Individuals often sat very light to religious practice: but even they assumed that they could no more escape God and the Church than they could jump out of their own skins. Formal religious instruction and doctrinal preaching existed, particularly in large town parishes, but huge numbers rarely came into contact with it. So Ignatius found that highly intelligent men like Favre and Xavier could conceal, under the outward appearances of academic learning and rationality, inner minds which were strange ragbags of religious legends, ancestral superstitions and primeval terrors. Ignatius himself was increasingly, if very slowly, moving out of this state and acquiring what he significantly called 'light' and 'a new mind'. But he did not and could not ever detach himself completely from the old mentality: he always remained more attached to it subconsciously than he realised.

Like the women of the town many students had only a vague and formal sense of sin. They could habitually behave in a sensual and highly unclerical way while being tortured with scruples about minor ritual mistakes. They rarely went to Confession and Communion except in the crises of life. Confession tended to mean standing before a priest and expecting him to cross-question you while you argued back. Communal life was thickly crowded with clergy and religious rituals, some formal and clerical, others antique and popular. Most people followed the crowd to great festival observances, but were distinctly casual about weekly Mass attendance. For most, prayer meant physical attendance at ritual observances. Once there most men stayed on the fringes of the crowd. They chattered, spat on the floor and made assignations. Thus in Portuguese India missionaries were compelled to have separate churches for Europeans and native converts, because the behaviour at Mass of the Europeans scandalised the converts.

The students' attitude to ordination was strangely mixed. They had a primitive sense that the 'oiling' of ordination (like the coronation anointing of kings) and the act of saying Mass were fearful divine mysteries. Writing in the 1570s of the Catholic England of his boyhood, the Englishman William Allen remarked that ordinands were terrified of undertaking the priesthood. No doubt this feeling accounted for Ignatius's very long hesitation about ordination and scruples about saying Mass for eighteen months after his ordination. Yet if the priesthood itself as a holy state was a fearful power, priests' benefices were regarded by the students and society generally as ordinary desirable offices of profit. Many students were driven on by economic and family pressures to acquire benefices. Then they were forced to seek ordination as the only way of securing their hold on the posts.

This mass of instinctive and often superstitious popular religion formed the background to a relatively small but important minority, 'the devout'. Ignatius joined the ranks of 'the devout' after his first conversion at Loyola. His account, in the *Auto-biography*, of his long-drawn-out initiation into 'devotion' stresses heavily his conviction that the whole process was supernatural and unique. As he saw it, it was a divine 'illumination' so that:

> 'all things seemed new to him as though he were a different man and had taken another intellect from that which he had previously . . .'

His account is so introverted that it gives an impression that all was from God directly and practically nothing of importance from human influences, though he never actually says this in so many words. In reality he was discovering for himself a spiritual tract of country which had already been well-charted and settled by a host of 'the devout' for centuries before his time.

From his childhood, and certainly during his service as a page and gentleman-retainer, he had observed from outside the behaviour of 'devout' people, their variety, and found out something of their practices. At Mass he saw different groups. At the back of the church and standing in the door and outside it would be ordinary folk, talking and fidgeting. There would be black-clad 'beatas' and pious men with rosaries, keeping up a steady *sotto voce* mutter of Pater Nosters, Ave Marias and Credos, sometimes kneeling, stretching out their arms in the form of a cross or prostrating themselves: occasionally they would get up, wander across to the statue of a saint to say Paters and Aves and kiss it. That would be the sum of their simple 'devotion', since they were quite illiterate. You could find some of them in the church any day or any time. They often banded together in parish guilds like Friendly Societies. Then there were people of a slightly higher social class with a little literacy. They had more complex ways of saying the rosary and a wide variety of prayer-formulas all originally culled from a copy of the most popular book of prayers, the *Primer*. Sitting or kneeling at the only benches in the church would be gentlefolk. Those of them who were 'devout' most likely appeared to pray from a book of devotions. It was not a missal, but might be a *Primer* or *Book of the Hours of the Blessed Virgin* in Basque or even Latin. These people were fairly literate and could often mouth the Latin psaltery of the Office convincingly and with a general knowledge of what it meant, even though they could not construe it for lack of Latin grammar. This class of 'the devout' undoubtedly belonged to confraternities and were strong on pilgrimages and gaining indulgences. Since they almost certainly had children or close relations who were monks, friars or nuns, they would be benefactors and *confratres* or sisters affiliated to religious houses, bound to special daily devotions to the founders, and entitled to be buried in the habit of an Order and in its cemetery. Such people had often learned from their *Primers*, or their association with an Order, little 'drills' for preparing for Confession and Communion. Preparation for Confession meant the use of some sort of *examen*, examining of conscience from the Seven Deadly Sins, the Ten Commandments, or any one of scores of other useful lists of possible sins. Most probably, as a sharp-eyed youth whiling away the hours in church, he had noticed, from the demeanour of the celebrant and the curates in the choir stalls, that the clergy varied greatly in their levels of 'devotion'. Some were very rustic and only at the devotional level of the 'beatas': they stumbled through the liturgical Latin like parrots. He wondered what they could possibly make of the Breviary Offices but recollected that most parishes had so many clergy that choir recital of the Office was fairly normal. The ignorant priest could say his rosary before his open book while his slightly better-educated fellows muttered the Latin in rough unison. In larger parishes the head priest was generally one of the 'Primer folk' and so a better confessor.

Lastly came the highest and rarest level of 'devotion' — 'meditation' or, as Ignatius later preferred to call it, 'contemplation'. Sharp observation in church could not have distinguished these people from 'Primer folk'. But Ignatius had, in his first job as a page, come under the influence of a small group of aristocratic 'contemplatives' so he knew something of their practices. These mostly derived from a widespread spiritual movement already almost two centuries old and sometimes called the *Devotio Moderna* — 'devotion for today'. Although the movement's aims and methods were remarkably practical and positively business-like, its leaders and most of its devotees tended to have university connections. The literature they produced quite lavishly even before the advent of printing, and after it more plentifully still, reflected the movement's mixture of educated sophistication and down-to-earth practicality. The overall aim was personal, individual conversion and sanctification. The authors warned their readers against falling into a pietistic craziness called 'Illuminism' — a deliberate cult of visions and miracles and extraordinary penances leading to wild ecstatic meetings and the formation of sects apart from ordinary congregations. Conversion was to be obtained by a variety of 'spiritual exercises'. Some, like the *examens*, were extensions of methods set out in the *Primers*. Others, involving ingenious ways of counting acts of virtue or sins in a notebook or on a rosary, or naming the rooms in your house after the virtues and practising them as you moved round, were original. Meditation or contemplation itself was an exercise which had many permutations and combinations, and involved pausing at numerous 'points' in the exercise to practise use of the faculties of the mind, memory, imagination and will on holy matters. Devotees were encouraged to read religious books meditatively and keep private notebooks in which they could record their spiritual thoughts and extracts copied from books. By far the most popular and widespread book in use was *The Imitation of Christ*, itself originally an 'extract book'.

Obviously no one could undertake meditation seriously unless he or she were well-educated, had servants and so adequate time for 'exercises', and access to books and to some spiritual director or confessor who was himself an adept of the system. Meditation was therefore practised in groups gathered in and round particularly devout religious houses or groups of unusually well-educated city clergy. Naturally the centres of the movement were in the areas of Europe which had the most population, urbanisation, economic activity and literacy — northern Italy and Flanders. By Ignatius's time almost every large town in Flanders had its group. Many were nameless. Others, of men, called themselves vaguely 'brethren', 'the devout' or 'brethren of the common life'; women's groups were called 'sisters' or *beguines*. In northern Italian towns they were even more numerous with names like the congregation of the Holy Wisdom, the oratory of Divine Love, the Paulists, the Barnabites, the Somaschi and the clerks of Chieti, Verona, Murano, S. Giorgio in Venice, Carpentras or Padua. As usual women's groups proliferated and were often nameless. The movement spilled over into some of the more backward areas of Europe, into south Germany across into Austria, to a few French towns, and a few centres in Spain.

The movement abounded in contradictions. The devotees felt passionately that the Church was grossly over-organised, its religion ultra-formalist and superficial: they were sent by God as reformers bringing a religion of grass-roots spontaneity, depth and simplicity. Some extremists among the devotees, spiritual Robespierres, talked of casting the dead husks of Catholic institutionalism on to the fire and rebuilding the Church on the movement. The moderate majority thought of themselves as a divine leaven, gradually re-educating and transforming the existing Catholic lump. Hence the movement appeared amorphous, shapeless, lacking in central direction. It had a multitude of educated, forceful individuals but no major leaders to lay down general laws. It produced a shower of 'occasional' literature, anonymous pamphlets, local groups' progress reports, collections of devotional hints and wise sayings, and conversion stories: but it produced no great spiritual writers. Its groups were a shifting ground. They rose and dissolved: they frequently changed shape and organisation. They fought shy of officialdom and Church regulation. Yet when we examine the groups we discover that their members had a positive passion for self-organisation, a mania for 'system' and 'method'. Some groups never developed beyond informal meetings of friends to swap experiences. Others infiltrated and took over existing local religious confraternities. Others organised themselves in a Napoleonic way as 'congregations' or 'oratories' or 'companions' with a simple common rule of life. They took private vows or yearly promises of chastity and poverty and shared a common purse. They undertook 'the apostolic life' — the way of life of Christ and his Apostles as they conceived it to have been. They set up private printing presses and published cheap, paperback devotional literature. They opened catechetical centres, cheap grammar schools and university hostels for poor students. They worked in hospitals and among the victims of famine and plague. They opened orphanages, Houses of Rescue for prostitutes, and 'Mounts of Piety' or loan funds for the deserving poor. They supplied chaplains and confessors to unhappy and disorderly convents of nuns.

Even more strikingly, devotees who, on principle, criticised traditional religious Orders savagely as haunts of formalism and decadence had long accepted a vocation to enter the Orders to convert them to 'meditation' and 'devotion'. Long before Ignatius's day and still in his time the influence of these strong-minded spiritual reorganisers worked inside the Orders like a violent purge or revolutionary force. There was war to the knife between 'Observants', fighting for a radical modernisation and the use of 'meditation', and orthodox 'Conventuals'. In some small Orders like the Carthusians and Camaldolese the war was over by the 1520s and the Observants victorious. In some bigger Orders there was an uneasy truce with Observant houses or even Provinces organised alongside the Conventual majority. The Franciscans had split completely and a set of totally separate Observant Orders appeared, the Observants, the Capuchins and the Minims, waging war on the Conventual rump.

All these extensive evangelistic operations led the devotees to systematise their methods of spiritual instruction. In their centres, the presbyteries of busy town parishes, the parlours of business men's houses, the Chapter rooms of Observant monasteries, masses of ingenuity and vigour were employed on what was a military campaign. With the utmost realism, befitting the children of successful business men and people with a knowledge of the world, they tackled the problems set them by mass illiteracy and a primitive religious system. They created a multiplicity of 'drills' graded in difficulty and varied for different types of person and case: drills for uneducated blockheads, for the semi-literate, for the educated who were pious but fully occupied in secular business, and for the educated with piety and leisure. There were simple and complicated methods for going to Confession and Communion, numerous ingenious methods for praying at odd leisure moments, methods for coping with temptations and scruples, methods for taking physical penance, and methods for detecting whether visions and voices came from indigestion, God or the Devil. For convenience and memnonic reasons, instruction and methods were divided and subdivided into 'headings' and 'points'. The Observant front in the holy war produced the movement's most ingenious handbook, Jan Mombaer's *Rosary of Spiritual Exercises and Holy Meditations*, the busy Observant religious's recipe book for spiritual progress. The book has a folding, pull-out engraving of a giant hand. Each feature of it is numbered and labelled after a divine person, our Lady, a virtue, or a spiritual idea. The table had to be learned by heart. Then 'the proficient' could use his outstretched left hand as a sort of meditation rosary. By 'touch-typing' its features in succession with the forefinger of his right hand he could connect up mentally the spiritual realities and the features represented and meditate on the connections. Mombaer pointed out the beauties of his method: an almost infinite number of mental connections could be made. Also once 'the proficient' was well-exercised, he could use his hand and mind to combine meditation with the saying of the Divine Office in choir. Thus choir psaltery would cease to be, as of old, 'a burden of divine servitude' and a physical chore, and would instead be turned into an occasion for busy meditation. Inevitably Mombaer and his associates put a high value on spiritual 'method' and 'exercise'. For them all learning and all moral and spiritual advance had to come through the destruction of bad habits and the formation of a multitude of good habits. For most people beginning 'devotion', the good habits must be crudely simple and physical. When the beginner became the proficient, the habits could be more sophis- ticated and the exercitant encouraged to understand what he was doing and to make an increasingly greater personal contribution. Mechanical devotional routines made physically habitual were not in themselves interior piety, but they were the gate leading to it. Hence the wheel was coming full circle for the movement. It began by rejecting orthodox religious Orders and ended by accepting them. It began by rejecting religious forms and rituals, and ended by creating them in great profusion. The hard-headed people who started the movement rejected emotionalism, visions, heavenly voices and mystical flights as dangerous self-deception and escape from the hard labour of spiritual 'exercise'. This remained a strong feeling among devotees. But emotionalism and mysticism periodically broke through their inhibitions. By the later 16th century the Observants had produced Teresa of Avila and John of the Cross.

Ignatius was very much a child of 'Devotion for today'. During his first thirty 'worldly' years he was once briefly, but ineffec- tually, influenced by some of the first Observants in Spain, the Observant Franciscans of his eldest sister's convent and the Carthusians of Seville. Immediately after his first conversion he thought of entering the Seville Charterhouse. On leaving his sickbed he travelled to a great Observant Benedictine centre, Montserrat. After that visit he began, at Manresa, to draft 'exercises' for himself. He was still presuming that he would enter a religious Order and only held back by doubts whether he should become an Observant or fight for meditation inside a Conventual house. On his way to Jerusalem and back he had plenty of opportunities to visit Italian 'devout' centres. In Barcelona he was in touch with Observants. The university com- munities of Alcala, Salamanca and Paris were peculiarly resistant to 'devotion'. He therefore had to attempt to form his own groups, relying greatly on sympathy and direction from nearby Obser- vants, particularly Carthusians. Once in Paris he made straight for the Montaigu hostel, the only 'devout' group in the university. His summer begging tours were principally directed to groups in Flanders. Back ill in Guipuzcoa he tried to found a group in the hostile environment of his home town of Azpeitia and then took refuge in the guest-house of the Charterhouse of Segorbe. Once settled in Venice he and his companions were caught up into association with what were probably then the most active and influential 'devout' groups in the whole movement.

The organisation and activities of the various university student groups Ignatius belonged to and his spiritual writings have often been described by hagiographers as if they were wholly unique and novel. In fact they fitted exactly into the pattern reproduced throughout Europe by the devotion movement. If the fortunes of the Society of Jesus happen to have given *The Spiritual Exercises* a currency and a reputation for timeless truth in the modern age, it remains a fact that the book belongs on the library shelves with *The Imitation of Christ* and Mombaer's *Rosary of Spiritual Exercises*. They are all historical period-pieces, heavily moulded by a mental climate and circumstances which have long passed away.

Ignatius, like almost all the many leaders of the movement, produced some 'occasional', practical spiritual writings but no real treatises. He displayed the typical contemporary mania for 'method' and 'exercise'. Everything is categorised and put into easily memorised formulas. Thus, for instance, *The Exercises* has three types of exercitants. Examinations of conscience are to be twice a day in one or other of five ways. Our thoughts come from three sources. There are three categories of sin. The Devil attacks us in three ways. There are three suggested ways of praying. Meditation must exercise in turn the three faculties of the mind. The exercise of imagination must, in turn, use the five senses. Penances are of three kinds and have three purposes. Prayer of asking must go to the Father by the proper channels in heaven: these take some learning. The process, like meditation, reads like a rather difficult drill.

The setting of Ignatius's writings was remote from that of today. He presumes that he is mostly addressing educated men who come from families of some property and breeding: that is to say persons neither drawn from the aristocracy nor the uneducated masses. Women are, not explicitly but by implication, regarded as minors. Society is elaborately hierarchical and each class has its duties to its superiors and underlings. This is even true of the free masses. Europe then contained many millions of serfs, and slaves were a familiar sight in Spain. Twenty years after Ignatius's death Seville contained some eight thousand slaves. Monarchy, thought of as a rather personal and capricious supreme power, prevailed in heaven and on earth. God the Father in *The Exercises* is always 'God our Lord' or 'the divine Majesty'. Aristocratic courts go with monarchy in heaven as on earth. Much in any underling's life depends on the 'grace and favour' or 'the pleasure' of superiors. As Ignatius says, religious acts must reflect that they are what they are because of the divine 'good pleasure' toward them and that 'grace' has usually to be merited and begged for persistently through the usual channels and mediators. This was a slow and complex business both in heaven and in Spain. Ignatius writes a great deal of 'offering service' and 'engaging in respect and obedience' to God. 'Honour' and 'a good reputation' are precious possessions for a man of breeding and religion: the greatest of all slurs is the charge of cowardice. Christians are clearly thought of as retainers standing in the earthly antechamber to heaven awaiting the divine Majesty's orders and 'good pleasure'. War under the standard of a king, and, even, more, crusading under God's standard, is honourable. The wording of Ignatius's two most famous meditations, 'The King', and 'The Two Standards', is so dated that today it has to be altered out of all recognition.

The mass of the people is hardly mentioned except as the recipient of charity. But their vast numbers and needs and the very limited resources of their betters render charity a token business. The greatest charity is to 'catechise' them, teaching them rude and primitive devotional exercises. As Ignatius remarked sadly but realistically he and his companions had only time enough to spare for a very little of this work.

Early 16th-century European society was very ill-policed and disorderly. It could not cope with the natural disasters of famine and epidemics which devastated it regularly. Ignatius eventually travelled from Venice to Rome through a countryside infested with bandits. He arrived at a Rome which had, some ten years before, been badly wrecked by a marauding army and then had its population reduced by a quarter by several years of plague. The early Society of Jesus lost almost a fifth of every noviciate by death from sickness. Naturally, therefore, the devout and Ignatius took a starkly severe view of life. Death and Judgement were ever-present realities. It had always been assumed by theologians that the great majority of the human race ended in hell. Ignatius's meditation on the Incarnation requires us to '. . . see what the people on earth are doing — wounding and killing and going to Hell.' His famous meditation on hell was not particularly rhetorical or dramatic. Its phraseology was typically matter-of-fact and terse. He knew that he only had to propose the barest outlines of the picture. The imagination of the average retreatant, fed since early childhood on sermons and painted Divine Judgements on church walls, would do the rest.

Ignatius shared to the full with the devout an intense religious emotionalism and a firm belief in supernatural phenomena, heavenly visions and voices, God-given revelations and portents, and appearances of the Devil and witchcraft. The *Diary* shows that violent outbursts of sobbing and floods of tears were an absolutely normal feature of Ignatius's devotions. His eyesight was often badly affected and his face swollen by the weeping: his clothes were sodden with tears. He was positively disconcerted when the weeping did not come. He was in no way peculiar in this. His devout contemporaries and a great weight of Christian tradition agreed with him. The Roman Missal contains a form of Votive Mass 'to procure the gift of tears':

> 'Draw from our eyes floods of tears to quench the burning flames of that punishment which is our due . . .'

In the *Exercises* directors are advised to make beginners repeat the meditation on sin as often as necessary until the 'gift of tears' comes as an assurance of true contrition and the favour of God: but holy tears can also be a manifestation of joy too intense for shouting and laughter. To Ignatius 'imagination' was somehow inseparable from devotion. He took it for granted that the average exercitant, without the slightest emotive prompting from a director, could get himself to 'see', 'hear', 'smell', 'taste' and 'touch' divine realities.

> 'Smell the indescribable fragrance, and taste the boundless sweetness of the divinity . . . Touch by kissing and clinging to the places where those persons walk or sit . . . Hear in the imagination the shrieks and groans and the blasphemous shouts . . . smell in the imagination the fumes of sulphur and stench of filth . . .'

Ignatius's own imagination, stimulated by such meditations and by holy pictures and images, ran riot frequently when he prayed, said Mass or even walked in the streets. He came to expect visions of a sort which occur in psychiatrists' casebooks: of the Holy Mother and Child as 'a great round something shining like gold'. At Manresa he saw the Trinity as 'three organ keys'. At other times he saw the Trinity as 'a burning ball somewhat larger than the sun' and the Godhead as 'a very powerful flash like lightning'. He saw our Lady as 'a sort of white body'. In March 1544 visions came to him frequently. For instance on the 22nd he had one and on the 25th he reported: 'I saw a vision of the divine essence in a spherical shape.' Another vision followed on the 26th and on the 27th he saw 'a vision of the divine essence in spherical shape as last time'. On 2 April it was 'a vision of the divine essence, sometimes like the Father in a spherical shape with many lights and internal understandings'. He had less pleasant visions, for instance, 'of a strange something with many glittering snake's eyes' or of a savage black dog. He heard heavenly music and 'voices' which seemed to come in bouts mysteriously interspersed with days or weeks of strange silence. Thus the *Diary* records no voices for months before 12 March 1545 when they suddenly came. On 12 March he heard 'voices and heavenly music'; on the 13th, 'interior voices'; and more voices on the 16th, 18th, 19th and 20th. On the 21st there were 'abundant voices'. They remained a daily occurrence until 30 September when they ceased abruptly, much disconserting him.

At other times he was violently affected by strange sensations. Sometimes his hair stood up on end and he felt a terrible trembling. At other times it might be strong oppression and heaviness, 'feelings even in the veins and other parts of the body'. He had a strange experience, repeated often enough for it to become familiar, of 'a certain devotion which was hot and reddish with much devout sighing'. Perhaps for him, as for Catherine of Genoa, constant vividly emotional meditation on Christ's Passion had imprinted on his mind the colour, heat and smell of fresh blood. Catherine (who died when he was in his teens) was so allergic to the sensation that any glimpse of red fabric or paint agitated her terribly.

Ignatius certainly tried to treat these floods of emotion and sensation with detachment. 'Devotion' had taught him that such phenomena might bring messages from God. His favourite book, *The Imitation of Christ*, had a section set in the form of a spirited dialogue between Christ and a devout soul. 'Devotion' had also taught him that the Devil and disordered human nature could both produce counterfeit ecstasies and revelations: a careful 'discernment of spirits' was needed to sort out true from false and interpret the meaning of the true. The 'proficient' must remain cool and collected through the storms of sensation. Ignatius worked out detailed guidelines for discernment, subject to the final judgement of the confessor. These safeguards might work fairly well in the more straightforward cases of self-deception by over-enthusiastic beginners and obvious pseudo-mystics. But in Ignatius's own case his judgement and that of his confessor often left him in the dark. He found it hard to determine the origins of his sensations and even harder to make out the meaning of ones he thought true. Divine messages in words were, according to contemporary hagiographers, a constant feature of the lives of saints. To his sorrow Ignatius received exceedingly little revelation of this kind, and then the words seemed vague or of doubtful meaning. He tended to attribute his failure to grasp what his 'voices' were saying to sheer inattention or wallowing in the pleasure of sensations. He once noted:

> 'It struck me that I was excessively pleased with the tone of the saying, and, so as to speak, with the timbre of the voice, without paying much attention to the meaning of the words . . .'

In 1545 when he was desperately anxious to get an explicit answer from God to a problem which was torturing him, he even tried to test whether God might be using a code to communicate with him. He noted as systematically as he could the passages in the missal text that he had reached in saying Mass when bouts of sensation came. There is a famous sentence in his *Exercises* which reflects his own unfortunate experiences. The exercitant, he says, is to hope that following the rules for discernment exactly will bring clear divine answers conveyed in sensations. But if no such clear answer emerges, let him turn aside his mind from the sensations and work out an answer from ordinary common sense.

In his cooler moments Ignatius wondered whether many of his sensations might not be caused by his ill-health, overheated imagination, mental stress and eyestrain. A doctor who carried out a post-mortem on his body after his death in 1556 found 'innumerable stones' in his kidneys and 'other organs' and commented that he must often have been in intense pain for a good many years. In a letter to Francis Borgia, Ignatius had remarked testily that ill-health, especially if caused by 'excessive mortifications' would render the soul unhealthy. Moreover, he wrote:

> '. . . without doubt there is more virtue and grace in being able to enjoy your God in various businesses than at the praying stool . . .'

These were counsels of perfection which Ignatius himself could rarely observe. To the end he remained quite undecided whether his visions and sensations were a spiritual help or a hindrance. At times he displayed a strong confidence in them and described them freely to his Jesuit associates. At other times he lost confidence and ordered them to burn all his spiritual diaries unread after his death. Then some who had known him well judged him a saint and a true mystic: others, like Pope Paul IV, said bluntly that he had been a tyrant and a charlatan. John of the Cross, who had been educated in a Jesuit school, perhaps had Ignatian spirituality in mind when, in his *Ascent of Mount Carmel*, he dealt with a devotion based on 'sensible sweetness'. His judgement was sympathetic and kindly, but very firm. He described vividly and in detail the strange sensations which haunted Ignatius, remarking that they were 'quite an ordinary thing with spiritual persons'. These sensations, fed by the practice of 'discursive meditation', often had a supernatural origin when they came to 'beginners' and were necessary for their advancement. 'Progressives' however should wean themselves from discursive meditation and 'fly' from visions, voices and extraordinary feelings. At this stage they become a terrible hindrance. A 'progressive' who remains dependent on them cannot attain real detachment. Also the whole process of 'discernment of spirits' becomes 'arduous and hindering'.

Most of us today cannot, with the best will in the world, feel at home in the thought-world of the 16th-century 'devout' and great mystics and share their standards of judgement and certainties. From our necessarily less exalted, more pragmatic, point of view, Ignatius's case is deeply interesting, very human, sometimes moving, but ultimately puzzling. We are in no position to pass judgement on him.

3

The Modest Beginnings of the Society
1537-1580

'I will show you favour in Rome . . .'

(*Autobiography of Ignatius*: the apparent meaning of 'voices'
heard in Vicenza and Siena, October 1537.)

The third period of Ignatius's life, his last two decades, was spent
entirely in the city of Rome. The great change in his life-style
from careless gentleman-retainer to anxiously 'devout' itinerant
student had been a severe shock to his system. He arrived in
Rome aged forty-six but prematurely old and chronically sick.
Now he endured a second change, perhaps a more severe one
than the first. He had to abandon most of his lay student spontaneity and informality and adopt the role of a priest-suitor for
favours from Roman clerical bureaucrats and politicians. He
became immersed in officework, administration, meetings and
political string-pulling. The atmosphere was both mentally and
physically unhealthy.

Rome was then an intensely uncomfortable place to live in even
by the low standards of comfort prevailing in cities throughout
Europe. It was no Venice, Florence, Milan or Paris. Early in the
century, probably due to a burst of papal activity and spending,
the population of the city had swelled rapidly from about 30,000
to 55,000, so ranking it among the great urban centres of Italy.
But when Ignatius lived there the population had sunk to under
45,000. After his death and in the last decades of the century
it was to shoot up to almost 100,000. In Ignatius's time whole
quarters of Rome were depopulated with many houses empty.
Modern ruins stood among the weed-covered remains of classical
Rome. Back streets were choked with rubble. Some parishes were
amalgamated and redundant churches left locked and tumbledown. St. Peter's was ill-repaired and partly in scaffolding, its
rebuilding halted because of lack of will and money. The city's
down-at-heel appearance was due to war, plague, famine and
galloping inflation. It still had not recovered from an efficient and

brutal occupation by an Imperial army of mercenaries in 1527. Plague was endemic and Ignatius was caught up in relief work among the sufferers soon after his arrival in the city. Famine was a constant threat. Food prices were soaring. The city's normal source of grain, the arable lands of the surrounding countryside, had dried up as landowners went over to wool-production. In bad years grain for the city had to be imported expensively from far afield. Unlike Bologna, also a papal city but thriving economically, and the great cities of northern Italy, Rome had no major industry. Its small foreign trade was handled by 'foreigners', Italian and Spanish. The people depended for their livelihood partly on farming and partly on small town crafts. But their prosperity hung entirely on the employment and custom provided directly and indirectly by the Papal Government. The Pope's own household alone employed upwards of seven hundred persons.

Plague, famine, malaria caused by adjacent stagnant swamps, and venereal disease made the city notably unhealthy. It had an abnormally large number of prostitutes attracted by the many unattached males, bureaucrats, suitors of papal courts, clerics seeking advancement, pilgrims, itinerant artists and mere adventurers. The wars had made Rome a refuge for beggars and abandoned children. Later in the century a visitor commented that 'you see nothing but beggars in Rome'. Church confraternities had multiplied in a vain effort to cope with the manifold social problems. Like all 16th-century Mediterranean cities with wealthy households, Rome had its quota of slaves, black and Turkish. The papal household usually contained a few of these. The city and the Papal States also had their quota of disorderly clerics and nuns. This was not surprising in the circumstances. 'Ecclesiastical persons' formed a large slice of the population: in one, probably fairly representative, quarter of the city in 1526 priests and male religious formed eight per cent of the residents. The Papal Government departments and households of the resident Cardinals contained numerous tonsured clerks who either delayed ordination indefinitely or had no serious intention of ever seeking it. Many of the latter class had contracted marriages and were raising families: the former class, who had an eye on promotion to posts which required ordination, often took mistresses. The two Popes whose reigns spanned most of Ignatius's time in Rome had both, in their youth in Rome, had mistresses and illegitimate children. Slack or disorderly 'Conventual' religious houses were so common that a Papal Commission in 1534 had seriously proposed that all 'Conventual' houses should be forbidden to receive any more novices.

Bandits plagued the roads leading in to the city and made irruptions into its suburbs, in spite of road blocks and a convoy system operated by papal troops. In times of an especially weak Papal Government, particularly high prices, high taxation and general unrest, the landowning and peasant population bred bandits as freely and innocently as Cornwall used to breed smugglers and wreckers.

These annoyances were by no means the chief unattractive feature of Rome for Ignatius and his companions. The majority of them were Spaniards. For years Italy had been a battleground for rival Spanish and French invading forces. The Spaniards were steadily gaining the upper hand and becoming the political masters of much of Italy. Hence in Rome Spaniards, even priests, and those Romans who consorted with them, were regarded with suspicion and dislike by self-styled 'patriots'. The Popes with whom Ignatius had to deal were generally anti-Spanish, even if they sometimes found it prudent to conceal the fact. Paul IV died of apoplexy brought on by a violent outburst of rage at Spanish arrogance. For their part the Spanish crown and episcopate, though solidly Catholic, stubbornly resisted papal interventions in Church affairs they considered purely national. Ignatius's friendship with some Italians and recruitment of a good many more into his Society did not, in the eyes of most Romans, offset his Spanish nationality, pride and lifelong inability to master the Italian language.

There were other, more complicated reasons for the distinct coolness of the reception accorded in Rome to Ignatius and his companions. The Papal Government was largely staffed by laymen thinly disguised as tonsured clerics. Their pay came partly from benefices in the Pope's gift, partly from their share of fees, and partly from the fact that they were allowed to purchase the life-tenure of their posts, to dispose of them to relations, and to appoint their underlings. The result was that a relatively small number of 'clerical families' monopolised large areas of the government for generations. They had a strong vested interest in the conservation of the whole system. Obviously the most prized office was that of Pope. For many years papal elections had been tough battles between rival parties of Cardinals. Some were 'Curials', indispensable departmental heads who were also the representatives of the families of bureaucrats. Others were 'Cardinal Nephews' grouped by families and owing their promotion to relationship to past Popes. Then there were outsider Cardinals, not usually resident in Rome. They owed their promotion to the settled papal policy of allowing Catholic monarchs and great religious Orders representation in the College of Cardinals. The electoral battles usually ended in stalemate and compromise: the election of a Cardinal outside the main parties but acceptable to all as unlikely to disturb the *status quo*.

This small Roman world, immersed in its own ecclesiastical and family politics felt itself to be under siege in the 1530s. It had been more shaken by the Imperial army's incursion in 1527 than it was willing to admit. Then had come the Protestant explosion in northern Europe and the collapse of papal authority over wide areas. More serious still, to the mind of the Roman bureaucrats, was the disturbingly widespread growth of an unsettled, highly critical temper among many well-educated and sincere Catholics. Talk of 'Church reform' was rife, and the opinion was freely expressed that reform should begin at Rome. 'Reformist' talk was common among 'the devout' and particularly direct and radical in 'devout' groups in Venice, Padua, Mantua, Vicenza and Naples. Worse still, from the point of view of most Roman bureaucrats, was the behaviour of Pope Paul III. He had been elected in 1534 as a typical 'compromise Pope'. He seemed to fit the part admirably. He came from the Farnese family which had a long record of service of the Papal Government. As a young man he had been made a Cardinal by Alexander VI whose mistress was Paul's sister. About twelve years after becoming a Cardinal, Paul was still unordained and living with a mistress by whom he had several children. In middle age, possibly due to the death of his mistress and some contact with 'devout' persons, he was ordained and in private assumed a more seemly and religious manner of life. Yet he did not, at any time, show signs of having adopted 'devout' ways. His outward style was entirely that of a thrusting politician, intensely devoted to advancing the fortunes of his children. This remained his style after he became Pope.

'Compromise Popes' were chosen for their advanced age, frail health and record of adherence to the conventions of Roman ecclesiastical politics. Periodically such a Pope, once on the throne, gained an astonishing new lease of life and vigour and displayed an alarming tendency to kick over the traces fastened on to him by long habit and the pressures of the Cardinals who had elected him. Paul III behaved in this fashion. He got in touch with the leaders of the 'devout' reformist groups in northern Italy, asked their advice and offered them advancement: some were made Cardinals. He accepted their ideas of a Reform Commission and a reforming General Council of Bishops where the Protestants would receive a hearing. One 'devout' group formed itself into an entirely new type of 'apostolic' religious Order, some degrees less monastic and more informal than the 'Observants'. This Order, 'the men of Chieti' or 'Theatines' received provisional authorisation from Paul III. Several other experimental 'devout' Orders were in process of formation. The founders proposed enthusiastically that these 'regular clerks' (secular priests leading a common 'devotional' life) should be made the officially approved pattern of the future for all religious in the Church.

These startling developments dumbfounded and alarmed the conservative Cardinals and bureaucrats. They regarded the Reform Commission as absurd utopianism and dragged their feet about preparations for the General Council. In private they agreed that the 'devout' reformists were covert Protestants. They opposed the authorisation of 'regular clerks' whom they regarded as monstrous hybrids, neither proper monks nor decently beneficed priests.

It was at this point that Ignatius and his companions arrived in Rome. In the universities they had gained something of a reputation as stern critics of conventional clerical life. They had shied away from 'Conventual' monasticism and most of them even had reservations about the 'Observants'. Some had scruples about taking formal vows, and others about ordination. These latter felt that canon law and custom treated ordination as an integral part of the ritualistic observances of monks and holders of benefices. Most of the group delayed becoming priests until they had secured an assurance from Rome that their ordination did not necessarily commit them to monasticism or benefices. They contrasted conventional clerical life with the 'apostolic' life of Christ and his disciples as seen in the New Testament. These 'way out' views, the group's addiction to lay evangelism, and their sometimes exotically 'charismatic' behaviour led them to be constantly accused of heresy.

In Venice they had associated with those same 'devout' reformist activists whose influence on Paul III was causing all the trouble in Rome. They met Cardinal Gasparo Contarini, Cardinal Gianpietro Carafa, Gasparo de Dotti, Reginald Pole and Dona Vittoria Colonna, Dowager Marchioness of Pescara. Contarini was a deeply converted lay diplomat who, though promoted by Paul III to the Cardinalate and a diocesan bishopric, steadily refused ordination. He made no secret of his belief that Martin Luther was, in spite of some mistakes, a much-maligned theologian with whom the Church must come to terms. Carafa was an equally converted Roman bureaucrat who had become a Theatine. He and Ignatius swapped devotional methods and Carafa urged that the Paris companions should join the Theatine Order. They considered the proposition but rejected it on the grounds that the Theatines were still some shades too conventionally monastic for their taste. Pole, an English aristocrat and layman who eventually combined the Cardinalate with a refusal to be ordained and with theological views almost as extreme as Contarini's, was never intimate with the Paris companions. But he was the originator of a famous saying which later came to be regarded as the epitome of Jesuit thought:

'Live as if you could only be saved by works; believe that you can only be saved by faith.'

Dona Vittoria was an intimate of Pole's and the warm friend of those reformists who were most obnoxious to the Roman conservatives, Contarini, the Spaniard Juan de Valdes of Naples and Bernardino Ochino, Vicar-General of the 'Observant' Capuchin Order and later a Protestant fugitive from Italy. Moving out from Venice some of the Paris companions became friendly with the d'Este court at Mantua and 'devout' circles in Vicenza. The court of Mantua had recently been a refuge for Protestants, and Vicenza was soon to gain notoriety as a haunt of Italian Baptists.

Inevitably, therefore, when the companions reached Rome they were only welcomed by a handful of people, 'devout' friends of Contarini, Carafa and Pole, and the Spanish ambassador, Dr. Ortiz. Since they lacked a regular income and official standing, they were compelled to disperse into free lodgings provided by their friends in villas outside the city. There followed two frustrating and painful years. The group was persistently accused of scandalously unclerical behaviour, of being vagrant clerics under no proper authority, and of teaching heresy. Ignatius had ample experience in coping with accusations. He published character-references and instituted law suits so that his defence of the group could be put on record. His actions staved off prosecution but did nothing to appease their enemies. The group's hopes of finding Paul III a friend and generous patron were soon dashed. He was alarmed by the storm against the reformists and increasingly absorbed in his schemes to forward the careers of his children and grandchildren. He was embarrassed by the group's frank expectation that he would take them under his protection. He merely suggested that they should undertake catechism classes for children in Roman parishes or, better still, disperse away from the city to offer their services to diocesan bishops in Italy as preachers, reformers of disorderly nunneries, and arbitrators in family quarrels. His urgings, and the group's awareness that the charity of their friends at Rome had limits, led most of them to move away to seek work in Siena, Mantua, Parma and Vicenza. Ignatius, because of his poor health and his ability in dealing with the authorities, remained almost alone in Rome.

The group was held together tenuously by its very democratic constitution accepted in its student days in Paris. The members made annual promises before God, voluntarily renewed each Lent, to pool their earnings, refuse all benefices, not enter religious Orders, and act jointly in all important matters after discussions which must end in unanimity. Any member could quit the group freely when his promises ran out in Lent. None of them had the right to impose his views on the rest. At discussions, usually when they assembled in Lent, they took it in turns to occupy the chair. Ignatius had always been the elder statesman and principal spiritual influence but his position in the tiny group was in no way, even in embryo, that of the superior of a religious Order.

Their usual meeting in the Lent of 1539 was well-attended, since they knew that the group was fast heading for dissolution. The discussion began with the crucial question: should they let events take their course, presuming that, in the eyes of God, the group had performed all the services it could? There is no evidence that most of the members had ever contemplated a permanent union. After a good deal of lively argument they agreed that they should at least try to stay united. The next question was even more crucial: their union could only survive if they altered and considerably strengthened their organisation. This, in effect, would mean an application to the authorities for permission to become a Congregation of 'regular clerks'. Were the members prepared to agree on this move? The discussion became more heated. They all knew that the Roman canon lawyers had compelled the 'men of Chieti' and other informal groups of 'devout' reformists seeking to become Congregations to accept a considerable amount of monastic discipline and observance. The view of the canonists, who had an immense weight of tradition and Roman authority behind them, was that there was no possible half-way house between monasticism and the secular priesthood: religious had to accept solemn perpetual monastic vows, absolute obedience to superiors, a community obligation to the performance in community of the very lengthy choir Office and penitential observances, and monastic enclosure. The 'Observants' had gained two concessions after exceedingly wounding battles with conservatives within their own Orders and the canonists. They were allowed to cut the length of their choir and penitential observances to a minimum and fill the time so gained with individually chosen 'devotional exercises'. They were also allowed to adopt a strange shift-system and Congregational form of government allowed to the Orders of Friars. The shift-system allowed the maintenance of monastic appearances by a minority while the majority were dispensed from most of it to pursue evangelistic works. The Congregational government combined short-term, elected superiors enforcing obedience with a relatively democratic 'parliamentarianism'. The 'regular clerks' were allowed 'Observant' rules with certain small extra concessions, such as omitting elaborate monastic music in choir and the uniforms customarily worn by religious.

Clearly most of Ignatius's companions were still exceedingly reluctant to accept even the sawn-off monasticism of the 'regular clerks'. They detested the idea of choir Office, of any common observances at all or any monastic enclosure. Solemn vows and regular obedience to superiors stuck in the gullets of some. They felt that any compromise on these matters would be a betrayal of what the group had stood for bravely since the first days in Paris.

Time was passing. Easter day came and went. A fortnight after Easter the exhausted members, some with relief, others with trepidation, agreed on the application to authority. Now they had to draft in detail the concessions they wanted. This was a highly delicate business. They knew well that the battle between reformists and conservatives in Rome was still in the balance. Paul III was no longer the adventurous free agent he had been earlier in his pontificate. If the group demanded too much, they might get nothing or an order to join the Theatines and have done with it. They agreed on a draft containing five sections. This followed the 'regular clerk' pattern in the main but had four differences from it. Two were boldly libertarian: they asked to be completely excused from choir Office and penitential observances. These provocative requests were prudently balanced by two others to which no conservative could possibly object. They asked for a major superior holding office for life, and for an extra solemn vow binding members to undertake any mission, however arduous, imposed on them personally by the Pope. The text phrased this last request dramatically:

'. . . whether he sends us to the Turks, or to the New World, or to the Lutherans or to others . . . infidels or Catholics . . '

The words were rhetorical. But the group's interpretation of this vow was modest. They thought that papal missions would be rare and exceptional and involve little interference with the Order's own, self-directed operations in Europe. In theory they would be binding themselves to the instant, blind obedience of every Jesuit to the Pope's lightest wish. In practice they expected missions to result from suggestions to the Pope by the Order. They spoke of the Order pressing the Pope to abandon the idea of missions judged to be impracticable. They pointed out that the Order would only be vowing itself to the performance of a duty of obedience to the Pope incumbent on all Catholics.

The group was well aware, as it drafted the requests, that Paul III already had in his mind the thought that some of its members could be used on diplomatic and intelligence missions. Pierre Favre was, with the Pope's approval, about to leave Rome on a fact-finding tour of Germany. A suggestion, endorsed by the king, had already arrived from Portugal that a few members of the group be sent to the Portuguese Far Eastern colonies to report on the missionary situation there.

The formal application once completed was handed to two influential 'devout' reformists, Contarini and a Dominican, Badia. They made sure that its phraseology was in proper, Latin Curial form, and then carried it themselves to Paul III. There followed a year of uncertainty and grave anxiety. The reformists did their best to rally their party to the support of the application. Ignatius, becoming an expert at lobbying, organised the collection of glowing character-references of members of the group from influential people likely to impress the Pope: the Duke of Mantua and his brother, Cardinal Ippolito d'Este, Cardinal Ferreri, the Government of Parma, the archbishops and bishops of half a dozen northern Italian sees, and the Pope's cherished illegitimate daughter, Dona Costanza Farnese. At first the Pope was bluffly approving without committing himself to paper. Then he carefully submitted the application to a committee of Curial Cardinals. They declared against it. Ignatius attempted to influence two of them and his efforts aroused their wrath.

At long last in September 1540 the Pope, by the Bull *Regimini Militantis Ecclesiae* gave a written, provisional consent to the formation of an Order or Congregation to be called 'the Company of Jesus' or, in Latin, *Societas Jesu*. Historians, with a great deal of hindsight, have greeted this Bull as a turning point in Church history. At the time, and, indeed, for another fifty years to come, it must have seemed a relatively small event and far from being a signal of victory for the group and the reformist party. Papal Bulls were not necessarily of great moment in those days. Some were issued to register decisions which were of their nature temporary. This Bull concerned a group of nine men — potentially thirty, if we include some two dozen probationer recruits collected by members of the group working in Rome, Parma and Cologne — who were more or less patiently awaiting the outcome of the application. These men were a very small segment of the 'regular clerk' movement and 'devout' reformist party. The papal approval was preliminary and provisional. Many details about the infant Company could only be decided as it grew and took shape — if it did. The papal approval was also grudging. The numbers of the Company were limited to sixty. The provocative requests in the application were the things the group had most at heart: one was flatly rejected by the Pope, and the other much whittled down. The Company was to have corporate penitential observances. They were excused choir recitation of the Divine Office. But they had to sing Masses in their houses and all their priests had to recite the whole Roman Office daily in private. Students had to recite daily the Little Office of our Lady. This was a particularly severe blow since there were respectable canonists who maintained that secular priests were not bound by Church law to recite the Office if they held no benefice, nor monks if they were absent from choir. Students were not in solemn vows and therefore, in current Church law, not religious. Also the Pope's Bull provided no insurance against future efforts by conservative Curialists or Popes hostile to the Company to amend its rules still more.

Inside the group itself the publication of the Bull in September 1540 did not automatically launch the Company. Most of its members had got into the habit of leaving Rome for evangelistic work and had not been there during the period of lobbying and suspense. An effort was made to summon them all to a meeting in Rome in Lent 1541 to elect a General, take solemn vows and make professions of obedience. Also the 'Five Chapters' of the application draft needed filling out into a set of temporary rules. When the meeting began at the start of Lent only six companions were present, and that included Ignatius and Broet, a French priest probationer from Parma hastily promoted into the thin ranks of the companions. As they marked time, waiting for the arrival of absentees, they debated rules inconclusively. They were reluctant to take over the Theatine rules *en bloc*. None of them had any practical experience of running a religious Congregation, and their future was uncertain. At last, well after Easter, the missing men arrived wearily and the election could proceed. The choice of Ignatius as General was a foregone conclusion. The only possible alternative candidates were Favre and Xavier and very few considered it worth taking their candidature seriously. Bobadilla, always a frank individualist and critic of Ignatius, declined to cast his vote.

Immediately after the election three of the companions left Rome hurriedly for their fields of work. Hence the solemn inauguration of the Company proved to be an extraordinarily modest affair. On the morning appointed, Ignatius and five companions left their several lodgings in the city and assembled in a parish church borrowed for the occasion. The Pope had already made over to the Company the use of a small, well-frequented but extra-parochial city church, Santa Maria degli Astalli, and its presbytery. The church contained a popular shrine of our Lady of the Streets which attracted beggars and prostitutes. Ignatius, who particularly liked working among these people, approved. Indeed the companions had recently rejected a bequest to them of a large house in the city because their dead benefactress had insisted that no woman should set foot inside its doors. But at the time of the inauguration of the Company Santa Maria was still not in their hands. Ignatius took possession of it in June 1541. He still lacked a General's office and residence for the Jesuits working in the city. At last, in 1542, he, his new secretary Polanco, a dozen professed Jesuits, a dozen probationers and a few lay servants moved from their several lodgings scattered round the city to take up residence together in a small, purpose-built house alongside their church of Santa Maria. This house, the first to be dubbed 'the Gesu', was of very modest proportions.

*   *   *

Like almost all great institutions, the Society had a difficult birth and an adventurous but stormy youth. Its pioneers were, like their kind in every age, men of much native force of character and at their best when improvising in difficult circumstances: most of them were rough diamonds and did not take kindly to discipline. The Society suffered all the usual growing pains. Periodically it outgrew its strength as new commitments outran the available resources and manpower. The pioneers repeatedly embarked on risky and daring ventures. Some, entered on without enthusiasm, paid off surprisingly and embarrassingly well and developed fast in quite unforeseen ways. Other ventures, dearer to the hearts of their originators, stagnated and foundered. The Society ran from crisis to crisis, and each time its very survival seemed in doubt. Acute overwork and strain, anxiety about the future, national differences, and the rugged individualism of the pioneers combined to produce a regular succession of resounding quarrels which drove men out of the Society and threatened to tear it apart. Ecclesiastical institutions, even when they contain persons of outstanding spiritual zeal and some destined to be canonised saints, are not exempt from these normal human processes of growth.

The northern Italian Congregations of 'regular clerks' grew out of very locally-based 'devout' groups and they continued to recruit in their home towns. Hence they tended to remain small in numbers, very regional and limited in their spheres of work. The Society of Jesus grew out of a student club of men of different nationalities used to travel. During the few years immediately before the foundation of the Society most of Ignatius's companions gravitated away from Rome and some made for their homes in distant countries. In the normal course of their evangelism, they all built up local 'connections' and enlisted followers, mostly students. These followers tended, on their own initiative, to enlist their friends. So, for instance, between 1538 and 1540, Pierre Favre visited Paris, Louvain and Cologne. In each of those places he interested a few students in the work of the Rome group. Pieter Kanis, a Dutch student whom he befriended in Louvain, moved to Cologne. He arrived there in 1541 after Favre had left the city on the long journey back to Rome to take part in the inauguration of the Society. Kanis found a group of nine Cologne students devoted to Favre and awaiting his return there. As they waited, Kanis enlisted several more student friends into the group.

Thus when Ignatius took over headship of the new Society in 1541 it consisted of nine professed members and a small but indeterminate number of associates or probationers. In Rome there were twenty one associates, about half of whom were Spaniards. There were seven or eight in Parma, three or four in Padua, a handful in Paris and Louvain, a dozen in Cologne, a few in Lisbon and most probably a few more in university towns in Spain. During, or immediately after the inauguration of the Society almost all the companions except Francis Xavier left Rome to go back to their fields of work and recruitment. Due to their pioneering efforts the Society continued to grow in numbers, but at first the growth was painfully slow and small. By 1550 overall numbers barely topped a hundred. The reports sent back to Ignatius by the companions attributed this depressing lack of success to two main causes. The first was a widespread contemporary distaste among Catholics for life in a religious Order. In 1550 Pieter Kanis, Favre's successor as leader of the Jesuits in northern Europe, reported to Polanco, Ignatius's secretary, that German Catholics in general had 'a positive horror' of vows and the religious life. The second cause for the Jesuit lack of success was the fact that the companions concentrated their attention on, and recruited from, university students. They tended to be 'kittle cattle'. Their ranks contained youths capable of great idealism, constancy and heroism, but most were fickle and unruly. A good many showed some initial interest in the Society of Jesus but relatively few of them submitted to probation. Of those who started probation or had completed it at least a third backed out or had to be dismissed as unsuitable. Even more disturbingly there were not infrequent cases of men who had been in the Society for some years and had then became extremely difficult and wayward. In the early 1550s Kanis reported that almost all the Jesuits whom he had, for lack of subjects, to employ as house superiors, were men of this type. Some of them had to be dismissed from the Society for grave faults or crimes: some then secured re-entry and later had to be dismissed a second time; and some decamped without leave. In Portuguese India Francis Xavier had exactly the same difficulties.

After 1550 recruitment suddenly began to pick up. When Ignatius died in 1556 overall numbers, including novices, probably exceeded seven hundred. Polanco placed the figure at about a thousand, but he was exaggerating. The sudden and sizeable increase was remarkable, not least because the loss-rate remained huge. A third of the novices left or were dismissed. One in five of Jesuits died young, either in the noviciate or as students. Dismissals of formed Jesuits remained quite common. It has been estimated that, of some 1,500 Jesuits who entered the

Society between 1540 and 1565 and whose records survive, 400 were dismissed and 300 died young. The increase in Jesuit numbers was not due to any change of heart among Catholics and, in particular, university students. It was very evidently the result of the foundation by local Jesuit groups between 1548 and 1556 of some thirty very small 'feeder schools' of lay boys. These schools were very modest affairs indeed and their continued existence was often in grave doubt. But their emergence at this time turned the course of Jesuit development. From 1550 their registers show a steady intake of batches of senior schoolboys: very often indeed they included groups of brothers. Ignatius was well aware of this change and did not like it. In 1556 he said flatly that he had been far too slack in his admissions policy and that he should never have allowed boys into the noviciate. He added darkly: 'He who is no good in the world is certainly no good in the Society.' There is even more striking evidence of the disappointment of Ignatius and his companions with Jesuit recruitment. The original practice of the 'Paris companions' was to take annual private promises or vows which could, at will, be renewed each Lent or ended. When the Society was inaugurated as a canonical Congregation of religious, canon law required that all its members must take solemn, perpetual vows. The nine companions did so. But they continued, with Ignatius's connivance, to impose only annual, private vows on new recruits to the Society. Probably on Ignatius's orders they restricted the taking of solemn vows to a very few men who had been well-tested by years spent in private vows. Normally, in these cases, such men were sent to Rome to be tested by Ignatius himself. Thus Pieter Kanis, who had been some years in private vows and had already succeeded the dead Favre as leader of the Jesuits in the Netherlands and Germany, was summoned to Rome and promptly set to work in the kitchens of the Gesu among the lay servants. Ignatius insisted that membership of the Society, and solemn vows, could only be accorded to men who had 'conspicuous integrity of life and learning' and he certainly found these qualities in very few of those recruited. In 1556, at his death barely thirty of the seven hundred men in the Society were in solemn vows. This situation aroused much adverse comment in Rome and elsewhere. One of the greatest theologians of the day, the Dominican Melchior Cano, said that the Jesuits were disobeying the terms of their official registration as a religious Order: the vast majority of Jesuits were clearly not religious at all and so not members of the Order. In 1546 Ignatius secured from

Paul III a written approval of his practice in denying solemn vows to many recruits and keeping most of them for many years, or even permanently, in private (or 'simple') vows. This papal approval was only gained with great difficulty. For the next half century the general opinion among canonists and the older religious Orders was that most Jesuits were not religious at all. Ignatius had to bow to this view. In the section of the *Constitutions* where he deals with the subject he ties himself in knots: only the solemnly professed are, he says, 'the professed Society'; the rest only belong to 'the body' of the Society 'in a certain interior manner'. The rest were, in a sense, perpetual novices without any voice in the running of the Society.

It is, however, an ill wind which blows no good. In the 16th century the canonists reckoned it to be exceedingly difficult for even the Pope to dispense religious from solemn vows. In cases, then very numerous, where religious proved dissident and rebellious or claimed that their professions had been extorted from them by fraud or outside pressures, superiors were expected to put them under restraint in conventual prisons. A great many such religious became fugitives. The common law of Catholic countries required the ecclesiastical and civil authorities to arrest the fugitives and return them to the conventual prisons for punishment. The Jesuit system of simple vows, which could be terminated at the will of superiors, in practice saved the Society from a multitude of embarrassments and it only had to maintain conventual prisons for the few solemnly professed who turned rebellious.

Modern Jesuit historians cannot decide whether their system of 'graded' membership was the result of chance or design. It was most probably a bit of both. Ignatius was very much a child of the 'devotion' movement and hence a man of a few very intensely felt spiritual principles. As always with such principles, their practical application was often disconcertingly difficult. Within the setting of tiny, informal and voluntary 'devout' groups practical application offered relatively few problems. But once 'the Paris companions' were committed to transforming their group and groups of associates into something which would meet the canonists' requirements for registration as a religious Congregation, the practical difficulties became increasingly worrying and insoluble. As General superior of the Society, Ignatius bore the major responsibility before the law and to the Pope for the process of transformation. Like all his original companions and most of the finer recruits to the Society he had a typically 'devout' belief in 'the inner freedom of the spirit' and a horror of mere legalism and formalism, 'the letter which kills'. Like them he could not help regarding conventional monasticism with deep suspicion: whatever the Society must become, it must never surrender to conventional formalism. It might have to take into its system a few of the outer forms of monastic Orders, but the Society itself, in its spirit and way of life, must be 'devout' and different. In a real sense, Ignatius sympathised with the 'positive horror' of vows and conventional religious life felt by so many contemporary Catholics. On the other hand he was committed at law. He and the original companions present at the crucial Lent debates of 1539 had foreseen that their groups had no enduring future in their existing form. The experiences of the Society during Ignatius's Generalate bore out this judgement.

For long after the foundation of the Society the tiny, widely scattered Jesuit groups improvised their own ways of life. Decisions were made at group discussions. The chair at these meetings and between discussions was occupied by election or by each member in rotation. Rules were few and made locally: they were easily dispensed with. Men joined or left the groups and the Society with startling casualness. There was no canonical noviciate. Those who persevered through a very short course of devotional exercises of a kind devised by the group at once made private vows and embarked on active membership. Ignatius did, as the law insisted, gradually set up Provinces of the Society and appoint Provincials and house superiors responsible to him in Rome. But this formal process happened very slowly indeed and was nowhere very evident before the 1550s. It was obviously totally impracticable when numbers were tiny, Jesuits peripatetic, proper residences simply non-existent, and works more tentative aspirations than settled realities. As numbers increased in the 1550s the new local superiors found that they had to act carefully. Manpower was still tightly extended. Many Jesuits were long accustomed to the old libertarian ways and to taking their own initiatives: they were pioneers whose temper was often uncertain. The superiors soon discovered that premature efforts to impose authoritarian rule could provoke revolt on an alarming scale. It was wiser to be tolerant of quite uncanonical behaviour. In any case a good many Provincials sympathised with the feelings of their subjects.

Moreover, long before 1550 wide divergences of opinion appeared about the Society's works and general policies. It was taken for granted by all that the Society existed to deepen the religion of its members by the life of 'devotion' and to teach that life to others. In Italy the Jesuits developed a distinct leaning towards a kind of religious 'social work' among the under-privileged and unfortunate classes of urban society. Ignatius himself shared this leaning to the full. He was always slipping away from his oratory and office in the Gesu to hob-nob with a few 'devout' lay friends and to go on to chaplain's work at 'the Martha House' for converted prostitutes, the orphanage, the hostel for deprived girls and the refuge for converted Moslems. No amount of ridicule or malicious gossip could deflect him from this course. This Italian way seemed inevitable in a country divided between rich and poor, where the rich were already fairly amply provided with 'devout' groups and the poor neglected spiritually and ravaged by plague, famine and inflation. In Spain and Portugal, on the other hand, the Jesuits had strong leanings towards 'contemplative' prayer and foreign missions to the Iberian colonies in America and the Far East. They lived among people who were passionately interested in these matters. They also shared to the full their compatriots' touchy and arrogant nationalism and rabid anti-Semitism. Ignatius was indelibly Iberian and never at home in Italy. No one could be more interested in 'visions' and 'voices'. He had close relations in the colonies overseas and a typically Spanish interest in, and fear of, Islam. The feeling for 'pure blood' untainted by Judaism was part of his inherited make-up. His attitude toward his Iberian colleagues was very naturally a strange mixture of sympathy and exasperation. At times he went along with 'the Spanish humour' of anti-Semitism. Yet he invited Spanish Jesuits of Jewish descent like Laynez and Polanco to Rome to share his work: once they were there he treated them with marked coolness. He accepted, though he in no way initiated, schemes to send a few Jesuits to the Portuguese eastern colonies, to Brazil, to the Portuguese Congo and to Ethiopia. By 1556 these schemes had produced little tangible result, except opportunities in Japan which then seemed an embarrassing accident. Ignatius might occasionally talk of missions overseas rhetorically and in general: in fact he showed no sign that he regarded them as a major Jesuit work.

At times he went along with his compatriots' passion for extreme penances and contemplative prayer: then, almost invariably, the scandals and furore caused by their wild practices roused him to furious anger. In the 1550s he was repeatedly involved in fearful and damaging quarrels about this matter. Francis Borgia, Duke of Gandia, a massive benefactor to the Society and a highly prestigious recruit to its ranks, created storms by encouraging his colleagues to spend hours every day in interior prayer and undertake extreme penances. When Ignatius remonstrated with him he threatened to quit the Society for a Carthusian monastery. Francisco Estrada, the Provincial of Aragon, was for ever demanding permission to retire to a mountain hermitage. Meanwhile in Portugal, strongly encouraged by their Provincial, Simon Rodriguez, one of Ignatius's original companions, groups of Jesuits carried their 'devotion' to strange extremes. Some became hermits, others departed without permission for the Congo, Goa or Jerusalem, others almost killed themselves with fantastic fasts and penances, others streaked naked through the streets of Lisbon crying woe on the godless city. The devotional mania spread to Portuguese India, where Francis Xavier found Jesuit superiors piling penances, fasts and long observances on their subjects. Ignatius, in a fury, removed Rodriguez from his Provincialship and ordered him to Rome. The Portuguese Province received a special punitive Visitation by Ignatius's Vicar-General, Jerome Nadal, carrying with him a strongly-worded *Letter on Obedience*. Practically half of the Jesuits in the Province promptly left the Society. In Goa, with Ignatius's approval, Xavier dismissed several Jesuit superiors from the Society. Rodriguez at first ignored Ignatius's order and made violent attacks on him in public. When he reached Rome he demanded leave to become a hermit or go to Jerusalem. Ignatius in fact treated him with indulgence and allowed him his hermitage.

Through all these Portuguese broils Ignatius laboured to try to solve the Spanish problem. Trouble in Spain affected the Society badly since by the 1550s the Spanish Provinces supplied well over half its total manpower. A steady stream of letters poured out from the Gesu to Borgia, to Antonio Araoz, Ignatius's nephew and the Provincial of Castile, and to Francisco Estrada, Provincial of Aragon. Sometimes the tone of the letters was sympathetic and concessive: Ignatius was willing to dispense Jesuits with real spiritual gifts from work so that they could spend hours in prayer; he would tolerate Borgia's lengthy and highly complex devotions and Estrada's desire to become a hermit. At other times the letters were abrupt and angry: they demanded obedience and asserted that a really spiritual Jesuit could be a contemplative on a mere quarter of an hour's devotion a day.

Then Ignatius appointed Borgia as his special representative in Spain with authority over the two Provinces. This was meant to draw him out of his contemplative shell and also to forestall a threatened move in Rome by the Spanish crown to release the Spanish Jesuits from obedience to the Gesu. But the appointment unleashed fury. As Ignatius lay gravely ill in 1555-6 the Provincials were openly calling him and Borgia tyrants and Ignatius the tool of expatriate Spanish Jesuits of Jewish origin. They were threatening to sever relations with the Gesu.

Meanwhile the Jesuits in France, the Netherlands, Germany and Austria had quite other preoccupations. Work with the under-privileged, high flights of prayer, missions to America and the Far East, and anti-Semitism meant nothing to them. They were obsessed with the Protestant threat, recruitment to the Society and the desperate need for Jesuit schools. Their nations had only been slightly represented among the Paris companions. For this and other reasons their Jesuit groups were still small and struggling in the 1550s. Dislike of religious vows and Orders was particularly rampant in northern Europe. Protestantism, or what seemed to be Protestant influence, was everywhere. The French Jesuits were shaken by the case of Guillaume Postel, which seemed to them very typical. He was a teacher at the Collège de France in the University of Paris, befriended the Jesuits in 1541, and travelled to the Gesu in Rome to be a novice in the Society in 1544. The following year Ignatius dismissed him because of his odd beliefs. In 1553 the Jesuits in Vienna heard that he had just been expelled from Austria as an aggressive Protestant evangelist. The future for the northern Jesuits appeared bleak. Their efforts to establish small Jesuit Colleges within the universities of Paris, Louvain and Cologne to protect their few Jesuit, and associate, students from what they considered dangerous influences were rudely rejected by the university authorities. In Paris and Louvain the authorities resented the Jesuit design as a slur on their Catholicism. In Paris, Spain was the old enemy and the Society regarded, with some justification, as a stalking-horse for Spanish political aggression. The efforts of Ignatius and his agent, a French Jesuit named Cogordan, to overcome resistance at Paris were ham-handed and counter-productive. The university authorities were enraged by the publication of character references for the Jesuits from French noblemen known to favour a *détente* with Spain, and by the bribes given to university dons by Cogordan. Another complicated intrigue by the Jesuits proved equally self-defeating. They became intimate with the Bishop of Clermont and, with Ignatius's reluctant approval, struck a bargain with him. They agreed to staff a diocesan seminary and grammar school he wished to found. In return he made over to them, without any endowment to maintain it, an episcopal residence, the Hôtel de Clermont, conveniently situated on the edge of the university quarter of Paris. The seminary and school occupied half a dozen French Jesuits whose services were desperately needed elsewhere and produced few recruits for the Society. The hôtel long remained a white elephant since the university authorities banned its use as a Jesuit College. In Cologne the archbishop was on the verge of declaring himself a Protestant and, on his orders, the university authorities refused to sanction a Jesuit College. In Bavaria and Austria Protestantism was so strong that many parishes had been abandoned by their priests, religious houses were almost empty, and universities denuded of teachers and students who had made off to Protestant centres of learning. The Duke of Bavaria and the Emperor urgently invited the Jesuits to assume teaching offices in the moribund universities. Ignatius hesitated, but was ultimately unwilling to affront great princes. Since the northern Jesuits had exceedingly few men of academic standing, he despatched the Society's best-qualified academics, Spanish, French and Italian to Ingolstadt and Vienna. The results were disastrous. The Jesuit scholars knew no German and were cold-shouldered by the local people: elevated to the position of university rectors and professors, they were immersed in administration and lectured to almost empty student benches.

The northern Jesuits were making no headway and they were terrified by the evidence all round them of Protestant inroads unresisted. They became convinced that the only possible solution to their difficulties was the building up of a system of Jesuit schools at all levels, theology, humanities and grammar apart from, and outside, the universities. Though the Society had been born in a university environment, bitter experience had proved that it would never grow and thrive there. Throughout Europe, in Alcala, Salamanca, Valladolid, Padua and Venice as much as in Paris, Louvain and Cologne, university teachers, whether secular clerics or religious of the older Orders, were entrenched in power and grimly determined that Jesuits should only enter their portals singly and as students subject to their authority. The situation in Ingolstadt and Vienna was an exception that proved the rule. Also Jesuit experience with university student recruits had been unhappy: they were unruly, opinionated and inconstant. If a totally Jesuit alternative system of schools could be set up, the lower ones feeding the higher, the Pope might be persuaded to create Jesuit universities authorised to confer academic degrees. Of course, the cost in money and Jesuit teaching manpower would be very great. But the northern Jesuits believed that these difficulties would solve themselves. By the 1540s an increasing number of great landowners, bishops and municipalities were anxious to establish grammar schools in their towns: they had funds and premises and all they usually lacked was competent teachers. The Jesuits could offer themselves as staff for these schools. Initially this would impose a tremendous strain on Jesuit manpower. But as the system developed, and if it succeeded, it should solve the Society's problems. Each educational establishment would ideally consist of two schools alongside each other. One would be a Jesuit students' College of the Humanities, and perhaps also of Theology. The teaching would, in the traditional fashion, mostly be done by students. Each Jesuit student would attend lectures in his subject and also teach his juniors lower subjects. Even the top classes could be taught by Jesuit priests who were in perpetual simple vows. They could also provide superiors and administrators for the schools. The adjacent Grammar School could be entirely staffed by Jesuit students in the lower classes of humanities in the College. The Grammar School and probably the humanities' classes in the College would admit lay boys. Even where the whole set-up was financed by a bishop and the Grammar School was a diocesan seminary the Jesuits could expect to recruit subjects from among the lay boys. Lay boys who became secular priests would retain for life an attachment to the Society. This system would provide the Society with a steady and ample flow of recruits who, unlike the students enlisted in the past, would be long habituated to discipline and Jesuit 'devotion'. As the system advanced the schools would incidentally produce generation after generation of 'devout' laymen and clergy friendly toward the Society. The northern Jesuits became sure that the system offered by far the best defence against the spread of Protestantism. Finally in 1548 they could point out that four Jesuit schools containing lay boys had already been established with Ignatius's approval, at Goa in Portuguese India, at Gandia in Spain, at Billom in the French diocese of Clermont, and at Messina in Sicily. Thus the northerners would receive support from at least some Portuguese,

Spanish and Italian Jesuits. Nadal and Laynez, two of Ignatius's closest advisers, were known to favour the proposed school system.

Between 1550 and the onset of his final illness in 1554 Ignatius did, in fact, consent to the establishment of no less than thirty-seven more Jesuit College-schools. Sadly for the northern Jesuits, sixteen were in Spain and seventeen in Italy. There were no new ones in France to stand beside Billom and only two very small ones in German lands, at Vienna and Cologne. The German College established in Rome in 1552 soon collapsed for lack of suitable students. As a whole the new Jesuit school system was very much on trial. By 1556 it had already greatly increased the flow of recruits into the Society: but the great bulk of the inflow came to the southern European Provinces whose preponderance in the Society was already an embarrassment. Almost all of the Colleges were scantily or insecurely endowed and some were teetering on the edge of closure. The general standard of teaching was low. The advent of the Colleges was to prove a great turning-point in the Society's history. Without them it would never have ranked above the Theatines and other Orders of 'regular clerks'. Eventually the Jesuit Colleges were to give the Society large numbers and great influence. Its other works would have to give way before the insatiable demands of the schools for Jesuit schoolmasters.

Still, in 1550-56 no Jesuit, not even Nadal, Laynez and Pieter Kanis, the warmest advocates of the school system, could foresee the scale of the change and its consequences for the Society. During those years the intellectuals of Europe were greatly interested in education, its principles and practice. Very few Jesuits shared their interest or read their books. Indeed the early Society was far from being a well-educated body. Laynez, Salmeron and Le Jay, who were accounted its learned men and who were despatched by Paul III to the Council of Trent as papal theological *periti*, had gained their doctorates by abbreviated courses. They did not rank among the great theologians of the age. Robert Bellarmine, who was admitted to the Society in 1560 as a lad of eighteen and who later became one of its really learned men, privately shook his head over the published works of Laynez and Salmeron, remarking that reprinting of them would only do the Society credit if the text were heavily amended. In the 1550s the Society contained numerous dunces. There were university-trained Jesuits who were incapable of teaching grammar: there were men who entered the noviciate as deacons but proved so illiterate that they were relegated permanently

116   *The Modest Beginnings of the Society*

to the kitchens as lay brothers.

Ignatius, like most of his colleagues throughout the 16th century, regarded the teaching of academic subjects with distaste: it was a necessary but menial chore hardly befitting priests and religious except as a penance. This view was traditional among spiritual people. The Middle Ages and the 16th century produced no real 'teaching Orders'. As a matter of necessity most religious houses had 'claustral' classes for young entrants and enclosed study houses of the Orders in university towns to provide the degrees, particularly in canon law which religious superiors needed. The Orders occasionally financed small Grammar Schools taught by outsiders: the pupils, bright charity boys, were needed as lay auxiliaries, secretaries, agents and holders of benefices in the Orders' gift. The small minority of parish clergy who had some book learning but little luck in the race for good benefices eked out a living menially by teaching school grammar to aspiring ordinands. Intellectuals in the 16th century were propounding a novel theory that academic teaching was an honourable profession with a spiritual value. But even they shrank from teaching, and the courses and methods they proposed were so advanced that none but the brightest teachers and pupils could attempt them. Education was still a tediously painful business involving long hours, endless dictation of notes, memorisation, set exercises and floggings. The 'devotion' movement shared the traditional view. Its leaders occasionally founded charity schools but rarely taught in them. The movement's spiritual distaste for schools was expressed in a grim chapter in Ignatius's favourite book, *The Imitation of Christ — Against Vain Learning.*

When Ignatius consented to the foundation of the Messina College in 1548 his mixed feelings were made evident. He asked the community at the Gesu for volunteers, making it clear that schoolteaching was a menial job not within the ordinary compass of duties for which his men were professed. Going to Messina to teach was, to his way of thinking, like going to India or America, a penitential, heroic, extraordinary choice. The band of ten who volunteered were treated as men going out of the ordinary rules and ways of the Society: even the students among them were allowed to vote for a superior. The sections on Colleges in the *Constitutions* breathe the same traditionalist, 'devout' spirit. Colleges must, no doubt, exist. The Society might even, exceptionally, have its own universities. On paper it already had one by 1556. Borgia's ducal influence in Rome was so great that he

got Paul III to grant university status to the tiny Jesuit College
he had founded at Gandia. But these educational establishments
were to exist on the very fringes of, or even outside, 'the professed Society' and fully professed Jesuits were not normally to
be involved in them. Lay boys received scant mention as inmates
of 'public schools admitted to association with our Colleges'
and incidental objects of charity. The *Constitutions'* treatment of
academic matters was perfunctory and austere. Teaching was to
be mechanical and authoritative. Frills were discouraged. Those
modern inventions, humanities (the Latin classics) and positive
theology (the study of the decrees of Church Councils and the
writings of the Fathers), subjects which Ignatius himself had
never studied, were admitted very grudgingly to the curriculum
as 'necessary for the times'.

Ignatius's distaste for Jesuit schoolmastering had another
source, his passionate attachment to 'apostolic poverty'. Jesuits,
he believed firmly, must own nothing, individually or corporately.
They must live on alms without accumulating large funds or
invested endowments. They must accept no stipends or fees for
the services they rendered and not solicit them. The Jesuit church
of Santa Maria in Rome had no collection boxes, not even for the
poor. The practical execution of these exalted principles cost
Ignatius much sleep and much consulting of his 'visions' and
'voices'. The acquisition of the Gesu and Santa Maria, of the
various Homes of Rescue and hostels in Rome, and then of a
steadily increasing number of Jesuit buildings, mostly decayed
monastic property, and Colleges caused him great anxiety. He
accepted the solution long adopted by the Friars, that the properties should belong legally to the donors or to trustees. This
arrangement left him with huge problems. What was to be done
with donations or bequests in cash? What was to be done if
donors of Jesuit buildings, as the owners, rebuilt or decorated
them in ways to suit themselves but very inconvenient and
embarrassing for the Jesuits? Thus the Messina College
buildings belonged to the town council of the place and they had
made provision for no less than fifty masters and several hundred
boys. In the years ahead the church of Santa Maria was to be
pulled down and rebuilt at vast expense by a donor utterly
regardless of the needs and susceptibilities of the Jesuits. Their
altars were left unfinished while most of the church was littered
with extravagant family tombs. Again, growing communities,
mostly of hungry young men, could not be fed, clothed, warmed,
provided with medicines, books, pens, ink and journey money

merely out of time-consuming door-to-door collections round towns, collections which would compete with Franciscan 'quests' and cause many resentments. Ignatius stumbled slowly and agonisingly into temporary solutions. Novices and the simply professed might, by a stretch of conscience, be regarded as not members of the 'professed Society' and so not subject to its stringent rules of poverty. He allowed these men in the Gesu to live from 'the Sacristy Fund', an invested endowment administered by a layman. But in the overcrowded Gesu professed Fathers had to share rooms with novices and the simply professed. For a time Ignatius insisted that the professed eat apart from the kitchen where the food was bought from alms. Then he accepted the suggestion that the professed be dispensed so that they could draw journey money and clothing from the Sacristy Fund. This arrangement was undoubtedly followed all over the Society: a hugger-mugger style of community life was then normal. Ignatius's conscience revolted against this. He agonised in prayer for another two years and then refused the professed at the Gesu leave to use the Sacristy Fund at all. The results of the decision were so absurd that he again resorted to a system of dispensations. One possible solution to his dilemma might have been the accumulation of 'Common Funds' in the hands of Provincials and the General to be used to support the professed Fathers and Colleges with small endowments and increasing communities. Since Ignatius's principles forbade the acquisition of endowments not tied to Colleges, Common Funds could only be clearing houses for general donations to be passed on instantly to deserving Colleges. Donations of this kind were very few up to 1556. Men who entered the Society with property — a rare breed — had a free choice on the day of their profession. They might return their money to their families, give it to the poor or give it to the Society. Almost invariably such a gift to the Society went to the Provincial's Common Fund and was, to Ignatius's way of thinking, soon squandered on dubious projects. The text of the *Constitutions* left by him at his death was full of loose ends. One of these was a plea, not an order, that 'profession gifts' of any size should go to the General, who would dispose of them for the real good of the Province concerned. This was a wholly impracticable suggestion. The Spanish Provinces were already enraged because Ignatius had persuaded Francis Borgia, on his profession, to give most of his remaining fortune to endow a large College to be built in Rome.

In fact Ignatius's scruples about poverty were never likely to halt the progress of Jesuit schools. His knowledge of the operations of Provincials was invariably defective and they constantly made decisions and implemented them long before their reports reached the Gesu. He was, in his last days, haunted by a premonition that breaches of his principles of poverty would destroy the Society. Yet after 1556 his scruples and complicated regulations, in spite of a multitude of dispensations to individual Jesuits and acceptance of breaches of rule, imposed curious restrictions on the free growth of the Jesuit economy with quite unforeseen and odd results. He had forbidden Colleges to charge fees. In the years ahead that awkward provision turned out to be a major cause why the Jesuit school system expanded so greatly and so fast. Ignatius had made endowments nontransferable. The result of this was, as the years passed, that some popular Colleges grew rich while remote and unpopular ones languished in acute poverty.

During his Generalate, Ignatius gained something of a reputation within the Society for bad temper and severe authoritarianism. Modern writers have gone much further, suggesting that he was at heart a soldier who thought of the Society as an army in battle against Protestantism and paganism, and who inculcated on his men a style of discipline and obedience equal to that of King Chaka and his Zulu 'Impis'. The truth is probably more complex, human and muddled. *The Imitation of Christ* was Ignatius's favourite book. Its teaching on obedience was allusive and extraordinarily complex. Everyone, even Popes and monarchs, is in a state of subjection to higher authority out of sheer factual necessity. Fallen human nature accepts this compulsion resentfully, even rebelliously, and unhappily. This is the common attitude. From a common sense point of view compulsory dependence and a rigid class system were the only insurances against chaos and so good. But from a spiritual point of view forced obedience was irreligious and bad for the soul. 'Devotion' and the growth in souls of a deeply religious view of life would inevitably make them see, and practice, obedience freely and devoutly, seeing God and his authority behind earthly rulers. In this way 'subjection' and obedience became a way to God, a deep spiritual experience, liberating the soul from the shackles of mere compulsion. Up to this point the teaching was profoundly simple and traditional. Then came subtle refinements meant only for 'proficients', well-advanced in devotion. They became the friends of God, receiving a direct 'interior light' from him conveyed through no human superior or intermediary. Normally this light would inspire the recipient to embrace ordinary vocations or acts or obedience to superiors with a heroic intensity, especially when the vocation was particularly unattractive or the orders given, from a common sense point of view, flatly absurd and misguided. On other occasions, however, the interior light might demand obedience to divine commands running quite contrary to the orders of superiors. The whole history of the early days of the 'Observant', 'regular clerk' and Jesuit movements reflected 'devout' people's strange conjunction of heroic obedience to Church authority and occasional firm disobedience in the name of God.

These ideas are surely the key to the apparent startling contradictions in Ignatius's teaching about obedience, his treatment of disobedient Jesuits, and his relations with the Popes and 'the hierarchical Church'. There are a number of passages in his letters (especially in a famous one to a Belgian Jesuit, Oliver Manares), in his *obiter dicta* recorded by his companions, and in *The Spiritual Exercises* which might have come from the *Journals* of George Fox, the Quaker leader. On the other hand there are a good many passages in his letters, the *Constitutions*, the *Rules for Thinking with the Church*, and his *obiter dicta* which teach a fantastically extreme form of blind obedience to superiors:

> '. . . obedience must be cultivated . . . first to the Pope, then to superiors . . . in execution, will and intellect . . . persuading ourselves that everything is just, suppressing every repugnant thought and judgement of our own in a certain obedience . . . They who live under obedience should permit themselves to be moved and directed under divine Providence just as if they were a corpse . . . or as the staff of an old man . . . To keep ourselves right in all things we ought to hold this point: what I see as white I would believe black if the hierarchical Church determined it so . . . Accept with docility the whole of . . . (your Professor's) . . . teaching without seeking to impose on it your own explanations . . .'

The wording of many of these phrases was copied from old monastic Rules by Polanco. But the spirit behind the words was all Ignatius and full of the emotional exaggeration he gave vent to periodically. They were the excited thoughts of a man who also said, for instance, that he would, on the Pope's order, sail out to sea in a leaky boat without oars, sails or food: that he meant to resign the Generalate and leave for North Africa to preach to the Moors and die at their hands: that, after he was dead, his body must be cast unceremoniously on the nearest midden in Rome.

Most of his time was spent in dealing with cases of ordinary, 'carnal' disobedience, often veiled in Spain by pseudo-mysticism. Hence the teaching on obedience in the public documents he left behind him is heavily weighted toward blind conformism. A minority of his cases concerned Jesuits whom he judged to be genuine mystics or possibly so. He could not legislate for these men, and the records of his dealings with them remained buried in the mountain of his correspondence. He could be habitually off-hand with Polanco, violently rude to Nadal and Laynez, and extremely angry with the plainly disobedient. With the outrageously disobedient and even insolent Simon Rodriguez and the lushly pious and erratic Francis Borgia, he wobbled between fury and indulgence since he was uncertain about their spiritual state. With men like Manares whom he judged to be 'proficients' under the direction of God, he was gentle and sympathetic. As Bobadilla later complained the text of the *Constitutions* was a jungle of contradictions. It repeatedly laid down great principles and then hedged them thickly with restrictions and exceptions. Ignatius's treatment of individuals, Bobadilla also complained, had lacked all consistency.

Many historians, picking on certain texts in the *Constitutions*, have insisted that Ignatius meant the Jesuits to be the Pope's special Janissaries, sworn to blind obedience to his lightest command. The texts in fact represent partly a shrewd move of the original companions in 1539 to counter the great hostility of the Curia, and partly a typical flight of Ignatius's 'devotional' fancy. He did sometimes write as if he constantly believed that acts of obedience to the Pope were the surest way of getting 'interior light' and the guidance of the Holy Spirit. But in practice he very rarely behaved as if he thought of himself as the Pope's retainer. The Bull *Regimini* of 1540 made it appear that Popes could despatch Jesuits on any mission at any time. Paul III did, in fact, send Broet and Salmeron on a dangerous and pointless mission to Scotland and Ireland, deprive Ignatius of his cherished secretary, Xavier, to send him as papal nuncio to Portuguese India, and send other Jesuits to the lengthy sessions of the Council of Trent. The Society's manpower was already thin and vastly extended and the papal missions, though prestigious, crippled the Jesuits for some years. Ignatius then extracted from Paul III, with much difficulty, two Bulls which delegated the papal power of mission inside and outside Europe to the General. Ignatius also never showed any hesitation in lobbying the Popes vigorously to get favourable decisions or avert unfavourable ones. In 1556 when he lay dying, the new Pope, Paul IV, was an old friend turned enemy. Paul was a Theatine who had striven hard to persuade Ignatius to merge the Society into the Theatine Congregation. Ignatius refused and Paul went against him and, from the start of his pontificate, took every opportunity to display his dislike of everything Jesuit. Though Ignatius was the General of an Order and protocol dictated that the death-beds of dying Generals should be attended by the Pope's doctors and agents bearing his final blessing no one came to the Gesu from the Vatican. Ignatius died surrounded only by his own community and lay friends.

*   *   *

When he was buried in the church of Santa Maria in an unpretentious tomb, the Society's greatest achievement was that it had survived for two decades. Other Congregations of 'regular clerks' were moribund. The largest Congregation, bigger than the Jesuits, the Theatines, was now in high favour in Rome under a Theatine Pope. It boasted its intention to unite with itself the remnants of all the other 'regular clerks', including the Jesuits. Paul IV made no secret of his support for the intention. He discontinued papal subsidies granted by his predecessor toward the establishment of a Roman College and German College under Jesuit control. He peremptorily ordered the Jesuits to conform to Theatine rules in two important respects: in the performance of the Divine Office in choir in all Jesuit houses containing more than one priest, and in the limitation of the General's term of office to three years. The Pope also gave his support to the view of most Curial canonists that, in spite of Paul III's decision, the Jesuit practice of putting the great majority of its men in perpetual vows was illegal. The canonists insisted that the Jesuit superiors should forthwith come into line with common practice in religious Orders: there should be a one year noviciate and on completing it men should either be dismissed or professed solemnly. If the Pope were to decide to enforce this rule on Jesuits the consequences might well be disastrous. Since the solemnly professed could not normally be dispensed from their vows and dismissed, many Jesuits in simple vows would prefer immediate dismissal. Those who chose, or were awarded, solemn profession might turn out badly and become embarrassing encumbrances. Moreover, once the whole Society, except novices, was solemnly professed either the Colleges would have to be given up, or the Jesuit rules of poverty drastically changed.

If Ignatius had been alive and well, he would undoubtedly have lobbied the Vatican with his usual vigour and tenacity and perhaps ultimately with some success. But in fact the Society had been in turmoil since 1554. In that year Ignatius's final illness began and he became incapable of governing. At his bedside were his three most prominent aides, Diego Laynez, Jerome Nadal and Juan Polanco. For years they had tried unavailingly to push an increasingly indecisive Ignatius into definite, consistent action on lines they thought right for the Society. Their view was that he had procrastinated and waited piously on events far too long while the Society drifted into near-disorder. For over ten years he had pondered, prayed and agonised over the text of the *Constitutions*. He was constantly making changes and it was still unfinished when he fell ill. Polanco carried out major researches into other Orders' rules, translated Ignatius's jottings in Basque-style Castilian into fair Latin, and prepared final drafts, section by section. Ignatius accepted them and laid them aside. Polanco was a scholar and an enthusiastic advocate for Jesuit Colleges. He did much research into curricula, consulted other Jesuits interested in such matters, and urged Ignatius to issue provisional rules for the Colleges, supplying him with ready-made drafts. He also urged that directives should be issued on devotional methods in the Society. Ignatius was actually persuaded to let Polanco put together a text of *The Spiritual Exercises* from numerous scribbled memoranda. Nadal, a much less tactful man, braved Ignatius's wrath and argued with him. He was eventually allowed to travel round the Provinces carrying some of Polanco's drafts to explain them to the local Jesuits. Between them Polanco and Nadal rallied numbers of the more intelligent and sensitive Jesuits in southern Europe behind the idea that the Society must order itself more strongly and uniformly round such of Ignatius's texts as could be made available.

Ignatius rallied a little in the course of 1554 and, by word of mouth, instructed Nadal to go to Spain as his special representative to try to settle the furious rows raging there among the Jesuits. He made little headway. The Provincials, Araoz and Estrada, challenged Nadal's authority. They had already refused to obey Borgia, who sulked and declared himself about to join the Carthusians. When the news of Ignatius's death in 1556 filtered through to Spain, all three Spanish superiors flatly refused to travel to Rome for an election of a new General. They demanded that the election take place in Spain, and that the headquarters of the Society be shifted there permanently. Philip II of Spain who was, to his embarrassment and disgust, at war with the Papal States because of Paul IV's Italian patriotism and hatred of Spanish domination, forbade all his Jesuit subjects to go to Rome.

Meanwhile affairs in Rome were also going badly. Shortly before his death Ignatius, by word of mouth, appointed Polanco his Vicar-General to administer the Generalate until the election of a new General. Ignatius's death and the news of this appointment produced violent debate and dissension amongst the leading Jesuits in Italy. The Society was still far from having a clearly defined and working power-structure. Ignatius had run the Generalate in a highly personal way full of improvisations and compromises, sometimes dictatorial and sometimes liberal. He had held consultative meetings in the Gesu very occasionally. The numbers of professed Fathers invited and able to be present were very few. In ordinary day-to-day administration he tended to rely heavily on a few favourites, almost all of them recruits into the Society after 1541. The *Constitutions* were supposed to define clearly the powers of the General, of the professed Fathers in and out of official meetings, and the Provincials. But in 1556 the *Constitutions* were neither printed nor in force. In any case their sections on constitutional matters were a strange and typical mixture of precision and vagueness. The future was to show that they could be legitimately interpreted in widely different ways: the General might be regarded either as an absolute monarch or as the executive head of a parliamentary government. Hence in 1556 there was much confusion. Bobadilla, one of the five surviving 'Paris companions' and a rough diamond, volatile and opinionated, led a party of Jesuits who demanded that the companions should be recognised as the natural rulers of the Society, the holders of authority during the interregnum between Generals, and the sole electors of a new General. As a Spaniard proud of his 'pure blood' he disliked Polanco, a Spaniard of Jewish descent. As a Paris companion Bobadilla was opposed to Borgia, Araoz and Estrada, whom he regarded as ambitious young men promoted too soon by Ignatius. Hence Bobadilla wanted the election to take place in Rome. He sent a strongly worded memorandum to Paul IV, urging him to intervene to restore order in a Society nearly wrecked by Ignatius's vagaries.

Laynez, another of the Paris companions, a Spaniard of Jewish descent (though he tried to conceal the fact) and a man of volcanic impatience and barrack-room language when aroused, led his own Jesuit party. He assembled them secretly in Rome and had motions passed deposing Polanco as illegally appointed and electing himself as Vicar-General. Then Nadal arrived in Rome from Spain, took issue with Laynez and formed his party. He rejected Laynez' authority as gained irregularly and asserted that he himself had been Ignatius's first choice as Vicar-General. Meanwhile Paul IV, having called off his military operations against Spain, was anxious for the moment to conciliate Philip II. He proposed that the Jesuit election should be held in Spain. Most probably he hoped that such an election would finally rend the Society asunder and the Theatines would then easily sweep up its Italian remnants. Laynez and Bobadilla, both rough frontiersmen, engaged in a public slanging-match and appealed to the Pope for a settlement. Eventually papal arbitrators awarded the Vicariate to Laynez and ordered the election to take place in Rome in the summer of 1558. So, after more than four years of fracas, a small electoral assembly of professed Fathers, surprisingly containing enough Spaniards to ensure them of a majority of the votes, easily elected Laynez as General. The assembly then made Jesuit constitutional history. It ordered that in future Generals should have Assistants chosen to represent the Provinces at the Gesu. In certain circumstances these Assistants might, on their own authority, summon a General Congregation to dismiss a General from office. The assembly ordered the promulgation of the *Constitutions* as fundamental law binding both the General and all Jesuits. The *Constitutions* were to be sacred and could only be amended by papal authority. The assembly passed on to reject firmly a relatively polite request from Paul IV for the promulgation of decrees establishing a three year limit for Generalates and imposing full choir Office on all Jesuit houses containing priests. A substantial minority of the assembly did, in fact, favour three-year Generalates. Paul IV angrily insisted on the decrees and the assembly reluctantly bowed to his orders.

The immediate threat to the Society's existence was over. It was bruised, battered, and altered and the promulgation of the *Constitutions* produced no instant solution to its grave internal problems. It was years before many areas of the Society had the manpower, stability and house-room sufficient to enable them to keep the laws consistently. The missions to foreign parts and

Protestant countries always had to be dispensed from observation of large sections. The Provinces had, however, worked or muddled through the long crisis relatively undisturbed. They had had long practice in improvising their own rules and methods regardless of the Gesu. The credit of the Society hardly suffered at all because of the unseemly crisis. By 1558 Jesuits still lacked popular support among Catholics and most Church hierarchs regarded them with deep suspicion. Anyway none of their chief enemies had any right to cast stones. The Roman Curia, in spite of Paul IV's 'devotional' thunders, remained its old self. In 1559, the year after the assembly, Paul IV invited the Society to undertake the invidious task of spiritually reforming the Datary, one of the oldest, most corrupt and faction-ridden Papal Government departments. Later that year he died, and, after a papal conclave which far surpassed the Jesuit crisis in intrigue and back-biting, he was succeeded by Pius IV, a Curial bureaucrat with three illegitimate children and a shameless nepotist. The old religious Orders, mostly hostile to the Jesuits, were still rent by fierce quarrels between 'Conventuals' and 'Observants'.

*   *   *

From 1558 to 1580 the Society progressed through a sort of early adolescence. It grew far too fast and this expansion often appeared ill-balanced and out of proportion. Yet it was, however confusedly and painfully, taking shape. The shaping was due far more to the pressures of outside circumstances and to local Jesuit initiatives than to effective central policy and direction. Central direction, such as it was, came much more from the efforts of two underlings, Polanco and Nadal, than from the three short-lived Generals whose reigns spanned the two decades. Polanco and Nadal had been Ignatius's closest associates and, indeed, the co-authors of his legislative efforts. Polanco's filing-cabinet knowledge of the Society and its records made him indispensable. He was private secretary to all three Generals until his death in 1576, Nadal, who survived until 1580, was given almost unlimited powers by the three Generals and ranged widely round the Provinces exhorting, commending, rebuking, dismissing and showering the Gesu with reports and advice. Some Jesuit historians were later going to name him 'the second founder of the Society '.

Jaime Laynez was a 'compromise' choice as General and far from being an ideal one. The Spaniards, the majority of the

Society, would not have a 'foreigner'. The surviving Paris companions would only have one of themselves, which ruled out Polanco and Nadal. Laynez was one of three Spaniards with this name, probably close relations, who entered the Society in its earliest days. One, Marco, died a novice in the Gesù. Another, Christopher, survived to become a Jesuit priest. But his temperament was so difficult and unruly that he was dismissed from the Society by Jaime in 1561, was re-admitted in 1567 when Jaime was dead, dismissed again in 1571, re-admitted for the second time in 1582, and died a Jesuit in 1592. Perhaps Jaime's characteristics ran in the family. Few of his colleagues ever contemplated asking for his canonisation: even fewer liked him as a man though many, long afterwards, were grateful for his stubborn constancy in what seemed impossibly difficult times. He was loud and plebeian in manner, volcanic in temper and given to shouting fits of abuse. He was often tactless. At the Council of Trent, where he was a papally-sponsored theological adviser to the Curial Cardinal-presidents, his over-ingenious defences of papal prerogatives upset the Pope, the presidents and the Spanish bishops. As papal agent at the oecumenical conference of Poissy in France, his violent refusal to enter into any real theological discussion with Protestants enraged the French Government. He was quite frequently absent from Rome on papal business and delegated his authority wholesale to Polanco, Nadal, his friend Salmeron, Borgia, and able young Jesuits whose careers he advanced. But Rome and Trent were unhealthy places and Laynez was dead at the age of fifty-three.

Francis Borgia, Duke of Gandia and grandee of Castile, was Laynez' successor as General in 1565. He also was a 'compromise' candidate and an extremely odd one. When he first came to Ignatius's attention in 1541 he was royal Viceroy of Catalonia, a married man, and the great-grandson of a notorious Pope, Alexander VI. He became a lavish benefactor of the Society and, after his wife's death in 1546, made a private vow to become a Jesuit as soon as he could divest himself of his public and family responsibilities. Two years later, on his insistence and after Ignatius's spiritual intuitions had led him to the decision, he was secretly and solemnly professed as a Jesuit and an ordained priest. Ignatius obtained a special dispensation from the Pope for this extraordinary transaction, without explaining the identity of the recipient. For the next five years everyone regarded Borgia as a layman: he continued in public office. Then he emerged into the open as a Jesuit, insisting that he should be treated exactly like his colleagues. He was exceedingly fat, fond of social life, and addicted to daily hours of prayer and penitential exercises of a lush and complicated kind. European society was then so constituted that a man of this kind could only have found real obscurity inside a strict monastic enclosure. He did, in fact, yearn for Carthusian life. Ignatius's solution for the problem was to make him his Commissary-General with authority over all Spanish Jesuits. They were secretly impressed by his dukedom and his reputation for holiness, but outraged by his sudden promotion and the oddity of his administrative decisions. During the great crisis of 1554-8 he contributed to the uproar by his support of the Spanish Jesuit demand that the headquarters of the Society be removed to Spain. When rebuked, he threatened to enter a Carthusian monastery. During Laynez' Generalate his strange career took a new turn. He was delated to the Spanish Inquisition for heresy. The evidence cited by the prosecution included passages from a volume of devotions he had written, and his open support of friends who had fallen foul of the Inquisition. It was mainly staffed by Dominicans who had long been hostile to the Society. Borgia was forced to escape from the Inquisition's jurisdiction into Portugal. He had always been a problem for the Jesuits: now he was an acute embarrassment.

Laynez liked and respected him and sought to help by procuring a papal mission ordering him to Rome. Nadal, who was in Spain striving to repair the damage, disliked and distrusted Borgia and did his best to hold him in Portugal contrary to the papal order. Borgia, in spite of his girth and serious illness, made a dramatic dash through Castile and France to Rome. There Laynez, about to set off for Trent, promptly made him his Vicar-General during his absence.

Apart from a papal mission to Spain in his later days, a labour which undoubtedly brought on his fatal illness, Borgia remained in the Gesu for the rest of his life. He became a much quieter and thinner man, due to his illnesses and the increasing intensity of his devotions. The comparatively well-attended General Congregation which elected him General in 1565 urged him to discipline the Society, check the haphazard foundation of Colleges, and put some order into the widely differing devotional practices current in the Provinces. Life at the Gesu in his day must have been peace indeed after the rows, shocks and constant comings and goings of Laynez' Generalate. The work of Polanco and Nadal and the presence at the Gesu of the Assistants and an increasing number of able and intelligent young aides seconded from the Provinces and housed in the Jesuit Roman College made it easy for Borgia to concentrate on the matters nearest to his heart. These were his own devotional life, the drafting of very detailed memoranda on the spiritual training of Jesuits, and his friendship with Pope Pius V.

The Generalate coincided almost exactly with the pontificate of Pius, another 'compromise' Pope, this time from very far outside the Curia, from a Dominican study house. He and Borgia were kindred souls, 'devout proficients', believers in 'visions', 'voices' and the inner light. It was, however, painfully evident to Borgia that his membership of the Society stood as a barrier between him and the other pillars of the 'devout reformist' movement, the Pope, the Theatines, Charles Borromeo Archbishop of Milan, and Philip Neri founder of the Roman Oratory. Borromeo would not have Jesuits in Milan and took as his Vicar-General a priest dismissed from the Society. The Pope, sharing the normal Dominican distaste for Jesuits, was set on reviving Paul IV's designs for reforming the Society, designs which had been quietly laid aside after Paul's death in 1559. Borgia was served with papal orders to re-start choir Office in all Jesuit houses and to phase out the Jesuit practice of keeping most of its members permanently in simple vows. Pius V was not the sort of man to be moved from designs he thought were the will of God by lobbying and a shower of representations in favour of the Society from princes. Borgia's spiritual friendship with Pius proved remarkably efficacious. Step by step the Pope retreated from the positions he had taken up. First Jesuit noviciates, and then Colleges, were dispensed from the choir order. For the rest of the Pope's reign he was content to know that in ten Jesuit professed houses valetudinarian Fathers in pairs, on a rota system, mumbled the Office together. Evasion of the papal order concerning vows took more time and agonising in prayer by Pope and General. In the end the Pope appears to have been satisfied with an assurance by Borgia that a rather larger proportion of Jesuits would be solemnly professed in future. However, Nadal opposed the decision, ostensibly on the grounds that Ignatius had meant to confine solemn profession to men who had completed a full four years of theology. Since he, and not the General, was on the spot in the Provinces where grades of profession were usually decided, his view prevailed. There is no evidence that Borgia was able to honour his assurance. By the end of his Generalate the proportion of solemnly professed men in the Society was lower than in 1565.

There were other Jesuit concerns on which Pope and General saw eye to eye from the start. All dispensations given by Laynez to communities in professed houses to enjoy the proceeds of endowments were cancelled: the communities had to live solely on alms. The result of this decision was a decline in the number of professed Fathers living in professed houses and an increase in those living in Colleges and noviciates. Hence the General Congregation of 1573 found it necessary to warn professed Fathers that their rank did not entitle them to disobey the superiors of the Colleges they lived in, superiors who were almost always in permanent simple vows. The other Jesuit concern was papal missions. Ignatius thought that he had, once and for all, persuaded Popes to delegate their power of despatching Jesuits on missions into the hands of the Generals. But Paul IV resumed the power to himself and now Pius V began to use it frequently. Sometimes these papal missions happened to fit in with the interests of the Jesuit Provinces and sometimes Laynez had managed to procure papal missions for purposes of his own. But Pius V's were generally highly inconvenient for the Society. Thus he lumbered them with responsibility for the Roman Penitentiary. He summarily ordered Pieter Kanis, the Provincial of Upper Germany and the mainspring of the still shaky Jesuit enterprises in German lands, to drop his duties and devote himself henceforward exclusively to historical research and writing against the Protestants. Pius ordered a score of Italian Jesuits out of their Colleges to carry out official visitations of the dioceses of the Papal States. In 1570 he ordered the General himself and a dozen prominent Jesuits to make lengthy tours of Europe to drum up support for a papally-sponsored crusade against the Turks. He ordered a dozen Jesuits to go to sea as chaplains to a war fleet sailing against the Turks. It happened that Borgia's piety included a very intense devotion to obedience to the Pope, so he raised no objections to the large number of missions the Jesuits were called upon to make.

The increasing number of Jesuits who hoped for a General who would have overall policies for the Society and a scale of priorities were disappointed in Borgia. The most 'devout' Jesuits later came to see a deep mystical significance in Ignatius's secret profession of Borgia in 1546 and to see the two men as joint-founders of the Society in God's eyes. This conviction helped to foster a cult of the two as twin saints and eventually to procure their canonisation almost simultaneously. But the Jesuit historians, whose standards of judgement were more earthly, firmly rated Borgia as a 'stop-gap' General.

When a General Congregation assembled in 1573 to choose Borgia's successor, it soon became evident that the age of pioneer Generals was over. Only three of the original Paris companions survived, Bobadilla, Simon Rodriguez and Salmeron. Death had also reduced the ranks of their first disciples: the only survivors of real consequence were Polanco, Nadal and Kanis. The General Congregation passed over all six men for a variety of reasons. By 16th-century standards they were old and the Gesu an unhealthy place. Bobadilla and Rodriguez, though now older and quieter, had deserved reputations for wild indiscretion. Salmeron had never previously been considered the stuff of which Generals were made. Polanco, for all his experience, was frail and of Jewish descent. Nadal had already been passed over twice in elections to the Generalate: he was an invaluable aide but would be unsuitable as a General. Kanis had been a great pioneer but was regarded as past high administration and many of his old subordinates in Upper Germany had reason to dislike him. So the attention of the electors turned to consider men professed in the 1550s, particularly those who had been seconded to the Jesuit Roman College and later employed in the service of the Generalate as Visitors-General, Assistants or Provincials. Such relatively young men were, of course, of the small elite of professed Fathers, and practised in the new bureaucratic ways of the Generalate office. The Society was now large, its operations complex and delicate, and it was unwise to continue having Generals so unversed in these ways that they had to leave administration to the bureaucrats.

The choice was difficult since there was little to choose between the suitable candidates. At this point the new Pope Gregory XIII, Pius V's successor, intervened. He announced that the time had come to break free of the Spanish control of the Generalate: all three previous Generals had been Spaniards. He indicated that he would like the Congregation to choose Everard Mercurian. Mercurian must have been on the Congregation's list. To commend him were the facts that he was a Luxemburger, not a Spaniard: he was a canonist, like the Pope; he had been trained and professed in Rome and had served Laynez and Borgia; and he was known to be a strong disciplinarian. This latter fact commended him to the Pope. Gregory XIII had been a curial official with a mistress and illegitimate child. He had been converted to 'devout reformism' by Charles Borromeo and was pledged to spend his pontificate in continuing the 'reformist'

work of Pius V. In spite of is curial past and association with
Borromeo, he was disposed to favour and make use of the Jesuits
more even than Pius V, just provided that the Society could be
put in good order by a strong General. The General Congregation
accepted the Pope's choice and Mercurian became General.

His Generalate was short and peculiarly colourless. He had
none of the prestige which accrued to the old Jesuit pioneers.
He entirely lacked Borgia's intense, mystical spirituality.
Mercurian's way of dealing with Jesuit 'spirituals' was to instruct
them that, for a Jesuit, prayer could not possibly be a principal
occupation, but 'an instrument to acquire virtue and perform our
ministries'. The words themselves might have been spoken by
Ignatius in one mood and they did faithfully represent one side
of 'devotion', but only one side. Mercurian flatly forbade all
Jesuits to have or read books of mystical theology and ordered
them and those whom they directed to use no other ways of
prayer but the ones set out in the pages of the *Spiritual Exercises*.

His reactions were those of a bureaucratic administrator not
a statesman. He did very little to stimulate academic progress
in, and improve the organisation of, the numerous Colleges
which had already become the places of work of the majority of
of Jesuits. His timid efforts to check and prune the haphazardly
growing mass of Colleges were swept aside grandly by Gregory
XIII. The Pope used his power of 'mission' extensively. He
lavished on the Society extraordinary powers entitling them to set
up Colleges within any Catholic university and to transform their
senior Colleges wholesale into 'pontifical universities'. These
establishments were to be housed in monastic properties com-
mandeered from the older Orders. Such high-handed actions
brought down on the Society's head a storm of abuse from the
university faculties, the old Orders and their powerful allies.
The Pope also proposed that the Society should take over existing
moribund diocesan seminaries for the training of secular clergy
and found new ones. For a start he summarily ordered Mercurian
to move into twenty seminaries, including the English College in
Rome. This action naturally roused furious resentment among
bishops and secular clergy and revolts among clerical students
in the seminaries.

During the Generalates of Laynez and Borgia very thinly-
manned and widely spread Jesuit missions had appeared in the
largely Protestant areas of eastern Europe, in Bohemia, Poland
and Transylvania, in the Moslem Near East, in the Portuguese
spheres of influence in Brazil and the Far East, and in the Spanish

Americas. The initiation and expansion of these missions owed little to the action of the Gesu. Communications with the missioners were slow and scanty. Complaints poured into Rome about violent clashes with the missioners of other Orders, with the civil authorities, with Protestants and Moslems: there were charges of gross breaches of Jesuit rules about poverty and obedience. Mercurian, much alarmed, despatched Visitors-General to most of the mission areas. But when he died he was still far from having a clear picture of mission conditions or anything that could be called a mission policy.

He had been chosen as a non-Spaniard. The Pope seems to have cherished a hope that, as a Luxemburger and northerner, he would be able to stand above the strife of national and regional interests which afflicted the Society. The General Congregation seems to have hoped that, as himself a trained bureaucrat, he would be able to check the rise of favouritism and careerism in the Jesuit Roman Curia. Both hopes were dashed. The Duchy of Luxemburg was part of the Burgundian inheritance of the crown of Spain: so Mercurian was, though no Spaniard, born a subject of the King of Spain. Although he spoke fluent Latin, Italian and a dialect of French, he preferred to use Castilian Spanish in his private memoranda and with his intimates. He was also guilty of using his power of rapid promotion and dispensation from rules to forward the careers of a small group of his intimates, mostly Netherlanders, Spaniards, and Italians from Spanish-held areas. By his death in 1580 this rank favouritism had roused furious resentment in the Society.

*   *   *

Jesuit views of the state of the Society during this period were sharply contradictory. During Borgia's Generalate Nadal addressed the Jesuit community of Coimbra in Portugal in these terms:

> 'Cast your eyes over our Society throughout the world and what do you see but exuberant vigour and fervour, afire for the great tasks of a strenuous charity, a Society never idle, never crying halt, never defeated . . .'

The letters of exhortation sent by Pieter Kanis to his communities in Upper Germany were full of the same resolutely pious language. Borgia explained patiently to Pius V that the excellent zeal and vigour characterisic of Jesuits proceeded from their attachment to forms of 'devotion' given by God to Ignatius: 'Conventual', and even some 'Observant', religious whose prayer was mainly the choir Office, conspicuously lacked that zeal and vigour.

Other Jesuit judgements flatly contradicted that buoyant optimism. Nadal passed from Coimbra to Andalusia where discipline was so bad that the desperate Provincial was resorting to imprisonment, the stocks and the whip. Nadal's private reports to the Gesu were pessimistic. Kanis's reports were even blunter. He could trust few of the Rectors of Colleges: his Province was bleeding to death as men were dismissed, fled or went over to Protestantism. Maldonatus, an Italian Visitor-General in France in 1579, much admired the devoutness of the French. But he reported that their complaints about the Jesuits working in their country were fully justified. 'The Society', he ended wildly, 'is destroying itself.' In fact the optimistic and pessimistic reports were all true. The Society was, astonishingly, in spite of glaring faults and human failings, displaying great vigour.

The rapid establishment of Colleges was producing an equally rapid growth in Jesuit numbers, though it will never be possible to calculate exactly the size of the growth. By 1580 the Jesuit Curia was demanding the keeping of detailed registers and regular returns of manpower. They were soon going to order that every Jesuit novice should write out his own biography for the records. The enforcement of these orders was slow and piecemeal because most superiors were overworked. The disasters which overtook the Society later in its history played havoc with the registers and returns. Entry into the noviciate or even entry and profession were one thing: survival to a ripe old age in the Society was quite another. The loss-rate by early death, dismissal or flight remained as high as in earlier days. In 1608 a Portuguese superior complained that so many Jesuits had left the Society over the course of the previous thirty years that Portugal contained more ex-Jesuits than serving members of the Society. No doubt Portugal at that date was an untypical Province: almost half of its Jesuits had left for mission work in the colonies. Of one batch of forty-three men who entered the Society in Italy between 1556 and 1558, twenty-one were gone by 1567 — eleven dead and ten dismissed. Of the nineteen Britons recorded as having entered the Society in Italy before 1565 and left records behind them, three died young and five were dismissed. Between 1563 and 1569 Pieter Kanis reported a steady series of defections in Upper Germany. At Dillingen eight Jesuit priests had been dismissed. At Innsbruck two Jesuits, one English and one German, had absconded to become Lutherans. At Augsburg a novice cook absconded with the house funds. At Ingolstadt dismissals had so emptied the house that the Rector had to undertake all the offices and also do duty as cook. It was the same story at Munich, Vienna and Prague. By no means all of the ex-Jesuits ended their lives in disgrace or obscurity. Two became diocesan bishops, one became Charles Borromeo's Vicar-General in Milan, and David Wolfe, a brave Irish Jesuit missioner in his native country before being dismissed for living unchastely, became a papal nuncio.

In 1580 the Society was overrun with teenagers and very young men. The recruitment of secular priests, university graduates and middle-aged men, common enough in more difficult days, was yielding place to a flood of schoolboys. The average age in noviciates was now sixteen: fifteen-year-olds were not uncommon and some novices were even younger. Edmund Campion was thirty-three years old when he entered the Jesuit noviciate at Brno in Bohemia and found himself among schoolboys, 'John and Charles, the two Stephens, Sallitzi Finnit and George, Tobias and Gaspar'. More than three-quarters of all Jesuits were unordained. The priests were desperately overworked and superiors preoccupied with speeding up students' courses so as to advance the dates of their ordinations. Even the superiors now tended to be much younger than had once been customary. The General elected in 1580 was only thirty-seven years of age and some of his aides much younger.

The reaction of senior Jesuits to these new conditions was not what we might expect. They were sharing the common lot. Europe in the 16th century suffered from a population explosion and a very high death-rate: it was overrun with children and young people. Campion himself became an Oxford undergraduate at fourteen and was a fellow of his College at seventeen. His academic career there was spent in teaching boys and teenagers, so the atmosphere of the Brno noviciate and the Prague Jesuit community was utterly familiar. In Catholic countries there was normally acute pressure on young people to find secure billets in the priesthood, the religious life or government offices. In many countries, particularly in northern Europe, clerical recruitment tailed off in the 1540s and 1550s in spite of these conditions, largely because of the Reformation crisis. The universities and the religious Orders lost men in great numbers and found recruitment hard. Some Orders, like the Capuchins, suffered much worse than the Jesuits. After 1560 the crisis eased in southern Europe and normal recruitment began again for almost all clerical organisations. In 1564, 200 students of Salamanca university entered religious Orders, fifty of them becoming Jesuits. By 1580 the Dominicans had 14,000 men. The Capuchins had a much greater efflorescence than the Jesuits. All the active Orders were flooded with the young and all were wrestling with problems of education.

The Society of 1580 had an even more decidedly Spanish flavour than in 1556. Now at least two out of every three Jesuits were subjects of Philip II of Spain, even if they were Italians, Belgians, Dutchmen or Portuguese. Since the growth-rate of the Spanish Provinces greatly exceeded that of the rest of the Society, superiors in France, Germany and Poland were still compelled to employ seconded Italian and Spanish priests, much to their embarrassment. Latin might be the official *lingua franca* of the Society, but in practice Italian and Spanish mattered more. Most Jesuits, especially in southern Europe, wore clerical clothes of a distinctively Spanish-Italian style topped in the street and in the invariably dank churches with a high, four-square 'Spanish Hat', one of the ancestors of the biretta. These Hispanic mannerisms were regarded with detestation by many French, German and English Catholics and all Protestants. But they were a widespread and inescapable feature of European Catholicism: all the major Orders were afflicted by them to a greater or lesser degree. 'Jesuit dress' was affected by many clerics who were not Jesuits: members of other Orders of 'regular clerks', Roman Curial officials, cathedral canons, secular priests who were ambitious papal chaplains or the attendants of Cardinals and noblemen or just well-to-do town incumbents.

Schoolteaching bulked large in the life of the Society in 1580 and absorbed a steadily increasing proportion of its manpower and energies. In 1556 teaching had been a small, fringe activity for the few, regarded by their colleagues as freaks or unfortunates. By the 1640s at least three out of every five Jesuits were schoolmasters and the Society's school system was uniquely well-organised and regimented. But in 1580 it was, like the Society itself, in an awkward, fluid state of transition.

The schools grew up as the result of hundreds of purely local arrangements designed piecemeal to suit local circumstances and needs and not any educational theory or policy of the Gesu. In fact Jesuit initiative, by Provincials or the Gesu, played relatively little part in the process. The biggest Jesuit initiatives proved failures. They were invariably directed towards the foundation of Colleges which would play an integral, teaching part in the life of major European universities. So at Paris the Society lobbied the crown, the Paris *Parlement*, the archbishop, the nobility and the faculties: they even resorted to a little judicious bribery and to camouflaging the local Jesuit community under a non-Jesuit name. It produced no effective, lasting result. In reality the Provincials had to wait, cap in hand, on patrons, sovereigns, nobles, bishops, town councils and Popes. Eventually they were offered educational opportunities which, though in some ways advantageous to the Society, more often than not turned out to be onerous and troublesome too.

A good many of the projected schools hung fire for many years. Pieter Kanis, the Provincial of Upper Germany, was fobbed off for years with empty promises from patrons before a single College took shape. Meanwhile, in order to show willing and achieve something, he had to accept the highly onerous and largely useless administrative responsibility for several moribund and ruined Catholic universities. There tiny Jesuit staffs, mostly ignorant of German, tried to teach handfuls of students in leaky buildings with collapsed endowments. At Toulouse, Rennes, Lyon, Bordeaux, Avignon, Marseille, Augsburg, Freiburg and Breslau, to name only a few examples, there were decades of promises, inconclusive negotiations, false starts of Colleges and Jesuit withdrawals before success was achieved. It was the same story in Rome itself. The Jesuit Roman College never got underway until Borgia supplied an endowment. The Popes gave only conditional and small support and the students had to attend lectures at the papal university. The College was lumbered with responsibility for, and staffing of, various national seminaries (German, English and Irish) which were unruly and always tottering on the edge of collapse. The *Germanicum* actually did collapse in poverty and disorder twice, in 1562 and 1572.

Once Jesuit Colleges were founded, the premises and endowments provided by the patrons often turned out to be grossly inadequate. In many cases a College had to begin life in one wing of an ill-repaired monastic house, sharing quarters with the aged survivors of the original religious community. Thus at Vienna the College started in part of a Dominican house and transferred three years later to a Carmelite one: in Munich it was an Augustinian convent, in Wurzburg a deserted Poor Clare convent and in Innsbruck a deserted charity hospital. In such cases the endowments generally were embarrassingly small. Some were monastic property far from the Colleges and difficult to administer; others were benefices, the ownership of which was formally forbidden by the Jesuit *Constitutions*. Elsewhere College premises remained town council property and the endowment a subsidy from local taxation, the yield of which fluctuated wildly. Thus there were Colleges, like Toulouse and Ingolstadt, which for many years received very little endowment income and had to live from hand to mouth by begging for donations.

'College' was a name which covered a wide variety of different Jesuit educational ventures carried on under the same roof or by the same staff serving different local schools. It was then quite usual for a Jesuit 'College to contain a Jesuit 'claustral' school, a university students' hostel, a day or boarding school for lay boys, a Jesuit noviciate and a catechetical school for local poor people — with a small diocesan seminary controlled by Jesuits from the same premises. In half a dozen university towns the mixture contained an extra ingredient — Jesuit faculty heads and professors teaching in the unversity. The Gesu and successive General Congregations repeatedly complained about these hugger-mugger arrangements. They demanded that noviciates should be removed out of Colleges into separate premises, and that boarding schools for lay boys and diocesan seminaries should be handed over to lay teachers or abandoned. These directions had a very limited effect indeed. Lack of money and buildings and the demands of patrons were strait-jackets from which no Provincials could easily escape. In 1579 less than half of the existing Jesuit noviciates were housed in separate buildings. The number of Jesuit-run seminaries and boarding schools slowly but inexorably increased, particularly in Belgium and France.

The Society found it steadily harder to provide its growing schools with teachers. In theory there was no problem. Throughout Europe much of the teaching burden was borne by 'auxiliaries'. Senior pupils were expected to combine their own course work with teaching junior classes. In large junior classes it was usual for one master to preside, assisted by a student 'usher' and a number of 'repetitors', 'decurions' or class monitors. These were pupils picked out of the class to relay the master's instructions to groups of fellow pupils, supervise their 'exercises' and hear them repeat memorised texts. The Jesuits naturally adopted this system and, indeed, could never have built up their schools any other way. However, the system put a severe strain on the student Jesuits. Although they were familiar with it, since they had recently been at the receiving end of its very mechanical complexities, few of them were natural teachers and their own course-work allowed them hardly any spare time for preparation of classes. They were hurried on towards ordination and expected to compress into four years of course-work what the average lay university student did in nine. Inevitably Jesuit students wilted under these extreme pressures. The Gesu became alarmed by the high incidence of tuberculosis and mental breakdown. Robert Bellarmine, one of their leading theologians, suffered constant ill-health because of overwork during his student days.

Provincials and rectors did their best to ease the teaching burden. Wherever it was possible they employed outside masters, secular priests or laymen. So at Pont á Mousson teaching at the diocesan seminary was shared out between Jesuits and secular priests. The Roman College in the 1570s employed at least two outside teachers, Antoine Muret, an able classicist layman from France, and Tomas Luis Victoria, a secular priest from Spain and a famous composer. In 1573 the *Germanicum* students, who had hitherto been lodged in the Roman College, moved out to occupy separate premises of their own: Victoria went with them as their chaplain and choirmaster. He celebrated the move by composing a setting of the psalm *By the waters of Babylon*. But hired teachers were an expense which most Colleges could not bear. The usual way of lightening the Jesuit teaching load was to shorten the academic day by an hour and increase the size of classes at the lower end of Colleges. The result by 1580 was that the larger and more successful Colleges commonly had lower grammar classes of over a hundred small boys. In 1583 the sixth class, of seven-year-olds, at Tournon College in France had over two hundred. The management of such huge classes was only possible by the employment of much increased number of 'repetitors'. They gradually became an important and integral part of the Jesuit school system. Necessity and piety were nicely combined by rectors who began to organise them into elite 'academies' or 'sodalities' as a reward for their extra work. Jesuit noviciates were largely recruited from 'sodalists'. This had the odd consequence that in future many a Jesuit's teaching experience began at the age of eight.

The organisation and lay-out of courses were matters which very few Jesuits caught up in the College treadmills had the time, energy or inclination to bother themselves with. Inevitably, therefore, rectors adopted ready-made syllabuses of which there were several in existence in the Society in 1580. All were slightly adapted versions of ones in use in the great Protestant schools of Germany, then the acknowledged educational experts of Europe. The Society did contain a few *avant-garde* educationalists who attempted to adopt, and popularise, their own syllabuses. In the 1570s Juan Maldonado of Salamanca, transferred to the Clermont College in Paris, caused a great stir by introducing his own theology course. At the same time Perpinien and his friend Muret at the Roman College, both fanatical classicists, tried to adopt their own humanities and rhetoric courses in the teeth of conservative Jesuit opposition. Perpinien was exiled to a new College at Lyon and eventually left the Society. Textbooks were another problem. The masters could not manage without them: senior pupils in Colleges could not be prevented from acquiring them. By the 1560s the only good textbooks in print for the courses from philosophy down to lower grammar were written by Protestant or radical Catholic authors. The Jesuits automatically adopted the books, only to find that ecclesiastical authority was beginning to ban their use. Pieter Kanis complained to the Roman authorities who eventually gave Jesuits secret permission to 'dissimulate': they might use most of the textbooks in plain covers until approved Catholic texts were in print. This curious arrangement stayed in force until, long after 1580, Jesuit teachers in Coimbra, Rome and Louvain found time to compile the textbooks which were eventually to be used in most of the schools, Catholic and, ironically, Protestant, in Europe.

Incidentally the rise of Jesuit Colleges exacerbated one of the Society's other problems — the lack of good servants. From its earliest days the Society, like all religious Orders, depended heavily on the services of lay brothers ('temporal coadjutors') and lay servants. In theory religious ought to have done their own household chores: in practice that was utterly impossible. Jesuit houses which, like the Gesu or the bigger Colleges, had communities of twenty or more priests and students, could only keep going with the manual labour of at least a dozen workers, including tradesmen, cooks, tailors, carpenters, painters and masons. Fortunately they did not need grooms, since Jesuits were forbidden to own horses or mules. The running of schools multiplied the manual work-load greatly. Long before 1556 it became obvious that the Society would always be short of temporal coadjutors and would have trouble with a good many of those it had. There was no shortage of applicants in most Catholic countries, but most lacked the particular qualities needed, a useful trade, natural piety, steadiness of character, and no lurking ambition for the priesthood. Hence by 1580 most Jesuit College Procurators had a servant problem. They had a few admirable temporal coadjutors, indispensable pillars of the College and more use than some priests, some useless and troublesome ones heading for dismissal, and a group of lay servants hired by yearly contracts. The lay servants were generally no more trustworthy than the run of their profession.

If these were the harsh realities of Jesuit schooling in 1580, was it successful? It is impossible to generalise. The Society's schools had not yet become fashionable and renowned. Some, but relatively few, sons of the great attended them. When they did they arrived attended by tutors and servants of their own and required, and got, special treatment. They rarely stayed long. It seems that many pupils of lower degree also left quite quickly. John of the Cross, later a famous Carmelite mystic, arrived at the Jesuit College of Medina del Campo in 1557 at the age of thirteen. He had already attended two other schools. He stayed in the College, then newly-founded and small, for about two years of grammar. He left, spent a year or two deciding between the secular priesthood and the Carmelites, and then entered Carmel. It is hard to detect any trace of his short Jesuit education in his works. Cervantes had arrived at the same Jesuit College at Medina two years before John: he came as a mere child, stayed about two years in lower grammar and was then removed by his parents. After some years of casual study under private tutors he had a brief spell, perhaps in humanities, in the unruly Jesuit College at Seville. Much later in life he praised his Jesuit teachers at Medina for their unusual gentleness, a rare quality in days when masters were expected to be severe.

Directly and indirectly the sheer mechanics and administration of the burgeoning school system seem to have exhausted most Jesuits in 1580. The Society had other fields of work, but for the most part they attracted few people. 'Devotional' evangelism among all classes, but especially the poor, had been a major Jesuit work in 1556. Now it was a fringe occupation. The Fathers in Seville, Paris and Rome, tied up in College work, spent their scanty leisure at hospitals, orphanages and Houses of Rescue. Pieter Kanis and his successors in the Provincialate of Upper Germany lamented that lack of time and linguistic ability prevented them doing much catechising of the poor. In Spain, and, to a lesser extent, Portugal, many of the Fathers and students resented College work and were more interested in foreign missions or their own personal life of 'devotion'. There was a well-known type of Spanish Jesuit called a 'Recollet' who lived an almost totally eremitical life of prayer and penance, and ignored teaching and pastoral work. By 1580 it was the Observant Franciscans, discalced Carmelites and Capuchins who were providing the lead in the 'devotion' movement, not the Jesuits.

'Dangerous missions' to the Protestants, Moslems and heathen had been as small a fringe activity of Jesuits as running schools in 1556. In those days their colleagues lumped enthusiasts for these missions with schoolmasters as 'rogue Jesuits', to be regarded with a mixture of respect and derision. The Curia treated both enterprises as strictly for volunteers who felt they had a special vocation for self-sacrifice. After 1556 teaching came to be accepted as a normal, indeed compulsory, task for all Jesuits mentally capable of it. Meanwhile, as we shall see in more detail in the next chapter, there was no similar change of Jesuit attitude toward 'dangerous missions'. A few tiny exploratory forays, covered by diplomatic immunity, into Protestant countries seemed to prove that Jesuit missions there would be not only dangerous but practically useless. In 1584 the General Acquaviva wrote coolly:

'To send missioners in order to give edification by their patience under torture might injure many Catholics and do no good to souls . . .'

By 1580 the missions to the Far East, Near East and America had swallowed up at least six hundred Jesuit volunteers, of whom less than half had lived long enough to do any mission work at all. The perilous sea voyage to the Far East took an enormous toll of the lives of the volunteers, and exhaustion and tropical diseases killed many on arrival in India. In one year alone pirates and storms killed fifty-three volunteers on their way to Brazil. Many members of the Society found it hard to believe that these risks, however glorious as a 'divine folly', brought any real advantage to the Church or to a Society fighting to keep its school system open. Most of the volunteers who survived overseas simply joined Portuguese and Spanish colonial establishments which were already overmanned with priests. The minority who tried to evangelise the natives reported home a long series of disillusionments. Hence in 1580 the Society very definitely put Colleges before 'dangerous missions'.

There was one last field of Jesuit work which had not existed in 1556. It developed from the 1560s but its growth was very stunted by the demands of the Colleges. The early Society was almost entirely innocent of intellectual interests. Among later generations of Jesuit students and teachers at Rome, Coimbra, Salamanca, Paris and Louvain there appeared an intellectual elite whose ambitions stretched far beyond the narrow bounds of College syllabuses and teaching. At the Roman College, each attended by a little group of student disciples, appeared Christoph Klau, a brilliant German mathematician and astronomer, Robert Bellarmine, an Italian theologian, and Perpinien and Muret, French enthusiasts for the classics. Klau's appeals for a modernisation of the Jesuit philosophy course and the training of Jesuit mathematicians went largely unheard at the Gesu. Bellarmine's efforts to modernise the theology course also foundered. He and Klau were kept heavily occupied in course-teaching and the writing of textbooks. Meanwhile the indiscretions of Perpinien and Muret had earned them the Gesu's displeasure. In 1580, at Coimbra, Francisco Suarez and Luis Molina, both brilliant 'modernist' pragmatists, were still struggling to give written shape to their ideas in the scanty leisure allowed to College professors. In Paris Juan Maldonado had already made his dramatic protest against the sacred tenets of traditional theological scholasticism: he was now back in Rome, a tired and dying man. In Louvain Leonard Lessius and Jean Hamel were following the same intellectual path, beset by the same obstacles. The intellectual 'mission' was almost as dangerous and thankless as the foreign missions. An unprejudiced observer of the Society in 1580 might have been pardoned for thinking that both had little chance of future success.

4

The Dangerous Missions
1540-1610

'I may have been in Pekin, or I may have been in
Paraguay — who knows where?'

(Fr. Holt SJ in W. M. Thackerary's
The History of Henry Esmond.)

In the early chapters of Thackeray's novel the hero, Henry
Esmond, an illegitimate child the circumstances of whose birth
are suitably mysterious, is being brought up in the household
of a Catholic nobleman. His tutor is Fr. Holt, a Jesuit, who does
his best to recruit little Henry into the Society. He tells him of

> '. . . the glories of his order, of its martyrs and heroes, of its
> Brethren converting the heathen by myriads, traversing the
> desert, facing the stake, ruling the courts and councils, or
> braving the tortures of kings; so that Harry Esmond thought
> that to belong to the Jesuits was the greatest prize of life and
> bravest end of ambition; the greatest career here, and in
> heaven the surest reward . . . so that he might join that
> wonderful brotherhood which was present throughout the
> world . . .'

Little Henry was quite carried away by the vision and might easily
have become a Jesuit and 'ended a martyr in China or victim on
Tower Hill' if his patron's household had not been broken up by
the crisis of the 'Glorious Revolution' of 1688 and Holt removed
to become a Jacobite secret agent. Much later in the story Henry,
now solidly Anglican, is an officer in the Duke of Marlborough's
army at war on the continent. He still has fond memories of his
old tutor and is fascinated and delighted when he meets him by
chance in a church in Brussels. Holt is disguised as an Austrian
army officer and is engaged on some highly secret mission.
Before the two men finally part Holt, with great delicacy and
kindness, reveals to Henry the true story of his birth and takes
him to his mother's grave: she died a Catholic nun. Henry's final

reflections on his old tutor are measured but kindly, even sympathetic. Holt, he thinks, is, like all Jesuits, a confidence man. He makes a virtue and a weapon out of a cloud of mystery about his and the Society's operations: they claimed to possess a kind of omniscience and to be backed by a divine mandate. Henry's Anglican moderation, British common sense and moral fibre rejected these claims outright. He could not approve of Holt's aims, the aggrandisement of the Society and the Roman Church, or his methods, which involved deceit. Nevertheless Henry cherished a sneaking admiration for Holt's courage and consistency.

Thackeray's feelings about Jesuit missionaries established him in the minority tradition among critics of the Society, Catholic, Anglican and agnostic. The majority tradition reserved its severest strictures for the missionaries. Sir Walter Mildmay, in moving a Bill against them in the House of Commons in 1581, called them 'a sort of hypocrites . . . a rabble of vagrant friars newly sprung up and coming through the world to trouble the Church of God . . .' Both he and contemporary German Lutheran writers compared them to body worms, or, more theologically, to 'the spawn of Hell' prefiguring the end of the world. French Huguenot corsairs felt they had done their religious duty when they made captured Portuguese Jesuits walk the plank off the coast of Brazil. Dutch Reformed corsairs made war on Jesuit missions in the East Indies. In the 19th century Sir Richard Burton, though himself famous for his wildly perilous expeditions to Mecca and elsewhere disguised as a Moslem and married to a stiffly devout Catholic, had no good word to say of Jesuit missionaries. 'They crushed out the man', he wrote, 'that he might better become an angel.' But there had always been a minority among the Society's critics who, while just as opposed to its principles and methods, excluded the great Jesuit missionaries from their strictures. Elizabethan Protestant gentlemen shouted to the executioners to let them hang to death before they were cut down to be ceremonially butchered. Sir Francis Bacon and John Aubrey approved of their learning and daring. Bishop Creighton, the great Anglican historian, and Newman expressly excluded Xavier, Ricci, de Nobili and the Jesuit missioners in Paraguay from their swingeing criticism of the Society. Robert Louis Stevenson wrote, after visiting Jesuit missions to the Californian Indians:

'How ugly a thing our Anglo-Saxon Protestantism may appear beside the doings of the Society of Jesus . . .'

Some Jesuit missionaries, particularly Ricci in China, the Reduction Fathers in Paraguay, and Pierre de Smedt in the early American far West, have enjoyed what almost amounts to a cult among non-Catholic writers.

The courage of many of the early Jesuit missionaries is beyond dispute, but it must be seen in perspective. Their physical courage was relatively unexceptional by the standards of their own age, when life was cheap, short and vastly uncomfortable for all. Many thousands of laymen faced the same, or far longer, voyages for honour, adventure and gain or to avoid gaol and their creditors. The physical sufferings of Xavier, Ricci, Anchieta and de Nobili were humdrum compared with the fantastic ones endured by Cortes, Pizarro, Almagro, da Gama, Albuquerque, Magellan, del Cano and their followers, *conquistadores* and explorers. For every Jesuit who went overseas there were twelve or fifteen other clerics, Franciscans, Dominicans, Augustinians, Carmelites or secular priests. Long journeys across plague-ridden and war-torn Europe, or even residence by choice in Colleges in filthy and unhealthy towns were quite as lethal as life in the foreign missions. Throughout Jesuit history the proportion of the Society actually engaged at any time in 'dangerous missions' has been very small. In the later 16th century it is probable that only one in ten of Jesuits was working outside Catholic Europe. Moreover, most of these missionaries were living in Portuguese or Spanish colonies organised as integral parts of the homeland with fortifications, troops, settlers, a civil government, parishes, bishops and small cathedrals. Life there was dull and familiar, if somewhat free and exotic. The average Jesuit missioner volunteered to go overseas during his student courses. Once he arrived at his station he was absorbed for years to ordination in College life little different from that at home. If he was of even moderate academic ability, and sometimes if his ability was slight, he found himself involved for the rest of his short life in a College at Goa, Macao, Malacca, Manila, Mexico City, Lima, Vilna, Poznan or Cracow. If he were judged useless for a College he was removed and sent into 'the bush' to some mission 'reservations' for 'reduced natives' — tribes hunted out of nomad existence by white troops and planted in segregated villages under the care of troops and priests. In Japan he would be sent to a station established by contract with a daimyo to instruct ready-made communities of the daimyo's tenants whom he had ordered to undergo Christian initiation. In either case the new Jesuit priest would find himself in a strictly subordinate position supervising the catechetical work of a small army of native underlings. His work would be limited to saying Mass, endless baptisings of dying babies and men, and trying to instruct the catechists in pidgin-Portuguese or Spanish. The native catechumens would be poles asunder from him. He could not understand their languages: at most he might know a few phrases in Tamil, Malayan or Japanese. He could normally have no dealings with women, who were instructed and even baptised by women catechists. In normal circumstances physical danger was slight: his chances of martyrdom were about as great as those of a Jesuit in Rome from death at the hands of local bandits, always possible but rare in practice.

The 'great' Jesuit missionary, celebrated for evangelisation over wide areas and for trying new methods, was inevitably a rarity. In the first sixty years of Jesuit foreign missions the Society produced no more than a dozen, all of them men with either rare linguistic qualifications or a specially privileged status in the Society.

Within the Society these men were certainly a race apart. They had to operate without much comfort and encouragement from their superiors in Europe. The passage of letters between America and Europe then commonly took from six to nine months each way, and from the Far East two to three years each way. At least half the letters were lost in transit. Ricci in China received no letter from Europe for nine years. In any case it was difficult for the Gesu to understand the peculiar problems of foreign missions. The Generals of the later 16th century were, like most Jesuits, utterly absorbed in European affairs and Colleges. To their minds the distant missions were peripheral affairs of relatively little consequence. They were usually unwilling to allow able men to go overseas. The printed Jesuit College courses of the period show that professors and students were extraordinarily uninterested in, and ignorant about, 'the new worlds' overseas. The Generals showed a steady disposition to suspect that the distant missions were lacking in proper discipline and regard for the letter of the *Constitutions*. The great Jesuit missionaries all suffered at the hands of a Gesu which was unsure of the value of their enterprises and increasingly suspicious of originality. They all found it advisable to phrase their annual mission reports carefully so as to make the most of their successes and offer no handle to their enemies in Rome. Xavier instructed the mission rectors in the Moluccas:

> 'Write detailed accounts of the work of conversion and let it be of edifying matters: and take care not to write of matters which are unedifying: remember that many people will read these letters . . .'

It was the common lot of these men to face official neglect, misunderstanding and censure. Pieter Kanis and John Gerard were rewarded for years of service in the field by summary removal from their posts, Kanis to historical research, Gerard to College and noviciate work on the continent. De Nobili suffered censure and a period of removal from his mission. Edmund Campion and Possevino were sent on ill-conceived and ill-fated missions which, as they knew well, mixed politics with evangelisation and were forced on an unwilling General by party lobbies inside and outside the Society.

These men also had much to suffer from their mission colleagues, European settlers, the missionaries of other Orders, and the native catechists and catechumens. In those early pioneer days the Jesuit mission staffs included a good many difficult characters. That was inevitable in the circumstances. The Society was very new and the *Constitutions* and rule books still only just coming into operation. Foreign mission communities were like those in Europe: most members were students or very newly-ordained priests and mature priests were in short supply. In the tiny set-up of the early foreign missions or the Colleges in the outer fringes of Catholic Europe Provincials had exceedingly little scope when choosing rectors. There usually was only one available older priest and he would be irreplaceable for years to come. The Provincial simply had to bear with his eccentricities and follies or try him out as rector of another mission. Outright rogues were few. Ignatius himself dismissed from the Society a Portuguese missioner in West Africa who traded in slaves and shared the proceeds with his relatives at home. Xavier dismissed at least four priests from the Society at Goa. One, the major superior, was wildly dictatorial and shifting him to other posts brought no improvement. Another was a fanatically austere novicemaster whose compulsory fasts killed half his novices. Xavier's best friends in the East, a Portuguese merchant in Malacca and a Japanese convert, both joined the Society but soon quitted it. Ricci and his Vice-Provincial at Macao did not agree on mission policy and Ricci fiercely criticised the methods of his Provincial in Goa. De Nobili's misfortunes were precipitated by violent denunciations of his methods notified to Rome by his Jesuit colleagues in India. The Jesuit English Mission was divided by serious quarrels and there were more ex-Jesuits than Jesuit missioners in the country by the 1590s. The Province of Upper Germany was full of difficult characters and Kanis's denunciations of them contributed to his removal from the Provincialate.

In every mission field except Japan the Jesuits arrived some twenty, thirty or even forty years after the missionaries of other Orders and secular priests. In most of these places the Jesuits were inevitably regarded as interlopers and competitors within the ecclesiastical establishment maintained by the colonial government of either Portugal or Spain, the *Padroado*. By long-standing special arrangements between Rome and the two crowns, missionaries were treated as agents of the civil power and at its disposition. They only sailed overseas with government leave, in government ships at the government's expense. Once in a colony they could not undertake any work without the governor's authorisation and depended very largely for their livelihood on his grants of agricultural land and forced native labour to work it. In effect the colonial government hired missionaries for three purposes. First they had to serve the religious and educational needs of the European and half-caste settler population. In the case of the Jesuits who could not take on parochial work without special dispensations from parts of their Constitutions, this meant Colleges of a European type. Secondly the missionaries had to shoulder part of the burden of running numerous native reservations. In these, natives, baptised without instruction *en masse* as a condition of settlement under colonial military protection, lived under a strict discipline enforced by the lash and gaols. As baptised Catholics the inhibitants were subjects and wards of the crown. The missionaries resident in or alongside reservations gave a more or less religious and paternalistic tinge to what otherwise was a form of prison existence. The third duty of missionaries was to cooperate in the extension of the colonial sphere of influence in the hinterland behind the colonies and among neighbouring independent native states.

The Portuguese and Spanish 'conquerors' had very early grasped that the 'new world' was ripe for European exploitation. It contained countless tribes of artless, primitive animists who were the prey of a number of powerful and comparatively sophisticated native empires, the Aztecs, Incas, Mayas, Moguls, Japanese and Chinese. Experience had shown that European armament, trading skill and technology could, when used boldly, enable mere handfuls of resolute whites to overthrow native emperors and take over their states. The *Padroado* therefore actively encouraged the entry of missionaries into Japan, Peking and Delhi, always provided they realised that they were the agents of European rule.

It never occurred to any of the early Jesuit missionaries to question the rightness of the *Padroado* and its principles, and their ultimate subjection to it. Its principles were not a conscious 16th-century creation but the inevitable consequences of old European attitudes and a way of life which Jesuits could no more reject than they could slough off their own skins. This did not, however, mean that they found life within the colonial set-up easy. There were pious governors and settlers. But most of the first generations of Spanish and Portuguese settlers, the 'conquerors', were rough-necks. Valignano, a Jesuit Visitor-General in the Far East probably voiced his mission colleagues' views on all settlers. He found the immigrant Europeans in general scandalously unedifying and totally incapale of accepting clerical life. Whites born overseas were even worse, effeminate and vicious. There were numerous collisions between Jesuit mission superiors and governors, government agents, estate owners and traders.

As in Europe, so in the colonies, the advent of the Jesuits was greeted coolly by members of other Orders and secular clergy. The first arrival of members of the Society was met with a kind of patronising interest. In Brazil the first arrivals became mission apprentices of the Franciscans. Anchieta, the first Provincial, was long an admiring pupil of that Order. In Goa Xavier was very glad to accept the offer of a Franciscan College. But this honeymoon period was short. Barely three years later Xavier returned to Goa from Malacca to find a war of words raging between his colleagues and the non-Jesuit clergy. The Jesuits found their subordinate position highly irksome. The other clergy thought that Jesuits arrogant upstarts bent on worming their way into ecclesiastical positions of power in the colony. On the whole, until 1600, the Jesuits only escaped from their subordinate position in one mission field, Japan. There shortage of manpower meant sharing the mission with members of other Orders. Though the Orders did their best to restrict entry to clerics willing to be subordinate to them, their efforts failed and the Jesuits rose in prominence. The old familiar story of strife was being repeated.

The great difficulties of the early Jesuit missionaries were increased by their mental isolation from most of their native converts and catechumens. The isolation was a reality, though we may suspect that few missionaries were sensitive to its depth. They were accustomed to linguistic difficulties in Europe. Since the great majority of them were Latins they rarely had to face serious linguistic barriers in southern European Colleges. But once they moved to northern Europe or overseas they had problems. Their academic linguists could rarely be spared from the big Colleges in Europe. It was this fact which made scholars like Ricci and de Nobili great rarities. Xavier, with his complete inability to learn more than a few simple phrases in Tamil, Malay and Japanese, was far more typical of his kind. Ricci, de Nobili and perhaps a very few other scholars concentrated their energies on mastering the infinite complexities of elite native tongues, literary Tamil, Telugu and mandarin Chinese. This brought them into contact with a few hundred native intellectuals but left them still further removed from the minds and tongues of simple peasants. Most missionaries had to rely entirely on the services of native interpreters and catechists, whose knowledge of Spanish and Portuguese was at best rudimentary. Religious instruction of catechists and converts was limited strictly to the parrot-learning of simple formulas. Preaching to natives was almost impossible. The giving of sacraments by Jesuits was severely limited. Most converts, including almost all females, were baptised by native clergy or catechists. Confessions by natives were heard almost exclusively by native clergy, of whom there were very few indeed. Native Catholics were communicated very rarely. Extreme Unction of the dying was probably the sacrament most frequently administered by the average Jesuit.

The result was the growth of a curious kind of mass 'catechumen-Catholicism' full of imported European religious practices, like penitential disciplines and rosaries mixed with antique native customs and ceremonies. No Jesuit was very clear about how to improve this situation. Some dreamed of an impossible *tabula rasa* or clean sweep of all native customs. Others were more philosophical, hoping that, after generations, the native converts would somehow mysteriously 'take' to Catholicism fully and so be admitted to full sacramental practice. Some missionaries were comforted by the thought that European

Catholic peasants and town poor were just as ignorant and super-stitious. Some Jesuits rejoiced because they thought, like Xavier, that they detected in the 'more advanced' native peoples large classes who thought and behaved like Europeans already. Xavier, after barely two years residence in Japan and without knowing the language, enthusiastically judged the Japanese better than Europeans. Other Jesuits flatly dismissed apparent similarities between European and native customs, civil and religious, as an illusion created by the Devil himself.

By 1600 events were occurring in Japan, the only really large and distinctively Jesuit mission field, which ought, in theory, to have provided objective answers to these doubts and ques-tionings. A massive and exceedingly violent pagan reaction and persecution set in, which tested the Jesuit missionaries. But the result of the test was quite inconclusive. Some showed the utmost bravery and died rather than renounce their faith. Others left the country hastily. Seven Jesuits, including the Provincial and two Vice-Provincials, gave way under torture and renounced their faith. Some of the Jesuit martyrs worked for years among their converts secretly, expecting arrest at any moment. Yet a number of their colleagues had helped to bring on the persecution by deliberately planning a Japanese Catholic revolt helped by Spanish naval and military intervention from the Philippines. The fiery trial also tested the depth and quality of the mis-sionaries' impact on their converts. In 1600 these certainly numbered over a quarter of a million, and, if we count every kind of catechumen or pagan 'enquirer', over half a million. Four thousand of these natives stuck to their Catholic religion heroically to the death. An unknown number, possibly some tens of thousands conformed to paganism outwardly while retaining dog-gedly, sometimes for generations, secret Catholic practices. The great majority abandoned their hold on Catholicism.

How, therefore, could the early great Jesuit missionaries work on through such a confused situation? Were they sustained by sheer ignorance of the size of the odds arrayed against them? And was this ignorance reinforced by a medieval crusading zeal? These factors were realities in the mentality of all the mis-sionaries, apparently more strongly in some than in others. With the exceptions of Ricci, a pupil of the great Jesuit mathe-matician and geographer, Christoph Klau in the Roman College, and perhaps de Nobili, the missionaries went overseas very ignorant of the geography of the areas they traversed and settled in and totally ignorant of their culture and history. What passed for geography in university and Jesuit College courses before the mid-17th century was a farrago of ancient speculation and a very little modern hearsay. At that time Jesuit philosophy textbooks made almost no reference at all to 'the new world'. Nothing had been done to disturb the future missionaries' prejudice that Europe was the Christian civilised world: the rest was marginal, uncivilised and fantastic. To new missionaries 'the new world' meant what outer space does to us today. The young missionary had little sense of distance. He was not helped by the fact that the seamen who carried him found it hard to calculate speed and distances. The ships waited months at intervening ports before putting themselves at the mercy of monsoon winds. The missionaries can hardly ever have seen maps or globes and were vague about the size and relative positions and shapes of continents. In a mind bred this way, mission experience, secluded from direct contact with the minds of natives, either confirmed deep prejudices or created a sense of insecurity and doubt.

There is plenty of evidence that many Jesuits in America and the Far East accepted and 'spiritualised' the crusading or *Padroado* view of their work. To their minds the conquest of the 'new world' simultaneously by the sword and the Gospel was the inevitable, too long delayed victory of Christendom over Heathendom. They could appeal to the words of Ignatius himself. The first key meditation in the Second Week of the *Spiritual Exercises* applies to Christ the image of a temporal king going to war, determined to bring under his control 'the entire land of the unbeliever', and calling on his vassals to follow him. The exercitant was expected to be familiar with the military rules of old days: the king could command service inside his country, but only take volunteers to fight outside it. Naturally also Ignatius assumed that the exercitant knew that ecclesiastics were forbidden to bear arms and shed blood: their part in the holy war was as chaplains to the military and converters of the conquered. In this meditation and others Ignatius insisted that, as with Christ, so with the Jesuit, the power to convert comes through suffering the 'white martyrdom' of labour and exhaustion or the 'red martyrdom' of death. But in other writings Ignatius had taken for granted that the missionary's teaching must ultimately be backed up by penal jurisdiction. He approved of the ecclesiastical tribunals of the Inquisition, Roman, Spanish and, he hoped some day, Portuguese. In a celebrated letter to Kanis in Upper Germany he regretted that the setting up of a German Inquisition was still 'inadvisable', but urged him to use his penal jurisdiction as a university rector fully and to try to persuade the Catholic civil power to deprive Protestants of offices and rights, imprison, banish or 'even execute' them if practicable.

Anchieta, the first Jesuit Provincial of Brazil and a very devoted missionary to the Indian reservations, wrote:

'there is no better way of preaching than with the sword and the rod of iron . . .'

He was talking of punitive expeditions by Portuguese colonial troops, accompanied by Jesuit chaplains, among the nomad tribes of the interior to drive them into reservations. Francis Xavier had proposed to the Governor of Goa military expeditions against Hindu and Moslem princes and a raid to Arabia to destroy Mecca. In India and Ceylon he encouraged his child catechumens to wreck pagan shrines, smash idols and break Buddhist holy relics. Valignano, a Jesuit Visitor-General to the Far East, complained that Jesuit missions could not function properly without the sort of penal jurisdiction they enjoyed over reservations in India and America. The Japanese converts, he wrote, 'will not suffer being slapped or beaten, nor imprisonment, nor any similar methods used as with other Asiatic Christians'. He suggested that it might be possible to get the missionaries granted powers of imprisonment and even execution by the Japanese daimyos. 'The Japanese', he observed, 'will not obey unless they fear death.'

But ignorance and crusading zeal were not the only ingredients of the early Jesuit missionary mind. We generally presume that apocalyptic ideas have been confined to extreme Protestantism. In fact from the 16th to the 18th centuries they were common ground for both Catholics and Protestants. For most religious minds they were a background which was taken for granted and rarely stressed: among the 'devout' they were often a burning preoccupation. The evidence that some Jesuits saw the foreign missions in an apocalyptic context is scanty but clear. Thomas Stapleton was an eminent Elizabethan English Catholic theologian living in exile in universities in Flanders. He soon became friendly with the Jesuit community in Louvain and it was there that, in the late 1560s, he published an anti-Protestant volume, *A Counterblast against Horne*. This ended with an extraordinary tribute to Jesuit missionaries:

'Now in these latter days, the Empire of Constantinople becoming Turkish, and in our own days, a great part of Europe . . . carried away by errors and heresies, God hath of his wonderful mercy and goodness . . . opened and revealed unto us as it were a new world, of which neither by writing or otherwise we ever heard anything before . . . He hath by his Providence ordained that the . . . countries of Asia and Africa have become of plain and open idolators, of Moors and Saracens, very good Christians, chiefly due to the Society of Jesus . . .'

He concluded sweepingly that the conversion of the new world might well be counted the greatest wonder in human history since the creation of the world and the Passion of Christ.

Ten years later, in 1579, Stapleton took up the theme again in more detail in the published edition of his university lectures in theology. He pointed out that, when seen in the light of the prophecies in the books of *Daniel* and the *Apocalypse*, contemporary world events could only have one meaning. One age of history was rapidly drawing to an end: the age dominated by two separate but twin Christian institutions, the 'carnal' Church and Holy Roman Empire. The old form of the Church was dying at the hands of Turks, Protestants, merely conventional Catholics, libertines and witches. (Like many contemporaries, Jesuit and non-Jesuit, Stapleton firmly believed that every European country was more and more infested with covens of witches.) The East Roman Empire had fallen to the Turks: the Western Empire was on its last legs. But, by the mercy of God, the inevitable end of the world and final Judgement were respited. A new 'spiritual empire' was arising like the phoenix out of the ashes of the old Church and empire. Led by the reformed Papacy assuming also the Imperial power, this spiritual force had power lacking to its corrupt predecessors: it was converting millions in 'the new world'. The reformed Church of true Catholics, the 'devout' was surely that 'reign of the Saints' which, according to the *Apocalypse*, was to last for a thousand years before the end of the world. At the time that he delivered these lectures Stapleton's association with the Jesuits was even closer. In 1585 he resigned his university posts and entered the Jesuit noviciate, though he left it of his own volition two years later.

Perhaps this apocalyptic view of the Society's vocation to reform and energise the Church and the whole world particularly appealed to the English. There are traces of it in Edmund

Campion's *Brag* of 1580, and, more clearly, the theme runs like a thread through some of the books written by Robert Persons, director of the Jesuit English Mission. It recurred very openly in the *Autobiography* of the most adventurous of all Elizabethan Jesuit missioners in England, John Gerard. The story of his mission work was, he wrote, full of marvellous direct divine interventions at every point since

> 'God chose me to do this because I was a member . . . of that Body which has received from Jesus its Head a remarkable outpouring of His Spirit for the healing of souls in this last era of a declining and gasping world . . .'

*   *   *

The voyages and land operations of the 16th-century Portuguese and Spanish 'conquerors' and the biographies of their main leaders have been described in much detail. The 'conquerors' themselves had no literary gifts: the great majority of them were barely literate. But a variety of circumstances combined to ensure that their work was recorded. They took secretaries and literate priests with them who were instructed to make records so that the leaders could claim support and privileges from their home governments. The brutalities committed by the victorious 'conquerors' led to protests by some missionaries and government intervention. Most of this went on record and provided ample material for colonial historians from the 17th century. Yet, in spite of this documentation, the lives, and often even the names, of the rank and file 'conquerors' are unknown. So, for instance, the only evidence that one of Ignatius's elder brothers was a companion of Cortes in Mexico is a casual reminiscence of a conversation with Ignatius.

The operations and lives of the 16th-century Jesuit missionaries were recorded to the same degree as those of the 'conquerors'. Though ostensibly a better-educated group of men, the missionaries were very rarely given to self-revelation in letters. From Ignatius's days Jesuit Provincials were bound to make annual reports on their charges to the Gesu. These 'Annual Letters' were of two sorts. One sort consisted of secret, uninhibited reports on the mission personnel and its problems. The tone of these letters was almost invariably gloomy and the details given discreditable to individual missioners. Because of the chance of the letters being accidentally lost in transit or captured, these reports were not made regularly. The other sort of annual report was an 'Edifying Letter'. This was a collation by the Provincial of reports by the rectors of missions written to a standard pattern. They had to include statistics of missioners, novices, auxiliaries, conversions, general Confessions heard, paupers and prisoners helped, and donations received. There followed 'remarkable events' thought to confirm the truth of the Faith or the divine mandate received by the Society — for instance, marvellous escapes from death, successful exorcisms of devils, acts of heroism by Jesuits, visions and miracles of healing. On arrival at the Gesu the secret reports were read and locked away. The 'Edifying Letters' were, when time permitted, edited with scissors and paste into privately printed circulars sent to College rectors in Europe. There, if the rector felt so inclined, they could be read to the community in the refectory or used as sermon 'examples'. There is little evidence that they were much used before the 1590s.

Besides this correspondence, there were many 'occasional letters' between the Gesu and the missioners in the field. Some concerned particularly troublesome missionaries. The Gesu took a keen interest in 'apostates' from the Society and their later history. They expected the apostate either to go from bad to worse morally and spiritually, or to return penitently to the bosom of the Society. The late 16th-century archives of the Provinces and of the Gesu usually contain anonymous documents in Latin with titles such as *The Divine Justice on Apostates* or *The Miserable Ends of Jesuit Deserters*. Thus, for instance, there are run-of-the-mill Jesuits about whom historians would know exceedingly little if they had not left the Society and the Catholic Church. Among the English examples are Thomas Langdale, a Yorkshireman, who fled from Loretto to England and became an Anglican. The Jesuit records suggested that he had become insane. There was Christopher Perkins, a Jesuit missioner in Upper Germany who became increasingly critical and obstructive. In 1580 he flatly refused to take part in the ill-conceived English Mission unless he were first allowed to take an oath of allegiance to Queen Elizabeth. He was dismissed from the Society, went to England and became an Anglican. He was later knighted and remembered as a distinguished member of James I's diplomatic service. The Jesuit records contain various rumours that he was in bad faith or that he degenerated into a libertine. There was Thomas Yate, an Englishman who became a Jesuit in 1574 and turned up on the Brazilian Mission by 1601. He fled from Brazil back to England and Anglicanism. The registers record a story that he was received back into the Church and the Society on his death-bed. In Goa there was Ferdinand Mendes Pinto who rated mention of a sort in local Jesuit records on several counts. He was originally a wealthy merchant in Malacca and became a close friend of Francis Xavier and a benefactor of the Society. After Xavier's death he became a Jesuit at Goa but soon quitted the Society. There is some mystery about his departure, since his benefactions were not returned to him but his name was struck from the registers. But apostasy did not win every troublesome Jesuit a place in the Society's records. Our only evidence of one Jesuit apostate comes from his Protestant nephew, the famous astronomer Kepler. Kepler recorded that his uncle Sebaldus became a Catholic and Jesuit in 1576 at Speyer, then left the Society 'against the will of his superior', wandered in poverty through France and Italy trying to make a living as an astrological practitioner, became a Protestant again and married a wealthy wife. Sebaldus was, wrote his nephew bluntly, a vicious man of impure life who died eventually of dropsy and 'the French sickness'.

Other ordinary Jesuits figured in 'occasional' Jesuit official correspondence because they were employed on special missions to politically sensitive areas. The English Mission of 1580-1 and the Swedish Mission of 1576-80, for instance, roused a great deal of comment, support and opposition inside and outside the Society. Hence the surviving official correspondence about the missions and their personnel is quite substantial and its size quite out of proportion to the relative unimportance of the enterprises. From the time of Ignatius onwards the Ethiopian Mission, a politically sensitive operation which repeatedly failed, filled whole boxes with papers in the Gesu archives. Some undistinguished Jesuits gained a mention in history books because they were very briefly involved in missions of this kind: for instance Holt and Samerie who were pawns in fruitless efforts to help Mary Queen of Scots' efforts of which the Gesu disapproved. Similarly Peter William Good, a native of Glastonbury, attained his modest place in Jesuit general history by a similar accident. He was an Oxford man and converted Anglican clergyman who entered the Society in Flanders in middle age. Directly after his ordination he was sent to Ireland for four years to attempt to pick up the threads of small enterprises started there by David Wolfe, a native Irish Jesuit lone operator who had been dismissed from the Society for flagrant immorality. To his relief Good was recalled to Rome and then chosen as secretary and 'Confession-companion' to a noted Jesuit diplomat, Antonio Possevino. He accompanied Possevino first to Sweden and then to Poland. In 1580, again to his relief, he escaped from the world of 'cloak and dagger' enterprises for which he was unsuited, and accompanied the rector of the College at Vilna, another Englishman, Adam Brooke, to Rome to a Jesuit General Congregation. The rest of his life was spent apparently in the decent obscurity he craved, in Rome and then in Naples. There he occupied his spare time with what really interested him, writing on the Anglican question and designing a large, diagrammatic table of the saints and monarchs of England.

A few Jesuit missionaries rated many references in the Gesu archives simply because of their pigheaded individualism and originality. The scholar-missionaries, Ricci, Ruggieri and de Nobili, drew much attention to themselves in this way. In Europe the two most noted 'rogue elephants' were Lauren Nielssen and Robert Persons. Nielssen was a Norwegian university student of mature years who became a Jesuit at Louvain in 1564. His superiors were deeply impressed with him. He was highly intelligent. He had a great influence over other Scandinavian students at Louvain and, indeed, was the organiser of their student 'nation'. Scandinavia was a *terra incognita* to almost all Jesuits: they knew nothing of its languages or its political and religious positions. Nielssen's native force of character and persuasiveness soon won him permission to operate his own private 'mission' to Scandinavia, aided by his student friends. In 1576-80 he inevitably became the expert director of 'the Swedish Mission', a project forced on the Gesu by political and papal influences to convert John III of Sweden, whose wife was a Polish Catholic. Unfortunately the Gesu were quite incapable of deciding what was truth and what was wishful-thinking in Nielssen's enthusiastic reports and modern historians of Sweden have been unable to decide on their veracity. If we are to take the reports at their face value, practically single-handed and disguised as a Lutheran minister, he almost succeeded in converting the nation to Catholicism. Possevino and Good, who had been sent hastily to Stockholm by a bemused General, to report on the real situation there, eventually urged the General to recall Nielssen to Rome and forbid him ever to set foot in Scandinavia again. Nielssen did hurry to Rome, where he talked to the General to such good effect that he was allowed back to Stockholm. To his death in his eighties in 1622 he was a legendary figure among the handful of Jesuits in northern Europe: 'the Jesuitarch'.

The Gesu left him mostly undisturbed in his complicated games. A charitable — and perhaps the right — interpretation of him is as a kind of northern European Matteo Ricci. Like Ricci he was a Professed Father and loyal Jesuit, but an incurable individualist who rode roughshod over the orders of superiors if they ran counter to his ways of thinking. Like Ricci too be believed in some degree of 'accommodation' of Latin Catholicism to the culture and ways of thought of peoples alien to it. Like Ricci he very possibly regarded such an 'accommodation' as a purely temporary device.

Robert Persons was, in some ways, 'the English Nielssen', though apart from one perilous year in England in 1580, he spent the rest of his forty years of advocacy of the Jesuit English Mission in bases in Flanders, Spain and Rome. Throughout that time the Gesu remained quite unconvinced of the soundness of his schemes for the mission and very suspicious of his methods, especially his courting of Philip II of Spain. Mysteriously his Jesuit enemies held up the establishment of an English Province of the Society until his last days. Most of the ablest of the English recruits to the Society were just as mysteriously sent to foreign Provinces and posted to the depths of Sicily or Poland, as far as possible from England and Persons. With great stubbornness, and in the face of numerous setbacks, Persons cobbled together a private army for the English Mission. Since he lacked English Jesuits, he staffed the small seminaries he founded for the mission in part with friendly colleagues borrowed from the Belgian, Spanish and Italian Provinces. He also made do temporarily with auxiliary secular priests trained in his seminaries and closely connected with the Society. Like Nielssen, Persons set his sights high, on the total conversion of his country, peacefully if possible, but, if not, with the assistance of Spanish naval and military forces. Both men thought it useless merely to create a Catholic minority sect or a Catholic nation of the easy-going, conventional, pre-Reformation kind. They believed that nothing less than full conversion to 'devout' Catholicism was essential and that the Society had been raised up by God for just that formidable task.

When Nielssen died his Scandinavian Mission was still a mere aspiration. But Persons left behind him a solidly established English Mission dominated by a newly-founded and rapidly growing English Jesuit Province. That was a remarkable achievement, but, in the eyes of the Gesu, fatally weakened by Persons' stubborn extremism. The Jesuit domination of the English

Mission and its association with Spanish power had deeply alarmed the English Government. It had also alarmed an increasing number of English secular clergy and lay Catholics who were turning sharply, even bitterly, against the Society. There is ample material available for a full-scale biography of Persons but no Jesuit historian has yet grasped the nettle.

There were other early Jesuit missionaries who gained a posthumous fame far outside the bounds of the Society because their work had a scientific interest. By the later 17th century many educated people, Catholic and Protestant alike, became increasingly interested in experimental science and technology. Geography based on exact surveying techniques and the scientific study of non-European cultures became popular. Some Jesuit College professors with a taste for these subjects began to collect materials amassed by missionaries. They turned first to old copies of the *Edifying Letters* circulated round the Provinces. Finding them bowdlerised and heavily edited, they got permission to search the Gesu archives for the originals, especially matter discarded as too lengthy, boring or shocking to pious ears. The result was a series of well-produced mission histories, copiously illustrated with engraved maps and drawings. The best of these histories, by Athanasius Kircher and du Halde, became European best-sellers and the names and work of that tiny minority of early Jesuit missionaries who immersed themselves in the study of native cultures and the exploration of distant countries became famous.

There were critics, usually men educated in Jesuit Colleges, who pointed out that a deep or scientific interest in mission countries and cultures was not characteristic of the ordinary run of Jesuit missionaries. The critics pointed out that journeys of exploration and the adoption of native dress and ways were only undertaken by a very few unusual missionaries whose purposes were evangelical and political not scientific. But Protestant readers of Kircher and du Halde brushed aside these criticisms. They were deeply fascinated by the exotic strangeness of Chinese, Indian and American society and enchanted by the courage of the Jesuit missionaries and the apparent novelty and boldness of their 'accommodations' to native cultures. Such readers soon attributed a quite legendary brilliance of learning and adaptability to all 'the Jesuit Fathers'.

For these Protestant *cognoscenti* their greatest discovery was Francis Xavier. Hitherto they had either never heard of him or dismissed him as a typical papist immersed in idolatry and superstition. Now they began to see him in a very different light, as one of the most brilliant and liberal spirits in history. It was he, they thought, who, far more than Columbus, Da Gama and Cortes, discovered 'the new world'. He originated the novel Jesuit policy of 'accommodation' of western ways to native cultures. He was credited with a great creative 'global vision'. This, his deliberate adoption of the dress and way of life of a Japanese bonze, and his famous admission that the Japanese were 'superior to Europeans in many respects' and 'the delight of my heart' all proved his greatness. Had he not particularly approved of the rationality of the Japanese and their relative freedom from the gross superstitions afflicting the less advanced peoples of Asia?

This image of Xavier in the dress of an 18th-century liberal bore little relation to reality. Xavier was probably the roughest diamond among the 'Paris companions'. Ignatius made no secret of the fact that he offered the toughest resistance to 'devotion'. He regarded university studies as an unpleasant necessity required to get him a comfortable benefice in his native Basque country. Only a fear of 'the French disease' held him back from a life of amorous adventure. Even after his conversion, Ignatius thought it wise to keep him closely by his side in Rome. It was therefore pure accident, not Ignatius's design, which led to Xavier's despatch to the Far East. The accident was an odd and embarrassing one. From 1539 John III of Portugal began to thrust his patronage on the 'Paris companions'. In that year, acting on impulse and the suggestion of a subject who was rector of the St. Barbe College in Paris, the king requested Pope Paul III to send six of the 'companions' to the Far Eastern Portuguese colonies. The Pope passed on the request to Ignatius. Ignatius was in no position to refuse it outright, though at that time the 'companions' were not yet an Order and their very scanty man-power was fully engaged. The acceptance of the 'companions'' request to become an Order still hung in the balance. Ignatius dare not offend the Pope or the king and had to set an example in treating papal missions as sacred. This event was, in fact, the start of an exceedingly difficult relationship between the Jesuits and John III. In the next dozen years he acquired a Jesuit con-fessor, patronised the Society greatly, and constantly treated it as his own possession, showering it with papal missions to his colonies in West Africa, Brazil and Ethiopia. The confessor grew arrogant and independent-minded. The rapidly-expanding Por-tuguese Province became by far the most disorderly and disobedient part of the young Society. Its demands and extremes threatened to distort the life of the Society badly.

Ignatius was in no position to give orders to the 'companions' in 1539: he had not yet been elected General. At a very thinly-attended general meeting they agreed that they must do something about the papal request. They decided that Simon Rodriguez and Nicholas Bobadilla must go to the Far East. No one else was available except Xavier and Ignatius insisted that he could not manage without his assistance. Bobadilla, who had no enthusiasm for the enterprise, fell ill. So Xavier had to go in his place, though Ignatius had many misgivings. When Rodriguez and Xavier reached Lisbon they discovered that John III was by no means clear why he wanted to send them overseas, or indeed that he really intended to send them at all. He pressed both men to stay with him in Portugal. Rodriguez decided to accept the invitation. After a great deal of hesitation Xavier obtained the king's definite permission to sail and was given some assistants — a couple of recent recruits prepared to throw in their lot with the 'Paris companions'. Xavier received a papal brief making him nuncio in the East. Although this gave him no power to interfere with the sovereign rights of the *Padroado* over clerics and religion in the colonies, it was intended to help smoothe his way with the Bishop of Goa and the superiors of religious Orders established in the Indies. John III provided letters appointing Xavier his agent with direct access to the throne by letter. This again was a doubtful asset and did nothing to impress Portuguese officials in outlying colonies. The purpose behind the mission remained obscure.

Xavier was not, by all accounts, a man to be inhibited by these confusions and doubts. He was personable, though by no means the aristocrat that legend later made him, and by colonial standards he was a highly educated cleric. He was certainly a fluent letter-writer, but devoid of real intellectual interests and he had no gift whatever for learning native languages, partly due to lack of ability, and partly because he was incurious about native cultures. He had all the astonishing courage, endurance, forthrightness and gambling instincts of his contemporaries, the Portuguese and Spanish 'conquerors', and, like them, no taste for the arts of diplomacy. His European prejudices and complete ignorance of seafaring and the life of Eastern people were characteristic of his breed. As with the 'conquerors', ignorance positively encouraged him in making crazy decisions and taking tremendous risks. His religious conversion, so slow and long-delayed, had at last 'taken'. He was no mystic, contemplative or even 'proficient' in the ways of 'devotion'. He performed the stock methods of 'devotion', exercises, prayer routines and taking the 'discipline' exactly. He retained a strong rustic and Basque belief in signs, wonders, miracles and devils. He had a strong, if naive, faith that Providence was with him. Unlike Ignatius, he did not agonise lengthily about spiritual decisions but decided quickly to go East, to stay there, then to move on to the East Indies, to Japan and to China. To a much larger degree than the Jesuit missionaries who followed him in the East, he constantly improvised. Thousands of miles of dangerous sea separated him from a Society which still had not fixed its *Constitutions* when he died. Decisions had to be made long before he could expect answers from Ignatius to letters which might well take almost two years to reach Rome and the answers as long to reach him. Xavier was a true Jesuit pioneer but hardly the 'typical formed Jesuit'.

His career in the East was brief and hectic. He left Lisbon in April 1541 in the company of the Governor-elect of Goa, his superior, and took thirteen months over the voyage to India, six months of which were spent roasting impatiently in Mozambique awaiting the monsoon winds. He then spent five frustrating months in lodgings in Goa prospecting for work. The colony of hard-bitten settlers was already more than adequately supplied with clergy and churches. The governor did not take kindly to his naive suggestions for forward military action against the Moslems. Then he and his companions were ordered to establish catechism posts among the Paravas, a poor tribe of fisherfolk long before taken under Portuguese military protection and forcibly baptised. The Governor of Goa undoubtedly followed the usual practice in the colonies of giving Xavier and his assistants civil and penal authority over their native charges. He did not dream of raising objections of principle against these strongly colonialist methods. The mechanical and wearisome chore of teaching large assemblies of Parava children a few religious formulas in Tamil (expecting that they would, in turn, teach their elders) was familiar enough. The 'Paris companions' used similar commonplace methods in the slums of Alcala, Salamanca, Paris and Rome. Xavier, like his colleagues, regarded this catechising as a grand penance and lesson in humility but a waste of the valuable time and ability of educated priests. Anyway the Jesuits had no great confidence in their pronunciation of the Tamil sentences they had learned parrot-fashion in Goa.

Meanwhile the number of his charges steadily increased. He served effectively as trainer of a Parava militia, built defensive hedges and dikes, and negotiated peace agreements with neighbouring tribes. The governor was impressed and sent Xavier as chaplain to punitive columns of troops which rounded up other tribes. They were committed to Xavier's care. In the process of conquest he saw plenty of brutality and bloodshed and took part in the mass baptism of the 'reduced' tribesman. The problem of finding catechist auxiliaries became very urgent. Enquiry in Goa showed that all the religious Orders had long been involved in the same mission process. They had, after a fashion, solved the problem of native auxiliaires by establishing Colleges. These were multi-purpose. They attempted to give a rudimentary education to lay boys, the sons of Portuguese settlers, and they also took in native boys, some of whom were of high caste, Brahmins or Ksatriyas. An effort was made to train these as 'Mass and confession priests' in the simplest possible way. A few climbed the great hurdles of clerical celibacy and learning a little Latin and were ordained. But as priests they often proved almost useless since they slithered out of celibacy and would not minister to native converts of a lower caste than themselves. The Colleges therefore also recruited up-country native convert boys to train them as lay catechists for the 'doctrinas' (organised villages of converts). Xavier borrowed a few catechists from the Franciscan College in Goa and eventually negotiated a Jesuit takeover of the premises. He also wrote to Ignatius begging him to send to Goa any Jesuit cast-off priests in simple vows who had proved too uneducated for work in European Colleges.

During his two years with the Paravas, Xavier, very much their patriarch, became fond of them but never displayed any real interest in, or sympathy with, their culture and history. When he was dealing with animists, Hindus and Moslems, and later with Buddhists and Shintoists he incited his converts brusquely to smash 'the idols' and desecrate the shrines. Like the other missionaries in India he wore European clerical clothes in Goa and a guru's gown when up-country. The practice was simply based on the observed fact that anyone who looked like a guru was immediately accepted with honour and given hospitality.

Directly a number of Jesuit recruits arrived in Goa from Lisbon in 1544 he quitted the Parava mission and set out on the restless and almost incessant travelling which occupied his last six years. Of the ten years he spent in the East more than a third of the time was spent in sea voyages. Another third was spent in direct missionary work, mainly in spells of two years with the Paravas and two years in Japan. The rest of his time was spent in restless movements on land and in administration. In India he visited the Malabar coast, Cochin and S. Thomé near Madras. Further afield he made brief visits to Bassein, Ceylon, Malacca, Amboina, the Celebes and Macao. Goa and Malacca both saw him no less than five times. Administration cost him a great deal of time and anxiety. His letters to the Gesu were almost always enthusiastic and confident. He dreamed of a large, widespread Jesuit mission establishment in the East. But trying to lay the foundations of it was appallingly difficult. The supply of Jesuits, mostly students, from Europe was small and practically half of them did not survive the journey out. The men who did survive too often proved insubordinate or odd, and he summarily dismissed three or four from the Society. There simply were not enough men to maintain even a minimal Jesuit presence simultaneously in Goa, the Parava country, Malacca, the Celebes, Japan and Macao. Like another Cortes, Pizarro or Legaspi, he brushed aside these difficulties and attempted the impossible. Moreover, the Portuguese colonial authorities bitterly resented his increasing independent-mindedness. Like Cortes, he never directly challenged their authority in principle and relied on their material help constantly. But also like Cortes he sometimes disobeyed the civil authority, hoping that appeals to the king and the success of his missions in spreading Portuguese influence would ultimately defeat local bureaucracy.

It was his missions to Japan and China which won him the applause of the 18th-century European *cognoscenti*. The Portuguese, long before his arrival, had opened up trade contacts, direct and indirect, with both these countries and they were well aware of them being the great powers in furthest Asia. They were anxious to penetrate the countries and draw them within the colonial orbit. Xavier became aware of the existence of Japan on his second visit to Malacca, in 1547. Much of his information came from his new merchant friend, Mendes Pinto, and from missionaries of other Orders established there. It seems that some missionaries had already planned to follow the traders to Japan and then China. Xavier also befriended Anjiro, an exile from Japan. In conversations with him through interpreters, he rapidly gained an impression that the Japanese were, quite unlike all the other Eastern peoples he had met, highly civilised, open-minded and, indeed, almost European in outlook. With his usual panache he decided to go to Japan. The visit was typically short, almost abrupt.

At first he and his two companions floundered helplessly in what seemed to be a hostile environment. They knew no Japanese. They were dressed as Indian gurus and so despised as pseudo-holy men. They did not understand Japanese customs and society. But Xavier was never ready to admit defeat. His mysterious foreignness, bravery and teaching transmitted through Anjiro made a few converts. He baptised them, left them with formulas written out, holy pictures, an altar frontal and a penitential discipline (with instructions to take it three times a week) and passed on to learn more about the country. He soon realised that his dress and begging for hospitality were mistakes. So he procured a bonze's silk robes from Portuguese merchants, hired servants and bearers, and displayed his commission as an agent of the King of Portugal. This famous action, and all his subsequent behaviour in Japan, in no way represented a profound 'accommodation' to Japanese culture. He abominated Buddhism and Shintoism and rejected customs he thought associated with 'idolatry'. It seemed elementary prudence for the time being to tolerate, or even adopt himself, apparently harmless (if grotesque) social customs. But, like Nielssen and Persons, he had no intention of merely founding a Catholic minority. His European heritage taught him that every civilised nation must naturally have one established religion enforced by law: religious toleration was an almost meaningless idea. Anyway a Catholic minority would have no more certain future in Japan than in any European country. Xavier needed no instructions from Ignatius to know that he must go straight to convert the rulers. In Japan, as in Europe, when rulers changed their religion they forced their subjects to follow suit. Japan, however, appeared to have no real monarchy except a feeble Shogunate and power lay with the feudal lords, the daimyos. Xavier was not distressed by this oddity and probably thought it much like the contemporary state of Germany and Italy. Japan's established 'Church', Shintoism, was badly organised, disregarded by most daimyos, and in decay. It would not need much persuasion, backed by offers of investment in Portuguese Far Eastern trade and Portuguese arms, to set most of the daimyos on the road to conversion, of course with their vassals.

As he spun the web of his schemes in his mind, he was soon imagining the time when the Catholic daimyos would defeat the pagan ones and grant penal jurisdiction and lands to support the Jesuit mission. Until that day the growing mission needed financial support. The daimyos had many vassals but little transferable wealth. The Portuguese colonial authorities could give little financial backing so long as Japan was an independent, pagan country. Xavier wrote to Ignatius suggesting a Jesuit investment in the pepper trade from the Celebes, and perhaps a Jesuit-controlled 'factory' (monopolistic trading post) at Osaka.

While most of this was still a pipe-dream and the Jesuit organization in Japan limited to three priests, a score of auxiliaries, half a dozen tiny mission stations and some twelve to fourteen hundred Japanese converts and catechumens, Xavier left for Goa. The unsatisfactory state of Jesuit affairs there called him. He was also already toying with another, still greater design. He had realised that Japanese culture was a pale reflection of that of the much greater Empire of China. By controlling China it would be easy to control Japan and almost any part of the Asiatic mainland. Two years after he had left Japan he arrived at Malacca intending to enter China with a few companions and interpreters. Mendes Pinto explained to him patiently that he would never get permission from the Chinese Government. The Portuguese Governor of Malacca, startled by Xavier's obvious physical weakness and afraid that, if he did trick his way into China his indiscretions might upset his own plans for increasing contacts with Canton, forbade the journey. Xavier evaded the ban and took ship in an ill-found Chinese junk which set him down on an island off the Chinese coast. There he died of exhaustion and his many ailments which he had never paused to have treated by doctors.

Xavier's posthumous fame among European scholars was undeserved and the result of misunderstanding. But, in his lifetime in the East, and, far more after his death, he gained a very different kind of fame. Like Cortes, or, in modern times, T. E. Lawrence and Orde Wingate, his personality made a deep impression on thousands of Indians, Cingalese, Malays and Japanese. They detected something Messianic in him and in his grand if crazy designs, his lightning decisions and holy certainties. Even if, as was usually the fact, they did not understand the complicated, foreign matters he was trying to teach them through a bad interpreter, they felt strongly that he was a great guru or even a divinity. They brought their sick to touch him, stole his belongings to serve as charms, and made images of him to pray to. He himself, quite unconsciously, furthered a cult which shocked him, by constantly presuming that God and the Devil were close behind the veil of everyday events in his life. Popular demand in Malacca led to the exhumation of his body and its transference thither. His tomb became thronged with Christians, Buddhists, Moslems and animists. There was nothing out of the way in all these manifestations. All these religions had their wonder-working saints and relics, and Christian holy men in life and death were easily assimilated into the pagan scene. In the 14th century the tomb of the Franciscan missionary and Archbishop of Peking, John of Montecorvino, was the centre for many years of a popular Buddhist and Confucian cult. Xavier's body was later transferred, with much difficulty, to the Catholic enclave of Goa by Jesuit superiors who were scandalised by the pagan cult and anxious to have a patron for the Jesuit missions as a whole. From that time all Jesuit recruits arriving from Lisbon in Goa were, if they could still walk, escorted straight from the ship to pray at Xavier's tomb.

By the end of the 16th century the Far Eastern mission superiors felt themselves to be remote from the Society, starved of effective manpower and sympathetic support at the Gesu. They did their best to step up the circulation of the *Edifying Letters* and information about Xavier. The effort came at a psychological moment in the Society's course in Europe. The enormous demands of the still growing College system and the increasing regimentation of Jesuit life was producing a sharp reaction, 'the spirituals'. These young Jesuits desperately wanted to revive the spiritual depth, initiative and informality which they felt had been crushed out of the Society in Europe. It began to seem that the foreign missions, particularly in the East, were the only places where true Jesuitry survived. Xavier's *Life*, now filled out with categorical accounts of numerous miracles, became immensely popular among 'the spirituals'. Xavier seemed a sign from God rescuing a corrupted Society. It was therefore a signal of triumph for both the Jesuit missionaries and 'the spirituals' when Xavier was canonised with Ignatius in Rome in 1622.

The texts chosen for the Mass appointed to be said on his feast day are full of reminiscences of him. The Introit (Ps.118) begins:

> 'Fearlessly did I talk of thy decrees in the presence of kings, and was not abashed . . .'

Indeed, when was he ever abashed? The Collect also breathes his naively confident spirit:

'O God, who by the preaching and miracles of blessed Francis wast pleased to bring into the Church's fold the peoples of the Indies . . .'

The Gospel (Mark 16) is Christ's missionary charge to preach the Gospel in the entire world. Those who refuse to listen will be condemned. Signs will go with the missionary: he will cast out devils, speak with strange tongues, walk unharmed over venomous snakes, drink deadly poisons and live, and heal multitudes by his touch. To the Jesuits in 1622 Xavier's career seemed an exact fulfilment of the Gospel promises. He was, it appeared to them, the first recipient of the special outpouring of the Spirit on the young Society, the harbinger of a new Apostolic Age. In this view the same Spirit rested upon the chosen generation of Xavier's successors in the East, especially Alessandro Valignano, Matteo Ricci, Rudolf Acquaviva, Roberto de Nobili and Benito de Goes. Through all of them the Spirit set in train an avalanche of conversions which was surely destined to bring all Asia within the Church.

*   *   *

To Kircher and du Halde and many writers who followed them Alessandro Valignano was (to quote the caption put under a favourite engraved portrait of him) 'the second apostle of the Orient, next after Xavier'. He, it has been held, recruited and trained Ricci, Acquaviva, de Nobili and de Goes. He placed them, like chessmen, in the most crucial and inaccessible parts of the East, in the Moghul Empire, along the Silk Road through Afghanistan and Tibet, in central India, in Korea, and in the heart of the Chinese Empire at Peking. Once there, under Valignano's inspired direction, they implemented his bold and unorthodox plan of 'accommodating' western Catholicism to the great cultures of the East. In this and other ways Valignano detached the Jesuit missions from all dependence, political and financial, on the Portuguese *Padroado*. It was he who inspired the conversion of half a million Japanese so that, by his death, the Christianisation of the whole country lay within the bounds of possibility. It was Valignano who, in the teeth of bitter European prejudice, opened the doors of the Society and the secular priesthood to Indians, Japanese, Koreans and Chinese. It was Valignano who, by his incisive reports and despatch of a band of Japanese convert noblemen to Europe, began to end the

Gesu's lack of interest in foreign missions. Thus in every way Valignano was the Society's 'architect of victory' in the East.

It was possible to maintain this traditional view of his career and importance so long as access to documentary evidence was slight. The thirty years of Valignano's residence in the East produced a considerable accumulation of his reports in the Gesu archives. Until recently they were almost the only evidence of his work and large parts of them were censored as too technical or liable to misconstruction. Today the whole text is available with its abundant evidences of Valignano's great limitations of outlook, his hidebound European prejudices, his lack of sympathy for, and interest in, native cultures, his extreme harshnesses of judgement and his changes of front. Today also historians have available to them complementary sources, European and native, and a great deal of knowledge of the Eastern world of his day. Inevitably therefore our view of Valignano has to be critical.

He entered the Society in 1566. His advanced age, good breeding and university degree in law set him apart from the bulk of his fellow novices who were mere schoolboys. Like other entrants of his kind he was destined for shortened studies, quick ordination and rapid promotion to administrative rank. In fact Mercurian, the General, despatched him to the East as Visitor and Vicar-General when he was still new in the Society and had risen to no higher than rector of a small provincial College in Ancona. Mercurian's choice reflected exactly his low view of the importance of the foreign missions. Valignano's brief was administrative and reforming, and his tour of duty intended to be relatively short. He was to enforce obedience to the Jesuit *Constitutions* by missionaries who had either never come across a copy of them or who judged them largely inapplicable in the East. He was also instructed to do his best to make the missions self-supporting in money and manpower by founding Colleges and seminaries and encouraging vocations among European settlers and native converts. Over the course of the next few years Mercurian shipped an extra large number of able Jesuit students to Goa to staff the new establishments.

Hence, just like Xavier, Valignano was sent to the East as a temporary administrator not a missionary: at that time he felt no particular sense of a divine calling to the missions. Like Xavier he had no gift for languages or real interest in native cultures, but both men eventually acquired a considerable, if superficial, familiarity with Eastern conditions. Both gained a feeling that they belonged in the East without in the least abandoning their deep European prejudices. There the resemblance ended. Xavier was a natural pioneer, driven on by a spirit of adventure and by sudden impulses which he almost invariably identified as divine imperatives. To him the East was, in spite of its surface mystery and complexity, basically a friendly environment wide open to European Christian conquest. Indeed in his day it was very unusually vulnerable to penetration by a handful of bold Europeans.

Valignano, on the other hand, was by training and habit of mind a lawyer and administrator, a pragmatist distrustful of impulses and visions and a very conventional man. By his day the Jesuit missions were solidly established, largely staffed, and spread over wide areas. The novelty of Eastern life had worn off and the weight of routine and commitments had grown fast. Furthermore during the 1580s and 1590s the political situation in almost every part of the East was changing dramatically and almost always for the worse from the Jesuit point of view. The Portuguese *Padroado*, which still remained the missions' base was now everywhere under heavy attack. In India its colonies were gravely threatened by the rapid growth of the powerful Moslem Moghul Empire. Spanish colonial power, based on the Philippines, was intruding busily and aggressively into the Portuguese sphere of influence, especially in Japan and China. It was hard for the Portuguese to repel this threat since Philip II of Spain had been King of Portugal since 1580. Meanwhile Dutch corsairs were systematically ravaging Portuguese colonies and vital sea lanes in the East Indies and China Sea. In Japan the peaceful days when every daimyo was a law unto himself were over. A power-struggle was raging between the major warlords. The prize at stake was the Shogunate and absolute control of the whole nation. Even the immense, strong and apparently changeless Chinese Empire of the Ming dynasty was starting to totter before the attacks of the Japanese and the Manchus.

By disposition Valignano was no daring pioneer. He was an anxious possessioner fighting desperately to conserve the missions in an increasingly hostile environment over which he had practically no control. To his intense discomfort he was repeatedly forced into hasty improvisations and painful decisions between evils. Like most of his clerical contemporaries he was a pessimist. He had a direct, naive belief in the miraculous power of God, but no trust whatever in the efficacy of human action by colonials, natives or even Jesuits.

The Jesuit missioner 'originals' of his day, Ricci, Acquaviva, de Nobili and de Goes, invariably made gestures of deference toward him as their major superior, the General's representative. In reality he did not plan or initiate their enterprises and took only an intermittent interest in them. When he did choose to interfere his directions were usually ham-handed if not outright disastrous.

The Chinese Mission had existed in embryo at Macao, on Chinese soil, since the 1520s. Valignano accepted its existence and its aspirations without much interest. When the rector of Macao College asked him for a capable Jesuit professor to learn and teach mandarin Chinese Valignano sent him Ricci from Goa. Ricci's sudden transformation from a College professor in a language he still hardly knew to a missionary deep in south China was due to a happy accident and the rector's initiative, not Valignano's design. During the long, precarious years of Ricci's mission in China his contacts with the Visitor were very infrequent and almost all unhelpful. Poor Ricci piously expected direction. When he did not get it he unhappily improvised mission policies. Periodically his anxious pleas to Valignano were answered by directions which upset those policies badly. The absurdities of the situation came to a head in the 1590s. By that time Ricci's patience had secured him official Chinese permission to reside in Peking. As he was travelling towards the Imperial city Chinese friends warned him to turn away and seek refuge in some obscure place in south China. News had arrived that a large Japanese army had invaded Chinese Korea with orders to move on to capture Peking and that the invaders had help from Europeans. The army had been sent by the chief Japanese warlord, Hideyoshi. Valignano was fearful that Hideyoshi would turn against the Jesuit mission in Japan. He therefore brushed aside all objections by his colleagues, courted Hideyoshi and did his best to back the invasion with forces supplied by Japanese Christian daimyos, Portuguese ships and arms, and Jesuit army chaplains. Naturally foreign residents in China became exceedingly unpopular. Ricci's infant mission was shattered. He himself lived in hiding for years daily expecting that his connection with the Jesuits in Korea would be uncovered and that he would be executed or deported ignominiously from the country. It was ironical that his life was saved by a pagan Chinese friend, a high official and the commander of the troops fighting the Japanese in Korea. Hideyoshi's death, the withdrawal of the Japanese forces, and a number of lucky accidents enabled Ricci to regain the ground lost by his mission and to take up residence in Peking.

Through all these tribulations Ricci's kindliness and piety triumphed over his common sense. He dismissed as devilish temptations all thoughts that the mission's troubles were due to Valignano. Now at last, as the Chinese mission really took shape Valignano's attitude towards it changed. He sent it missioners, he offered it money, and, in his last illness in Macao in 1606, he talked of it constantly and proposed, if God spared his life, to make a tour of its mission houses. When the news of his death filtered through to Peking Ricci wrote loyally in his journal that the Chinese mission was 'orphaned'.

The 'Mogor Mission' of Rudolf Acquaviva to the court of Delhi in 1580 was another startling enterprise in which Valignano played little part. In that year the Jesuit Provincial at Goa received an invitation from the Moslem Moghul Emperor Akbar to send priests to his court. The invitation had been engineered by *Padroado* officials. The rapid rise of the Moslem Empire had upset the balance of power in India and threatened the Portuguese colonies. Portuguese diplomats set up an embassy in Delhi in 1578. Akbar, like Hideyoshi of Japan and other intelligent Asian rulers, was trying to make up his mind whether to root out the Europeans or make use of them. The Portuguese diplomats seemed to have tipped the balance in favour of the second course, the opening up of trade with Goa and the inviting into the empire of European traders and technicians. Akbar was also now willing to tolerate the presence of Catholic priests at his court as chaplains to foreign residents. When his invitation was relayed to Goa College in 1580 there was much uncertainty whether it should be accepted. The diplomats were in favour of it pointing out that Akbar was an unusually tolerant Moslem and his new empire had a majority of non-Moslems. The Governor of Goa, on the other hand, urged that the invitation should be rejected. He pointed out that missions to Moslems had never been successful and that a Jesuit presence might easily touch off a strong Moslem backlash which could be fatal to the Portuguese colonies.

Valignano was thus confronted with the sort of decision he hated. He settled for acceptance, without enthusiasm. The College at Goa contained only one man, a Persian convert, who knew the languages of the empire and the nature of Islamic practice. Only three Jesuits could be spared — the Persian was to serve as an interpreter and expert (although his origins would not endear him to ardent Moslems) alongside Acquaviva and Montserrate, two young College professors with no gift for languages or real understanding of Islam. The party set out with much trepidation. For the rest of Valignano's life the Mogor Mission remained a commitment of the Province of Goa and was served by a rapid succession of short-service missioners. It made excedingly little impression on the Moslems. From the point of view of Kircher and du Halde it had two achievements to its credit: it manifested the willingness of the Jesuits to undertake the impossible, and it produced the epic journey of Benito de Goes. De Goes was a Portuguese lay-coadjutor and ex-soldier. He set out from Agra in 1603 in disguise to establish whether the old Silk Road route overland to China through Afghanistan was practicable for Jesuit missionaries who found the normal route by sea to Macao infested with Dutch corsairs. The enterprise must have had Valignano's consent, though he was dead long before de Goes staggered to the edge of China and died there of exhaustion. For some Jesuit scholars, though not for Valignano, the journey had a second purpose: to find a lost Christian country called Cathay which was supposed to lie somewhere in western Asia. In the event de Goes' sufferings produced no positive result. The Silk Road route was clearly impracticable for missionaries, and Cathay was a myth.

In 1606 while Valignano lay dying in Macao the Provincial of Goa, in the course of his ordinary appointments, moved a very young and enthusiastic Jesuit priest, Roberto de Nobili, from the Parava coast to the Madurai Mission up-country where he was to be curate to the chief missioner, Fernandez. Without express permission from the Provincial or Fernandez, de Nobili started up his separate and highly controversial mission to the Madurai Brahmins. It is very unlikely that Valignano heard of the affair or knew de Nobili who had not long been in India.

Thus the Visitor was in no way responsible for assembling and training an elite band of Jesuit 'originals' to carry out a far-reaching policy of 'accommodation'. This was not surprising since he never had such a policy. Throughout his career in the East he accepted completely, and without ever criticising it, the current missionary practice of treating peasant or lower class native converts of all races like children and herding them into *doctrina* settlements under very strict clerical supervision. He took for granted the principle that, apart from a few vernacular devotions, *doctrinas* must gradually train the inmates in the ways of western Catholic liturgical, sacramental and devotional practice. His only recorded complaint about the

Jesuit *doctrinas* was that those in Japan and China were not sufficiently strictly disciplined. It was, he reported to the Gesu, very regrettable that recalcitrant Japanese and Chinese lower class converts could not be flogged and imprisoned as their Indian counterparts were.

When he first arrived in the East he carried out the General's instructions by ordering the Provincials and rectors to establish more Colleges and seminaries and to recruit candidates for the Society and the secular priesthood from among the colonial settlers and upper class native converts. He pointed out that Rome intended to despatch Jesuit bishops to Japan to speed up this policy. Some of the newly-arrived Jesuit students, including Matteo Ricci, strongly supported the policy. But the established missionaries in both India and Japan fiercely opposed it. At first Valignano was alarmed and indignant at this insubordination and for some years tried to ride roughshod over it, disciplining recalcitrant superiors. But by the 1580s his increasing experience of Eastern conditions and his strong, if originally latent, European prejudices combined to bring him round to the side of the rebels. He now reported to the Gesu that Portuguese India would never have its own clergy, Jesuit or secular. The Portuguese settlers born in Europe were almost entirely irreligious and of bad character: the few who were pious were so illiterate that there could be no place for them in the clerical establishment except as Jesuit lay-coadjutors, a job which most colonials regarded as only fit for natives. Valignano dismissed all male Portuguese born in India and half-castes as 'effeminate, useless and despicable'. He was even more cutting about upper class Indians of the Brahmin and Ksatriya castes. He dismissed them all, without exceptions, as 'beneath contempt'. He was well aware that, years before he arrived in India, the Portuguese authorities had massacred all the Moslems in the Goa enclave and forcibly baptised the Hindus. Then an ecclesiastical Inquisition had been established to hunt down the converts who showed signs of reversion to Hinduism. The Jesuit College at Goa had trained a small number of Indian secular priests. Opinion about them varied among the Jesuits. But Valignano firmly aligned himself with the majority view that these native priests were idle and a source of scandal. The General replied that the need for clergy in India was so great that Valignano must enforce the new policy: bad priests were better than no priests at all. Valignano accepted this directive glumly. But henceforward he put little pressure on the superiors in India. Relatively few natives were ordained to the secular priesthood and extremely few received into the Society.

When Valignano first visited Japan he ordered the opening of seminaries, the removal of the bar within the Society preventing Japanese entrants from rising about the lay-coadjutorship, and the recruitment of a few Capuchin missionaries to work under Jesuit direction. Indeed Valignano's initial impressions of the Japanese upper classes were very favourable. It seemed to him that all Indians were 'niggers', but educated and well-bred Japanese uniquely 'white, courteous and highly civilised'. He was therefore outraged by the stubborn resistance offered to the new policy by almost all the Jesuits headed by their Vice-Provincial, Cabral. Cabral remarked bluntly that the Visitor had so far only seen the good side of the Japanese character. It had hidden, mysterious and barbaric depths. Since Xavier's time there had been an avalanche of conversions of daimyos and their followings. In many cases the conversions were superficial or even political and only years of instruction could turn these nominal Catholics into real ones. Meanwhile the missionaries felt swamped by a movement liable to get out of control. Cabral estimated that if the new policy were implemented a horde of Japanese would seek ordination for the status and mastery of European learning it would give. Then the European clergy would be completely outnumbered and gradually lose control of a national Church which would slide into syncretism.

Valignano reacted in Japan much as he had done in India. After much hesitation and with an outward show of compliance with the Gesu policy he quietly went over to the rebels. His reports to Rome became steadily more and more pessimistic. He detected treachery and falseness in the Japanese character. They were, he wrote, bestially cruel and given to sodomy which 'they account a virtue'. He was soon ordering the superiors to put a brake on admissions of Japanese to the Society and the seminaries. Two Jesuit bishops reached Japan. One, made ill by scruples, sailed back to Europe for treatment. The other marked time, ordaining very few Japanese. By the end of Valignano's life there were only half a dozen Japanese in holy Orders.

The Gesu, Valignano and the Jesuit missionaries always took it for granted that the religious practice of the Japanese upper class must be completely European. The Japanese clergy must learn Latin and be instructed in European philosophy and theology to operate the Latin liturgy and sacramental system and

European devotions. They must, like the Jesuits on mission duty, wear European soutanes. By Valignano's time Jesuits only adopted the dress of bonzes when they were on diplomatic missions in pagan areas. The Visitor himself was wont to don a bonze's robe of Chinese silk indicative of his high rank when he went in state to do business with the warlord Hideyoshi.

He only tolerated far-reaching measures of 'accommodation' in one area, the Chinese mission. But this tolerance was really an exception which proved Valignano's rule. After a great deal of anxious consultation he allowed Ricci to abandon his bonze's robe for the dress of a Chinese graduate or civil servant. Chinese mandarin converts were allowed to practice the ancient rites of respect for their dead ancestors. Ricci was permitted to make some use of Confucian terminology in his expositions of Catholic doctrine. These concessions were granted grudgingly and merely as temporary tactical measures, on the understanding that, if the Chinese mission really took root, the converts would be brought over to European ways.

The survival and remarkable success of the Japanese mission were certainly due, in a large measure, to action by Valignano. But this action was political and financial not pastoral and spiritual. He arrived in Japan an innocent, pledged to enforce the letter of the Jesuit *Constitutions*. He was shocked to discover that ordinary mission houses were not living on alms but accumulating endowment funds. The Vice-Provincial, he discovered, was deeply involved in commercial transactions. He had obtained a lease of the port of Nagasaki and had arranged with the Portuguese authorities in Goa that the annual 'treaty ship' trading between Goa and Canton should put in at Nagasaki and no other port in Japan. The Vice-Provincial had then invested Jesuit funds extensively and profitably in the ship's trade in silk, silver and gold. Many Japanese daimyos also wished to invest in the ship's cargoes. By the use of his hold over Nagasaki and the ship's captains the Vice-Provincial had gained great prestige and influence among them. Valignano also found that the Vice-Provincial was deeply, if secretly, involved in Japanese politics. He was attempting to band together the fast-increasing number of Christian or sympathetic daimyos into a political and military alliance which eventually, with some help from the Portuguese *Padroado* or the Spaniards in the Philippines, could overthrow the warlord Hideyoshi and set up a Christian Shogunate over the entire country.

All of these practices were contrary to the *Constitutions* and the Gesu's standing order that Jesuit missionaries in the field were to dissociate themselves entirely from politics. In these, as in so many other matters, Valignano soon came round to the side of the missionaries. The establishment of Colleges, especially at Nagasaki, brought the Jesuit endowment funds within the letter of the *Constitutions*. To legitimise Jesuit trading was a much more difficult business. The Visitor wrote frankly to the General:

> 'Your Reverence must understand that, after the grace and favour of God, the greatest help we have hitherto had in securing Christians is that of the Great Ship . . .'

He pointed out that the Japanese converts, even the daimyos, could never sustain the missions financially. Subsidies from the Pope and the king were small and slow in reaching Japan. The cost of maintaining the entire Japanese mission was relatively small — no more than the cost of a single large European College. Trade was the only way to raise the money and it did not really enrich the Jesuits. After much negotiation the Popes and the Gesu accepted a compromise. Trading by Jesuits would remain officially forbidden. But Rome gave the Japan mission a secret and provisional dispensation from the ban. Then Valignano began to extend Jesuit trading on the 'Great Ship'. Shortly before his death he was proposing to Rome that a Jesuit bank should be set up in Nagasaki.

It was easier to get round the Roman ban on Jesuit political activity. It was always taken for granted by the Popes, the Gesu and Valignano that succesful missionary activity must always, sooner or later, be backed up by political or even military action. This should be left to Catholic sovereigns. But occasionally, especially where such state action might be counter-productive, special Jesuit envoys might be employed in diplomacy and political action. It was not difficult for Valignano to get the Gesu's permission for him to remove all political and military matters from the hands of the Vice-Provincial into his own. He considered that the Vice-Provincial's plan for a revolt by the Christian daimyos with European military assistance was far too dangerous. He therefore quashed it and negotiated a firm alliance with Hideyoshi, and then with his successor, Ieyasu.

Reading between the lines of his reports we can detect that Valignano was never very happy about these secular activities. He was well-aware that he was choosing between evils. Jesuit commerce gained the Society enemies in the East and in Europe. The *Padroado* was always threatening to do a deal with Hideyoshi and move the 'Great Ship's' port of call from Nagasaki to Osaka. The superficiality of many Japanese conversions was only too painfully evident. The future of the Japan mission depended on the continuing goodwill of Hideyoshi and his successor, Ieyasu, men of very uncertain temper who might any day double-cross the Jesuits. Valignano was a brave and likeable, if unoriginal, man. He was fortunate in the time of his death: not long after it his political and financial system and the Japan mission collapsed in ruins.

* * *

Matteo Ricci, the first Jesuit apostle of China, enjoyed no fame in Europe in his own day. A contemporary French Jesuit writer of philosophy textbooks for Colleges wrote vaguely that 'some Spaniards' had recently gained a foothold in China. Long after Ricci's death in Peking Kircher and du Halde unearthed his letters from the Gesu archives and introduced him to the *cognoscenti* of Europe as the European discoverer of Chinese civilisation and the prototype of all Jesuit scientist-missionaries. Still his fame remained small until, early in this century, a copy of his manuscript account of his mission was discovered. This was so detailed that it has provided copious material for biographers and for the theory that he was far ahead of his time and a great pioneer of the extensive 'accommodation' of Catholicism to Eastern cultures.

Ricci was certainly an exceedingly rare type of Jesuit and missionary. His background outside and inside the Society was the small esoteric world of the 'natural philosophers', the primitive, embryonic stage of the European 'Scientific Revolution'. His father was a provincial magistrate and pharmacist in the Marches of Ancona. Hence Matteo was brought up in the atmosphere of a 16th-century pharmacy full of herbs, distilled drugs, dried snakes and bats, amid charts of the stars and elaborate astrological calculations. His father automatically cast his horoscope when Matteo was born. Through the influence of a Jesuit tutor and a Roman Jesuit Sodality Matteo was persuaded to quit law studies and enter the Jesuit noviciate against his father's will. After the noviciate he was chosen to join the elite philosophy class taught by the natural philosopher Christoph Klau. The course was a very strange mixture of ancient and modern. The medieval philosophical categories derived from Aristotle and Ptolemy were taken for granted. But, on the other hand, a large part of the course was devoted to the learning of very practical techniques, of geometrical calculation and surveying, cartography, astronomical observation and calculations of calendars, the construction of sundials, clocks, simple machines, spheres and astrolabes. Ricci revelled in all this and was an apt pupil. But the *Spiritual Exercises*, taken in the Sodality and in the noviciate, had had a very profound effect on his mind. Left to his own devices and his father's advice he would undoubtedly have become a lay official in the Papal Government and a devoted amateur of 'natural philosophy'. Once within the Society if he had followed his natural bent and the advice of Klau he would undoubtedly have ended his days as a professor of philosophy or even mathematics in the Roman College. But this seemed too easy and pleasant to be the will of God. Such a life would not bring that humiliation and suffering which the *Exercises* said were the way to God. Therefore Matteo volunteered for the Eastern missions. At first he was considered too useful and too immature for relegation to what the Gesu still considered a backwater. Then he was drafted to Goa to teach rhetoric in the College while doing his theological studies. His superiors seem to have found him angular and difficult. His 'scientific' activities made him a rarity and probably not a popular one. His behaviour fluctuated between an ultra-pious conformism and a disturbingly critical independence of mind. Though very new to the East and junior in the Society he took it upon himself to write a very sharp letter to the General criticising his superiors' opposition to Valignano's policies on the ordination of natives. The Provincial, probably to discipline him, had him prematurely ordained and put to a spell of mission duty in Cochin. Then he was recalled and despatched to Macao.

The Portuguese and the Jesuits had long been aware that the Chinese Empire was the key to an East which was dominated by its culture and enormous economic resources. But their chances of real penetration into the empire appeared slender. Unlike India and Japan, China was a powerfully unified state which, on principle, had no dealings with outsiders unless they wished to submit to its rule and religion. 'Barbarians' were only allowed inside the empire as strictly supervised visitors come to present tribute. There were religious minorities in the outlying parts of the empire but their status was regulated by ancient treaties. The Portuguese had been able to establish themselves by treaty on the peninsula of Macao near Canton. Their presence there and the annual visits to the markets of Canton were tolerated because they offered no military threat and were of use in supplying Japanese silver. The Jesuits in Macao had made a few Chinese converts and accompanied the traders to Canton and, very occasionally, to up-country markets. But there was no question of a proper Jesuit mission of the Japanese kind being tolerated within China. Moreover the Jesuits could not even communicate with Chinese officialdom since they found its language, Mandarin, impossibly complicated and difficult to learn. It seems that Ricci, who was not wanted in India, was sent to Macao on the off-chance that his peculiar capabilities might enable him to master Mandarin and teach it to his colleagues.

After a year in Macao he could not have endeared himself to them. Most of the younger members of the community, Pasio, Ruggieri, Langobardo, d'Almeida and Dias, were later to do stints inside China with him and to disagree with him strongly. Ruggieri, his first mission companion, never got on with him. Moreover, even Ricci's intelligence and skill with mnemonics enabled him to make little progress with Mandarin. He filled in his time with teaching rhetoric in the College and with making glass, clocks and maps. Then in 1583 Ruggieri, the most adventurous of the community, had a stroke of luck. He was able to visit Canton and get as far up-country as 'Ch'ao-ching in Kwangtung Province. There, through an interpreter, he roused the interest of the Chinese Governor in some of Ricci's 'toys'. The governor actually invited Ricci and Ruggieri to pay him a visit. When they did he offered them a permit of residence. Acceptance of it amounted, in Ricci's view, almost to apostasy from Catholicism and the Society. They could stay provided they promised solemnly not to leave the town, to dress as bonzes and follow in every detail the Chinese way of life, to obey Imperial law and import no other barbarians. They could, however, import one Chinese servant from Macao. Ricci accepted the permit after a great struggle of conscience. It is quite certain that at the time the contracting parties were quite unaware of each others' beliefs and cultures. The governor knew nothing of Europe and Christianity. He presumed, from their pidgin-Mandarin and illiteracy in it, their strange manners and dress that they were wandering Buddhist teachers from some peripheral part of the East. As such they would be no danger, since the various 'ways' of private devotion of Buddhism were commonly and easily combined with conformity to all the rites of the Chinese religion. Bonzes were usually despised in China as uneducated vagabonds and layabouts. Normally the governor would have deported them.

But his curiosity was greatly roused by Ricci's skill with scientific and mechancial appliances. Skills of that kind were as rare in China as in contemporary Europe. But in China they went with a high grade of literary education. So Ricci appeared to be a very odd anomaly.

For their part the two Jesuits were very ignorant about China and, as yet, quite unaware of the extent of their lack of knowledge. Ricci could only hope piously that their camouflage as Buddhists and acceptors of Chinese religion would not compromise their Catholic loyalties or confuse prospective converts. Only time and experience could answer that question. He spent over six years in Ch'ao-ching, most of the time alone with his servant, since Ruggieri returned several times to Macao. During those opening years of the mission Ricci made slow progress with spoken Mandarin. Even twelve years after his entry into China his speech was so ungrammatical that it always betrayed his barbarian origins and lack of Chinese education. He made even slower progress with written Mandarin. Meanwhile, using his 'toys' as bait, he tried to make converts. Naturally he used the standard methods he had learned at Goa. First he translated the ten Commandments into Mandarin along with a few prayers, taught them to visitors who showed interest, and tried to get them to make an examination of conscience. He was, after some intitial shocks, wary of displaying his crucifix and teaching the Creed, since the reaction of most catechumens was of either blank incomprehension or hostility and disgust. In the event he took a chance and baptised some thirty men whose demeanour, for no very rational reason, impressed him. He then had them, in small groups, to his Mass. He dare not communicate them. Chinese custom barred him from instructing women or receiving them at Mass. One married women was instructed and baptised by her husband. At this early stage in his ministry and mastery of the language and religion of China he had the haziest of notions about the mental processes of his converts. In later years, after he had left the town, he discovered, sadly but without much surprise, that most of the converts had lapsed back into a paganism laced oddly with Christian devotional practices. It was very hard indeed to convey to the Chinese that Catholicism was not just one more Buddhist 'way' of private devotion. Converts could not abandon the innumerable Chinese rites of respect for their ancestors and the tutelary dieties or spirits of the family, the town, the province and the empire without cutting themselves off entirely from their people and making themselves

aliens. *Doctrinas* were the solution. But they were only practicable in the peculiar political conditions prevailing in America,
India and Japan: such things could not work in China.

In 1589 there was a change of governor in Ch'ao-ching. Ricci
very narrowly escaped deportation back to Macao, and was forced
to move to Shao-chou where he spent four very unhappy and
uncomfortable years. The place was unhealthy and two Jesuit
companions sent to him from Macao both died of fever. The
mission house was repeatedly stoned by hostile local people and
Ricci was assaulted and wounded. He began to wonder whether
he should not close the mission and leave China. As his knowledge of spoken and written Mandarin increased together with
his knowledge of the mentality of the educated Chinese he met,
he began to realise the depth of his ignorance and the folly of
posing as a bonze. He could only meet the Chinese ruling class as
an equal and as one in whom they would be willing to confide if he
became as proficient in Chinese literary culture as any 'graduate'.
He set out grimly to acquire this proficiency, spending all his time
on memorising the characters, reading Chinese classics and
amassing a huge glossary of Chinese terms and their shades of
meaning if translated into Italian, Portuguese and Latin. Very
few contemporary Jesuits or European scholars would have been
capable of such an exhausting task. He soon realised that the
terminology of western Catholicism was almost inextricably
interwoven with classical Greek and Latin concepts. At first he
was in despair, thinking that the Chinese classics belonged to a
quite different thought-world, so that translation of Catholic
doctrine would be impossible. Then he began to toy with the
theory that these ancient thought-worlds, European and Chinese,
were basically one. His reasons for inclining towards this theory
were not linguistic but doctrinal and devotional. He recalled from
the days of his truncated theology course Aquinas's idea of 'the
man in the woods' who had never heard of Christianity but who
could attain salvation if he made a decisive act of faith in some
primitive, world-wide divine revelation. Ricci also dimly recalled
hearsay that Catholic missionaries had preached the faith in
China centuries before: it might well be that memories of that
preaching had seeped widely into the Chinese classics. The more
he considered these ideas and the feeling of rapport that he had
with some of his closest Chinese acquaintances the more he was
tempted to think that the theory was right. Perhaps Confucius
was Seneca in Chinese clothes. Perhaps a belief in the incarnation
of Christ and the redemption by him was already lurking in

an inchoate form in the classical tradition of the educated Chinese.

On the other hand this lonely and intensely scrupulous man had agonising doubts. His original missionary tactics had been approved by Valignano. If Ricci now abandoned them as mistaken he would be committing an act of disobedience contrary to his religious vows. He would also be saying that Valignano had erred and was ultimately to blame for the lack of success of Ricci's first years in China. Ricci's scrupulosity went further. The way to God was through humiliation and suffering. Life as a bonze offered an unlimited amount of that. If Ricci could achieve acceptance as a 'graduate' and apply his new theory with great success, many souls might be saved and God honoured but Ricci might damn himself by choosing the easy road contrary to his calling to suffering.

He manifested his scruples to Valignano by letter. The Visitor gave him permission to seek graduate status but reserved judgement about the new theory. He did not explain to Ricci that Hideyoshi's invasion of Korea and China had already been launched with his approval, accompanied by Jesuit chaplains. The Visitor's letter and a lucky accident combined to haul Ricci out of his deep depression. A Chinese official of his acquaintance procured him a permit to visit Peking, the Imperial capital. He set out thither. But when he was nearing the capital his euphoria came to an abrupt end. His Chinese patron warned him suddenly that the Japanese invasion made it very inadvisable that he should show his face in the city. At first Ricci was sure that the crisis could only be temporary. He took up residence at Nanking, the second city of the empire, and confidently assumed his new role as a graduate. He acquired a graduate's silk robe and cap, a sedan chair and a retinue of servants. He produced for inspection by the Nanking officials a sample of his writings in verse and prose in the style of a proficient in classical Mandarin. But instead of receiving the respectful welcome he expected he was served with an expulsion order. The war scare had reached Nanking. So he fled south and took refuge uneasily in Nan ch'ang in Kiangsi Province.

There he passed five years alternating between moods of deep depression and confidence. His colleagues in Macao and Valignano had always regarded his intellectual theory about the mission with bewilderment and dislike. They had regularly blamed his self-will for the failure of his mission and had exhorted him to use more orthodox methods. He should, they considered, dress himself as a potentate, go boldly in state to Peking as the envoy of either the king or the Pope, and persuade the emperor to grant him and other Jesuits permission to preach the faith in a normal manner throughout the empire. Hitherto Ricci, though shrinking from open disobedience, had not readily complied: his experience told him that his critics' methods would be fruitless or even disastrous. Luckily both the king and Rome had refused him the title of official envoy. But now in Nan ch'ang, in the depths of depression, he persuaded himself that he had been wrong: the Japanese invasion and the consequent ruin of his own plans must have been Providential. A 'vision of God' seemed to confirm his conversion. Valignano gave him some small official status by appointing him superior of the mission and urged him to approach the emperor through the Princes of the Imperial Blood.

Ricci left Nan ch'ang for Nanking and Peking to carry out these instructions. The results were humiliating and almost disastrous. His application to the princes in Nanking was greeted with a storm of disapprobation from his graduate acquaintances. One of them informed him that the princes were ambitious persons of no political worth or power. So he moved on to Peking to hand in his presents and petition to some graduate government department there. Now he ran into a second humilation. Applications to the emperor had no hope of acceptance unless they were made through the corps of Imperial Eunuchs. They were notoriously venal and hostile to graduates. Ricci would get no satisfaction from them unless he dissociated himself from the graduates and gave the eunuchs very large bribes. He left Peking. On the road back to Nan ch'ang his depression returned so badly that he fell gravely ill.

He had now been seventeen years in China. In spite of his incessant labours and the deaths of three Jesuit colleagues the mission had achieved very little success. But in 1600 his tortuous career took a turn for the better. The Korean war ended and he was warmly invited to take up residence in Nanking. When he reported to Valignano the setback in Peking, the Visitor went so far as to approve of Ricci's taking up again, at least temporarily, his graduate plans. Valignano furthermore took action to silence Ricci's critics and approve of his very tentative judgement that converted Chinese graduates might continue to do obeisance to their ancestors' souls and the spirits of the towns and the empire. For years Ricci had agonised over this problem. His converts and prospective converts were all graduate Imperial officials and these rites formed an integral part of their official duties. If conversion to Christianity meant no rites many would jib at conversion and the few converts would be ostracised and ruined. Ricci's reading and enquiries eventually made him think it probable, but by no means certain, that the rites, though originally religious, now had a merely social significance for the officials. Valignano's decision enabled Ricci to go ahead with the practice with a fairly clear conscience. But both he and the Visitor knew that opposition to the practice would be very strong in Rome, among the missionaries of other Orders, and within the ranks of the Society. The two men simply hoped that, in the not too distant future, some sort of Imperial edict of toleration for Christians would make it possible to withdraw the permission to converts to use the rites.

Once in Nanking Ricci, now 'the graduate Li Ma-ton', was much courted. He published a map of the world which caused a great sensation. His samples of prose and verse in Mandarin were widely read and judged to be extraordinary feats for a mere foreigner. He was in demand as a tutor, especially in mathematics. A large empty house was made over for his use and that of three other Jesuits whom Valignano drafted from Macao. The house stood empty because it was said to be haunted by evil spirits. Ricci took the matter very seriously and exorcised each room with bell, book and candle satisfactorily. Enquirers thronged to see him.

In 1601 he felt that his prestige among graduate officials was high enough for him to make a second effort to take presents to the emperor. It was also, he felt, high enough for him to request that the Visitor should allow him to withhold the petition for religious toleration for some years. Valignano agreed. Once in Peking Ricci did battle with the eunuchs, a battle which proved even tougher than he had feared. After many humiliations and strange turns of fortune, the emperor demanded to see the presents which naturally consisted mainly of scientific 'toys' made by Ricci. Among them was a rhino's horn, a sovereign specific against all known poisons. The reception of the presents at first produced no mark of Imperial favour. Then suddenly he was summoned to the palace to wind the clock he had presented. Thenceforward he became, in effect, a prisoner in the outer wards, kept to service the clock and to advise the Imperial mathematicians who drew up horoscopes and composed the official Kalendar.

When he died in Peking in 1610 the emperor paid for his

funeral and consented to the appointment of another Jesuit pupil of Christoph Klau, dé Ursis, to take his place. Right up to the time of his death Ricci refused all suggestions from Europe and Macao that he should petition the emperor for religious toleration. The empire contained only a few hundred Chinese converts. A dozen Jesuits staffed the houses in Ch'ao-ching, Shao-chou, Nan ch'ang, Nanking and Peking. They said Mass quietly and privately in the houses, baptised the male children of converts and blessed the graves of the dead. The great majority of the converts only confessed and were communicated on their death-beds. Almost none of the missionaries outside Peking knew much Mandarin. These very low-profile and strangely inactive missions were only left undisturbed by the authorities and the often hostile local populations because of the Imperial favour to the odd 'scientific mission' at the palace. The Jesuit China Mission then and for the next two centuries exactly reflected the strange personality of its founder.

5
The Triumphant Years
1581-1681

'I hope the Portuguese will forswear fratricidal strife with the Spaniards and bathe their swords in the blood of heretics in Europe, in the blood of Moslems in Africa, the blood of the heathen in Asia and America . . . conquering and subjugating all regions under one Crown and under the feet of the successor of blessed Peter . . .'

(Antonio Vieira SJ, a sermon in Lisbon, 1642)

'The more inward we are, the more we may undertake outward activities; the less inward, the more we should refrain from trying to do good . . .'

(Louis Lallemant SJ, c.1630)

The achievements and mentality of the Jesuits in the 17th century have always fascinated a host of distinguished writers as various as Pascal, Kircher, du Halde, Voltaire, Thackeray, Thomas Macaulay, Shorthouse, Mrs. Humphrey Ward, Dumas, Michelet, Charles Maurras, Henri Brémond, T.S. Eliot, Thomas Hardy, Sir Richard Burton, Boehmer, Lord Acton, Baron von Hügel, Somerset Maugham, Aldous Huxley, Ronald Knox, Berthold Brecht and Koestler. Jesuit traditionalists have always regarded the 17th century as the Society's really 'Golden Age' of formative period and Claudio Acquaviva (General from 1581 to 1615) as incomparably the age's greatest Jesuit. Acquaviva, they have insisted, was the Society's greatest General and its 'second Founder', who pulled it out of the awkwardnesses, uncertainties and internal conflicts of its adolescence into its vigorous and well-coordinated adulthood. It was he who devised so very many of those minutely detailed regulations, directives and drills which gave the Society its modern identity and its ability to be at once very orthodox and yet immensely flexible. He was responsible for an almost fourfold increase in Jesuit numbers. He built a haphazard jumble of Jesuit educational establishments into a teaching system which was the envy of all western Europe. By his death the Society had become the greatest force in Counter-Reformation Catholicism: Jesuits were the normal confessors and advisers of Popes, ruling sovereigns and great nobles. He taught the Society, by the use of the school and the confessional, to adapt a medieval religion to a European society becoming steadily more modern and a western religion to non-European cultures. Hence in the 19th century, when Generals were struggling to resurrect a shattered Society, they inevitably regarded the 'days of Acquaviva' as their pattern in every respect.

On the other hand Jesuit dissidents down the years have had hard things to say of Acquaviva and his system. In his own days active rebels like Acosta, Hernandez, Mariana, Vincent and Hoffaeus went so far as to call it a 'tyranny'. In the mid-17th century there were sharp criticisms from Lallemant, Surin and other 'spirituals'. By the end of the 19th century thoughtful young Jesuits like Henri Brémond and George Tyrrell agreed that 'Acquavivaism' was the source of that 'Jesuitism' which they abhorred, the destroyer of 'Ignatianism' and a disaster for the Society. By 1958 so distinguished and mature a Jesuit publicist as Cyril Martindale could safely write:

'How could the original spirit of the Society survive Acquaviva's Generalate . . . the production of a closed company of good, spiritually middle class men, hommes *à tout faire*, averse to all innovation, almost a Church within a Church, aloof from the older religious Orders, and very self-satisfied?'

During the 1960s the Society in fact relegated most features of Acquaviva's system to its lumber rooms. Its historians mostly lost interest in 'the days of Acquaviva' and turned their attention to unravelling the obscurities of 'the Ignatian age'. Acquaviva has become so neglected that he has yet to find a biographer.

So it is the view of all historians, admirers and enemies of Acquaviva alike, that he has a very major place indeed in Jesuit history, perhaps a greater one than Ignatius himself. But what sort of man was he? The fact that he found no biographer even in the days when his credit stood very high in the Society is in itself significant. He seems to have been that biographer's nightmare, the 'organisation man'. The original sources for his career are vast but depressingly monochrome. They consist for the most part of files of administrative papers: reports, memoranda, directives, decrees and business correspondence. There is very little personal material and most of it is gossip or casual hearsay about factions among the leading administrative assistants who

filled the Gesu's outer offices and the local positions of importance in the Society. Like Philip II of Spain, his older and much
greater contemporary, Acquaviva was the autocratic head of a very
widespread and complex organisation the workings of which
were clogged by the inefficiency and factiousness of underlings,
shortage of manpower and money, and painfully slow channels of
communication. Like Philip he had an obsessive sense of duty
and direct responsibility to God for the whole organisation. Like
Philip he disliked delegation of authority and so condemned
himself to endless hours chained to his desk coping with moun-
tains of paperwork and making countless decisions, many of them
about minor matters. Like Philip he came to identify himself
utterly with the organisation. Its interests and 'good' became his
own. The two men rarely allowed themselves the luxury of
distractions or leisure.

Acquaviva became an 'organisation man' from an early age.
He was the younger son of a Neapolitan duke with Spanish
connections. After education in a Jesuit College he embarked on
the dull technicalities of a long university course in canon and
Roman law at Perugia, a course which could fit him for nothing
but a career in Church administration. At the age of twenty-four
he, like so many of his contemporaries educated in Jesuit schools,
made a late entry into the Society's noviciate. Once there his
mature age, very special academic qualifications and aristocratic
status readily assured him of an unusually swift, privileged
passage to ordination and posts of responsibility. Within little
more than twelve years after his entry into the Society he had
occupied two very important administrative posts, the Pro-
vincialates of Naples and Rome. By 1580 he was the bureaucrats'
candidate in the election to the Generalate though he was still
only thirty-seven years of age.

His election was, in itself, a demonstration of the growing
power and political skill of the Jesuit bureaucrats. The Provincial
Congregations, and the General Congregation they elected to
choose a new General, were composed exclusively of Professed
Fathers and local major superiors promoted to their positions of
authority by the General. In theory, and to some extent in practice, the General Congregation was therefore a docile and
conformist assembly. Mercurian had decreased the already very
small number of annual admissions to Profession of the four vows
and had tried to pick major superiors with care. However,
'difficult', independent-minded men and outright dissidents
were so numerous in some large Provinces that it had been

impossible to exclude them all from promotion. The temper of the General Congregation was therefore uncertain and a source of anxiety to the bureaucrats. At the outset of the debates they suffered a humiliating setback. There was a rowdy outburst of fury directed against Manare, Mercurian's Vicar-General and the President of the Congregation, and, through him against the whole class of bureaucrats. Manare was, in effect, put on trial on charges of unseemly and underhand practices designed to forward the careers of the bureaucrats' favourites: he was found guilty and deposed from office. Yet it was the humiliated bureaucrats who triumphed signally in the end. Congregational decrees meant to restrict a new General were watered down. Manare was retained at the Gesu, and Acquaviva, whose career manifested all the tendencies most abhorred by the dissidents, was elected General. As we shall see, henceforward they vented their indignation on him, and his Generalate was a stormy one.

His ten years training in canon and Roman law undoubtedly contributed much to the narrowness of his views on government. He loved absolute autocracy and detested elections. He had a naive faith in the efficacy of intensive drilling of his Jesuit subjects by showers of detailed directives and hosts of minute regulations. Men, he believed, should be kept in line by these things and by inquisitorial procedures where information was obtained by means of secret delations and compulsory 'manifestations of conscience' in Confession to superiors. As often with canonists his rigid legalism was oddly tempered by a great skill in exploiting loopholes in the law and interpreting it unrestrictively, especially where the interests of the Society were at stake. All this made Jesuits like Juan Mariana, the most forthright of the dissidents, regard Acquaviva as a uniquely monstrous phenomenon. But they were exaggerating. In his day the Roman Curia, the ranks of the superiors of all the other religious Orders and the higher civil servants of sovereigns were full of men who thought and reacted as he did. The upper echelons of European society were in the grip of a powerful wave of reaction against what they regarded as the formlessness, laxity and chaos of earlier generations. Europe was full of 'Puritans' who wanted discipline, uniformity, government planning and enlightened autocracy. So Acquaviva's ideas were the fashionably conventional ones of his day and a good many within the Society were disposed to welcome them long before his election. Thus he and his 'system' were more the products of the reactionary movement than its creator.

Moreover, in his case, as in that of other contemporary Puritans, a frightening single-mindedness was tempered by a variety of human weaknesses and inconsistencies. The absoluteness of his autocratic principles and practice went with a constant insistence in his directives that law and authority must be exercised in love: superiors must be 'the fathers, mothers and physicians' of their subjects who therefore must love the rod. He condemned favouritism and human respect. But he was often very indulgent toward individuals whom he instinctively liked (for instance Nielssen, the odd pioneering Scandinavian), his Neapolitan fellow-countrymen, sovereigns and noblemen. He lectured superiors on the great evils of random over-extension of the College system at the expense of manpower and evangelism. Yet his letter-books show him often intervening to allow the foundation of Colleges in small towns where Jesuit resources would be taxed and results meagre. He insisted on a rigid policy of selection in recruiting. Yet after his death his trainee and successor as General, Vitelleschi, was aghast at the way he had allowed the Society to be stuffed with hastily recruited and badly screened youths.

Acquaviva was genuinely horrified at the idea of Jesuits being involved in politics and the sleaziness of court life. Yet he himself was an adept politician. In his day numbers of Jesuits became deeply involved in politico-religious affairs and the confessional direction of kings with his nervous acquiescence. He was distressed when he came across grammatical mistakes and crudity of style in his subjects' Latinity. He wanted the Society to get a reputation for academic excellence. Yet he had no intellectual interests whatsoever. His elaborate corset of regulations for Jesuit studies, the *Ratio*, did much to stifle real academic life and spontaneity in the Colleges. His timidity and lack of interest caused him to stamp on every sign of intellectual originality in the Society. He wanted Jesuit churches in Europe to be more impressive than those of other religious Orders. But his own tastes in architecture and decoration were both Puritan and Philistine. He preached in season and out of season the necessity for a deep Jesuit spirituality. But mysticism alarmed him and he was no devotional 'proficient'. He equated spirituality with a great exactness in the regular performance of devotional observances and a taste for miracles and portents. Like all the reactionaries his views on sexuality were exceedingly narrow. He grew very angry and repressive when he received evidence that some of his subjects were professing mildly liberal views on the subject or on the position of women in the Church. In mentality and character Acquaviva was a model of that safe, respectable 'golden mean' to which he wished all Jesuits to conform themselves. Most of them were only too willing to obey.

* * *

During the thirty-five years of his Generalate the offices of local Jesuit superiors were deluged with paper from the Gesu. His personal acquaintance with local conditions was limited to Italy. In the early 1580s he was still willing, if unable, to tour France. Thereafter he resisted all efforts to draw him far from the Gesu. With his advent to power the bureaucrats at last came fully into their own. The relatively amateur and primitive officialdom of earlier years now developed fast into a complex machine relying almost entirely on paper and the postal system. The sheer volume and expense of these postal operations became immense. Acquaviva required his local superiors to render him regular reports in due form and in great detail and to submit even minor matters to his judgement. The reports were cross-checked against other sources of information, the national Assistants in Rome and numerous unsolicited incoming packets from individual Jesuits, complaints against superiors, petitions, requests for favours and delations of offenders. The correspondence was sifted by a band of secretaries. They and amanuenses wrote out most of the General's answers at his direction or dictation. At his requests the Assistants or Commissioners regularly made digests of information from the files and compiled memoranda on specific subjects. From these memoranda Acquaviva compiled his many directives, most of which were regularly amended and redrafted in new editions as the result of reports on their enforcement in the Provinces. At each redrafting the directives became more comprehensive and more complex.

It appeared therefore that the General must be supremely well-informed and much better placed to plan the Society's life and operations than any of his predecessors. It could be argued that his administrative machine had become the most efficient one in Europe. It had, it might seem, an edge over civil governments since, unlike them, it was able to command obedience by vows from men who were better-educated than their civil service counterparts and detached from family commitments. It seemed also that the Jesuit machine was more effective than the Roman Curia (which relied on nuncios rather than bishops, who were more the servants of kings than of Popes) and the curias of other religious Orders. But in practice the 'Acquaviva system' was self-defeating. The European postal system, Jesuit and public, even in Acquaviva's last days was very slow and faulty. He was making use of a system which had hardly existed in Ignatius's time but which still operated at a speed of no more than six or seven miles a day. The handwriting of letters, the coding and decoding required in times and places subject to war or civil dissension, and waiting for the arrival of permissions and directions vastly complicated and hampered the carrying out of Jesuit operations in the midst of swiftly-changing political circumstances. Thus in France negotiations over the foundation of Jesuit Colleges commonly dragged on for ten or even twenty years. The General also came to be separated from his subjects by a wall of paper. His view of Jesuit realities was distorted by the ignorance and prejudices of his many informants. His liberty of action was more and more circumscribed in practice by the growing hedge of regulations, precedents and protocol. He became increasingly the prisoner of his own system and unable to adapt his policies significantly except by an increasing use of dispensations from his own rules. Individual Jesuits also suffered under the system. By 1615 it was becoming practically impossible to keep the multiplicity of new rules. Projects and petitions could easily get lost in the post or founder for lack of priority status in the complexities of the 'proper channels'. Both General and subjects seemed now to be mere cogs in a faceless, if holy, machine, 'the Society', to the maintenance and interests of which all their own private opinions, likes and dislikes must be sacrificed. Acquaviva's directive of 1602 to the Jesuit confessors of kings illustrates very well this dangerous development. He directed that the confessors, in the performance of their duties, must always keep in mind the right order of their priorities. The first consideration must be 'the advantage and conservation of the Society': after that comes 'the edification of the people', and lastly 'the utility of the prince'.

Acquaviva's directives ranged very widely. Some were long sermons on the theological bases of Jesuit life. The 1609 edition of an officially inspired devotional volume called *The Letters of the Generals to the Fathers and Brothers of the Society of Jesus* has 620 pages and twelve letters. Two letters are by Ignatius, one each by Borgia and Laynez and no less than eight by Acquaviva occupying 500 pages. Then there were directives combining instruction on principles and regulations on practice. By 1615 these covered almost every aspect of Jesuit activity and most of them had been amended several times and increased in size. They covered novicemasters and noviciate rules, student life, rules and syllabuses for all College courses, rules for the 'tertianship' (a second noviciate at the end of studies), the manner of giving *The Exercises*, Jesuit prayer in general, retreats, apostolic work, confessing kings, nobles, women, communities of nuns, directing Orders of women, the observance of poverty and obedience, the allotment of 'grades', the duty of professors to avoid uncommon or contentious matters when teaching, the censorship of Jesuit books, the duties of rectors, procurators and Provincials, the decoration of churches, keeping clear of commerce, penances, and even on personal cleanliness and seemly deportment. Acquaviva introduced a more extensive use of private printing presses by the Society to produce works of propaganda, devotion and controversy for public consumption and instruction manuals for strictly private circulation among Jesuits. The latter were in small format to fit conveniently in a Jesuit's pocket. They included a rule book, digests of the *Constitutions*, digests of special directives, *Maxims* and *Sentences* from Ignatius's and Acquaviva's long directives on principles, and meditation books. All the manuals were copiously interspersed with exhortations to exact obedience to rules and observances, to prayer and hard work. Some manuals were interleaved with blank pages so that they could be used for particular *examens* on rule-keeping.

New official histories of Ignatius and the Society formed another, more oblique, form of directive. Existing standard biographies of Ignatius by Ribadeneira and da Camara and histories by Rodriguez and Orlandini were quietly withdrawn from circulation for revision. The Gesu bureaucrats had been complaining before 1580 that these books made Ignatius appear far too human and informal: something was needed to stress hard the elements of method and severity in his government and of the miraculous and other-worldly in his piety. The result was the publication of completely recast versions of the books by Ribadeneira and da Camara, the relegation of Rodriguez' biography to the dustbin, and the publication of an entirely new history of a 'Roman' type by Sacchini. Simultaneously the hitherto rather haphazard methods of censorship of books by Jesuits were much tightened up and centralised. In order to pass the Society's censorship a Jesuit author now had to prove far more than just that his book was free from doctrinal error. The censors would require it to be so well-written, uncontentious, edifying and timely in its appearance that its publication would redound to the Society's credit.

Acquaviva and his supporters hoped that, by this great work of remodelling the Society they could free it once and for all of dissidence, slackness and scandals and thereby reduce its enemies to silence. He considered that the root of the trouble was the Society's lack of stable religious communities able to build up that strong house-observance, discipline and corporate spirit enjoyed by the monastic Orders. His solution to the problem was to try to turn the Jesuits into a set of individual monks without real monasteries but with a peculiarly tight community spirit centred on the whole Society personified in the General. Each Jesuit must be very intensively drilled in, and then carry round with him individually, a set of observances more thorough and effective than those of any orthodox monk. At the same time he must be indoctrinated with a great regimental loyalty. These ideas could be found, in part and in embryo, in Ignatius's writings together with a great deal else which Acquaviva regarded frankly as either unnecessary or misguided.

The new directives imposed compulsorily and uniformly on all Jesuits a much more monastic regime than many of them had hitherto known. So far there had been Jesuit houses, especially in Spain, which had an almost Carthusian monastic regime and many others where some individuals pursued a home-made course of devotion while others lived practically the life of secular priests. Some Jesuits had always used the *Spiritual Exercises* often and intensively. Others never used them at all and found their spiritual nourishment outside the Order. It had been common for entrants to the Society to be professed after a noviciate lasting only a few months. A great many Jesuit students had had their studies foreshortened or broken because of College teaching duties. Now the noviciate was to last a full two years and its regime be Spartan, monastic and governed by regulations. Every effort was to be made to keep up monastic observances and a strictly regulated life during the studentship. Wherever possible students were to do a significant part of their studies in segregated houses with few teaching duties. Only academic dullness might now excuse a student from a full seven years of studies. After that course he was to do a second noviciate or 'tertianship'. In order to ensure that Jesuit priests kept up their monastic observances they were now bound by rule to an hour of prayer every day, a day of recollection every month and a long retreat every year. The *Spiritual Exercises* now became by law a large feature of every Jesuit's life. He must take them in their entirety three times in the course of his career and parts of them frequently. In every way his spiritual food, forms of meditation and prayer and pious reading must be distinctively Jesuit.

As, and if, the 'Acquaviva system' gained a grip on the Society he expected that its members would become the real modern monks. He regarded the old-fashioned monks and friars as relics of a past age, doomed to vanish with the last traces of the medieval social and economic conditions which had formed their ways of life. Thus the Jesuits would acquire a great sense of identity and, incidentally, superiority. That, at least, was the General's programme. It remained to be seen whether it would really be accepted in the Society and, if it did, whether its effects would be quite what he expected. Much to the indignation of the German superiors he had excluded history as a subject from College syllabuses. It seems that he knew very little, and cared less, about the realities of monastic history. If he had known more about them no doubt his policies would have been less severe and utilitarian.

*   *   *

By his death in 1615 the Society and the system appeared to be successful. Numbers had risen from 5,000 to 13,000. The system was well launched and he had at last inflicted a really crushing defeat on the Jesuit dissidents. The results were impressive but they had been gained at a high price. The battle with the dissidents dragged on for thirty years, was tough and damaging to the Society and cost Acquaviva himself much anxiety and humiliation. Even when the open fighting was over and the original dissidents dead, dispersed, reduced to outward compliance or ejected from the Society the defects and pressures of Acquaviva's system begot a new kind of dissidence, as stubborn as its predecessor but underground. Also, during this battle, the great increase in Jesuit numbers, activity and influence touched off a new and very heavy attack on the General and the Society by a heterogeneous collection of outside enemies, Popes, Roman curial officials, the older religious Orders, bishops and secular clergy. Lastly, by 1615 some of the blighting effects of Acquaviva's *Ratio Studiorum* on the Colleges were beginning to appear.

In theory he could have crushed the dissidents instantly by dismissing them wholesale from the Society. There was a notable precedent: on one occasion Ignatius had summarily dismissed more than 130 Portuguese Jesuits. The *Constitutions* spoke of the vast majority of Jesuits as helpers kept on temporary contracts only so long as their superiors judged that their association with the Society was to its advantage. But in practice Acquaviva was never in a position to pursue so draconic a policy on any large scale. 'Dissidence' is a convenient omnibus term to describe a hydra-headed phenomenon, the exact size and extent of which was obscure even to Gesu officials with all their impressive sources of information. It was endemic throughout the Iberian Provinces and their American dependencies, strong in France and Germany and troublesome in the Dutch and English Missions. There were Spanish dissidents like Toletus, Acosta and Mariana, who seem to have headed a fairly well-organised protest group circulating manuscript manifestos widely. Their mentality was libertarian and nationalist and their methods political. They had their counterpart groups in France (represented by Auger, Vincent and Coton), in Germany (headed by Hoffaeus, the German Assistant at the Gesu), in Holland and even in England (which produced the most political of all contemporary dissidents, the Yorkshireman, Thomas Wright). Each of these groups felt strongly that strict Gesu control and policies were terribly damaging to Jesuit efforts in their countries: there could be no progress without a great deal of decentralisation in the Society. Then there were specialist groups who resented the way in which Acquaviva's system steam-rollered over their special projects. Some mystics and ascetics saw no salvation for the forms of devotion they practised except in the formation within the Society, but semi-detached from its ordinary rules, of a 'contemplative Province'. Progressive academics and intellectuals like Christoph Klau, Leonard Lessius, Thomas Sanchez and even Robert Bellarmine were restive as the Acquaviva system limited their freedom of teaching and research. Missionary leaders, including even Valignano, had their struggles with the Gesu and their bitter complaints about its autocracy and ignorance of mission conditions.

The leading dissidents were all eminent Professed Fathers who, as such, could only be dismissed from the Society by special papal dispensations which could not be obtained readily or quickly, especially at periods when Popes and Roman curial officials were at war with the General. Indeed Acquaviva found himself continually at war on two fronts simultaneously. The fronts at some times and in some places were quite separate but often they coincided disconcertingly. The dissident leaders almost always had friends at Court: the Spaniards were closely associated with Philip II; Auger was confessor and adviser to Henri III of France; other rival French dissident Jesuits had the Guise family as patrons; Thomas Wright had friends at the English Court including the Earl of Essex. Hence there was a real possibility that a wholesale dismissal of the 'difficult' might precipitate schisms in the Society and the formation of national 'Jesuit Orders' with much official support from outsiders. Such embarrassing events were commonplaces in the broad field of monastic history. At best wholesale dismissals would bring a landslide of voluntary defections which could hamstring the Society's operations.

Acquaviva's wars began soon after the election of a new Pope, Sixtus V, in 1585. The Gesu had been hoping and expecting that their great patron, Cardinal Farnese, would be elected. Instead they were now faced by a Conventual Franciscan who had inherited all of his Order's dislike of the Society. The infant Society had grown up under the wing of the Observant Franciscans and the Carthusians. By 1580 this alliance was at an end and all the Orders of monks and friars were regarding the growing Society with alarm. They had, over the course of centuries, fought their own battles with Rome, the bishops and the secular clergy and had established for themselves a legally-safeguarded, established place in the Church's economy. The growing Society had begun to challenge them. A series of papal grants to the Jesuits, culminating in Bulls issued to Acquaviva by Sixtus V's predecessor, had given them legal privileges surpassing those of the older Orders. In particular the Jesuits were dispensed from various regulations made by the Council of Trent for all religious Orders. They were empowered to set up theological schools within any university without the permission of the heads of the existing schools there, secular and regular. Sixtus V's predecessor had frequently used his supreme power to make over to the Jesuits existing religious houses of other Orders and their endowment properties, on the grounds that the houses were grossly under-manned or moribund. The vast Franciscan family of Orders, Conventual, Observant, Capuchin and Minim contained six times as many men as the Society in 1615. Between them the Franciscans bore most of the burden of evangelism in Europe and the foreign missions. The Dominican Order, a much smaller organisation but containing over 30,000 men in 1615, had long had a great and deserved reputation as the Church's finest theological teachers and most daring and original foreign missioners. Their tradition of government was strong and relatively democratic. Their opposition to the Society was even more bitter than that of the Franciscans.

The first shots on both fronts were fired in 1586. Trouble had begun in a small way in 1582 in a number of universities and seminaries. In the universities of Coimbra, Salamanca, Louvain and Douai the professional and academic enmity between Dominican and Jesuit theologians, deep and real but dormant for some years past, now flared up again more violently and persistently than ever. The first occasion was a law suit in a Church court in the Spanish city of Avila. An ex-Jesuit who had married was denied an inheritance by his relatives on the grounds that he was an ex-religious. By old law legal dispensation from the vows of religion was grudging and very partial: normally it left the subject incapacitated for life from marriage and inheritance. The ex-Jesuit's confessor, a Dominican, alerted his colleagues at Salamanca. They all undertook the man's defence with suspicious enthusiasm. They insisted that the ancient rules applied only to true religious professed in solemn vows. The ex-Jesuit had been simply professed. Hence, the Dominicans urged, he had never been a religious at all but only a lay student who had made a temporary, private promise to associate himself with the Society's works. This line of argument was not new and the Society was allergic to it with good reason. Although it had a fine array of past papal documents approving of its system of 'grades' and of simple but perpetual vows, its enemies had never ceased to insist that the documents were worthless since no Pope had the right to set aside fundamental traditional principles: hence the only real Jesuits were the handful of Professed Fathers and nine-tenths of the Society was an illegal sham.

The quarrel spread like a forest fire. Next the Dominicans, helped by some Jesuit dissident underground literature, charged the Society with basing its discipline on a massive and scandalously ungodly confidence trick — the practice of extracting confidential information from subjects compulsorily in confession and then using it in government. Finally, and even more fundamentally, the Dominicans launched for the first time a block-buster of an attack on the Society which has operated right down to today. They insisted that Jesuit theologians were not traditional Catholic believers but liberal minimisers of the Faith, watering it down greatly by applying humanistic rationalism to its central tenets. Some, it was said, were teaching a distortedly simplistic view of the high spiritual mystery of the interaction of human free will and divine Grace. Others were interpreting the Bible as if it were human literature and doctrinal Tradition as if it were a human code of law: in both cases the line of interpretation was very minimising. Some Jesuit theologians, said the Dominicans, were teaching that a Catholic need not believe doctrines which were peripheral to the central core of the Faith. Some minimised the severity and length of Purgatorial punishment of the dead. Hence when the Society got hold of old religious houses founded by other Orders and still burdened with the obligation of saying many yearly Masses *gratis* for dead benefactors, the Jesuits announced flatly that the obligations only lasted for ten years. This of course, said the Dominicans sharply, released many Jesuit priests from the burden of saying Masses for medieval benefactors and set them free to accommodate the needs of modern patrons.

It was at this time also that the Dominicans and secular priest theologians in Flanders began to charge Jesuit moralists with grossly scandalous watering down of traditional Catholic moral teaching. This teaching, mainly of medieval monastic provenance, was exceedingly narrow. Extenuating circumstances like ignorance and passion were almost entirely disregarded. Trade, money-lending and sex were treated as immensely dangerous for the soul. In sexual matters the great principles were that every offence, however slight, must be a grave sin, that virginity was the truly Christian life and marriage a base necessity for some inferior souls, and that intercourse in marriage could rarely be performed without grave sin. Much of this teaching was buttressed by the authority of the writings of Augustine of Hippo which were said to rank closely after Scripture. But for centuries the monastic austerities of the principles were greatly eased in practice. Society in general quietly accepted a double standard which was practically, if not theoretically, endorsed by the silent consensus of clerical casuists and rustic confessors. Periodically in history there were religious revivals of a monastic kind accompanied by a drive towards moral Puritanism: such a revival was taking off in the 1580s. It became increasingly fashionable to condemn as scandalous and unchristian the lax opinions of casuists. At Louvain there was a violent attack on Pieter Kanis's celebrated *Catechism* for laxism. In Spain the most celebrated Jesuit casuist, Thomas Sanchez, an expert on marital cases, came under heavy fire.

These grave Dominican charges against Jesuit theologians were mostly lacking in substance. The contemporary reaction toward doctrinal traditionalism and moral Puritanism was strong throughout Europe among both Protestants and Catholics. Liberalism and 'laxism' were in full retreat. Pockets of both still existed bravely in all camps, even among the Dominicans. In the main the Jesuits, Acquaviva included, were ardent supporters of the reaction: their 'humanists' and liberals were few, very moderate, and cautious. Leonard Lessius, a Louvain Jesuit who was regarded by the Dominican majority as an arch-heretic, certainly defended unfashionably liberal views on Grace and usury, but was unbendingly 'Augustinian' on sex and marriage. Thomas Sanchez' casuistical forays into sexual liberalism were hesitant and slight. The Puritans were mostly outraged by the clinical realism (though veiled in scholastic Latin) of his published works. Those few Jesuit theologians who, like Robert Bellarmine and Juan Mariana, mildly challenged the fashionable view that absolute autocracy, papal and royal, was the only right form of government ran into trouble inside and outside the Society and were soon compelled to cease publication of their shocking opinions.

While these violent academic broils were gaining momentum a series of unseemly student riots broke out in a number of Jesuit-directed seminaries for the training of candidates for the secular priesthood. Although these seminaries were normally fairly fertile recruiting grounds for the Society it had never been anxious to undertake responsibility for them. Almost all 16th-century seminaries had a stormy history of rebellions and closures. Acquaviva's tightening of Jesuit discipline undoubtedly precipitated further student revolts in the 1590s but the roots of the trouble existed long before his day. Now it was evident that the rebel leaders had some sort of association with Jesuit dissidents and with members of other religious Orders. When rebels were expelled from Jesuit seminaries they not infrequently took refuge in Benedictine, Dominican or Franciscan houses. Acquaviva's reaction was a strong desire to withdraw the Society from all seminary work. In a few cases this happened willy-nilly. Carlo Borromeo, Archbishop of Milan, ordered the Jesuits out of his diocesan seminary. The General begged the Pope in vain for permission to give up the rowdy English seminaries at Rome and Douai.

From 1586 these troubles developed swiftly into a major battle.

The Dominicans realised that they practically controlled two great weapons, the Spanish and Roman Inquisitions. These were very active and powerful ecclesiastical tribunals which had the right to investigate the affairs of any religious organisation and to arrest and try suspected heretics, the writers of unorthodox books, and all clerics thought to be guilty of major crimes, particularly sexual ones. The tribunal concentrated especially on heresy, breaches of the confessional seal, and the use of confession as a way of seducing female penitents. These were considered to be relatively common crimes dealt with far too mildly and ineffectively by the ordinary episcopal courts. The liberal few hated the Inquisitions and their autocratic methods: most people, however, regarded the tribunals as completely necessary guardians of orthodoxy and public decency. The Inquisitors always claimed that everyone, however exalted in ecclesiastical or social station, was subject to their authority. Most large religious Orders (apart, of course, from the Dominicans) had, for many years, been fighting a legal battle to establish their complete freedom from Inquisitorial juris-diction. They could, and should, they maintained, deal with their own offenders with the lash and with prison sentences. The Franciscans were fighting a particularly determined action against the Inquisitions: ultimately they lost it. The Jesuits, particularly in Spain, presumed that that their papal privileges definitely exempted them from the Inquisition's authority.

But now a dissident who had been expelled from the Society in Spain delated a number of his former colleagues to the Inquisition. He accused them of covering up a few cases of heterodox doctrine and seduction in the confessional. Normally Jesuit superiors dealt with such cases expeditiously. If the accused were in simple vows they were generally dismissed from the Society at once. In some areas, particularly in Germany and Portugal, ex-Jesuits were numerous. Professed Fathers were few. When they became trouble-makers superiors were in real difficulties. Sometimes, especially in Germany, the offenders simply fled and became Protestants. If they did not, and moving them to other houses produced no improvement in their behaviour, they could be sent to Rome to be imprisoned. Vincent, a Jesuit dissident at Bordeaux, actually delated Ignatius's *Letter on Obedience* to the Roman Inquisition. For this and other dissident acts he was removed to Rome, apparently treated as mentally ill, and confined for the rest of his life. In 1586 the Spanish Inquisition arrested the accused Jesuits, including two superiors. Their pleas of papal privilege were rejected. Instructed by Acquaviva they applied to the Pope.

As the months passed the case gathered size and momentum. The whole Dominican Order weighed in and the Inquisition's charge-sheet was vastly extended to cover the General and the whole Society while the charges now ranged from condoning heresy and seduction through huge breaches of canon law to 'laxist' heresy. The Spanish Jesuit dissidents, now tactically on the side of the Dominicans, persuaded Philip II to ban the appeal to Rome and to order a full investigation of the *Constitutions* and the Spanish Jesuit Provinces by the Inquisitors and a Spanish diocesan bishop.

At first Acquaviva's counter-measures seemed effective enough. He played on Sixtus V's hatred of Philip II and his unwillingness to admit in public that his predecessors had erred in approving of the Jesuit *Constitutions*. Sixtus responded and went so far as to issue a declaration partly exonerating the Society and to browbeat Philip II into allowing the Inquisition's case to be removed to a Roman court.

However, from that point onwards the General's affairs took a disastrous turn for the worse. His troubles seemed endless. He was deeply worried about the involvement of various Jesuit cliques in politics in Spain, England and France. In Spain it was the Jesuit dissidents who seemed to enjoy Philip II's confidence. Robert Persons was running the English Mission as if it were his own private Order. English Jesuits who opposed his schemes were ousted because '. . . (they) do not walk in step with Father Persons . . . following (their) own private notions and ideas . . .' He was involving the mission in Philip II's design to send an armada to invade England. Meanwhile Mathieu and a number of other French Jesuits, associated with Persons, were ardently supporting warlike operations by the Catholic *Ligue* to exclude from the French throne its legitimate but Protestant heir, Henry of Navarre. The General had no objections in principle to politico-religious action carried to the point of fomenting armed rebellions. Most probably he judged that the plans of Persons and Mathieu were theoretically right. But he was obsessed, understandably, with the perils of these operations and the likelihood that they would bring down more odium on the Society, particularly at a moment when its whole future existence was at stake in Rome. He was therefore appalled when Sixtus V entered into negotiations with Philip II using as his main emissaries Acosta, a leader of the Spanish dissidents, and Persons. The dissidents were encouraged by this signal mark of papal favour and Persons could now persuade himself that his designs had the highest backing. The bitterest pill for the General was the fact that the Pope's mission was successful. Philip II called off the threatened Spanish investigation into the Society's affairs.

But this was only the beginning of sorrows for Acquaviva. Sixtus V, a man of volcanic energy and temper and given to unpredictable impulses, now turned sharply against the Society. He set up a special commission in Rome to report on the *Constitutions*: its members were mostly Franciscans and Dominicans. There was a strong suspicion that the commission received suggestions from the Spanish dissidents. By 1589 the commission gave its report to the Pope and he issued orders to the General. They came as a severe shock. The Society's enemies had always regarded the name *Societas Jesu* as a piece of offensive arrogance. Now it was to be changed, omitting the holy name. The Jesuit 'grades' were to be abolished: in future all were to be unprofessed novices until the time came for their ordination. Then they were either to be dismissed or solemnly professed. The General was to leave the admission of novices to Provincials, provided that no bastards or persons of Jewish descent were accepted. Jesuit obedience had to be redefined in a less absolutist way. Secret 'syndications', delations and compulsory confession to superiors had to be abolished. Jesuit rules on poverty had to be brought into line with those currently in force in the Orders of friars.

During the months before the Pope's decision and even after it he became the focus of a babel of Jesuit argument. The dissidents showered him with proposals and encouragements. For his part the General used every possible means to delay the decision and, once it had been taken, to delay its promulgation and avoid having to obey it. He lobbied sympathetic Roman curial officials with some success as well as the few well-disposed Cardinals. He procured from friendly kings, ruling princes and other influential persons a sheaf of testimonials. Armed with these he besieged the Pope in audiences, belabouring him with arguments for the Jesuit *status quo*. Sixtus was a sick man, weary and increasingly enraged by Acquaviva's stubborn disobedience. Then, at the last moment, a strange combination of circumstances lifted the black cloud from the General and gave him three years of respite. Sixtus died, his unpromulgated orders died with him, and Rome had no less than four Popes in rapid succession, three of whom achieved little.

Acquaviva made use of this breathing space to perform a vital task which bore him in good stead later. He despatched a trustworthy Gesu Vistor-General to Spain with detailed instructions on the administrative reforms and stratagems he must employ to break the power of the local dissidents. The Spanish Provinces were redivided and otherwise reorganised, with many incidental new links with the Gesu and changes of superiors. Some dissidents were relegated to remote houses. Others, spiritual coadjutors, were dismissed from the Society. At least two major leaders, both Professed Fathers, were pushed and persuaded into changing Orders voluntarily, one moving to the Dominicans and the other to the Capuchins in Italy. The moves were perfectly canonical since they were voluntary and the recipient Orders were accounted 'stricter' than the Society.

By the end of 1592 the breathing space was over with the election as Pope of a vigorous autocrat, Clement VIII, an old enemy of the General's. He had every intention of continuing the effort to reform the Society radically. He intended to use his supreme power but was well aware of his own mortality and Acquaviva's proved stubbornness. Hence he decided to move, as far as possible within the legal bounds of the Society's existing *Constitutions* and with a great show of consultation. But he launched the enterprise autocratically. With prompting from Philip II, himself advised by dissident Jesuit courtiers, Acosta and Mendoza, Clement, on his own authority, summoned an extraordinary General Congregation to meet in Rome in 1593. Against Acquaviva's advice he promoted an eminent dissident theologian, Toletus, to the cardinalate and groomed him for the presidency of the Congregation. The Pope seems to have calculated that, at the very least, the Congregation must have a great body of delegates hostile to the General and capable of cutting down his power or even deposing him from office. It was probably at this time that Acosta suggested for the first time moving the General to a see in southern Italy.

Acquaviva was making his own preparations for the crucial trial of strength. He made a great show of consultation and desire for reform. Provincial Congregations were instructed to collect criticisms of the Society's government and reform proposals even from individual Jesuits and forward them to a Reform Commission at the Gesu. The General Congregation assembled. It soon became evident that although, as many of the reform proposals sent to Rome showed, discontent and alarm were widespread, the disposition of the majority of the delegates was to give Acquaviva another chance to prove that his autocracy could work better. Toletus was voted out of the chair and proposals for structural reform of the Society put forward by dissident delegates rejected out of hand. The General then dramatically asked the assembly to investigate closely the record of his administration since 1580. The result was a strong vote of thanks and confidence.

At this point Clement VIII, astounded and enraged by the turn of events, visited the Congregation in person. He demanded a second vote on the dissidents' proposals in his presence: for the second time they were voted down. Then Clement delivered an angry address, asserting that the delegates were vastly mistaken if they imagined that things would ever improve under the existing administration and *Constitutions* and threatening draconic measures unless definite reform decrees were passed. According to one observer, an admirer of Acquaviva, the General now rushed forward, fell on his knees and kissed Clement's feet as a sign of absolute obedience. Then began a strange process of bargaining between the Pope and the assembly. In the end he extracted from them grudging acceptance of three reforms, the third taken only after the registering of a strong protest. In future rectors and Provincials were to hold office only for three years. Provincials, on relinquishing office, were to summon their Provincial Congregations and submit to their judgement an exact account of the Provincials' stewardship. General Congregations were to be held, not simply to elect new Generals, but also automatically every six years. Acquaviva must have disliked these changes intensely. But he was now so skilled in self-defence that he knew well that they were of minor importance. The dissidents seemed at last to be on the run, the *Constitutions* and Acquaviva's system were basically intact, and Philip II and Clement VIII could not live much longer. The General Congregation, before departing home, passed a very strongly worded decree demanding the punishment or dismissal from the Society of all 'malcontents . . . false and degenerate sons, disturbers of the common peace . . .'

Acquaviva might now feel safer, but he had no occasion to feel complacent. The reform proposals which had poured in to the Reform Commission showed disturbingly that dissidence to the point of demanding structural reforms was still strong in Spain, in parts of Germany and in the French Lyon Province. In France and England Jesuit *Ligeurs* and supporters of Persons' schemes for the forcible Catholicisation of England were still active.

During the height of his troubles in Rome Acquaviva had been negotiating with Clement VIII and the French Provincials the delicate business of the conversion to Catholicism of Henry of Navarre. In theory this event should have won the gratitude and favour of the new king, Henry IV, and put an end to the intrigues of the fanatically *Ligeur* faction of Jesuits bitterly opposed to Henry. In practice suspicion of the Society and its own internal divisions died hard. In 1594 a fanatic, associated with the Jesuit *Ligeurs* tried to assassinate the king. The result was the arrest and execution of some of the *Ligeurs* and the expulsion of the Jesuits from much of France. Meanwhile in England Persons' policies had, as Acquaviva had always feared they would, roused bitter resentment among the Catholic laity, a good many secular priests, and even a few Jesuit missioners. The latter, mostly ejected from the Society, campaigned bitterly against Persons and his supporters.

Acquaviva was faced with other humiliations. All efforts to punish the two great surviving dissident leaders in Spain, Mendoza and Mariana, foundered because they were Professed Fathers and protected by the Pope and the new king of Spain, Philip III. Both men now wrote fine statements of the dissidents' case and the manuscripts circulated widely. Even as late as 1607 the dissidents were still strong enough to secure the passing of reform resolutions in several Spanish Provincial Congregations. In 1604 Mendoza revived the plan to get Acquaviva moved from the Generalate to an archbishopric. Clement VIII took up the idea and persistently offered Acquaviva the archbishopric of his native city, Naples. When this effort failed Mendoza devised an alternative scheme. At his suggestion Philip III warmly invited the General to pay a state visit to Spain to settle once and for all the differences between the Escorial and the Gesu. The conspirators hoped that once Acquaviva was in Spain means could be found to prevent him ever seeing the Gesu again. But he declined to walk into the trap, pleading ill-health. Clement VIII, who knew of the secret plan, then peremptorily ordered him to accept the invitation. Delaying tactics, including business preoccupations, tactical illnesses and the usual sheaves of testimonials failed to soften the Pope. In the end Acquaviva steeled himself to undertake the journey. Then the Pope died in 1605.

The next Pope, Paul V, was an unknown quantity. Some years later he became well-disposed toward the General. But in the meantime his uncertain temper combined with a series of disasters within the Society to cause Acquaviva much anxiety.

In his eyes the leaders of pressure groups and 'private empires' among Jesuits were almost as dangerous as outright dissidents. He had always predicted that the intrigues of Robert Persons and his supporters would bring ruin on the English Jesuit Mission and discredit on the whole Society. Now his predictions seemed to be fulfilled in the Gunpowder Plot (1605). The Jesuit missioners were widely, even among English Catholics, accused of involvement in the plot: Garnet, the superior, and several other missioners were arrested and executed. John Gerard, the most effective missioner, narrowly escaped the same fate and was so discredited in many quarters that he had to be removed from the mission permanently. Meanwhile in France the efforts of a number of Jesuit moderates had persuaded the king to offer to allow the Jesuits back into the main part of the country on certain stringent conditions. These included the posting of Coton and a number of other Jesuits permanently at the royal Court, ostensibly as chaplains but really as hostages for the good behaviour of the fanatically *Ligeur* element among their colleagues. This was a sensible precaution since assassins — paid by the *Ligeurs* — had already made at least one attempt on the king's life and were ultimately to achieve their purpose. The hostages had to take a special and thorough-going oath of loyalty to the king, the terms of which seemed to put his interests above those of the General and the Pope. With good reason Acquaviva was deeply disturbed. It was not the first time, and would not be the last, that some French Jesuits had displayed an even more extreme nationalist separatism than their Spanish colleagues. Moreover, both Coton and Acquaviva were terrified by the prospect that one or other of the Jesuit court chaplains was bound to be invited to become the king's confessor. As Coton wrote to the General, it was one thing to exercise *epikeia* — a kind of easy tolerance — in social converse at Court, the centre of which was a king who was reckoned to have had fifty-six mistresses, it was quite another matter to deal with the king in 'the rigour and vigour of the Sacrament' of Confession. The Dominicans and others were loudly accusing the Jesuits of moral laxism in teaching and confessional practice. If it were known that the king, whose womanising was the talk of Europe, had a Jesuit confessor and was seen receiving Holy Communion the Society's enemies were bound to think the worst. Acquaviva naturally stressed this 'political' aspect of the matter. Later, when Coton was forced for a short time to occupy the dangerous position of royal confessor he expressed his feeling to the General:

'How indulgent we are towards the faults of princes . . . yet when I read the books of the old Fathers of the Church I am terrified by their great strictness and zeal . . . it makes me tremble . . .'

In a later letter he wrote:

'Thanks to the pope's blessing, the graces of the Jubilee, and your Reverence's prayers, the king has lately set his conscience in order. He has good intentions which I think he will keep, at least in part . . . I am torn between fear and hope . . .'

Quite recently also the General had been upset by other evidences of Jesuit groups taking the law into their own hands, this time in such remote and barbarous areas that he had very little chance of restraining their misjudgements and fanaticism. In Poland and Russia there had been the wild, fairy-tale affair of 'the False Demetrius'. The King of Poland had taken it into his head to invade Russia in order to put a Catholic Russian refugee on the throne of the Tsars: he took with him also a band of Polish Jesuits led by Peter Skarga, a highly independent-minded, pioneering man. For a brief period 'Demetrius' actually was the Catholic Tsar and on paper the Russian Orthodox Church was forcibly Catholicised. Then the whole mad adventure collapsed. Meanwhile in Japan and China, almost at the furthest limits of the Gesu's postal system, Valignano and Ricci had long learned to make and execute their own daring decisions: the General only heard of them three or four years later if the letters did not miscarry.

Back in Rome a papal commission of theologians, nearly all Dominicans and Franciscans, had been for years going through the published writings of Jesuit theologians in order to acquire sure proof of heresy. By 1606 the commission's work was nearly complete and the Dominicans said that the evidence was damning. But this stroke against the Society was again warded off by unforeseen events. Quarrels between the Venetian Republic and the Papacy were endemic. In yet another round the Jesuits were expelled from Venice on the grounds that they had defended the rights of the Holy See. Paul V was much impressed and overnight became much more favourably disposed towards the Society. Very possibly for this casual reason he decided to leave the report of the commission unpublished, merely ordering the theologians of both sides to keep the peace in future. That was not the only good consequence of the Venetian affair. By the

Pope's favour, Philip III of Spain was prevailed on to tell the dissident Mendoza to accept the offer of a bishopric in Peru. The collapse of dissidence was sealed in 1608 when Acquaviva at last felt it safe to summon a General Congregation. It was a very docile assembly which gave the General an enthusiastic vote of confidence and urged him to dispose of the last relics of dissidence. He needed no prompting.

*   *   *

By the time Acquaviva died in 1615 the celebrated Jesuit educational system of the 17th and 18th centuries had definitely taken shape. Very many educated people, Protestants as well as Catholics, regarded it with something akin to awe as one of the greatest wonders of the age.

In sheer size, almost doubled during Acquaviva's Generalate, the system was certainly impressive. It was made up of eight complete universities, some thirty Academies which were small universities in all but legal status, over 400 Colleges (or Grammar schools), a dozen seminaries, and a number of learned Jesuit societies containing a galaxy of scholarly talent. There were theologians, headed by the famous Bellarmine and Lessius, moralists like Sanchez and philosophers like Suarez. There were historians like Sirmond, Petau, Labbe and Rosweyde. Christoph Klau's renowned Roman training school for Jesuit mathematicians and astronomers had *alumni* in Colleges across Europe combining ordinary teaching with amateur astronomical observation. This host of schools was planted in every Catholic state except the Republic of Venice, from the Russian border right across to Sicily. They formed the only large, centrally-organised educational system in Europe taking in lay schoolboys and ordinands as well as clerics. By 1615 Europe was enjoying a remarkable educational boom. Schools for boys whose parents could afford fees proliferated everywhere. Discerning people were beginning to think that they had become altogether too numerous. But the vast majority of schools were isolated units utterly dependent on local talent and financial support. They were in a constant state of flux. The arrival of a reputable master, the entry into his school of the sons of influential local people and the absence of outbreaks of famine, plague or warfare in the district almost invariably allowed a school to flourish. Contrariwise the arrival of a bad master, the withdrawal of pupils and local outbreaks of famine, plague and military operations almost always destroyed it in a very short space of time. It might, or might not, have been resurrected years later. But it appeared that the Jesuits, because of their strong system, were insured against the worst disasters of this kind: the system endured with a rock-like solidity and uniformity, always growing.

Another admirable characteristic of the system appeared to be the superior skill and thoroughness with which it was organised. Its schools had unusually large staffs of teachers who were said to be trained and disciplined to a unique extent. Boys in Jesuit schools were, it was said, 'brought on' amazingly. The Jesuits had their own textbooks which were so widely admired that they were often used, in somewhat bowdlerised forms, in Protestant schools. It was common knowledge that the Jesuits preferred persuasion, competitions and a variety of teaching games to drilling and the rod. No pupil in a Jesuit College got his 'ascent' to a higher class until he had genuinely earned it. The general view was that Jesuit schools had a distinctive *cachet* about them: there was something about the conversation and demeanour of their ex-pupils which made them as immediately recognisable as, say, Etonians today. On the strength of this great reputation Catholic kings and princes were beginning to insist that their sons must have Jesuit tutors.

It was therefore very easy to believe, especially if one had never set foot inside Jesuit schools, that they were perfectly run and that the system was, in every detail, the brain-child of some genius. In fact, as we have already seen, the system grew up in embryo in the early years of the Society more by accident than design. By the time that Acquaviva became General it was already growing fast. This was still not due to a clear decision by the Gesu to make it the Society's main work, but because the more active Provinces were pushed into developing it by public demand. An increasingly large number of parents desperately sought, in an inflationary age, to diversify their families' sources of income. Minor landowners, tradesmen and yeoman farmers wanted their younger sons to get one of the secure and relatively well-paid jobs in government service which Catholic monarchs were creating. A decent schooling in Latinity and sometimes a university degree were essential qualifications for such posts. The Jesuits happened to be the only religious Order available and willing to supply this sort of schooling for lay boys in Acquaviva's time. It was only later, in the mid-17th century that other Orders and educated secular priests began to compete with the Society whose school system by then had built up a commanding lead. Moreover, Jesuit principles formed the organisation of their teaching in ways which commended them greatly to parents. The Society's rules of poverty prevented them from charging tuition fees. Acquaviva's strong monastic tendencies caused him to limit boarding facilities in Colleges to the sons of nobles and Catholic boys sent to the continent from Protestant countries. Hence most of the Jesuits' pupils lodged inexpensively with parish priests in the vicinity of the Colleges. It was not surprising that, in these circumstances, Acquaviva and his Provincials were continually deluged with requests to open new Colleges or to extend their intake into existing ones. All they could do was to struggle, sometimes quite unavailingly, to be selective in their acceptance of requests and to put a modicum of order, method and uniformity into the welter of Jesuit educational expansion. The draconic and rigid character of many of the General's school regulations proceeded not only from the tidiness and autocratic temper of his mind but from his terror that the system was getting out of control.

The realities of Jesuit schooling in his day often bore only a distant relationship to the tidiness of his regulations. These poured out of the Gesu from 1586 in successive editions and appendices which were gathered together into the famous code of 1599, the *Ratio Studiorum*. A modern reader of the *Ratio* is bound to find the system it ordains foreign, narrow and repulsively repressive. Jesuit teachers at every level were to use precisely the same teaching methods. They were to be 'readers' or 'lecturers' automatically transmitting by word of mouth completely traditional material, Latinity of a Ciceronian and Virgilian kind, Aristotelian philosophy of the simplified and stereotyped form produced in medieval schools, and medieval scholastic theology. The syllabuses were fixed by regulation as were the textbooks. The Jesuit teacher was limited to reading the prescribed text to his class, section by section, pausing only to dictate notes (summaries and explanations) which were also almost invariably traditional. The *Ratio* deliberately left masters exceedingly little freedom of action and interpretation. Acquaviva knew only too well that a highly intelligent minority of Jesuit teachers given real liberty of choice would use it to experiment with new kinds of syllabuses and with daringly new interpretations of the traditional material. There were also daily 'exercises' which consisted of compositions and, in the higher subjects, scholastic disputations in proper form. The preparation of these was reckoned by the *Ratio* to need five hours a day in some 'study place'. When the exercises were performed, individuals or groups were invariably pitted against each other in 'battle'. The winners and the most pious received rewards. They were made 'repetitors', 'decurions' or 'praetors', given fast promotion to higher classes, and, if working consistently, promoted into the ranks of elite societies called 'academies' or 'sodalities'.

Both Jesuit masters and pupils were to be kept under strict surveillance. The masters were subject to 'syndications'. The boys were watched and informed on in College by their 'repetitors', 'decurions' and 'praetors' and also by 'secret censors', usually members of sodalities. Out of College supervision was left to the 'censors', the warden of the *internat* or hostel and the police services of the town. The pupils' scanty leisure was to be carefully filled in with attendance at religious services, super-vised games of an approved kind in the College's enclosed quadrangle, and rehearsals for College theatricals. Gesù regulations required that the theatricals must take place inside or near the College and be of material which was conducive to piety and exercising classwork. Since the use of the vernacular was forbidden in Colleges, the plays, like the classes, compositions and disputations, had to be in Latin of a highly formalised sort.

In fact the *Ratio* regulations were perfectly typical of the age. The governing bodies of almost all 16th-century schools, even remote English grammar schools, were addicted to elaborate school rules. Since the Jesuits normally had no boarders, their rules were less full than those of most schools. Strict super-vision by masters, a very full use of boy-monitors, delation, drilling and flogging were absolutely standard. Persuasion to learning by competitions and by theatricals of an artificial kind were common form. Lutheran schools in Germany were particularly famous for their Latin and Greek plays.

With the Jesuits, as with most other 16th-century school-masters of note, the minute regulations were at once an ideal and a desperate safeguard against the ignorance, rebelliousness and ebullience of schoolboys, students and junior masters. Some were of such a disposition that they could be moulded by constant drilling and supervision: others were driven by such methods to secretly organised, undercover forms of evasion and protest or, where there were bold leaders, to open demonstrations and even violence. The Jesuits had their fair share of all these troubles.

It was not merely love of truth and academic creativity which accounted for the almost schoolboyish combativeness of most of the greatest Jesuit scholars of Acquaviva's day. They were practically all Professed Fathers and steadily observant religious, yet became habitual evaders of the letter of the *Ratio*. Leonard Lessius spent years upsetting his Provincials and the Gesu, the Dominicans and university faculty boards. He experimented with less scholastic, more 'positive' ways of theologising. He set the universities of Louvain, Douai and Paris in an uproar with his pointed, reasoned attacks on a scholastic traditionalism which had become a hard orthodoxy. At Salamanca University Luis Molina attacked the Dominican theory of Grace head-on and Thomas Sanchez made a great furore with his treatise on marriage. Lessius supported Molina's theory warmly and attacked its Jesuit critics, Suarez and Bellarmine, ferociously. But Bellarmine himself and his fellow professors at the Roman College, Toletus and Klau, all had their moments of creative ebullience and paid for them with humiliating rebuffs from authority. One of Bellarmine's books was put on the *Roman Index of Prohibited Books* and others narrowly avoided the same fate. Klau, the friend of Galileo, an ex-pupil of the Society, was compelled by the Gesu to desert him. Suarez, the most widely admired Jesuit after Bellarmine, insisted on teaching philosophical notions which could hardly be squared with the *Ratio's* directives.

Where the great Jesuit scholars led, the most vigorous minds among the younger Jesuit professors, often their pupils, followed suit. They compiled their own introductions to courses and substituted longer expositions of their own for the brief, standard official 'dictates'. They habitually skipped fast through parts of the syllabus they regarded as obsolete in order to find time for texts and subjects which formed no part of the prescribed syllabuses. Acquaviva battled furiously with their taste for classical authors whom he thought pornographic or pagan and for extra-curricular incursions into history and geography. He was enraged by their contempt for Aristotle and Galen and their concentration on mathematics, astronomy, optics and mechanics. Some provincial Colleges, like Bordeaux, became as notorious for free-thinking as the *Romanum*.

Even Provincials and rectors sat light to the *Ratio* where common sense, patrons or parents insisted. The Society's flood of recruits included a great many quite incapable of profiting from the *Ratio's* course of scholastic theology, Hebrew and Greek. One way round this difficulty, used especially at the *Romanum*, was to defer the entry of boys into the noviciate and place them in seminaries not bound by the Society's rules. There they could be put through a very short course of studies for ordination in 'positive theology' and 'cases of conscience' well-adapted to the capabilities of dullards. Immediately after ordination such men were received into the noviciate and so spared the Society's prescribed training. Some rectors went further and either set up an illicit, simplified, intensive course for the dull consisting of 'positive theology' and 'cases of conscience', or allowed students to truncate their course of scholastic theology. In 1610 no less than one in three of all Jesuit priests had been ordained without doing the full, prescribed course. Of fifty-three Jesuits working in England in that year thirty-seven had done the scholastic course (though one of them never managed more than a year of it), fifteen were *positivi*, and one, a *humanista* and most likely a lay coadjutor, had done no theology at all.

The rectors and Provincials were also inclined to bend the rules concerning lay boys. In some large city Colleges they were driven by public demand to admit far more boys than their staffs could manage effectively. Lower Grammar classes of 100, 140 or almost 200 boys under one master were not infrequent. Boys were admitted who were so illiterate or dull of understanding that 'Rudiments' or preparatory classes were started in some Colleges in spite of Acquaviva's sharp disapproval. The consequence was that a great many pupils spent years in the lowest classes without getting any 'ascent'. Young men with beards sat there alongside small boys. Many left Grammar voluntarily or were superannuated by the rectors as incapabale of Latinity. But at the other end of the scale the Jesuit system contained many highly intelligent and literate boys who could be ready to enter philosophy at a very early age. It was they and their parents who grumbled about the rigidity of the *Ratio* syllabus. In some places they exacted from the Jesuit authorities illicit 'extras' like mathematics, astronomy, horsemanship, dancing lessons and sessions with a fencing master. The rectors knew well that if they did not bend the rules the boys would quit the Colleges for private tuition or Academies run by secular persons.

There were other types of parent whom the Society dare not accommodate. The *Ratio* very firmly excluded teaching in canon law. Parents whose minds were set on preparing their sons for lucrative careers in Church administration invariably withdrew them from Jesuit Colleges at the end of Grammar and entered them in secular colleges in prestigious universities. Partly due to policy but mostly because of the violent opposition of most university authorities and the other religious Orders to the Society the Jesuits in 1615 were still unable to offer their own students and boy pupils places in the great universities or within Jesuit establishments incorporated into them. The university section of the Jesuit system was one of its weak points. They had to make do with an academic second best: they set up small universities of their own with papal authorisation or, especially in Germany, took over completely largely moribund and empty old universities. In these cases the faculty staffs were all Jesuits and the universities did not offer courses in law or medicine. Otherwise a Jesuit student or lay boy pupil could go to a Jesuit Academy of higher studies located within the township round a greater university. But the Jesuit professors in such an Academy were denied official status in the university and their students forbidden the right to matriculate and graduate in it. It was not surprising that so many bright lay boys in Jesuit Colleges showed no desire to continue to university studies under Jesuit masters. This situation, however, as the case of Matteo Ricci showed, did not necessarily alienate the boys from the Society.

Then there were boys who could not be accommodated in Jesuit Colleges for other reasons. A map of Europe marking the sites of Jesuit Colleges in 1615 shows that their geographical disposition was very irregular. Some areas, like Brittany, contained very few Colleges largely because of the local language problem: Breton boys were averse to speaking in Latin: when they did their masters could not understand their strange pronunciation and the boys could not cope with the Italianate pronunciation of their French masters. In other areas, for instance the greatest shipping and commercial towns of France, the dominant local merchant community refused to have Jesuit Colleges because their syllabus was medieval and clerical. As the anti-Jesuit opposition gained ground in England, an increasing number of Catholic gentry parents felt the same way. In Germany there were Catholic nobles who sent their daughters to board in French convents and their sons to the Protestant Dutch University of Leyden. On the whole Jesuit Colleges were more likely to be found in urbanised areas than in rural ones. Thus in Portugal the twelve Colleges were congregated mostly in and round Lisbon, Oporto, Coimbra and Lagos. In the Province of Naples of the sixteen Colleges seven were tightly packed in and round the city of Naples and eight others in large coastal towns. The Colleges were overwhelmingly middle class institutions. Some did accommodate the sons of ambitious peasant farmers who travelled to visit them every market day bringing food stores. Dull peasant boys never reached even the higher Grammar classes: bright ones, if they and their parents' purses could stand the course, were transformed by a College education into middle class clericals and office-holders.

In matters of College discipline Provincials and rectors were forced to go far beyond the *Ratio's* small concessions to the social habits and needs of parents and boys. The *Ratio* set its face firmly against the schoolboy and student clubs with elected 'dukes' which could often terrorise masters and university authorities especially in France and Italy. Offensive weapons were to be kept by College porters during classes. Very few holidays were to be allowed. *Internats* were to be regularly and closely inspected by rectors. Sodalities and Academies within Colleges were meant to steal the thunder of the student clubs. A senior boy who might otherwise become a secret 'duke' could find an outlet for his passion for leadership in being a 'praetor' or 'decurion'. Even Acquaviva, however, was forced to bend a little before College realities. He reduced class time and instituted a Thursday holiday every week. Provincials and rectors went further, granting longer and longer *vacances* during the wine and grain harvests. They became cautious about imposing public floggings after numbers of mass 'walk-outs' by boys, and resorted more and more to fines and expulsion. Occasionally Colleges went through very bad patches of pupil rebellion and mass truancy: the English seminaries and the *Germanicum* at Rome had a particularly bad record in this respect. The municipal regulations about schoolboys in College towns in France indicate what sorts of crimes rectors had to deal with. Boys were forbidden to frèquent brothels or the lodgings of known prostitutes, professional or amateur: they must not enter *cabarets*, carry weapons on the streets or fight duels.

The financing of the Jesuit educational system proved even more of an anxiety than student rebellion. Acquaviva inherited a Gesu policy which barred boarding schools and the foundation of Colleges without solid assurance of adequate endowments. He began by giving dispensations to a few Colleges which took in English, German and Hungarian boys and to some wholly boarding establishments in Flanders (which deserved well of the Society since it supported more than forty of its Colleges) and

Germany (where the need for schools was greatest). Later, stung to indignation by accusations that these schools were making large profits from boarding fees, Acquaviva withdrew the dispensations granted in Flanders. College endowments remained a perpetual worry. In many places they consisted of municipalities' grants of old, disused school buildings and quarterly payments out of the proceeds of local property taxes and market tolls. Elsewhere ecclesiastical Chapters granted tumbledown Church premises along with the proceeds of prebends and benefices. Elsewhere Popes and princes made available to the Jesuits empty or moribund religious houses and hospitals and parts of their scattered endowment lands loaded with encumbrances, the payment of pensions, the stipends of secular priests and the maintenance of old Mass foundations. By 1615 it had not yet become possible to pull down these inadequate buildings and replace them with purpose-built school premises. In larger Colleges therefore classes were crammed hugger-mugger sometimes working on a shift system. Endowments, especially in Germany and in France until recently torn by religious war, commonly included isolated lands which were largely or totally unproductive because they were in the hands of Protestants. A lot of College endowments were in the form of tithe payments the actual yield of which fluctuated wildly from year to year because of plague, war, famine and inflation. In times of famine country Colleges' revenues shrank and the intake of boys and novices became small. By 1615 few Colleges were regularly breaking even financially. Most were in debt, some heavily. Here and there Colleges closed their doors for years or quietly packed up. The circumstances of the times and the severity of the sections devoted to religious poverty in the *Constitutions* gave Provincials little scope for the accumulation of substantial emergency funds and prevented them using the endowments of better-off establishments to help out those in trouble. The main possible source of emergency funds was donations from well-to-do Jesuits just before profession. But the Society's system of perpetual simple vows and easy dismissal even after years of service made the free use of these donations perilous: if the donors left the Society Provincials had to repay the money or face law-suits. Acquaviva was particularly allergic to accusations that Provincials habitually fished for wealthy novices. The accusations persisted, particularly in the writings of Jesuit dissidents.

It is difficult to make a fair judgement on the Jesuit schools of

1615. On the one hand their mere survival and growth in the face of so many difficulties was a great achievement. The existence of the system between the 1550s and 1615 gave Catholicism vital help since its other educational resources happened to be at a very low ebb at that period. Then quantity probably mattered more than quality. The Jesuits for the most part provided a 'utility' kind of education without much in the way of experiment, academic excellence or material splendour. Critics of the short-comings of Protestant schools and other Catholic ones of those days had no difficulty in plumping for admiration of the Jesuit achievement. By 1615 these other schools were just beginning to make up lost ground. More far-seeing critics were just starting to point out the glaring omissions and defects in the Jesuit system. Its most daringly creative efforts were untypical of the system and condemned by the Gesu. Its average standard was humdrum, a little old-fashioned and stuffy. It contained a sizeable bottom layer of schools where the teaching was bad and discipline poor. The Jesuits' almost total exclusion from the great European universities could have been pure gain for them. Those univer-sities, though they were more prosperous materially than they had been for many years, were mentally hidebound and reactionary. The Jesuits could have used their freedom from the shackles of the system to promote a real and creative intellectual life in their own small, rival group of universities and Academies. They had small groups of scholars who were disposed to take that path and who tried to set out along it. But their promising efforts were largely thwarted by the Gesu, and, still more, by the stolid conformism of most of their colleagues who were content to settle down in a mental rut even narrower and more conservative than that of the old universities. Acquaviva must bear some, if not all, of the blame for these missed educational opportunities.

*   *   *

Mutius Vitelleschi, his successor in the Generalate, has proved even less attractive to Jesuit biographers than Acquaviva. Like him he was Italian and a bureaucrat, utterly and narrowly devoted to the interests of the Society and the desk-work of administration of an ever more complex, highly regulated and successful organisation. Like Acquaviva he was young enough at the time of his election to have an unusually long reign, from 1615 to 1645.

In his time the Society continued to grow and its works to proliferate with a kind of inevitability: nothing breeds success like success. It is true that the rate of increase in the numbers of Jesuits slowed down. In Vitelleschi's thirty years numbers only rose from 13,000 to 16,000. At the outset of his Generalate he issued a stern warning that the Society had been growing too fast for its health and ordered that entry into noviciates should be tailored to the real needs of the Provinces and unnecessary small establishments closed down. But events and the demands of patrons, in his case as in Acquaviva's, took control. A sharp decline in the hitherto high rate of general population increase throughout much of Europe due to famine, plague and war most probably did much more than Vitelleschi's orders to reduce entries into Jesuit noviciates. On the other hand political changes compelled Provincials to found a great many extra, and often small, Colleges and houses. In Austria, Bohemia and Germany Catholic sovereigns began the Thirty Years' War, an all-out attack on Protestantism. The Jesuits in those areas were forced to move into the large conquered areas and to cooperate vigorously in their forcible Catholicisation. In France the Catholics had won the wars of religion and the French Provinces were caught up willy-nilly in a similar work. In the Far East the collapse of the Japan Mission led to a wider and more experimental redistribution of its missioners in India, Tibet, Siam, Indochina and Ceylon. In South America the expansion of the white and half-caste population led to an increasing demand for Jesuit Colleges and expansion into the jungle interior brought the spread of Jesuit *doctrinas* or 'Reductions' to protect the native tribes. In North America, French and English colonisation in Canada and Maryland pushed the Jesuit Provincials into following the flag and the colonists. Vitelleschi's part in this considerable expansion was, like Acquaviva's before him, mostly limited to deep anxiety, solemn warnings of disaster and reluctantly given permissions for processes already in train.

However, his time saw the Society attain, rapidly and apparently almost automatically, great goals which Acquaviva had striven for painfully but never reached in his lifetime. Almost overnight the Jesuits ceased to be held suspiciously at arm's length by the greatest Catholic potentates. The Society was not only accepted by them: it seemed to become an integral and privileged part of the core of the Establishment, a major power within the Church.

Down to 1621 the Generals had rarely, and then only uneasily and for short periods, felt that they enjoyed papal favour. Now all that was dramatically changed. With very few exceptions the

Popes from 1621 to 1676 were educated in Jesuit Colleges: most of them had studied under Jesuit professors in the *Romanum*. They had warm friendships with leading Jesuits, normally chose Jesuits as their confessors, and saw to it that the Society was well represented in the College of Cardinals. In the 1620s Ignatius, Borgia and Xavier were all canonised as saints. The Society now had no less than four newly restored and decorated churches in Rome, the Gesu, S. Stefan Rotondo, S. Vitale and the Quirinale: it was soon to have a fifth, S. Ignacio. In 1640 Urban VIII insisted on paying for and organising lavish celebrations for the centenary of the foundation of the Society. These very remarkable developments were primarily due to two factors. First, the Roman Curia had undergone great changes in Acquaviva's time. Like most European monarchies and the Society itself it now had a government which was at once highly autocratic and bureaucratic. The number of officials and departments had been greatly increased while the power of Cardinals and department heads to check the Popes' freedom of action had much decreased. Hence if a Pope now chose to grant favours to the Jesuits, curial opposition would be very muted. Secondly, also during Acquaviva's time, a considerable number of ex-pupils of the Jesuits had gained offices in the Roman Curia. Even before 1621 there were enough of them to form an influential pressure group. The Society's enemies said that this was due to a deliberate manoeuvre by Acquaviva. They could point to the facts that Jesuits had long been spiritual directors to a number of curial departments and that Acquaviva had been quick to rely on the influence of 'Jesuited' officials during his hard struggles with Popes. It is, on the other hand, very likely that the growth and popularity of Jesuit Colleges in Italy automatically produced recruitment of their ex-pupils into the Curia without any particular encouragement from rectors, Provincials or the General.

The Jesuits soon found that papal favour had its limits and that their new privileged status aroused alarm and jealousy in many quarters. It became evident that the election to the papacy after 1676 of candidates drawn from the muted but inveterate anti-Jesuit opposition in the Roman Curia would be the signal for attacks on the Society of an unheard of violence and strength. Meanwhile it still had to endure a great deal of petty but humiliating annoyance. In Rome the 'Jesuited' Popes and their Cardinal-Nephews might profess the utmost devotion to the Fathers, but their patronage was usually inexpensive. The Gesu church was open for public worship and the main symbol of the

Society. Yet when Vitelleschi died and for years afterwards its interior decoration was haphazard and of poor quality. The Society still had no authority over the choir and nave: control there belonged to the legal heirs of the founder, Cardinal Alessandro Farnese. The Jesuits could not afford to hire professional decorators for the side chapels, even that of Ignatius. Consequently some were decorated in a crude, amateur fashion by lay coadjutors who were more house painters than artists: others were decorated at the expense, and to the very individual tastes, of lay patrons. None of the 'Jesuited' Popes, not even the great friend of Bernini, Urban VIII, ever offered to finance the complete redecoration of the Gesu by experts to an overall design. In the 1620s the celebrations for the Jesuit canonisations had to be on a modest scale to suit Vitelleschi's purse. When Urban VIII condescended to pay for the centenary celebrations in 1640 he merely had the inner walls of the church discreetly hidden behind painted canvas screens. Meanwhile the Jesuits had the humiliation of knowing that the Capuchin mother church in Rome, built at Urban VIII's expense, was accounted the most tasteful and impressive building in the city: second came the Oratorian church and third the Theatine — the Gesu came nowhere in the competition. The other three Jesuit churches in Rome were not rated at all. They were merely used as domestic oratories for the noviciate and Colleges and had been decorated to Acquaviva's directions and at his expense in the cheapest and crudest manner possible.

No amount of papal favour and grants of legal privileges could protect the Society from a host of petty annoyances. Throughout Europe even papal and royal orders could not budge university authorities from their refusal to admit Jesuits and their pupils. In England and Holland bishops, Vicars-Apostolic and Chapters of secular clergy fought the Jesuits and successfully defied papal orders. In Spain the Spanish Inquisition finally won its case against the Society before a Roman Congregation and the Pope decided not to intervene in such a notorious hornets' nest. The Jesuit solution to the problem, tried out briefly and unsuccessfully after Vitelleschi's day, was to use royal influence to give the Society practical control of the Inquisition. The new Roman Congregation *de Propaganda Fide* spent all of Vitelleschi's Generalate in trying persistently to gain ultimate authority over Jesuit foreign missions. The General repeatedly beat off these attacks by appeals to the Pope. But the Congregation would not admit defeat and waited patiently for anti-Jesuit Popes.

In 1626 Cardinal Ludovisi, an ex-pupil and warm friend of the Jesuits, was reported to have said frankly that one of his main reasons for admiring the Society was '. . . the power and authority they have over nearly all our Princes . . .' In the same year the papal nuncio in Vienna wrote to the Pope:

> 'The Jesuits have attained overwhelming power. They have the upper hand over everything, even the most prominent ministers of State, and domineer over them if they do not carry out their will . . .'

What Ludovisi and the nuncio were saying had already become a European commonplace. Most statesmen now reckoned that the Society was a major force in politics, an international Great Power, acting primarily for its own interests. This, it was held, was a far greater Jesuit triumph than their influence over the Popes.

Before the 1620s Jesuits had long been royal confessors. Ignatius had issued warnings and directives on the subject and Acquaviva a celebrated set of instructions in 1602. So far the persons affected were ruling sovereigns of small states or Austrian archdukes. In Acquaviva's later days Henry IV of France and then the Regent, Marie de Medici, the Duke of Bavaria and Philip III of Spain took Jesuit confessors. Vitelleschi's Generalate saw the practice extended so widely and completely that by 1640 every Catholic ruler, except for the King of Poland and the Doge of Venice, was under Jesuit spiritual direction. In 1648 the chances of family history and politics were to bring a former Jesuit novice and Cardinal, John Casimir, to the throne of Poland. Nothing like this had ever happened since the golden age of the Dominicans and Franciscans in the 13th and 14th centuries.

Most contemporary political commentators, Catholic and Protestant alike, refused to believe that this astounding development was accidental, or that Jesuit direction stopped short at the monarchs' personal religion and morality. It was asserted confidently that the direction was vastly extended as the major weapon in a Jesuit master-plan to subject the rulers to themselves and weld them into a militant force crusading to destroy Protestantism once and for all and set Catholic states permanently under the Popes' sway. Incidentally, it was said, the Society was protecting its own interests. It would prove to Rome that the Society was incomparably the most powerful of clerical organisations, more efficient than papal nuncios and the other religious

Orders. Moreover 'the confessional policy' would gain the Society such a hold over Catholic rulers than even anti-Jesuit Popes would never dare to attack it.

To the commentators the Jesuit confessors' strategy was plain. They ensured that their power would be permanent by capturing every member of each royal family, especially the heirs. They arranged all royal marriages, helped by the fact that the inbreeding of European royalties meant that every betrothal needed expert Jesuit canonists to sort out degrees of consanguinity and affinity and secure papal dispensations. As guardians of sovereigns' consciences Jesuit confessors were generally entrusted with the vetting of all royal appointments, Church and secular. This enabled the confessors to plant their former pupils systematically in positions of importance and exclude known enemies of the Society. It seemed no secret that the confessors of the emperor and the Duke of Bavaria saw to it that key German bishoprics went to priests educated in Jesuit Colleges and at the Jesuit-directed *Germanicum* in Rome. The system extended to furthering the careers of the Jesuits' clients and providing them with profitable marriages. Thus the great Czech mercenary soldier, Wallenstein, was, so rumour said, converted from Protestantism by a Czech Jesuit, married off by him to a wealthy Moravian heiress, and then promoted by the emperor's Jesuit confessor to high commands in the Imperial army. It was no secret that Tilly, the celebrated Imperialist commander, rose in his career the same way. He had been in a Jesuit College, and then directed out of a Jesuit noviciate into the army.

The commentators habitually wrote of the Jesuit confessors and Vitelleschi as major European Powers. Richelieu, it seemed, feared Fathers Suffren and Caussin, not their penitents, the Queen Mother, Marie de Medici, and Louis XIII. When the emperor and the Duke of Bavaria seemed at odds, it was a personal vendetta between their confessors, Fathers Lamormaini and Contzen, ironed out only by the authority of Vitelleschi. The fall from power of Wallenstein and his murder by Imperial officers was interpreted as an act of hostility by Lamormaini against a man who had thrown off his subservience to the Society. It was taken for granted that Father Vieira, confessor to John IV of Portugal, decided his policies and personally negotiated his treaties.

The political commentators reported, as if it were a matter of course, very close involvement of Jesuits in almost all the political and military debates and operations of the age. Thus, for instance, the sensational seizure of Donauwörth in 1609 by Bavarian troops and its forcible Catholicisation involved Jesuit confessors and missioners. The event was celebrated enthusiastically in indifferent Latin verse by several German Jesuit College professors. At the famous 'defenestration of Prague' in 1618 two of the Imperial envoys hurled out of the palace window on to a heap of manure by Czech Protestant rebels were Czech Jesuit priests. Jesuit confessors were habitually present, sometimes in their capacity as Councillors of State, at the planning of military operations during the Thirty Years' War. Grave clashes of interest between the great Catholic states, especially the pro-Protestant policies of Richelieu, the French statesman, produced anguished consultations between Vitelleschi and the confessors of the sovereigns concerned. There was Jesuit lobbying and the printers were kept busy turning out Jesuit books designed to teach Catholic statesmen their religious and moral duties. Richelieu was stung and infuriated by vigorously written little books with titles like *Mysteria Politica* and *On Heresy*. Jesuit army chaplains accompanied troops into battle and were killed or wounded on almost every major battlefield of the time from Lützen to Basing House. Shock brigades of Jesuits were drafted hastily from College professorships into newly-conquered Protestant territories to work closely with the occupying forces in evicting determined heretics and converting wavering ones. They distinguished themselves especially in the Catholicisation of Bohemia, Moravia and the Palatinate. As the Thirty Years' War progressed they dodged perilously in and out of areas which changed hands several times: Jesuit Colleges were improvised in places like Nuremburg, Heidelberg and Rinteln and then just as hastily abandoned. German, Belgian and French Jesuits became the 'hammers' of witchcraft which was widely regarded in the Society as a consequence of the spread of Protestantism. The age's standard textbook on witchcraft, covens, demonism and the detection and trial of offenders was written by a Belgian Jesuit. Jesuits were prominent in hunts for witches in Germany: Jesuit specialists were at the heart of cases of demonism in France at Loudoun, in Brittany, in Spain and even in southern England. Ardently political or militaristic sermons by Jesuits became commonplace. In Brazil and Portugal Vieira, the greatest Jesuit orator of the age, exhorted his congregations to arms. In Brazil he thundered:

'Are we going to lie down and let heretics take over Brazil, all South America, Portugal and Spain — or are we going to fight for our faith?'

He was the epitome of Portuguese armed resistance to Dutch attacks in Brazil. Back in Portugal he helped his colleagues to engineer the overthrow of Spanish occupying forces and the establishment of national independence under the House of Braganza. In England, during the Civil Wars and Interregnum, the Jesuits maintained a prudent detachment from politics but the Provincial took part in secret negotiations in 1651 between Catholic leaders and Independent generals and politicians.

In grave emergencies the Jesuits themselves took up arms. At Prague Father Plachy, a professor of Scripture, led seventy armed colleagues in the defence of a section of the city walls against a Swedish army assault. In Macao Adam von Schall, always choleric and then still a Jesuit student preparing for the Peking Mission, saw action in skirmishes with Dutch corsairs attacking the colony. Later in Peking during the chaotic years of the collapse of the Ming dynasty and irruption of the Manchus, he once defended his mission house effectively, wielding a Japanese sword against armed marauders. Jesuit missionaries trained and led Indian militia units beating off the raids of São Paulo slavers on the South American Reductions. In the English Civil Wars a few Jesuits courted dismissal from the Society by taking up arms as gentlemen-volunteers in the forces of Charles I.

The commentators could also report on Jesuit skill in the acquisition of landed property and in commercial transactions. In Seville the lay coadjutor-procurator of Spain's largest Jesuit College tried to tide over a slump in rents and dividends by disastrous investments in the Atlantic shipping business. The English Provincial took up shares in Lord Baltimore's Maryland Company, occupying his 'Adventurer's allotment' of Indian lands with missioners, English farm settlers recruited at a London office and negro slaves. In the Far Eastern missions most Jesuit procurators still tried to make ends meet by dabbling in exchange and bullion transactions and in the China trade. In South America and the Antilles Jesuit procurators worked *haciendas* and Reductions by organising forced labour and the export of cinchona, tobacco, cacao and sugar to Europe. In 1629 the emperor's confessor, Lamormaini, secured the grudging consent of his master to a famous Edict of Restitution. This ensured that every scrap of old Church property in German Protestant hands should be reclaimed without compensation as occasion (mostly military conquest) offered. The Papacy and the crown were to get their fair share, and the Society the choicest parts of what was left for distribution. Thenceforward German Jesuit superiors became notorious for their appropriation of the best recovered Church properties and beating off the counter-claims of bishops and other religious Orders. It was said that Wallenstein's disenchantment with the Society stemmed mainly from his indignation at their barefaced avarice: they habitually got hold of the most productive lands in his allotment of north German duchies, demanded his protection from counter-claimants and Protestant attackers, and frightened out of the duchies most skilled labour because the workmen happened to be loyal Protestants. Meanwhile in Portugal the services of the Jesuits to the House of Braganza were rewarded by John IV with lavish grants of ecclesiastical sinecures, the abbacies and priorships of mostly extinct religious communities with large properties and rent-rolls. Such grants were flatly contrary to the *Constitutions*. But orders from the General to give up the grants were denied promulgation in the kingdom by John IV.

No other single achievement of the 17th-century Jesuits brought them more publicity, prestige and enmity than their Court confessorships and political activities. The legend of their political skill, confessional 'expertise' and sheer Machiavellianism became very strong and enduring. Hence in the 18th century when the Society had lost many of its confessorships, its papal and royal enemies planned its destruction nervously with the sort of show of police and military force normally required against a powerful hostile state. Even in the later 19th century when the restored Society was weak, otherwise well-informed politicians still credited it with a quite unique political skill and influence.

How much truth was there in the legend? Many features of 17th-century 'Jesuitry', real or legendary, were widespread among practically all groups of Catholic clergy. The very strong religious movement of reaction and Puritanism which historians call 'the Counter-Reformation' had gripped the Roman Curia and the Popes. Commentators frequently refer to the zelanti of the curia, who were distinct from its 'Jesuited' members and often critical of them and the Society, as altogether too worldly. The Popes of Vitelleschi's day needed no memories of their schooldays under the Jesuits or promptings from the General to pursue rigorously theocratic and crusading policies.

Gregory XV, for instance, ordered the papal flag to be flown alongside the Imperial colours into battle with Protestants. He encouraged the emperor in uncompromising language:

> 'The almighty God of vengeance has chosen you to be the instrument of his wrath against his enemies . . .'

Gregory issued detailed instructions to his nuncio in Germany, Carafa, who was supervising the forcible Catholicisation of Bohemia and the Palatinate. The nuncio was to set his face against the political, compromising attitudes of Imperial officials and chaplains — he needed no urging. He had already complained bitterly of the mildness towards Protestants of the emperor's former Jesuit tutor and confessor, Martin Becanus. He now reported:

> '. . . under the pressure of fear many hastened to be instructed . . . and since then God, little by little, has purified their dispositions and they have embraced the Catholic religion . . .'

Urban VIII approved, and Carafa supervised, military *dragonnades* in Austria to liquidate surviving Protestant enclaves. Carafa's reports had as their theme a text from Isaiah: 'that suffering may teach them'.

The other great religious Orders, new Congregations, bishops and educated secular priests were not by any means behindhand in 'Counter-Reformation' zeal. In Germany Capuchins, Dominicans, Franciscans, Augustinians and even Benedictines shared in the work of Catholicising conquered areas and 'resuming' Church property. The Capuchins, who were more numerous than the Jesuits and not, like them, so often tied up in College teaching in relatively safe and solid Catholic districts, bore the main burden of the work. In France the whole country was a swarming hive of clerical activity, of 'reforming' lax, neglected or moribund monastic or women's Orders, founding seminaries and schools, holding intensive missions across the countryside, and running large hostels for the 'newly converted' Protestants who had been peacefully but somewhat forcibly converted to Catholicism and who were ostracised by their families and destitute. This great ferment of earnest religiosity hitting a country where laxity, scepticism and reversion to superstition had been paramount during the half century of religious war produced a monstrous crop of psychological and mental disorders and demonism. Astrologers, magicians and exorcists flourished in such an atmosphere. In the turmoil Jesuit efforts often seemed swamped by those of very numerous fellow workers. Great nunneries cheerfully received reforming help simultaneously, or in rapid succession, from Carmelites, Recollets, Jesuits, Capuchins, canons and secular priests. The system of Jesuit Colleges and seminaries seemed overrun by similar establishments run by Oratorians or Congregations of secular priests. In many cases the founders of these Congregations, very able men like de Condren, de Bérulle, Eudes, Olier and Gibieuf, were ex-pupils of the Society. Almost to a man they had grown up peacefully in its ways, then had very seriously considered becoming Jesuits before sheering off to follow independent and rigoristic paths of their own making. In the process their originally friendly relations with the Society degenerated into rivalry and criticism and then into outright hostility.

What was even more disconcerting for the Jesuits was the mushroom growth of a strong, hostile 'episcopalianism'. This was an idea that, by divine law, the natural directors of the Church's affairs and 'Counter-Reformation' evangelism were the secular clergy led by their bishops and not the Papacy and Roman Curia or the religious Orders. The main propagandists for this theory were the founders of the French Congregations, especially Pierre de Bérulle, a man of great charm and force of character and well-connected at Court. He insisted that an adequately trained secular clergy would have all the skills and good points of the active religious Orders and none of their faults and shortcomings. In his vision of the Catholic Church of the future there was practically no room for active, evangelistic religious Orders linked to Rome and so privileged by it that they were practically independent of episcopal jurisdiction. Thus the Society would become completely redundant. The Jesuits had tended to think of the secular clergy as a multitude of ignorant, peasant Mass-mongers best brigaded as auxiliaries of the Orders under the guidance of an elite of Jesuit-educated priests, themselves devoted to the Society. The practical Jesuit idea of the episcopate was of a host of aristocratic, ignorant absentees and idlers kept on the shelf by a Jesuit-educated elite of bishops anxious to cooperate with the Society.

The 'episcopalian' movement began with a noisy battle of books in the 1620s. The existing English secular clergy opposition to Jesuit dominance of the English Mission had a great stroke of luck. The patronage of Charles I and his French Catholic Queen, Henrietta Maria, secured from Rome the appointment of the first English bishop not bound by the terms of his commission to bow to Jesuit influences, Richard Smith. Smith, a university graduate and convert from Anglicanism, was long a student and teacher in Jesuit seminaries. He underwent a violent conversion from ardent 'Jesuitism' to 'episcopalianism' under the auspices of his friend de Bérulle and was the theological tutor and friend of the great Cardinal Richelieu. He was an angular, choleric, combative man with no gift of diplomacy. Once in England he issued a shower of episcopal directives of a very uncompromising kind and made a head-on attack on Jesuit privileges. De Bérulle and the French Congregations took his side with great vigour and the affair became a great propaganda effort for their movement. Jesuit influence in Rome was strong enough to defeat Smith. He eventually withdrew sulkily to Paris, refusing to haul down his colours. He was a renowned spiritual director and pillar of 'the Counter-Reformation' and widely regarded by his party as a saint and martyr. His tombstone in the graveyard of an English convent in Paris had an inscription directed at the Society:

Betrayed by false brethren.

Meanwhile the 'episcopalian' flag was going into battle elsewhere. An increasing number of French bishops, even those educated by the Jesuits, favoured the Congregations. François de Sales, the greatest evangelist and hammer of heretics of them all and the author of the century's classical work of spirituality, *An Introduction to the Devout Life*, was an ex-pupil of the Society and accounted its devoted friend. Yet even he showed signs of wavering. Vincent de Paul, not a bishop but an immensely influential French 'apostle of the poor', showed a quiet but increasing sympathy for the 'episcopalians'. The French assembly of bishops empowered the Bishop of Rouen, with backing from the Roman *Propaganda* to exercise ordinary jurisdiction over French Canada and put an end to the practical monopoly of the Jesuits there. In England the secular clergy Chapter set up by Bishop Smith to exercise episcopal authority in his name after his departure from the country negotiated with the *Propaganda* to get the Maryland Mission taken away from the Society and transferred to secular priest missioners. In Italy the 'episcopalian' movement had unusually deep roots running back through Carlo Borromeo, the dictatorial Archbishop of Milan. It now took on a new lease of life as local Congregations were founded in large numbers to take over seminaries, reform convents, evangelise the countryside and open schools. In war-torn Germany and Austria the Society had hoped that it had the favour, or at least the measure, of most bishops since it had educated the best of them in its Colleges or the *Germanicum* in Rome. But there were now disturbing signs of concerted episcopal opposition to the Society led by the arch-bishops of Vienna, Prague, Olomouc and Cologne. Kesl of Vienna and von Harrach of Prague, both Cardinals, were particularly bitter opponents.

In Vitelleschi's last years Spain produced the most formidable of all 'episcopalian' leaders, Juan de Palafox y Mendoza. Though the illegitimate son of a marquis and a favourite of Philip IV's chief minister, Olivares, Palafox was no mere aristocratic careerist. He was a great patriot, a dedicated Church reformer and evangelist, a mystic and a writer deeply influenced by de Bérulle's ideas. In 1639 he arrived in Mexico as Bishop of Puebla and the Government's Visitor of New Spain. Within a short time Olivares had secured his appointment as viceroy and archbishop-primate and backed his radical reforming schemes wholeheartedly. The downtrodden Creoles, the secular clergy and, for reasons all their own, most of the other religious Orders supported his assault on corrupt officials, clerical concubinage and the Jesuits. He set about creating an episcopally-controlled network of seminaries and schools to challenge the Jesuits' monopoly of the higher reaches of education. He also challenged sharply the Society's legal immunity from episcopal visitation and certain forms of taxation. When Vitelleschi was dying in 1644 the 'Palafox Affair' was gathering momentum right across South America and back to Spain. Young Jesuit firebrands were staging demonstrations by pupils and supporters and planning an aggres-sive march on Puebla. Vitelleschi was despatching a stream of appeals and protests to the Pope and the King of Spain. Arch-bishop Palafox was destined, far more than de Bérulle, Richard Smith or Cardinal Kesl, to become the uncanonised saint of the 'episcopalians' as their movement endured on strongly into the 18th century.

If the Society had no monopoly of 'Counter-Reformation' zeal it was also far from being unique in its touchily defensive reactions, its hunt for positions of influence, its building up of cliques of supporters and its taste for intrigue. The ecclesiastical world of the 17th century 'Counter-Reformation' was crowded with organisations, old and new, all ruled by autocrats. The crowding produced very strong competition for positions of influence. Autocratic rule had now crept into old Orders which had always prided themselves on their democratic Chapter rule: autocracy was rife even in the new Congregations. Large elements of Acquaviva's Jesuit discipline were borrowed by these organisations which were its hot rivals. In spite of his charm of manner and exalted spirituality de Bérulle ruled his penitents and the Carmelite convents under his direction with a rod of iron. When the Jesuits sought help from the Pope, his nuncios and the King of France, de Bérulle naturally applied to his penitent, the royal Duke of Orleans, and to Cardinal Richelieu.

In the 17th century and long afterwards the Society's enemies accused it of having a secret intelligence service of agents, male and female, secretly vowed to its service but dressed and living as secular priests, bishops, nuns, laymen and laywomen. The great storm aroused by Mary Ward's *Institute* or 'Jesuitesses', the ferocity with which the Roman Curia dissolved it, and the speed with which the General dissociated himself and its supporters among the English Jesuits from the venture was something more than merely a manifestation of male chauvinism. The Jesuits certainly did have associates and supporters of many kinds. In the 'dangerous missions' it had some hundreds of secular clergy who worked under obedience to Jesuit missioners. These men, called 'Ignatians' by their opponents in England, had been educated in Jesuit-run seminaries, were directed spiritually by Jesuits, and sometimes had taken private vows to enter the Society. In English mission-conditions, where no Catholic clergy wore clerical costumes, it was often impossible for even Catholics to identify Jesuits with any certainty. To this day there is no certainty whether Toby Mathew, a distinguished English convert priest much around the Court of Charles I, was a Jesuit or not. Papal agents asserted confidently that he was: Jesuit historians have reported that there is no surviving evidence either way. A great many ex-pupils of the Jesuits retained for life their membership of College Sodalities or Congregations of the Blessed Virgin. The Society had a few oblates whose precise relationship to it was always obscure. Although the *Constitutions* expressly forbade Jesuits to undertake regular direction of communities of nuns the rule was often dispensed. By the early 17th century the great majority of English convents on the continent had regular Jesuit confessors. The practice was widespread and that of borrowing Jesuit forms of discipline and devotion even commoner. There were numerous women penitents of Jesuits. These penitents could take private vows of obedience to their confessors and live, in effect, as pious confraternities under their direction. Finally there were, in addition to Jesuit lay-coadjutors and hired lay servants in Jesuit houses, male *donnés* or pious, unmarried lay tradesmen who took service in French Canada with missionaries.

Jesuit apologists have always firmly denied that this host of 'followers' ever had anything more than a spiritual connection with the Society or that they were ever employed as weapons in politico-religious lobbying. They point out that the veil of secrecy was simply and solely a necessary part of a confidential, confessional relationship with the Society. The apologists have, though much less emphatically, pointed out that almost every other religious Order in the 17th century and some secular clergy had their 'tails' of followers and secret societies. Pious societies of every kind proliferated in Catholic society. The wills of the well-to-do devout almost always revealed that they belonged to a multiplicity of pious societies. The Carmelites, Capuchins, Dominicans, Franciscans, Recollets and monks all, as a matter of course, had private followings of confraternities, convents, oblates and strings of closely directed penitents. Vincent de Paul was the founder of a rash of secret '*AA*' societies and de Bérulle formed committees to drum up support for Carmelite convents. France's most powerful, and eventually most-hated, religious confraternity, the *Compagnie du Saint Sacrement*, concealed the names of both its directors and its members.

In such a world therefore why should Jesuit secret societies have been singled out for special censure? The reason cannot have been their mere existence, their size or their secrecy, none of which features made them specially remarkable. Their underground activities in support of their directors seem to have been neither more nor less sinister than those of the supporters of other religious bodies. It is rather unlikely that Jesuit societies displayed any very unusual degree of exclusiveness. The Society had its inner circles of supporters who would have nothing to do with 'alien' groups: but other Orders and Congregations aroused the same sort of narrow devotion. On the other hand Wallenstein's lack of that type of exclusiveness was not so rare. He founded a Jesuit College on his Bohemian estates, supported the Capuchins and Carmelites, built a Carthusian monastery and chose to site his family mausoleum in its chapel. Lamormaini found such liberalism sinister but other Jesuits did not. Eminent French Jesuits like Coton and Surin had happy relationships with their brothers and sisters who had joined other Orders. A considerable number of ex-pupils of the Society joined other Orders or became secular priests. Megerle, a German Augustinian superior and preacher of great distinction, was formerly a pupil in a Jesuit College and then did his theological studies in a Benedictine Academy. He, like a good many others of his kind, remained friendly with the Society.

The Jesuits, of course, had no monopoly of ecclesiastical and political intrigue. The prevailing autocracy of civil and ecclesiastical government bred, as it still does today in similar circumstances, a remarkably high degree of outward conformism and moralism combined with a mass of secret intrigue and evasion. Even the holiest and most scrupulous of persons living under such a system automatically acquired a high degree of dexterity in using influence, lobbying, bribery and intrigue. François de Sales used extraordinary manoeuvres in his battle to keep his Order of the Visitation free from canonical enclosure. Vitelleschi used exactly the same means in his fight to keep the Ursuline sisters free from the same restrictions, a fight needing all the more subtlety since his opponents were not only the Roman Curia but a large body of Jesuit opinion.

In 1645, taking into account all these circumstances and its size, the Society was undoubtedly the tidiest and most respectable of all Orders except for the Carthusians. It had its fringe of villains. In 1621 a Jesuit priest in South America, Gaspar de Villenas, was arraigned before the Inquisition for soliciting at least ninety-seven women, including nuns, in the confessional and having sexual intercourse with thirty of them on church premises. In 1649 Adam von Schall, superior of the Peking Mission, was nicknamed 'the old Adam' or 'the Adam who fell' by his mission colleagues. They forwarded to the Gesu a round robin asking for his dismissal from the Society because of his scandalous manner of life, brutal arrogance and compromises with paganism. There were certainly Jesuit careerists. The General Congregations of 1615 and 1645 complained about the increasing numbers of Fathers who found every excuse to hang for years round the Gesu in Rome soliciting favours or appointments or who devoted all their influence to furthering the careers of their relatives. De Vermi, the Jesuit confessor of the Viceroy of Naples, travelled without leave to Madrid to wangle an appointment to a bishopric for himself. After his dismissal from the Society he did become a bishop. Antonio de Dominis, an Italian Jesuit student, cherished the same ambition but voluntarily quitted the Society before his appointment to the Archbishopric of Spalato. Later he became a great embarrassment to the Roman Curia and the Society. He took the side of the Venetian Govern-

ment in its quarrel with Rome, fled to England to embrace
Anglicanism and become Dean of Windsor, repented and
returned to Rome where the Curia committed him to the care of
the Society. He joined a select band of eccentrics and oddities
for whose perpetual confinement the General was made responsible. They included Jesuits like Antonio Vieira (rescued from the
Inquisition's gaols in Brazil where he was under sentence for
his wild apocalyptic speculations) and Didier Cheminot, and
non-Jesuits like the Dominican heresiarch, Campanella.
Cheminot, who had been confessor to the Duke of Lorraine, had,
in 1637, openly defended his penitent's bigamous marriage, and
was for a time excommunicated.

However, these Jesuit scandals were relatively infrequent.
The Society had the facility, denied to almost all its rivals, of
promptly dismissing offenders who were in perpetual simple
vows. The other Orders were compelled to carry heavy burdens
of eccentrics, the mentally unstable and villains, trying to cope
with them by floggings, confinement in the Orders' prisons or
more or less deliberate provocation to take refuge in flight. In
the estimation of good judges, the average Jesuit was a gentleman, better bred, cleaner, and better educated than his monk or
friar counterpart.

The judgement was a relative, not an absolute, one. For a
combination of religious, social and economic reasons western
Europe contained a great surfeit of civil officials and clergymen.
An abnormally large slice of the male population entered religious
organisations, the Society included, and brought with them their
native variety of dispositions which even Jesuit training could not
eliminate. A relatively small minority of Jesuits embraced the
principles and disciplines of the Society and the 'Counter-
Reformation' with a specially literal, even fanatical, intensity.
Lamormaini, Contzen, Vieira, William Weston, perhaps John
Gerard at times, Garasse and some unrepentently ferocious
French Jesuit *Ligeurs*, and German Jesuit haters of Protestants
and witches like Mayrhofen and Binsfeld came in this category.
They were often hair-raisingly absolutist in their ideas on
authority and unbalanced in their ferocious persecution of
Protestants, Jews, 'New Christians', French converts from
Protestantism, liberals, scientists and harmlessly eccentric old
women. Some of these fanatics dabbled in astrology, apocalyptic
theories and Rosicrucianism. From their extreme views proceeded their 'holy follies' which provided Protestant controversialists and political commentators with an abundance of

'Jesuitical' case-histories. Most of the Jesuit fanatics bore a charmed life in the Society, protected from expulsion by the four vows of Profession. They endured severe reprimands by the General but rarely suffered any disciplinary action worse than being moved to a higher post in a quieter area. Vieira's wild apocalyptic eventually landed him in an Inquisition gaol in Brazil. Vitelleschi's successor as General instructed him to resign 'voluntarily' from the Society and enter some other religious Order. But the King of Portugal, with some connivance from Vieira, blocked the execution of the General's instruction and negotiated a compromise. Vieira was released and rusticated to the Gesu. There his intelligence, charm and marvellous sermons so moved the General that he was eventually allowed to return to Brazil for the rest of his life. John Gerard's association with the Gunpowder Plot in England and his enthusiastic support of Mary Ward's 'Jesuitesses' led eventually to his rustication to the continent for good. The move was humiliating and painful, but the blow was tempered by promotion to Profession of the four vows.

Jesuit major superiors formed a different category: they were in no way fanatics or disposed to master-mind crusades or grandiose schemes for increasing the Society's power. They accepted the Acquaviva system and the 'Counter-Reformation' automatically and conventionally, without deep reflection or passion. Their profession and disposition of mind inclined them to an habitual pessimism, great caution and a taste for compromises. Vitelleschi, like Acquaviva, made no secret of his grave doubts about almost every major Jesuit enterprise, the new Colleges and universities, the Court confessorships, the wholesale acceptance of captured German establishments, the missionary advances in Canada, Maryland, Peking and India. These superiors were, often in a bumbling way, incessant intriguers. But their intrigues, elaborate compromises and cover-ups had little about them of the crudity and murderous ferocity favoured by the fanatics.

The Jesuit monopoly of Court confessorships was not consciously planned by either Acquaviva or Vitelleschi. Like the Society's hold on Catholic schools it grew up very gradually, partly by accident, partly due to local initiatives by Jesuit fanatics or careerists, partly by rather grudging Gesu concessions to the demands of sovereigns. By ancient custom all European sovereigns maintained large clerical establishments of chaplains, deans, almoners, confessors, secretaries, tutors, musicians and choristers. As far as possible these establishments were paid for out of Church revenues. During most of the 16th century respectable clergy avoided service at Court whenever possible. With good reason Court clerics were reckoned laxists and racketeers. Incursions into this dangerous ground, particularly in Portugal, by Jesuit pioneers in the Society's early days had all ended in scandal and disaster and the Gesu banned further efforts. But by the later 16th century a combination of new circumstances forced a very reluctant Acquaviva to relax the ban. The 'Counter-Reformation' effort involved 'the reform of Princes', an operation regarded by the devout as quite as hazardous and meritorious as trying to convert sailors and prostitutes or going on 'dangerous missions' to the heathen. The new-found reputation of the Jesuits as schoolmasters automatically provided them with what seemed a safe and honourable way of influencing Court life for the better. Royal persons began to demand Jesuit tutors for their sons. The task, as experiments conducted at Ingolstadt and in France showed, could not be performed in a seemly manner inside Colleges. Kings were pleased because the Jesuit tutors would not (except in Portugal, always a trouble-spot) take pay in cash or benefices. The Jesuit fanatics were pleased because it was a short step from being a tutor to becoming the pupils' confessor and lifelong mentor. The death rate among royal children brought up in the grossly insanitary atmosphere of Courts was so high that every royal prince, however low in the legal order of succession at the time of his birth, had a sporting chance of ending his life as sovereign. Moreover, as the fanatics pointed out to the Generals who were especially moved by this sort of argument, if the Society did not sieze its Court opportunities they would be forestalled by the Capuchins, or, worse, the Dominicans with disastrous consequences.

There was yet another factor which helped to move the Jesuits in force into Court service. This was their growing popular reputation as the kindest, most sympathetic and skilled of confessors for the wayward and backsliders, types found in great numbers at Court. In 1640 a group of Belgian Jesuits produced *Imago Primi Saeculi*, a small volume to commemorate the Society's first centenary. It abounded in rhetoric and exaggerations and its publication is today dismissed by almost all Jesuit historians as a minor disaster. But its text does convey what many Jesuits and their supporters thought about the Society. The writers exulted in its success in the confessional:

'. . . a Society of angels . . . changing the face of Christendom . . . they have become besieged by crowds seeking confession and piety, and have put more gladness and joy into piety and penance than there is in sinning . . .'

Private confession to priests occupied a surprisingly modest place in the traditional Catholic scheme of religious practices. It was quite dwarfed by a massive alternative system of public penance, public admissions of guilt, dramatic and almost ceremonial public penances, and dramatic, publicised reconciliations. Notorious sinners were solemnly reconciled to decent society. Vendettas were settled by ceremonies in which long-standing enemies kissed each other and took oaths of eternal friendship. This elaborate business was conducted in part in Church law courts by archdeacons, bishops' representatives and Inquisitors, and in part less formally by parish priests and visiting missioners, friars, monks or Jesuits. The public system left little room for private confession except for the very scrupulous needing reassurance, the dying and intending communicants. Even for these classes of penitents, it was difficult to find opportunities for really private confessions. Churches at or just before service-times were tightly packed and confessional boxes were still rare in 1645. A private penitent would have to shuffle forward through the press of people into a queue and then confess very briefly and baldly standing within easy earshot of many. Churches on weekdays were places of secular business not of quiet religiosity. Most priests and penitents were so ignorant that any sort of confession could only be extracted by the simplest and bluntest of questionings. Death-beds and child-beds, where private confession might seem most appropriate, were usually very crowded and public occasions. The internal arrangements of most mid-17th century houses, even mansions, were such that few inmates and visiting priests could enjoy much unhindered privacy. Most people communicated exceedingly rarely, many only once or twice in a lifetime.

The clergy, living in presbyteries or religious houses of the old Orders, undoubtedly used private confession much more than any other class in society. This was simply because most of them were priests and bound to say Mass on certain fixed occasions. Nevertheless they used private confession much less than we might imagine. Most of them said Mass only once or twice a week. Many lived such disorderly lives that they avoided confession for years. The old religious Orders lived a life which, by rule, reflected the religious customs of ordinary society. They had a highly developed system of public penance, with compulsory open confessions in Chapter, public penances, floggings and conventual prisons.

It was the great movement of 'devotion' in the later Middle Ages and 16th century which developed private confession from a rather obscure formality into a complex and vitally important part of popular religious practice. The 'devout' saw immense potentialities in it as a means of Grace almost as important as Holy Communion, a real Sacrament. They made much of its power of forgiveness and penance, but more still of its power to give deep self-knowledge, spiritual direction and rapid progress towards holiness. The 'devout' developed techniques of frequent and general confessions, of direction by confessors, of private vows of obedience to them. All these novel techniques were institutionalised by the 'Observant' Orders including the Jesuits. The *Constitutions* of such Orders invariably made such practices compulsory for their members and supporters and either much reduced, or almost totally abolished, the old conventual systems of public confessions and penances. This new ideal of the private, individual spiritual life brought with it structural changes in Observant religious houses and in parish churches used by the 'devout'. The old common dormitories and cloisters were partitioned off into private 'cells' and wooden, free-standing confessional boxes lined the side walls of some city parish churches. The advent of the vogue for intensive private confession swept the urban areas of Catholic Europe through the 16th century and took a still deeper grip on them in the 17th century. But the ancient public system died very hard and slowly. In 1645 it remained a popular attraction in towns, especially in Spain and Italy, and still dominated rural areas.

The Jesuits were born into the 'devotion' movement and Observant confessional practice. From the start their students were educated not only in scholastic theology but in 'Cases'. This was a special training course for private confessors mainly created by Dominicans at Salamanca. It was purpose-built to meet the needs of confessors who were now expected to be 'doctors of the soul'. The old system of penance took practically no account of sinners' intentions or of factors like inadvertence or ignorance which might have reduced their culpability. The 'Cases' course had to train priests in the art of deep cross-examination of penitents to discover their mental processes. They had also to know how to train regular penitents in self-knowledge and self-examination. The course included practical exercises where the professors or selected students 'went to confession' to the class, simulating various types of penitents in different sorts of difficulties. At table during students' meals the professors propounded knotty 'cases' and the students were expected to debate how to deal with them. As the courses developed the ingenuity of the professors led them into 'confessional research'. They got permission to spend holiday periods confessing penitents in particularly difficult areas like seaports. Their research taught them that the cut-and-dried traditional moral code, designed many centuries before to go with the system of public penance, often bore little relationship to the realities of 16th- and 17th-century life. Its code of sexual practice in part reflected the austere mentality of medieval monks and in part the anxiety of administrators of a primitive and violent society to stamp out every threat to the security of family life and private property. The old code treated merchants and moneylenders as public enemies, a view which might have been tenable in the Dark Ages but which was demonstrably unjust in the 16th century. Moreover, that century had a host of moral problems about which the old code gave no real guidance. These were the products of the spread of education, commerce and banking, the European colonisation of America and the Far East, the growth of governmental and Church autocracy, bureaucracy and regulations, and the confusions produced by the Protestant Reformation. Inevitably therefore the casuists, headed by the Dominicans at Salamanca, began very cautiously to modify and supplement the rules of the old code.

The early Society took over piecemeal the Dominican system of training in 'Cases'. The early Jesuit confessors were busy, practical, unintellectual men and the Society's training and discipline still makeshift. So there was no uniform Jesuit confessional technique and their 'Cases' courses tended to be distinctly conservative compared with those of the Salamanca Dominicans. By the time of Acquaviva and Vitelleschi things had changed. Training and discipline were far tighter. Casuistry was booming in universities and Academies. Every Order and the secular clergy now had acknowledged masters of casuistry who all published textbooks. There were brisk academic wars over disputed judgements on particularly difficult cases. The Society now had its own master casuists the greatest of whom were Thomas Sanchez, Vasquez and Laymann. It also had its own distinctive style of preaching, devotions and confessional technique. It was popularly supposed that while the confessors of some Orders, particularly the Capuchins and Dominicans, were constantly inclined to err on the side of severity, and those of other Orders to be slack and slovenly, the Jesuit confessors were particularly thorough and yet marvellously flexible. They tended, it was said, to adjust their manner to each penitent's disposition. If he or she were a proficient in devotion, the confessor would be very severe, even brutal. With beginners or habitual sinners he would be all encouragement and gentleness until the penitent was converted: then the iron hand in the Jesuit velvet glove would begin to appear. Penances were used flexibly. Even in cases of grave sin they could be light or nominal. In cases of small sins committed by the devout they could be very severe. Absolution might be granted immediately: in other cases it might be withheld until a course of penance had been completed. Jesuit confessors expected to be obeyed absolutely. They granted Communions or withheld them. They decided vocations, packing off some penitents into Carmels or Charterhouses or ordering others to leave noviciates or move from one Order to another. Jesuit confessors were even flexible about the highest matters of principle. They could instruct proficients always, in questions disputed even by the master casuists, to follow the hardest and 'safest' of the opinions: they could order painfully scrupulous souls to follow the most libertarian of the opinions, even if only one single master casuist had proposed it in the teeth of all his colleagues. In fact lay enthusiasts for Jesuit confessional direction asserted boldly that they were the best of all the Orders, the greatest converters of hardened sinners, and the surest guides through all the moral complexities of life. Whether that judgement was true or not is disputed. What cannot be disputed is that a great many 17th-century sovereigns, courtiers and aristocrats believed it to be true.

In the last decades of the 16th century as the reactionary 'Counter-Reformation' movement gained momentum there were increasingly widespread and harsh criticisms of the rationalistic approach of the great casuists to moral problems and their modifications of the strictness of the ancient code. The use of a kind and indulgent manner toward penitents also came under fire. Among Jesuits the casuists Vasquez and Thomas Sanchez were attacked violently. Sanchez' treatise on marriage caused great anger and he was labelled prurient, a sensualist and a laxist. Acquaviva and Vitelleschi, exactly like the major superiors of all other Orders, did their best to clip the wings of their casuists and caution confessors. Jesuit students were instructed to use only the 'Cases' textbook of Laymann, a Jesuit of unimpeachable conservatism and a sharp critic of his colleague Sanchez. By the 1640s the Dominicans, who had, for the most part, now abandoned their moral liberalism for staunch conservatism, insisted that, in spite of the Society's officially conservative moral doctrine, its casuists and confessors habitually tended towards laxism. The popularity of Jesuits as confessors among sovereigns, courtiers and libertines in general was, the Dominicans said, based on a cheat. The root of the trouble, they insisted, was not merely human respect and a love of popularity but a false theology: the Jesuits were humanists not orthodox Christians. This was something more serious than another flare-up in the long running battle between Jesuits and Dominicans: in the 1650s the Dominican charges were to be supported widely among all the Society's enemies.

Naturally the brunt of the attack fell on the Jesuit Court confessors. They were also unpopular in the Society at large and at the Gesu. General Congregation after General Congregation, speaking for the Provincial Congregations, complained about their arrogance, independent attitude toward the General and involvement in politics and patronage deals. The Generals had plenty to complain about. In Portugal Vieira's successor, Nunez, accepted a seat on the Council of State, took gifts of abbeys and priories for his Province, and sheltered himself from Gesu reprimands behind the king's protection. In France a succession of royal confessors, Coton, Suffren and Caussin, became hopelessly involved in the political opposition to Richelieu and were dismissed from office by him. Coton, in particular, carried devotion to the crown and French nationalism to extremes. In Bavaria and Austria the Court confessors were constantly in trouble. Becanus and Masen were censured by the Roman Curia and the Gesu for their support of Court factions which favoured the toleration of Protestantism. Lamormaini and Contzen habitually put their duty to their princes before obedience to Rome and the General and were censured for their murderous fanaticism. They could not be removed from office without grave danger to the Society's interests in the empire. Cheminot in Lorraine and de Vermi in Naples were convicted of grossly scandalous behaviour. The track-record of the Court confessors was appalling. Meanwhile the Courts they served, though outwardly more moral and religious than in the 16th century, were far from being schools of piety. From the point of view of the

'Counter-Reformation' and the Jesuit fanatics themselves the Court confessors failed. They did not arrest the steady decay of Spanish power. They did not prevent Richelieu and Mazarin from pursuing a nationalistic policy which repeatedly saved the Protestant cause in northern Europe. In Germany the confessors actually fomented bitter quarrels in the ranks of the Catholic crusaders and so bore much of the blame for what the fanatics and *zelanti* regarded as the shameful and godless compromises of the Peace of Westphalia in 1648. The Gesu could take scant comfort from the fact that the few Court confessors and politicians drawn from other Orders had been equally unsuccessful. In Spain, Philip IV's long flirtations with a Carmelite nun director and a Carmelite confessor did not make the Court more pious or Spain less depressed. The pious-political schemes of Richelieu's agent, the Capuchin Joseph du Tremblay, were even more tortuous and perverse than those of his Jesuit opponent, Lamormaini. The French Capuchin confessors at the English Court of Queen Henrietta Maria signally failed to budge Charles I from his stolid Anglicanism. The confessors themselves mostly behaved scandalously: one or two took flight from their Order and others were gravely suspected of gross immorality.

For their part the Jesuit Court confessors felt aggrieved. They insisted, with good reason, that their critics wildly exaggerated the extent of their influence. Most Catholic sovereigns were subject to powerful non-Jesuit influences. Louis XIII often paid more attention to Richelieu and de Bérulle than he did to Suffren and Caussin. Even du Tremblay had a following in the royal family. Philip IV paid more attention to his nun, Maria de Agreda, than he did to Nunez. The emperor often listened longer to his liberal councillors and Wallenstein than he did to Lamormaini. As for confessional practice, the Jesuits asserted indignantly that suavity and *epikeia* outside the confessional were one thing and treatment of royal penitents 'in the rigour and vigour' of the Sacrament quite another.

In 1645 Jesuit uniformity concealed the presence within the Society of another difficult type of subject, the 'spiritual'. 'Dissidence' of the old kind might be dead, but Vitelleschi had to cope with a hydra-headed kind of unrest lurking in the Colleges. It manifested itself in many ways. Juan Mariana's manuscript criticisms of the Acquaviva system were spirited out of Spain and published simultaneously in several places in northern Europe in spite of every effort of Vitelleschi to have the books siezed. He was forced to issue a statement that the text was the work of enemies outside the Society. Balthasar Gracian, the Jesuit rector of Tarragona, published his *Handbook Oracle* of maxims which was perhaps a satire or perhaps a serious attack on Spanish clericalism and hypocrisy. In Austria, Becanus and Masen seriously proposed schemes for a reunion between Catholics and Protestants, and Guldin, a Jesuit scientist, befriended the Protestant polymath, Kepler. In Germany, Adam Tanner and Friedrich von Spee roused their Jesuit colleagues to a fury by roundly attacking the witch-craze and the wholesale condemnation of eccentric old women on the most fanciful of grounds. Von Spee made no secret of his intense unhappiness and tried in vain to get secondment to Italy. He published his very critical *Cautio Criminalis* secretly and without leave of his superiors. Meanwhile in scores of Colleges young Jesuit professors were quietly substituting texts and dictates of their own choice for those prescribed. René Descartes, a former pupil of the Society, and the creator of a revolutionary new philosophy which outraged the orthodox, received a good deal of sympathy and quiet support from some of his old Jesuit teachers.

The unrest came to a head in 1626, the year when von Spee published his *Cautio* and Vitelleschi received a large bundle of delations of the French Jesuit 'spirituals'. If the delators were to be believed there was a large and dangerous conspiracy afoot to destroy the Society from within. The arch-conspirator was, they said, Louis Lallemant, a College professor of theology, and he had a well-organised body of disciples in cells within Colleges at Paris, Lyon, Bordeaux, Nancy, Dijon, Poitiers, Limoges, Bourges and elsewhere. The conspirators were said to be 'Illuminists' working to overthrow all proper authority in the Society and the Church to make way for a vast charismatic movement operating under the direct guidance of the Holy Spirit mediated through inspired 'prophets' and ecstatic 'prophetesses'. It was noted that the movement included a number of notorious women ecstatics. The implication of the accusations was that the movement, like similar 'Illuminist' ones in past Church history, would end up in orgies of immorality.

At first Vitelleschi was panic-stricken. He showered the Provinces with admonitions, instructions, and demands for enquiries and reports. The accused Jesuits all had, in accordance with Acquaviva's standing orders, compiled spiritual autobiographies. These, their letters and private papers, were collected by their superiors and forwarded to the Gesu along with detailed reports from the Provincials. The General read through the mass of material carefully. The Provincials clearly thought that Lallemant's ideas were innocuous. He was deeply upset by the frantic activism of so many of his colleagues and was sure they needed a deeper spirituality. This, he thought, could best be secured by making Acquaviva's invention, 'the tertianship', a full year and a much more intensive affair than it had become. It ought to produce 'a second conversion' and a lasting, contemplative habit of mind and prayer. This, Lallemant had written, was what Ignatius had intended. It was evident to Vitelleschi that the 'spirituals' were, in most cases, pathetically anxious to be loyal to the Society. They had averted their attention from what would inevitably happen if ever their programme spread to the whole Society: the pace of Jesuit activity would become much slower; many Colleges would be run down or closed; many regulations would become obsolete; the spirit of Jesuit obedience would become far less military. The spread of Lallemant's ideas was undoubtedly due to the fact that many Jesuits were unhappy about the increasing superficiality and formalism of their many devotions which had become compulsory, uniform 'observances' of the kind which Ignatius had sought to avoid.

The spiritual autobiographies revealed, over and over again, the influence of the contemplative spirituality of Carmel and of devout women in general. Some of the 'spirituals' had been allowed to read Teresa of Avila's works during their student years. Others had lived for years in the Society feeling increasingly alienated from its way of life. Crasset, a disciple of Lallemant, wrote:

'I have lived eleven years in the Society like a poor wretch abandoned to great temptations, hated, desolate, suffering from spiritual pains and quite inexplicable bodily torments . . .'

Then, like others, he gained the beginning of relief and peace of mind from a chance meeting with a Carmelite prioress. Jean Rigoleuc endured similar agonies until the influence of Armelle Nicolas, a poor servant girl and ecstatic, and Lallemant brought him peace. Other 'spirituals', like Jean-Jacques Surin, came from families very closely associated with Carmel convents and entered the Society with habits of prayer which their superiors discouraged. Surin's family founded a Carmel convent which his widowed mother and sister entered. Jean-Jacques was practically brought up in the convent parlour. When, after many struggles of conscience, he entered the Jesuit noviciate he did so on a condition imposed by the General that he should conform himself utterly to Jesuit 'practical prayer'. The tremendous effort he made to obey was ultimately a failure and sowed in his mind the seeds of mental disorder.

Vitelleschi decided to compromise with the 'spirituals'. Lallemant was allowed a brief stint as director of a tertianship house before being put back into College teaching. His disciples were based on Colleges but, under discreet supervision, allowed to communicate with each other, to direct pious women and, if they wished, to undertake missions in the wilder parts of rural France. From the administrative point of view the compromise was a fair success. Most of the 'spirituals' gave little trouble. They lived in, but apart from, College communities and were treated by them with a mixture of dislike, contempt and amused tolerance. A dozen 'spirituals', frustrated beyond the bounds of endurance, quitted the Society but only one of them, Jean Labadie, who ended as a Protestant, attacked it. Others sought refuge in the Huron Mission in French Canada. Rigoleuc proved awkward. He was a man of many enthusiasms and at his death was writing a *Life of Palafox*, the arch-enemy of the Society. Surin was destined to become a true 'prophet in Israel' for the movement. His later life seemed to the devout a divinely-given 'similitude' or parable of Lallemant's teaching that the true contemplative must suffer and become a laughing stock for world-lings. In 1635, due to the folly of his Provincial and his own *naïveté*, he was sent to exorcise the hysterically 'possessed' Ursuline nuns of Loudoun. In that sick and intensely dangerous atmosphere, amid mass hysteria, blasphemies and obscenities two enthusiastic exorcists of other Orders had already lost their lives. Surin was caught into the vortex and went insane. For the next quarter of a century he was confined in a Jesuit private asylum. In the end he recovered his wits.

The 'spirituals' had laboured in vain. Their movement lingered on into the early 18th century. Pierre Champion, a devoted disciple of Rigoleuc, gathered up the writings of the 'saints', especially of Lallemant and Surin, and published them in an edition which was promptly buried on the remoter shelves of Jesuit libraries. The Society's observances remained unreformed.

* * *

At Vitelleschi's death in 1645 the Society seemed to be at the peak of its power. At the papal conclave of the previous year the

Cardinals seriously considered holding their assembly in the Jesuit *Romanum* College. One of the leading Cardinals, much fancied as a future Pope, was de Lugo, a Jesuit. The conclave's official confessor was a Jesuit. Innocent X, the new Pope, was very devoted to the Society and took as his confessor a Jesuit, John Paul Oliva. The new Cardinal Secretary of State, Chigi, destined to be the next Pope, was utterly 'Jesuited'. He had been educated by the Society: his confessors were all Jesuits as were most of his intimate friends. Yet the next fifteen years to 1661 proved catastrophic for the Society. Its whole structure, recently so solid and majestic, was gravely shaken and tottering. There followed two decades of marvellous recovery (1661-1681) under a great General, Oliva. His reign was to be remembered fondly afterwards as the Indian summer of the old Society, its last years of success and glory before the long, slow and painful decline towards collapse in 1773.

During most of the fifteen catastrophic years, 1645 to 1661, the Society was in effect without a General. No less than five times it went through the very long-drawn-out business of assembling a General Congregation. Of the five Generals elected three were dead within the space of five years: one actually died before the end of the Congregation which elected him. A fourth General was a complete invalid during most of his reign and incapable of performing his duties. Though the Acquaviva system had created a bureaucratic mechanism it was devised in such a way that the personal intervention of a General was needed at every level for almost every decision of any moment. Without that personal leadership the mechanism soon faltered.

The root cause of the Gesu's troubles and of much else that now went wrong in the Society was what historians call 'the general crisis', which afflicted European society very widely in the 1640s and 1650s. The last stages of the Thirty Years' War saw particularly ferocious fighting by states which were anxious to capture as much territory as possible before the opening of the general Peace Conference of Westphalia. Wide areas of northern France, Flanders, south Germany and Austria were devastated by marauding troops. The occupations by hostile forces and the terms of the peace treaties of 1648 compelled the Jesuits to evacuate some Colleges and universities hastily. The universities of Heidelberg and Molsheim were lost, and those at Bamberg, Freiburg and Prague wrecked. Famine and plague ravaged the war-torn areas. Many Colleges lost half their pupils: smaller ones were closed. Throughout France and the 'German

Assistancy' noviciates were almost empty and the Jesuit death-rate much exceeded recruitment. From 1648 to 1653 France was greatly upset by the wars of the Fronde and by peasants' revolts. The English Mission was largely disrupted by the Civil Wars and the overthrow of the monarchy. The Dutch Mission was upset by civil disturbances and revolution. Large areas of Poland were devastated by the revolt of the Ukrainian Cossacks and Russian incursions. Meanwhile the Portuguese revolution of 1640 led to fighting with Spain and in Spain itself there were large-scale revolts of Provinces and peasants in Catalonia and Aragon. Of all European countries Italy suffered worst. There was a savage revolt against Spanish rule in Naples in 1647 and an appalling succession throughout the peninsula of outbreaks of plague, famine, banditry and peasant revolt. It was therefore not very surprising that Jesuit Generals died of plague or of other infections caused by famine, that the death-rate at the Gesu was so high that the Society temporarily ran out of Italian candidates for the Generalate, and that there was an acute Jesuit manpower crisis. Even as early in the troubled years as 1646 a Jesuit Congregation decided that it could do nothing to redecorate the tomb of Ignatius in the Gesu church 'because of the Society's extreme poverty and the disastrous times'.

As the Jesuits attempted to weather the situation most of them spared little attention for the firing of the first sighting shots in a new and dangerous attack on the Society. In 1643 Antoine Arnauld's *De La Fréquente Communion* was first published: by 1648 it was a best-seller throughout Europe. In 1656 Blaise Pascal began to publish his series of *Lettres Provinciales* which eventually roused even more interest and excitement.

The reign of John Paul Oliva began in 1661 when a special General Congregation made history by appointing him Vicar-General of the Society with right of succession to the moribund General. Oliva, a middle-class Genoese of remarkable vigour, tact and charm, had long been the most outstanding and influential Jesuit of his time. He had been the close friend and confessor of two Popes, was immensely popular in the Roman Curia and an intimate friend of the great architect Bernini. At Oliva's touch the shaken Society regained strength and morale. His policy of recruitment filled the noviciates and brought Jesuit numbers up to 18,000 by 1681. His taste, contacts and diplomacy with patrons performed the miracle of giving the Society the three most splendid churches in Rome. At long last the Gesu got its superb ceiling and the tomb of Ignatius its magnificence.

Bernini volunteered to rebuild S. Andrea al Quirinale. He and Oliva discovered the talent of Andrea Pozzo, a lay coadjutor, and set him to redecorate S. Ignazio. Here in Rome, and in provincial-city Gesu churches which began to rise all over Europe, Jesuit Baroque was born. Its style was theatrical and unoriginal. But its message was powerful: the Society is, by the will of God, the Church's greatest mainstay.

Jesuits could be pardoned for sharing this feeling of exultation. The Colleges became more successful than ever in attracting custom, in the teeth of increasing competition from other Orders. The Jesuit Court confessors now seemed immensely influential. In Spain Johann Nithard, the Queen Regent's confessor, Councillor of State and Inquisitor-General, in France La Chaise, Louis XIV's confessor and dispenser of the crown's Church patronage, in Vienna Leopold I's dear friend and confessor, Baron Friedrich Wolff, in Poland Maurice Vota, confessor to that devoted ex-pupil of the Society, the soldier-hero King John Sobieski and in Portugal Nunez, a Councillor of State, were all even more powerful than the Lamormainis and Cotons of past decades. Their careful combinations of diplomacy and evangelisation were proving much more successful than the crude efforts of their predecessors. One after another the reigning Lutheran houses of Germany which had resisted Catholicisation by force of arms in the 1630s accepted it voluntarily in the 1680s and 1690s. Even in England Charles II was nearly a Catholic and had a Jesuit illegitimate son. His brother and heir, the Duke of York, was a convert of the Jesuits.

In so many ways Oliva's Generalate restored the Society's faith in itself. Even violent attacks on the Society now seemed to end with a whimper. The 'Jansenist' attack in France unleashed by the books of Arnauld and Pascal seemed squashed by the pro-Jesuit moves of Rome and Louis XIV. The fury of the 'Popish Plot' scare in England cost Jesuit lives: but by 1681 the Duke of York's succession to the throne was assured. The Jesuits could be pardoned for feeling that the future could hold no terrors for them.

6
The Decline and Fall of the Old Society
1681-1773

The judgement of the devout Jansenists:
'The Jesuits have tried to combine God and the world, and have only earned the contempt of God and the world . . .'
(Blaise Pascal, *Pensées*)

Of the liberal and 'enlightened':
'It is their fault (the Jesuit Colleges) that we are a great nation which uses up all its choler in lawsuits and only uses its manual skill in writing books. When a whole nation is ill with Logic and Poetry and spends all its practical ability on devising spheres and astrolabes instead of other necessary things, all that is a sure sign of its approaching ruin . . .'
(J. L. Guez de Balzac, *Le Prince*, 1631)

'She had the idea of approaching a Jesuit . . . there were grades to suit all levels of society. Just as the Lord has prescribed different forms of nourishment for the various species of animals, he has ordained that the King shall have his confessor, known to all who seek benefices as the head of the French Church. After him come the Princesses' confessors. Ministers do not have them: they are not so stupid. Then there are the Jesuits for the common herd, and, in particular, Jesuits for the ladies' maids, from whom their mistresses' secrets are learnt: a most important piece of work this. The lovely St. Yves approached one of the last category, who was called Father All-Things-to-All-Men . . .'
(François Marie Arouet de Voltaire, *L'Ingenu*)

Of civil administrators:
'The Society of Jesus by its very nature is inadmissible in any properly ordered State as contrary to natural law, attacking all temporal and spiritual authority, and tending to introduce into Church and State, under the specious veil of a religious Institute, not an Order truly aspiring towards evangelical perfection, but rather a political organisation whose essence consists in a continual activity, by all sorts of ways, direct and indirect, secret and public, to gain absolute independence and then the usurpation of all authority . . .'
(Decree of the *Parlement* of Paris, 1762)

Catholic religious Orders are very tenacious of life. Like plants they have a remarkable capacity for survival even after apparent extinction. In the early 16th century their hold on northern Europe was almost totally destroyed by Protestant action while sheer demoralisation very gravely weakened their hold on the south. Yet in the late 16th and 17th centuries the Orders revived massively in the south. Between the 1750s and the early 19th century liberal governments almost completely destroyed this new crop of religious. During the early decades of the 19th century they had a very shadowy and threatened existence. There followed an extraordinary resurrection. By 1914 religious had penetrated every part of Europe and were relatively more numerous than they had ever been.

But, paradoxically, the Orders are extremely vulnerable because of their extensive infrastructure, international character and uncompromising ideology. Even the most apparently economically self-sufficient of religious houses have often succumbed because of inflation, changes in markets, famine, plague or just incompetent management. During the general crisis of the mid-17th century a good many religious houses succumbed and Rome formally suppressed at least a dozen struggling and depopulated small Orders. In the mid-18th century the failure of Law's Bank in Paris, inflation and increased taxation led to the closure of many small religious houses, French, English and Belgian. It was wartime naval blockades in the Atlantic which ruined the sugar exports of Jesuit houses in the West Indies and so precipitated the crisis which led to the expulsion of the Society from French territories.

A large infrastructure and international network made the Orders hostages to fortune in wartime. 'Alien' religious were regularly expelled from enemy countries. The Spanish, Portuguese and French monarchies excluded almost all alien religious from their territories even in peacetime. In war, even between Catholic Powers, religious houses in war zones were subject to pillage.

Religious were also affected by the ordinary processes of social change. The friars and the Jesuits had largely abandoned 'questing' for alms by the 17th century as being counter-productive. Church law bans on moneylending, mortgages, investment in shares and commercial transactions by religious were practically unenforceable by 1700. The pious, illiterate religious was a rarity by the later 17th century and all Orders had acute difficulties in recruiting lay brothers. Orders established for practical purposes like defending the Holy Places in Palestine or ransoming Christian slaves from Barbary were facing grave crises or dissolution as their *raison d'être* became obsolete. As modern liberalism gained a grip on the educated it became progressively harder for parents to pack their children off willy-nilly into religious houses. The minimum age for taking solemn vows was increased from fourteen or sixteen to eighteen by most Catholic governments in the teeth of Orders' *Constitutions* and general canon law. More and more newly-founded Congregations copied the Jesuits by instituting perpetual simple vows which allowed relatively easy release. For their part diocesan bishops vigorously opposed this development. They had no desire to shoulder an increasing burden of finding employment and sustenance for religious released from their vows after ordination.

As institutionalised religious movements or even revivals, Orders are naturally subject to ordinary psychological processes. There is a discernable rhythm in most of their histories. They gain strength and prosper and morale is high. Then comes the inevitable loss of steam with declining numbers and morale when an Order can collapse or gain, painfully, a second wind. By the 17th century monastic outlooks and practices dating from the Middle Ages — a great strain for more modern, faster-moving minds and less rugged physical constitutions — were shouldered enthusiastically and as a matter of deep principle. Thus, for instance, the foundation of La Trappe and other fantastically severe and medievalist Cistercian houses in France drew large numbers of recruits from lay life and from less severe Orders. The loss rate by disease and sheer mental and physical exhaustion was very high. By the 18th century this cult of medieval asceticism was waning rapidly. The acute psychological tensions produced by it undoubtedly accounted for the very large proportion of religious, Jesuits as well as Trappists, Benedictines and friars, who defected immediately the governmental drive to dissolve 'socially useless' Orders began.

Lastly religious Orders can never be a law unto themselves. They are always greatly dependent on public opinion and the support of government, civil and ecclesiastical. In the mid-16th century and again in the later 18th century nominally Catholic public opinion over large areas of Europe turned against the Orders with fatal effects. In late 19th-century liberal Protestant England the very strictly enclosed English Benedictine convent at Stanbrook in Worcestershire found it advisable to site its high enclosure wall in such a fashion that the people of the adjacent village could, standing in the village street, easily see over the wall into the enclosure. That device did much to reduce local hostility which could, if unchecked, have forced the nuns to move elsewhere. No central or local Catholic government has ever been willing to give the Orders complete freedom of operation. Even in the later Middle Ages every royal government had *Mortmain* laws restricting the steady accumulation of monastic property and was quite capable of expelling from the kingdom Orders which were regarded as alien or anti-social. From the early 16th century governments began to exercise a far stricter control, as the Jesuits discovered to their cost. Thus in France whole sections of the Jesuit *Constitutions* were declared null and void at French law by the *Parlements*. The French Provincials were forced to sign undertakings to accept this and also distinctly local and minimalistic interpretations of canon law. The continued existence of the Society in France depended directly for two centuries on the acceptance by French Jesuits of the principle that their duty to the king must always come before their duty to the Pope and the General. Undertakings of a very similar kind were made by Jesuits in most other Catholic states. They were repeatedly expelled for long periods from states like Venice, Malta and Portugal for transgressing such undertakings in relatively minor details.

Within the narrower, complex, much overcrowded clerical world of the 18th century the Orders were just as dependent on higher authority and public opinion. That world contained a bewildering multiplicity of corporations, organisations and parties whose interests often clashed. The 17th century had been an age of Counter-Reformation expansion for clerics: the 18th century saw that movement gradually grind to a halt and give way to a steady recession. On all sides clerical groups complained anxiously of increasing difficulties with recruitment, finance and lay anti-clericalism. Anxiety and strong competition for shrinking resources bred an ultra-touchiness. The clerical world was rocked by violent quarrels. The Counter-Reformation Papacy had established a tighter legal grip on the clergy of all groups. It was therefore more involved than ever in trying to maintain a just balance between opposing interests and to keep the antagonisms from passing the bounds of decency. In practice papal policy combined a tough autocracy with a talent for subtle, face-saving compromises, infinite patience, and an ability to bend gracefully and temporarily before clerical public opinion when it proved especially determined and united. The atmosphere of the incessant clerical warfare of those days was a strange mixture of extreme legalism and blatant evasion of the law, viciousness and high idealism befitting clerics and nuns who were some degrees better ordered and educated than in any previous age of Church history. In that genteel jungle the Society was generally acknowledged to be the king of the beasts. Its teeth and claws, its hold on Popes and kings, its ability to drum up an impressive body of influential supporters in any emergency, and its proven skill in controversy were renowned and much feared by its rivals. Yet there was always a distinct possibility that if the leadership of the Society were ever to falter and its opponents to unite to pull it down Popes and kings might show no disposition to save it.

In spite of all these difficulties the Society's self-confidence remained high. Most Jesuits, now that the traumatic years of the mid-17th century were forgotten, seem to have assumed that the Society was practically invulnerable. Other Orders might totter but it would never fail. Superficially there was a good deal of evidence to support this view. At a time when other Orders were having recruitment problems, the Society continued to grow in numbers. In 1681 there were 18,000 Jesuits, in 1710 nearly 20,000, in 1750 22,600 and even in the fatal year 1773 23,000. The number of Jesuit Colleges also rose greatly from the 580 of 1681 to 612 in 1710, 669 in 1749 and nearly 800 in 1773. The statistics show that the Society had at last overcome one of its great weaknesses, the old heavy predominance of Portuguese, Spaniards and Italians. By the 1760s recruitment had levelled off in Italy, Spain, Portugal and France: in some Provinces it was slightly declining. Meanwhile there was a tremendous spurt of recruitment in the old 'German Assistancy', in England, the Low Countries, Germany and eastern Europe. Residences had multiplied greatly in those backward areas and many of them had quite new and splendid Baroque Colleges and churches. Another significant change for the better was the 'coming of age' of the South and Central American Provinces. They now recruited Creoles so fast that the flow across the Atlantic of Portuguese and Spanish Jesuits declined.

The Jesuit hold on Rome seemed solid and unalterable. The long line of Popes who were ex-pupils of the Society continued, with relatively few breaks, right down to 1773. Even the few Popes who were not 'Jesuited', including the Dominican Benedict XIII, were generally careful of the Gesu's susceptibilities. All this was hardly surprising since most 18th-century Popes had been curial officials and the Curia was as full as ever of men who had either been educated by, or owed their advancement to, Jesuits. In 1762 Bernardo Tanucchi, the main Neapolitan Minister of State, estimated, perhaps wildly, that no less than three quarters of the curial staff were 'Jesuited'. At this period the Consistory of Cardinals invariably contained a couple of Jesuits: for some years early in the century it had three, of whom one was also the Spanish ambassador to the Holy See and another the leader of the Imperialist faction in the Consistory. In 1770 a French Minister of State reckoned that twenty-five of the forty-three Cardinals were 'Jesuited'.

The city of Rome was considered, with good reason, to be the hub of the great international network of Jesuit influences. Protestant tourists, mostly English and German, flocked there. They were always particularly anxious to see the splendours of the Gesu church, the Pozzo ceiling in S. Ignazio, and, above all, the macabre and theatrical representation of the death-bed of the young Jesuit saint, Stanislas Kostka, set up deliberately as a tourist attraction in his old room in the Roman Noviciate. The main papal university in the city, the *Sapienzia*, and the Dominican *Minerva* were quite overshadowed by the size and vigour of the Jesuit *Romanum* with its ring of satellite national seminaries, the *Germanicum, Hungaricum*, English and Irish Colleges. The *Romanum* was much attended by ambitious secular ordinands since it was well-known that the professors looked after the careers of their pupils. Old *Romanum* students were numerous in the papacy itself, the Consistory, the Curia and high ecclesiastical offices in Italy. *Germanicum* men got a flying start in the race to acquire similar offices in their native countries. Jesuits had been spiritual directors of numbers of curial departments for many years and the masters of a small but crucial office, the Sacred Penitentiary. The Jesuits' hold on this was commonly supposed to be one of the main reasons why they were in such demand as confessors by aristocratic 'hard cases', since it was the source of various types of unusual papal dispensations and especially wide confessional faculties.

The Jesuit hold on Court confessorships and the officialdom of civil governments remained extensive down to the 1760s. It was so deeply-rooted and long-standing that it seemed, especially in southern Europe, to be an essential part of the fabric of governmental and social life. This was especially true in Portugal. Early in the century, Clement XI, a 'non-Jesuited' Pope, made an unusual and vigorous effort to clean up scandals connected with the court confessors there. His foray did little to alter the local system but it did reveal the completeness of Jesuit penetration into the heart of Portuguese government. In 1754 the confessing of the entire royal family occupied the time of five Jesuits. The ministries and main provincial offices were monopolised by 'Jesuited' men. The 'non-Jesuited' clergy, functionaries and aristocrats, from whose ranks the destroyer of the Society in Portugal, Pombal, came, were bitterly resentful but almost powerless. Things had gone almost as far in Spain and its dependencies, Naples and Sicily. Charles III, who became King of Spain in 1759, was a liberal reformer who had spent most of his life out of the country. He found the 'Jesuitical' system so deep-rooted that he felt powerless to attack it. He dismissed his predecessor's Jesuit confessor, appointing a liberal Franciscan in his place. But Jesuits had to be retained as confessors and tutors for the rest of the royal family. Charles picked as chief ministers of Spain and Naples two of the ablest liberals he could find, Aranda and Tanucchi. It was significant that both had Jesuit connections. Aranda was reckoned by the strongly 'Jesuited' to be a rank atheist. In fact he regularly attended Mass, had cousins in the Society, and was warmly attached to his old Jesuit tutor. Tanucchi belonged to one of the Society's most prestigious confraternities and his regular confessor was a Jesuit. He reported to the king that the entire Court at Naples was 'Jesuited', as were the provincial governors. The heiress of the Neapolitan throne, an Austrian archduchess, was 'full of Jesuitism'. Charles III had also to reckon with the fact that Jesuit influences ran through almost all sections of Spanish society in a hidden way, rather like the tap roots of a great tree. Occasional crises tended to reveal that the roots had penetrated into very unexpected places. Thus military commands and provincial governerships were almost monopolised by aristocratic *colegiales*, so-called because they had been educated in exclusive royal academies, the *Colegios Mayores*. Few of these had ever been staffed with Jesuits. But most entrants came from Jesuit preparatory schools and the *Colegios* tended to have Jesuit chaplains. That immensely popular and powerful, if absurdly antiquated, national institution, the Spanish Inquisition, though in the past accounted anti-Jesuit had long been a staunch ally of the Society and protector of its interests. Also, as Charles III was to discover at his cost, the Jesuits and their church confraternities were popular and influential in Madrid, Barcelona and Seville where their decorated carts, giant figures of saints and highly-dressed contingents of supporters were the highlight of the processions on all the many fiesta days.

In France, northern Italy and the countries of northern and eastern Europe the Jesuit network was less massive and ancient but still widely pervasive. After the death of Louis XIV, that highly possessive lover of the Society, in 1714 the Jesuit Court confessors were quietly edged out of direct control of all royal Church patronage. But they retained, as a matter of course, their confessorships and tutorships of most members of the royal family to the very day when the Society fell from power. French politicians, 'Jesuited' themselves or not, had perforce to be very well-informed about all the ramifications of a 'Jesuitism' which stemmed from the unplumbed influence of the Court confessors, the tutorships of the nobility, the Colleges, the Sodalities, the confraternities and the 'Jesuited' convents. The politicians were especially concerned about the Society's strongest 'friends', the *rouliers* or *Jésuites de courte robe*. Among the 'Jesuited' were all the womenfolk of the royal family, especially Louis XV's Carmelite daughter, considerable sections of the provincial aristocracy and episcopate, a large part of the *noblesse de robe* and a substantial number of officers in the army and navy. Every *parlement* had its 'Jesuited' members and they had a clear majority in the *parlements* of Aix, Besançon, Alsace and Flanders. What was unexpected was that the Society had always made special provision in its Colleges for preparing boys for entry into the army at fourteen or fifteen directly or through a royal academy, and that many naval officers were trained in royal schools of navigation and hydrography under Jesuit direction set up by Louis XIV in most of the great ports on the Atlantic coast. Moreover, the politicians had to take account of the long roll of eminent Frenchmen who had been educated by the Society. These included: among politicians, Choiseul, Turgot and the Cardinal de Bernis; among Churchmen, Bossuet, Fénélon and Pallu along with Archbishop de Beaumont of Paris; and among men of letters and the world, Voltaire, Montesquieu, Fontenelle, Diderot, Condillac, Condorcet, St. Simon, Malesherbes, Desfontaines, the Abbé Prévost, the Marquis de Sade, Rameau, Buffon, La Rochefoucauld, and, though they were dead, the living influence of the great Molière and Corneille. 'Jesuited' mathematicians and scientists were not numerous but no one was likely to forget Descartes and Mersenne. The worlds of music, painting and science might be enchantingly free of 'Jesuitism': the greater world of literature certainly was not.

In the Austrian Empire the reign of the great Empress Maria Theresa from 1740 produced a similar scaling down of the direct, political pull of Jesuit Court confessors. But, as in France, they retained spiritual direction and tuition of a good many members of the Imperial family, especially the archduchesses, down to the day of the Society's suppression. The usual fine, mysterious network of Jesuit influences ran out from the Court confessors, tutors and confessors to the nobility, the Colleges and their Sodalities, the Jesuit-directed seminaries for secular ordinands, the 'Old Boys' of the *Germanicum* and *Hungaricum*, the city Church confraternities and the very numerous small town missions set up by the Society throughout Hungary, and, for that matter, right across eastern Europe along the borders of Russia and into old Polish Catholic territories now incorporated into the Russian Empire. By the 1750s the Society was reckoned to have upwards of a hundred seminaries in Austria, Bohemia and Hungary alone and not far short of a million members of confraternities. They included Glück, the Imperial Court's favourite composer of operas, if not Mozart or Haydn. 'Jesuited' archdukes and archduchesses often proved unofficial ambassadors for the Society. They carried their Jesuit mentors and affiliations with them to the rule of satellite Austrian principalities, to prince-archbishoprics in southern Germany and to state marriages in Dresden, Munich, Madrid, Paris and Naples.

If 18th-century Jesuits still nervously required proof of the Society's strength they had only to cast an eye over the recent achievements of its missioners outside the bounds of Catholic Europe. These achievements, and even the mission failures, displayed a spirit and expertise conspicuously lacking among most non-Jesuit missioners. In Holland and England, missions in the main created by Jesuit vigour, the Society could still claim that it maintained a quarter, or, in the case of England perhaps a third, of the mission establishments: it certainly had 'Jesuited' a large proportion of the wealthiest gentry and was making a steady dribble of conversions among Protestant notabilities. It was the crass stupidity of James II and the naïve complacency of his Jesuit confessor, Edward Petre, which in 1687-8 threw away a golden chance to make big advances in England. The blame could not be laid at the doors of the Gesu or most English Jesuit missioners. Also from 1688 to 1745 the cause of the Catholic Stuarts still had a possibility of recovering its lost ground.

In Protestant Germany and Scandinavia the Jesuits alone had

made real, even startling, progress, while other Catholic missioners floundered. The conversion of Queen Christina of Sweden by two Italian Jesuits in 1650 set the pace. There followed, over the next decades, a string of Jesuit conversions of German Protestant ruling houses, Saxony, the Palatinate, Neuburg, Württemburg, Anhalt, Brunswick, Hesse and, though this did not in the end work out, Hanover. The converts mostly took Jesuit confessors who fought to keep the Catholic succession going in the tiny Courts, linking the families, wherever possible, by dynastic marriages with the old Catholic Courts of Vienna, Munich, Paris and Warsaw. In return the new German Catholic rulers entrusted to the Society the building up of missions in their still almost entirely Protestant states. The Jesuits now, in fact, developed effective techniques of negotiation with Protestant rulers and nobles. They were repeatedly called in to negotiate the best terms possible for the Catholic party in those aristocratic 'mixed marriages' which had long been a feature of high life in Germany. By private agreement between a Jesuit Provincial and the great Protestant warlord, Frederick the Great, King of Prussia, Jesuits received favoured treatment in his territories including a practical monopoly of the Catholic parishes and schools in the province of Silesia which he had conquered from Austria. Just as astonishingly other Protestant rulers in the north, including the kings of Denmark and Sweden, swallowed their prejudices against the Society and engaged Jesuits as chaplains to Catholic mercenary regiments and Italian stuccoists in their service.

By 1740 the salons and coffee houses of London, Paris, Vienna, Prague, Dresden and Berlin were buzzing with interest in, and praise of, Jesuit foreign missions in Paraguay, Canada, California, Indochina and Peking. The intense interest was stimulated partly by good Jesuit publicity and partly by the growing contemporary fashion for everything romantically strange, exotic and primitive. Many, if not all, liberals and a good many educated Protestants regarded the Jesuits and their Reductions in Paraguay with deep admiration, an admiration perhaps not unaffected by the fact that most of the missionaries there were Germans, Austrians and Hungarians. The liberals saw the Guarani Indians of Paraguay as typical 'good savages' in the real 'state of nature' which so fascinated 'philosophers'. They saw the Jesuit missionaries as statesmen, scientists and 'philosophers' determined to preserve the Indian way of life intact from exploitation and the manifold corruptions which came from westernisation. The more devout liberals went so far as to see the Reductions as Utopias, ideal Christian societies meant providentially to shame the depraved godlessness of Europe. Likewise pious Catholics were deeply moved by the traditional, 'antique' heroism and sufferings under torture of Jesuit missionaries in Indochina and among the Canadian Hurons, feats worthy of the early Christian martyrs. Liberals, on the other hand, were so strongly impressed by the 'philosophical' spirit of enquiry of the more reflective Jesuit missioners that they were cheerfully willing to forgive them their Catholic dogmatism as a temporary aberration. They were particularly impressed by the scientific observations of the Californian Indians and terrain by the Jesuit travelling missioner, Eusebio Kino, fresh from his College professorship in Ingolstadt. The observations and mathematical skills of the French Fathers of the Peking Mission were also greatly appreciated. The collapse of the Peking Mission in 1742, destroyed by hostile non-Jesuit missionaries, the Roman *Propaganda* Congregation and Pope Benedict XIV, was roundly condemned in Europe as a shameful triumph of basely narrow-minded Catholic superstition over Jesuit humanity and 'enlightenment'.

This extraordinary outburst of liberal esteem for Jesuit foreign missionaries, members of a body which the 'enlightened' habitually regarded as a great bastion of medievalist reaction, was by no means an isolated phenomenon. As we have seen, the corset of highly disciplined orthodoxy which Acquaviva fitted on the Society had not prevented a good many Jesuits from continuing to profess and practise one or other of two kinds of religious liberalism. One was orthodox in doctrine but flexible in tactics, willing to be 'all things to all men' in order to win them ultimately to orthodoxy. The other was deeper, dissident liberalism, always hovering uneasily on the edge of leaving, or being cast out of, the Society. Both of these kinds of liberalism existed fairly vigorously, if somewhat covertly, in the 1740s in the bosom of a Society which was strongly coloured by the prevailing religious conservatism of the clerical establishment. The Jesuit liberals had friends and even admirers among the 'enlightened'. They regarded their own work and contacts as a far greater strength to the Society than its large 'Old Boy' network and far more likely to save it in the forthcoming major assault of the 'enlightened' on the Catholic establishment. Liberal tendencies were, it was true, to be found in almost every section of the clerical body, even in unlikely areas: in Spain two of the greatest liberals were monks, a Benedictine, Feijoo, and a Cistercian; in Belgium there were 'enlightened' Dominicans and Carthusians; and there were 'enlightened' English seminary professors. But the liberal Jesuits hoped and believed that they formed the largest and best-equipped single body of effective, liberally-minded apologists for Catholicism in an increasing hostile age.

The heavily conservative, even reactionary, face of the Society was there for all to see. At almost every General Congregation the exclusive little body of delegate Professed Fathers, especially those from Spain and Germany, voiced the same list of complaints about the disgracefully lax behaviour and opinions of the younger generation of Jesuits. These 'laxists' insisted on having a bourgeois, not a traditionally monastic, standard of living in their houses. They demanded as of right, tea, coffee, chocolate and forks, and furtively smoked that narcotic weed, tobacco, though experience showed only too plainly that addiction led inevitably to vice and apostasy. Worse still, the 'laxists' excused themselves from traditional devotional exercises and bodily penances, justifying such outrageous behaviour by saying that they followed the 'pernicious mildness' authorised by libertarian moral theologians called 'Probabilists': these theologians held the convenient opinion that in moral matters one might safely follow any lax judgement provided it was in print and the author a qualified moral theologian. General after General echoed the complaints of the General Congregations in long Latin *Instructions* entitled: 'The Evils of the Times', 'On the Spirit of our Vocation', or 'On the Promotion of the Desire for, and Study of, Spiritual Things'. For years in the 1670s Tirso Gonzalez, a Jesuit College professor in Salamanca, headed a strongly conservative pressure group which bombarded the Gesu and the Popes with urgent petitions. Gonzalez and his friends were died-in-the-wool academics. They were convinced that there was only one perfectly effective way to stop the laxist rot. This was for authority to burn all 'Probabilist' textbooks and impose on the Society the obligation under pain of grave sin to use nothing but strict, old-fashioned 'Probabiliorist' ones. The campaigners were, unfortunately, dissatisfied with the array of available 'Probabiliorist' books and so proposed to compose more suitable ones themselves.

Unfortunately for the Jesuit ultra-conservatives in general and Gonzalez in particular these were the days of the great 'Jansenist' dispute. Ultra-conservatism remained a common enough phenomenon in most clerical groups throughout the 18th century but its adherents were usually devoid of literary gifts and a flare for publicity. From the 1650s there arose from their ranks in France and Belgium a number of people of very unusual ability and force of character, university professors, religious, including some very forceful nuns, members of the Oratory and other Congregations, a few bishops, and some hundreds of gifted laymen. They had no single leader. Although the Jesuits later chose to dub them 'the Jansenists' after Cornelius Jansen, a Flemish bishop, his influence on the movement was relatively slight. It arose immediately after the publication by two French laymen, Blaise Pascal and Antoine Arnauld, of brilliant, best-selling books which read very like political party manifestos. From the start no conservative Jesuits were associated with the movement. It proposed itself not merely as another protest against 'laxism' but as a crusade to reform the whole Church and bring it back to the simplicity and strictness of the early Christian Church. The 'Jansenists' announced that they regarded the Society as the principle cause of 'laxism'. They suggested strongly that this was not merely because of its moral degeneration but due to a far deeper cause: heresy. The Society had abandoned the old, spiritual theology of the early Fathers of the Church. It had even abandoned in the main classical medieval Thomist theology, and had gone over to 'Molinism', a modern 'instant' theology which was more humanist than Christian. In effect, therefore, the 'Jansenists' called on the Jesuits' 'friends' and penitents to abandon them if they valued their souls: they called on all decent, observant, conservative Jesuits either to put the Society's house in order radically or quit it.

Faced with this highly embarrassing threat the Gesu and the Provincials had little difficulty in rallying most Jesuits, conservative or liberal, and their most influential 'friends' to battle to defend the Society's good name and existence. The outcome of the battle could not be in much doubt though open fighting was going to last for over sixty years and the guerilla tactics used by the defeated 'Jansenists' many more. The Gesu could rely mostly, if not quite always, on the support of Rome. So long as he lived Louis XIV was a tower of strength.

Because of this battle Gonzalez' petitions at first produced no tangible results. The Gesu wished to put its house in order and silence its most blatant 'laxist' teachers. But it had no desire to copy the arguments of the 'Jansenists'. Then, very surprisingly, in 1686 Pope Innocent XI, one of the rare 'non-Jesuited' Popes and a man who had some sympathy with the 'Jansenist' point of view, intervened at the election of a new General and imposed Gonzalez on the Society. He proved, as General, a grave disappointment to the Pope and the ultra-conservative Jesuits. They complained as much as their more liberal colleagues that he avoided his ordinary desk duties and remained engrossed in preparing a string of his own 'Probabiliorist' textbooks for the press and frantically petitioning a series of embarrassed, 'Jesuited' Popes for changes in the *Constitutions* to make the books orthodoxy for the Society. His efforts were in vain. The Pope kindly proposed to remove him from the Generalate to a bishopric. But a General Congregation, basically sympathetic towards Gonzalez' general outlook, if not towards his methods, decided that such a move would cause more scandal than his continuance in office. So they put up with the professor-General and his incessant writing until his death in 1705.

Meanwhile up and down the provinces conservative professors published 'Probabiliorist' textbooks steadily with only a little difficulty from the Gesu, and their liberal colleagues had acute difficulties in getting permission for the very occasional publication of a mildly 'Probabilist' one. 'Probabilist' or 'Probabiliorist' books, however, were certain to be word-for-word the same in their treatment of one subject, the sixth Commandment, sexual matters. Here, in Jesuit textbooks at least, a very rigid medieval monastic standard prevailed. We may guess that liberal Jesuit confessors when doing long stints in rural parishes were somewhat less strict. Alphonsus Liguori, who was educated in moral theology by Jesuits in an area of Italy where liberalism was unknown, went out into pastoral work as a secular priest assuming that 'Probabiliorism' was the only possible confessional system. It was only years later, when he was the founder of the Redemptorist Order, that hard experience of rural congregations taught him its absolute impracticality.

Backwood Jesuits, especially common in Poland and England, continued to raise their voices petulantly against 'laxism' and the 'moderns': their liberal colleagues behaved with more circumspection. The letter-book of Lewis Sabran, a Frenchman but of the English Province, gives us a fair idea of the mentality of the conservative majority. Sabran was the son of a French marquis and therefore quietly ear-marked from his earliest days in the Province for the pleasanter jobs requiring grace and manners. He was a procurator in Brussels, a military chaplain in Flanders, a chaplain to James II in London and then at St. Germain in France. He became assistant to the Provincial and attended more than one General Congregation in Rome. He died in Rome in 1732 after a long stint as Spiritual Father in the English College. Sabran was tetchy about the servant problem. He was let down and deceived so often by lay coadjutors who appeared angels but turned out repeatedly to be scheming monsters fleeing into the Society to avoid their creditors. He was on edge about young Jesuits: 'Fr. J. Constable', for example, was seeing too much of 'the young' and of young English ladies; there was a 'frowardness' in him. In 1715 Sabran was preoccupied, without any sign of misgivings, in helping on the plea of the Imperial Director of Instrumental Music, Matteis, and his English wife that they should separate by papal dispensation so that Matteis could become a Jesuit and his wife a nun. Late in his life, in Rome, he was keenly involved in plans to get a Jesuit on to the staff of the Holy Office. He wrote: 'No Jesuit of a long time hath any place there.' His judgements on the English Vicars-Apostolic were *parti-pris*: one was 'a rank Jansenist', another only a shade inclined that way.

The Jesuit liberals could, in an odd way, feel grateful to the 'Jansenists' for preserving them from much heavier ostracism in the Society. In 1734 Francis Mannock, an English Jesuit of the ultra-conservative type, was in an embarrassing position. He had, not long before, been removed from a house-chaplaincy to a thoroughly 'Jesuited' gentry family in Warwickshire, the Fitzherberts, and then moved to the Bar Convent in York. In Warwickshire he had been roused to a fury by the attitude of the Fitzherberts. They were even more conservative than he was, yet they insisted that they could not understand why a party with such impeccable conservative principles as the 'Jansenists' could possibly be regarded by the Society as a pack of heretics. Mrs. Fitzherbert actually waved in Mannock's face a 'Jansenist' pamphlet entitled *The Imaginary Heresay*. Safe in the haven of the Bar Convent, an utterly 'Jesuited' community attached to conservative devotions and Jacobitism, the centre of a cosy network of like-minded Catholic gentry, Mannock sat down to compose a petition to Rome. The text was the usual catalogue of the enormities committed daily by Catholic 'laxists', clerical and lay, culminating in a list of seventy-seven 'laxist' opinions worthy of immediate condemnation by papal authority. Mannock knew well that the Society, and even the very conservative English Province, contained notorious liberals. But his petition had to pass through the hands of a secular clergyman, the Northern Vicar-Apostolic. Hence he made no mention of Jesuits and confined his attention to the faults of 'the clergy'.

What did liberally-minded Jesuits achieve apart from hopefully 'philosophical' observations about the native cultures of Paraguay and China? By the 1760s a mild degree of 'tactical' liberalism was fairly widespread among those Catholic clergy, Jesuits included, whose pastoral work brought them into contact with the cultured laity. By that time all over Europe the cultured minority had acquired a fashionable veneer of 'enlightened' opinions and phraseology. In urban churches much frequented by such people the old Latin liturgy and sacraments were now generally lodged in a setting of vernacular prayers and sermons in the 'enlightened' idiom. This development had become so marked, even in backward England, that the English Benedictine superiors observed that young monks preparing for the mission in monasteries abroad must be taught the idiom thoroughly, even from Anglican books: if they were not their ministrations would be condemned by genteel congregations as outlandish.

Other Jesuits undertook 'tactical liberalism' in a more deliberate way. In 1701 the French superiors put up the money to establish at Trévoux a busy literary apostolate designed to protect the cultured laity from the rank irreligion of 'enlightened' extremists. The Trévoux Jesuit press mostly produced religious tracts and straightforward works of controversy. But occasionally the Jesuit authors adopted fashionable 'enlightened' literary forms. For more than sixty years they produced a monthly review, *Memoires pour Servir a l'Histoire des Sciences et des Beaux-Arts*, commonly known for short as the *Journal de Trévoux*. This ancestor of the 19th-century Jesuit periodicals like *Etudes, Stimmen aus Maria Laach* or *The Month* tried to attract cultured readers by articles on the very latest scientific and 'philosophical' topics while taking, more or less openly, an orthodox Catholic line. From 1704 the authors of the *Journal* brought out successive editions of a 'guide to modern knowledge', the *Dictionnaire de Trévoux*. The only other Jesuit Province with the energy, interest and money to attempt a similar apostolate was in Poland. There a Jesuit group took over a Piarist Church magazine, *The Warsaw Courier*, in 1740 and gave it sections copied from the French *Journal*. Also in Warsaw in 1765 a Jesuit poet who was slowly going over to 'doctrinal liberalism', F. Bohololec, started *The Monitor*, a copy of the English *Tatler*.

The larger Jesuit Colleges proved natural recruiting grounds for liberalism, both 'tactical' and 'doctrinal'. The 18th century saw the progressive collapse of most of the prescribed curriculum

for the Colleges. The old philosophical and theological courses
were based on a traditional Aristotelianism which was completely
discredited among the learned of Europe. The classical arts
course had always over-stretched the mental capacities of most
Jesuit teachers and their pupils. It was now worse taught than
ever and unpopular with 'enlightened' parents. Jesuit Generals
and General Congregations insisted, to the bitter end in 1773,
that the old syllabus must be maintained intact. In practice many
professors, like their colleagues in the study houses and
seminaries of other Orders, quietly departed from the old courses
more or less extensively. The Jesuit 'philosophers' tried a variety
of eclectic arrangements. At first they imported matter into
their still nominally Aristotelian courses from Descartes, who,
for all his devotion to his old Jesuit mentors, was much disliked
by the Gesu, or Malebranche the Oratorian. Then, as Car-
tesianism was exploded, daring professors borrowed material
from Isaac Newton directly or through the medium of pirated
'Jansenist' school textbooks. In Germany the more liberal
professors became tributaries to Wolff, a Protestant academic
exile from Berlin who fetched up in Catholic Dresden, and even
Kant. Scientists and mathematicians had always formed a very
small elite among Jesuit 'philosophers' since the Gesu always
refused to give them wholehearted support. Their ranks in
the Jesuit Colleges were made even thinner by drafts sent to
maintain the Peking Mission and to man the French royal schools
of navigation and hydrography. Hence few Colleges in the 18th
century devoted much of their philosophy courses to science.
There were rare, celebrated examples of the Jesuit scientist.
Laurence Guzman of Coimbra was the first Portuguese to con-
struct a hot air balloon and make an ascent in it. Giuseppe
Ruggiero Boscovich was one of the two Jesuits who achieved
a Fellowship of the Royal Society of London. He was a Serb
converted from Orthodoxy by the Jesuits of Ragusa and was long
a professor of philosophy in the *Romanum* where he published
a Latin treatise on the composition of matter. In the 1760s Dr.
Samuel Johnson and his circle of friends received 'Dr. Boscovitch'
with acclamations during his visit to England.

Hence Jesuit professors of theology found that their classes
were full of young men quite unfamiliar with the scholastic
categories of Aristotle on which the old *Ratio* course was based.
Even conservative-minded professors were forced to improvise,
producing new courses which were little more than expositions
of defined Catholic doctrines backed up with a little history of

doctrine and apologetics. The more adventurous and liberal professors attempted to expound doctrine in Cartesian, Wolffian or Newtonian terms. Some, in France and Germany, actually evaded the Society's censors and published theology textbooks in the modern idiom: such books almost invariably ended up on the Roman Index of Prohibited Books. In France two Jesuit theologians, Jean Hardouin and Isaac Berruyer, raised an even greater storm when they followed the same path. Berruyer's books were officially condemned by the Holy Office in Rome, the Sorbonne in Paris and the Paris *Parlement*. The Archbishop of Paris gave the French Provincials funds to enable them to buy up and destroy as many copies as possible. At his insistence the Provincials even had handbills distributed among the congregations in Jesuit city churches warning them not to imperil their souls by reading Berruyer's books. The 'Jansenist' Bishop of Soissons distributed round his diocese a violent Pastoral Letter attacking the books. The published edition filled four volumes. Yet, oddly enough, after a brief pause Berruyer resumed publication unrepentantly and without incurring any more censures.

Berruyer and his master Hardouin were genuine 'doctrinal liberals'. They were exceedingly sceptical about the trustworthiness of the text of the Bible and the ability of moderns to understand and interpret such ancient writings. Hence to their minds traditional Catholic apologetic needed radical recasting. Like other liberal Jesuits they were deeply influenced by a revolution in historical studies which had been building up since the mid-17th century and particularly the textual criticism of Richard Simon, an Oratorian, and of the Maurists, a team of French Benedictine historians. In Belgium the Bollandists, a team of learned Jesuit historians, were engaged in a massive research project on the lives and legends of the saints, a subject only slightly less explosive than the Bible. The Belgian team was tiny and always struggling to survive. Its superiors, terrified that its publication would injure the Society's good name, gave the team little financial support and encouragement. The Bollandists were working their way very slowly and thoroughly through an immensely long list of saints, major and minor, historical figures and figments of pious imagination, arranged in alphabetical order. The articles on each of the saints when completed were put together into volumes. The publication of a new volume was necessarily a rare event and almost always led to a noisy broil. Early in the century the whole Carmelite Order rose up in arms over a suggestion by the Bollandists that there was very little truth in the traditional account of the Order's origins. The offending volume of *The Lives of the Saints* was put on the Roman Index and the Bollandist team barely survived. Thenceforward they phrased their articles cautiously and tried to bury the most contentious material in the small print of footnotes.

Indeed it was hard for any Jesuit historian writing to be a conservative or to avoid controversy. The work of Denis Petau, perhaps the greatest Jesuit historian of the age, was pirated and used extensively by the 'Jansenists'. Louis Maimbourg, a French professor at the *Romanum*, wrote a series of books on early and medieval Church history in which he severely criticised traditional Roman views on the development of the papal primacy. All of these books were put on the Index. Then he published a history of Lutheranism in which he insisted that much of the blame for the Reformation cataclysm lay at the door of the Papacy and Roman Curia. Innocent XI was so affronted that he forced Maimbourg to leave the Society. Louis XIV obligingly provided the penniless scholar with his protection, a pension and 'grace and favour' apartments in a royal *château*. Maimbourg died while engaged in research into the question of the validity of Anglican Orders.

'Doctrinal liberalism' even existed vigorously in the most backwood parts of the Society. In China a dozen Jesuit missionaries maintained a defiant but 'respectful silence' about the Roman condemnation of the Peking Mission's 'accommodations' to Chinese beliefs and customs. In Paraguay a score of Jesuit missioners flatly refused to obey the orders from the General and the Pope to cease resistance to the Portuguese and Spanish troops attacking the Reductions. In the Republic of Venice, a curiously self-detached little segment of the Society for complex historical reasons, there were very liberal Jesuits who eventually greeted the suppression of their Order with relief and approval. The South American Jesuit Colleges were regarded in Europe as stagnant academic backwaters. In fact many of them, especially in Peru, Guatemala and Mexico, contained Creole professors who were ardent liberals and nationalists: Landivar, the great Guatemalan poet, was one of this group. There were Jesuits of the same mind in Tuscany and in the Bohemian and Polish Provinces. The Czech liberals included the historian Beckovsky, the preacher Dobrovsky, and the great nationalist writer and preacher Balbin, whose books were regularly refused publication or heavily censored by his superiors. The Polish liberals included the poets Naruszewicz, later a bishop, Kniaznin, later accounted a libertine, and Bohololec. Even the English Province had its determined liberals. Charles Maire was a Newtonian astronomer. Charles Wharton, an American, carried his liberalism to the point of abandoning the Jesuit mission in Worcester, the Society and the Catholic Church. John Carroll, another American, was to be a very ardent supporter of the Berington group of liberal English clergy in the 1770s and later the first Bishop of Baltimore.

* * *

In the 1740s the Society was very large, still growing steadily in numbers, well-supported and, in spite of its divisions between conservatives and liberals, still fairly vigorous pastorally and intellectually. Why therefore did it collapse so suddenly and resoundingly between 1759 and 1773?

There were two rival contemporary explanations for the great disaster. The first was that cited somewhat baldly and summarily by the Portuguese, Spanish and French governments when they began the Society's destruction and largely endorsed by Pope Clement XIV when he completed the process in 1773. This view was at least two centuries old in practically every detail. Long before the 'Jansenists', Voltaire, Diderot and the other 'Encyclopaedists' gave the charges a new degree of wit and cogency they had been voiced, bluntly and passionately, over and over again by an imposing array of the Jesuits' enemies, Philip II of Spain, the Spanish Inquisitors, Roman Curial officials and irate Popes, French *parlements* and the Sorbonne, Dominicans, Franciscans and Oratorians, Bishop Palafox, and Dutch and English secular clergy. Some of the more fundamental charges had been voiced bravely and clearly by distinguished Jesuit dissidents. According to this view the early Society, a small, relatively informal 'devout' Congregation, had speedily and finally changed into a massive, completely self-centred, power-hungry organisation bent on endless expansion. In principle and practice the organisation subordinated all other considerations — its duty to the moral law, to Popes and sovereigns — to its own interests. Hence, whenever those interests seemed to require it, the Society was prepared to justify equivocation, cheating, and breaking any law of Church and state, and inciting its 'friends' to murder, armed rebellion and war. It had been responsible for the assassinations of Henry III and Henry IV of France and for attempts on the lives of Elizabeth I and James I of England. The Society professed to steer clear of politics but in fact interfered in them constantly, withdrawing subjects from their natural allegiance. Jesuits had been responsible for the murder of Wallenstein. The Long Parliament's belief that the English Civil Wars were caused by a 'Jesuitical conspiracy' was on record. Hence, very typically, the Jesuits were at their old games in the 1750s. Some of them officered private armies which were waging war in Paraguay on the royal forces of Portugal and Spain. Others were actively fomenting rebellion against the Portuguese crown in Brazil. Others were plotting the assassination of the King of Portugal while others fomented popular uprisings in Madrid. Clement XIV, in his Suppression Bull, *Dominus ac Redemptor*, of 1773 added that the Society had, in effect, enslaved the Papacy, extorting from it by undue influence great and unheard-of privileges and monopolies. It had used the same sort of influence to defeat, one by one, a long series of efforts by 'non-Jesuit' Popes to reform it radically and reduce it to obedience. The Society was therefore, according to the greatest authorities in Christendom, thoroughly evil. Its complete and permanent suppression was amply justified and very long overdue.

This tremendous indictment did not fade into history after 1773. It remained practically a dogma among liberals and Protestant conservatives to the end of the 19th century. It blocked all efforts to restore the Society before 1814. After the restoration it only allowed the new Society a very hobbled and anaemic life until the middle years of the century, excluding it almost totally from South and Central America and from much of Europe. The same indictment caused the expulsion of the Society for years from France, the German Empire and other European countries later in the century.

The second explanation for the suppression was that voiced by a few heavily-preoccupied Jesuits during the traumatic years between 1759 and 1773. The ideas were reflected on, and shaped into a case for the restoration of the Society, by scattered groups of ex-Jesuits and 'Jesuited' supporters down to 1814. Neither the Papal Bull of restoration in that year nor the superiors of the new Society in the 1820s and 1830s made much of the case. The enterprise, carried out in the teeth of liberal and old-fashioned conservative opposition, was insecure and the Jesuits' energies swallowed up in a struggle to survive. But by the 1840s they had taken root strongly and their growing self-confidence manifested itself in lengthy and eloquent statements of their case by the Jesuit preacher, de Ravignan, and the 'Jesuited' lay

historian, Cretineau-Joly. Their explanation of the disaster of
1759-73 was clear and forceful. The old Society was martyred
by a conspiracy against it engineered by the Devil. Only a direct
intervention by Satan himself could account for the way in which,
after 1740, so many parties whose real interests were mutually
exclusive could have united to destroy the Society, 'enlightened
deists and atheists, 'Jansenists', Popes, monarchs and the other
religious Orders. The 'enlightened' extremists, who were the
prime movers of the conspiracy, knew that the Society was the
greatest single active force upholding the Catholic order they
wished to destroy: destroy the Society and the rest would easily
succumb. Hence the campaign against the Society was organised
like a war. Every trick of warfare was employed, barrages of lies
and rumours, the division of the enemies' ranks, and a surprise
attack using large forces of troops. Clement XIV, a weak and
stupid man, and the Empress Maria Theresa, a good but ageing
sovereign handicapped by her sex, were frightened and brow-
beaten into enforcing a total suppression of the Society, imagining
that if it were gone the 'enlightened' would leave the rest of the
Church undisturbed. That hope, of course, speedily proved vain.
By the 1790s the Catholic Church in most of Europe was in a far
worse state of disorder and collapse than it had ever been in the
worst years during the Reformation crisis of the 16th century.
The Popes who followed Clement XIV and Catholics who were
relatively untainted by either 'Jansenism' or 'enlightened'
extremism could now see clearly that, as in the later 16th century,
so now far more in the early 19th, the proper Catholic ordering
of society could not be rebuilt without the Jesuits.

There is some truth and a great deal of wild exaggeration in
both the rival explanations for the suppression. In the early
1750s the Society's position seemed reasonably safe. There
were, to be sure, evident signs in many quarters that the
'enlightenment' was passing beyond the stage of being a mere
intellectual fashion and becoming a powerful political force.
There were already more or less 'enlightened' monarchs and
'enlightened' ministers of state were a commonplace. These
ministers were eager to undertake expensive programmes of
administrative and social reform. 'Medieval' religious conservatism was becoming steadily more unpopular. Governments
were beginning to prune clerical privileges and increase taxation
on clerical properties. They clearly intended to break up large
Church properties and use the proceeds to provide elementary
schools. Redundant religious houses were threatened with

closure. Papal and royal governments alike showed an increasing disposition to interfere with the internal affairs of clerical corporations. The Gesu had recently been forced by Benedict XIV to come to terms with the Roman *Propaganda* Congregation. Jesuit missioners overseas and in Protestant Europe now owed canonical allegiance to *Propaganda's* Vicars-Apostolic.

These developments were upsetting for clerical administrators and canon lawyers but not really alarming for the Gesu. Clerical conservatives pointed out in deep alarm that there were areas of the European countryside where religious practice was minimal and paganism rampant, and that in large cities and the upper classes deists and professed atheists were now so common as to pass unremarked. Modern French historians go so far as to write of the 'dechristianisation' of 18th-century Europe. In fact, as the French Revolutionary crisis was to show, religion still had a great grip on every country and on most of the 'enlightened' minority. Frederick the Great of Prussia, still Europe's only real 'enlightened despot' in the 1750s, approved of the Jesuits as schoolmasters and supported their establishments in his kingdom through all their troubles. Catherine II of Russia, who was to come to her throne in 1762, felt the same way. Maria Theresa of Austria, a pious woman who generally allowed her minister, Kaunitz, to pursue a moderately 'enlightened' policy, was not 'Jesuited' but took for granted that Jesuit establishments were an integral part of any Catholic nation. 'Jansenism' as an open movement had long been crushed and discredited. Though its influence was still strong, its militants had to work underground where they produced illicit periodicals. The 'Encyclopaedists', a good many of them ex-pupils of the Society, were sharply critical of many features of 'Jesuitry' but seemed in no way immediately dangerous. Voltaire still had Jesuit acquaintances and his strongly anti-Jesuit tales, *Candide* and *Berthier* were not published until the onset of major troubles for the Society in 1759. D'Alembert's famous article, *Jésuites*, in the *Encyclopèdie* lay far in the future. Also, if only to give a sop to his conscience, Voltaire gave house-room to an ex-Jesuit priest after the expulsion of the Society from France and wrote of its expulsion from Portugal as 'a superfluity of the laughable with a superfluity of the horrible'. And d'Alembert, though he owed nothing to Jesuits in the past, found it advisable to write in his article, *Jésuites*:

'I have not written these things out of hate for, or resentment against, the Jesuits. My aim has been to justify the act of government which expelled them . . . and to teach the religious of that Order who will one day try to reestablish themselves in this kingdom (if they succeed, as I believe they will) on what conditions they may hope to maintain themselves here . . .'

Crusading against the Jesuits for ideological reasons was only one of several factors which combined to bring about the Society's ruin, a very complex process which dragged on for more than fifteen years. Pure accident, administrative necessity, and human weaknesses on all sides were other important factors. Until the very last stages of the operation there was no really general conspiracy to bring about the total suppression of the Society. Also when the conspiracy did take shape the parties who took part in it were drawn into common action by practical and political necessity not a shared ideology.

The whole affair stemmed originally, and surprisingly, from the indiscreet zeal of three small, separate groups of Jesuit missionaries in America. The first group, based on the Paraguayan Reductions, consisted of some forty men, mostly northern and eastern Europeans, Germans, Austrians, Hungarians, Poles and even a few Irishmen and Englishmen. The second group was of Portuguese and Brazilian Jesuits living in and round the Maranhao Reductions near the mouth of the Amazon. The third was a tiny group of French Jesuits in the West Indian Antilles. It was ironic that the mission work of the Jesuits in the Reductions had been almost universally admired by the 'enlightened' in Europe. In his early articles in the *Encyclopèdie* Montesquieu wrote of them in very glowing terms. His praise contrasts oddly with the mocking condemnation of the Reductions in Voltaire's *Candide*, published years later after their destruction.

In 1750 the governments of Spain and Portugal signed a frontier treaty which provided for an exchange of territories in South America as part of complicated schemes to revitalise the economies of the mother countries. The practical result of the treaty was that the superiors of the Jesuit Reductions in Paraguay were ordered to abandon most of their native missions and transfer the inhabitants elsewhere. Also neither government would any longer guarantee to the missions their hard-won exemption from policing, taxation and the impounding of forced labour by colonial officials. The Jesuits and missionaries of other Orders fought for many years against corrupt officials, rapacious settlers and slave-raiders to secure these legal immunities.

The Jesuits had been much more successful than other Orders in this effort but had never gained practical immunity from slave raids by officials and colonial troops. Sad experience had gradually compelled the Jesuits, in a lawless frontier area, to counter force with force. They surrounded their missions with fortifications, trained a native militia, and imported muskets and light artillery. Very understandably the Jesuit superiors suspected that the drawing of the new frontiers and the irruption into the Reductions of troops claiming to have commissions from the Portuguese and Spanish governments were due much more to greedy settlers than to the governments in Europe. They therefore sustained a vigorous military resistance and sent messages to Lisbon, Madrid and the Gesu asking for justice. The affair dragged on until 1754 when the General, frightened of the effects of adverse publicity about it in Europe, ordered the missionaries to lay down their arms and evacuate the Reductions. Most of the missionaries obeyed with bad grace: some continued to fight. In Lisbon, Pombal, a new Portuguese Minister of State and the author of an ambitious programme of economic and social reform, issued furious attacks on the Reductions. He naturally emphasised that the Jesuits had borne arms, raised rebellion against lawful authority, and organised extensive trade links with Europe. He did his best to destroy the good opinion the 'enlightened' had of the Reductions, pointing out that their inhabitants were treated like serfs and that the Jesuits everywhere in America raised no objection to negro slavery. The whole matter was then, and is still today, very contentious, but Pombal's propaganda achieved its aim. Opinion in Europe hardened against the Reductions.

Simultaneously Pombal ordered the liquidation of the Maranhao Reductions and the foundation of a monopolistic, Lisbon-based trading company to dominate the economy of Brazil. A good many Brazilians whose livelihood was threatened by the company organised a rival organisation to fight it, the *Mesa do Bem Commun*. The Jesuit missioners evicted in Maranhao warmly supported the *Mesa* and undertook to rouse their colleagues in Portugal to lobby the king against Pombal's schemes. Benito da Fonseca, the Maranhao superior, actually undertook the paperwork of the *Mesa* and Ballester, the most celebrated Portuguese Jesuit preacher in Lisbon, held forth from the pulpit against Pombal. Pombal was furiously angry. His 'enlightened' opinions were genuine but naïve and mingled in his mind with a bitter animosity against the Society inherited from his family which was of the official class and contained distinguished secular clergy. He began to think that underground networks of Jesuit influences linked the wave of civil disobedience in Brazil with aristocratic dissidence in Portugal. His fright bred ferocity. He ordered the arrest of the leaders of the *Mesa* and their Jesuit associates and began to look for evidence of dangerous collusion between aristocrats and Jesuits.

Meanwhile Lavalette, a Jesuit procurator in the Antilles and his associates, had been in serious trouble with the Gesu for illicit trading. In 1753 he was summoned back to France and prosecuted by the Government. Two years later the matter appeared to be closed. The prosecution was withdrawn and the General allowed Lavalette back to his post in the Antilles on certain conditions. The procurator could, with some justice, say that trading by missionaries was a very long-standing practice in all Orders and often the only practicable way of financing missions. The Gesu and the Papacy had repeatedly turned a blind eye to the practice except when it gained adverse publicity. But unfortunately for Lavalette rapidly changing war conditions in the Atlantic confounded all his ingenious commercial schemes. His cargoes were captured by the British Navy: his agents in France went bankrupt, and his secret company founded to trade with the Dutch collapsed. His creditors in France sued him there for the enormous sum of five million francs.

By 1755 the Brazilian, Paraguayan, Portuguese and Antilles affairs were creating grave embarrassments for the Gesu. Pombal roused the King of Portugal to dismiss the Jesuit Court confessors and forwarded to the Roman Curia through the Lisbon nuncio a long list of charges against the Portuguese and Brazilian Provinces of the Society. He asked for the appointment of a papal Visitor, not a Jesuit, with summary powers to punish the chief offenders. The General, Centurioni, did his best to get the matter shelved in Rome indefinitely. Meanwhile he was searching hard for ways and means of satisfying Lavalette's creditors quietly. With luck the Gesu might just have managed to give a *quietus* to these awkward affairs: it had passed safely through worse storms in the past. But now misadventure piled on misadventure. The King of Portugal was a libidinous weakling. Pombal's personal vendetta against the Jesuits was peculiarly violent. Centurioni, an able diplomat, fell ill and died at a crucial stage in the delaying operations and there was an interregnum of months before the election of a new General. The General Congregation's choice, Lorenzo Ricci, was an odd one. He had spent a good many years as a spiritual director at the *Romanum*, was noted for his timidity and indecisiveness, and was totally inexperienced in administration and delicate diplomacy. On top of this Benedict XIV became moribund and incapable of doing business.

Affairs now rapidly got out of control. During the Pope's final illness and the vacancy in the Generalate, Pombal pressed his cause in Rome and secured, probably by the use of bribery, exactly what he wanted. Without consultation with the Gesu, the Roman Curia granted a Brief empowering Cardinal Saldanha, one of Pombal's relations and supporters, to carry out a visitation of the Portuguese Jesuit Province, reform it in any way he pleased, take secret proceedings against offenders and withhold from them their right of appeal to Rome. In 1759 he began by formally inhibiting all Portuguese Jesuits from teaching, preaching and hearing confessions pending the completion of his reforms. Then came a chance event which gave Pombal an excuse for crushing his enemies. The King of Portugal, on his way to an assignation with an aristocratic lady, met her husband who fired several shots at him. The result was a 'Portuguese Plot' which rivalled in mystery, horror and sheer absurdity the English Gunpowder and Popish plots. Pombal had the nobleman, his wife and household, including three Jesuit confessors, arrested, tortured and executed. On the strength of undisclosed information, said to have been extracted by the tortures, a number of leading noblemen and over 180 Jesuits, a third of the Province, were arrested and charged with complicity in a plot to assassinate the king and Pombal. Among those who were executed was Malagrida, an old, pious and highly eccentric Jesuit accused of inciting the plotters with charms and dire prophecies. Then, acting with great speed to forestall protests and demands for information from the newly elected, and 'Jesuited', Pope, Clement XIII, Pombal and Saldanha jointly ordered the siezure and sale of all Jesuit property in the kingdom and its colonies overseas. All the Jesuits in Portugal, the colonies in America, Africa, India and elsewhere in the Far East, apart from those already in gaol, were expelled and shipped forthwith, with a great deal of brutality, to Civita Vecchia in the Papal States.

The affair of Lavalette in France developed just as badly but more slowly. Ricci, after much hesitation, allowed Lavalette to leave the Society and then tried desperately to settle his debts. It proved impossible to do this by selling the Jesuit properties in the Antilles since the islands had just been occupied by British naval forces. Ricci then suggested that the French Provinces might club together to find the money, if necessary borrowing and selling or mortgaging a number of small Colleges. The Provincials pleaded poverty and pointed out that the *Constitutions* made each individual Jesuit College or mission responsible for its own debts. While Ricci hesitated the Provincials squabbled, lost their heads, and took the initiative unwisely. Simultaneously they urged the General to persuade better-off Provinces in Italy, Spain and South America to make voluntary contributions and appealed to Louis XV and the *Parlement* of Paris. They asked for a legal acknowledgement that liability for the debts rested solely on the Antilles mission. Clearly they expected no effective help from the General and put all their trust in their 'Old Boy' network in France. The matter hung in the balance for a year. Then in 1761 the *parlement* arrived at a decision. The ex-pupils of the Society on the bench were outvoted. The whole Society was declared liable to pay the debt and the *parlement* demanded that the *Constitutions* should be submitted to their judgement since some clauses in them manifestly conflicted with the common law of France. Delaying action by the Provincials proved fruitless. In 1762 the *parlement* formally declared the *Constitutions* illegal. The Jesuits must either leave the kingdom or reform them to bring them into line with French law in every particular, turning the Provinces into a purely French Congregation separated from the Gesu. Pending the Provincials' decision on this the *parlement* ordered the noviciates to be closed down and all French Jesuits to cease from teaching.

There was nothing particularly new about the *parlement's* decisions. Ever since the 16th century the Society's position in France had rested on a series of compromises. Its superiors had repeatedly subscribed to declarations that they put their allegiance to the crown and common law before their duty to the Pope, the General and the *Constitutions.* They professed to the *parlement* that their subscriptions were sincere, and to the Gesu and the Roman Curia that they were merely formal and extracted from them by force. This peculiar gentleman's agreement had often been attacked by French officials who were not 'Jesuited' and by zealous Popes and Curial officials. It had endured through storms and controversy because it had suited kings of France who held the Papacy and the Gesu at arm's length but were much attached to their Jesuit confessors. The arrangement was tolerated uncomfortably by 'Jesuited' lawyers and by Jesuits who had somehow to combine intense patriotism with real devotion to the Society.

Louis XV was annoyed that the Provincials and Lavalette had roused a hornets' nest about their ears but sincerely wished to find some compromise solution. For political reasons he dare not try to call the *parlement* to order by summoning them to a *Lit de Justice*. He therefore proposed that the General should quietly alter the *Constitutions*, grant the French Provinces at least the outward appearances of independence of the Gesu, and let the French Jesuits make yet another, and very public, declaration that their allegiance to the crown came before all their other loyalties. This scheme was warmly supported by a good many leading Jesuits, including the Court confessors, and a body of 'Jesuited' lawyers. Unfortunately both Clement XIII and the General were timid and deeply scrupulous men. They agonised over the problem and finally declared that they could not, in conscience, accept the compromise scheme.

The *parlements* of France now went into action. Among their members were men of every type. Some were thoroughly 'enlightened' and very anti-Jesuit on principle. Some, though not many, were free-thinkers. Some were certainly secret 'Jansenists' who had old scores to settle with the Society. Some were not 'Jesuited' but generally well-disposed towards the Society. A good many were ex-pupils of the Jesuits but not all united in their view of the crisis. The outcome of the voting in the *parlements* was therefore by no means certain in advance. In fact the *parlements* of Paris, Bordeaux, Rennes, Roussillon and Rouen decided to sequester all Jesuit property in their jurisdictions, declare the Society an alien body, and expel all Jesuits. In a good many other *parlements* there were long and passionate debates, party intrigues and eventually the swamping of the 'Jesuited' or their exclusion from office. The French bishops were equally divided. They received Briefs from Clement XIII urging them to defend the Jesuits. But as *parlement* after *parlement* declared for expulsion and expropriation and the anti-Jesuit forces in society surfaced with a sudden and wholly unexpected ferocity and unanimity even the 'Jesuited' bishops took fright. Louis XV was quite disinclined to go along with the tide. But he was deeply offended by the General's rejection of his efforts and could not afford to cross swords in public with the *parlements* at a time when he desperately needed their approval for extraordinary financial levies for the war effort. When the Archbishop of Paris ventured to speak up in favour of the Jesuits the king packed him off to confinement in the grim Cistercian monastery of La Trappe. Government officials put seals on the doors of all Jesuit establishments evicting the inmates most of whom were hustled out of French territory. In a few areas where they were widely popular they hid in the houses of friends and were left undisturbed.

These dramatic events in Portugal and France stirred up a mass of publicity, speculation and heated debate throughout Europe. Charles III, who had become king of Spain in 1759 at the height of the Portuguese crisis, was stirred to action by the news. He was a rigidly pious man with a devotional life not far removed from that of the well 'Jesuited'. But he had long been a convert to very moderately 'enlightened' ideas which, in a country like Spain, socially very backward and far more dominated by clerical influences than France, were commonly regarded as 'atheistical'. He had no illusions about the strength of clerical and popular opposition to his policies for modernising the country. With good reason he saw the Spanish Jesuits as the most active and dangerous of his opponents and was pessimistic about his chances of reducing their power. Then a rapid succession of events changed his mind and decided him on strong action. There was very serious rioting in Madrid, touched off by his decree forbidding the wearing in public of archaic garments adopted consciously as tokens of traditionalist resistance. The rioters insulted the king and beat up his guards. The death of Charles's mother, who had been very devoted to the Society, removed an obstacle to action against it. The news from France, where Jesuit influence was reckoned to be very strong, inclined the king to think that a similar, but much swifter, expulsion of the Jesuits, if carefully planned, had a good chance of success. News from Naples suggested that action would have to be undertaken there very soon or postponed for many years.

The Government's action in Spain, Naples and the colonies in 1767 was planned carefully like a military operation against a strong enemy. As far as possible the Jesuit network of influences was paralysed in advance. 'Jesuited' officials and aristocrats were dismissed from their posts, sent overseas or persuaded to hold their hands. The bishops were easily brought over to the king's side by concessions and promises. They and the other religious Orders needed little persuasion to leave the Inquisition, the Society's staunch ally, isolated. The royal decree of banishment of the Jesuits and sequestration of their property was executed simultaneously in many places in each area in such a way as to bewilder, mystify and neutralise popular opposition. Strong forces of officials and troops made dawn raids on Jesuit houses, packed the inmates into covered wagons and hustled them under close guard to the ports of embarkation for the Papal States.

By the end of 1767 the Society was very hard hit. Of its 23,000 members, approximately half, 11,608, had now been officially ejected from the countries in which they worked. The superiors of those expelled realised that they would have no means to support novices, students and many of the simply professed. Most of them therefore immediately offered these men and the lay coadjutors release from their vows. The civil governments usually added an inducement by promising to give small pensions to those who quitted the Society but none to the simply professed who stayed in it and went into exile. These offers were accepted at once by about a third of the whole number scheduled for expulsion: they quitted the Society and were allowed to go home to their families. During the first few years of the exile of the expelled Jesuits a rapidly increasing number of them gained release from their vows. Among these were some of the Professed. The movement out of the Society was especially brisk among the liberally-minded and South American Creoles. The harsh and crowded conditions of life as exiles without work caused the ancient quarrel between Creoles and native Spaniards to flare up and the two groups soon ceased to speak to each other. Thus in a very short space of time the Society was bled of more than a quarter of its membership. In the great majority the men who left were those on whom the stricken Provinces most depended for their survival, novices, students and young priests. Noviciates and student houses could not be improvised in the conditions which prevailed among the exiles so the grave losses could not be made good. Thousands of mostly middle-aged and old, often ailing, Jesuits were dumped unceremoniously in lodging houses in the Papal States and Corsica. The pension money promised to the Professed was long in coming. When it was received some of the recipients refused to share it with their less fortunate brethren. These were compelled to beg or try to get casual work as tutors or journalists. Morale among many of the exiles was low.

Clement XIII and his Consistory of Cardinals were not very helpful. The Pope had issued a Brief affirming his support for the Society. The Cardinals argued that if it were known that the Pope was willing to house all expelled Jesuits in his States governments would assume that he accepted the legitimacy of the expulsions and, worse, was ready to accept any who might be expelled in future years. That would positively encourage other sovereigns to turn against the Society. Therefore shiploads of South American Jesuits arriving at the entrance to the papal harbour of Civita Vecchia were greeted with warning shots and forced to discharge their passengers in Corsica. That move soon proved no solution to the difficulty since French troops were in process of occupying the island. As they did so they packed the South American Jesuits into small boats and sent them to the Papal States. This time they were rather grudgingly allowed to land but strictly forbidden to come anywhere near Rome. The General, without much hope of success, tried to levy money from the surviving Provinces to support the flood of exiles.

The governments of France, Spain and Portugal now consulted together about their next moves. Their example had been followed by Parma and Malta. Tuscany and Bavaria drew the line at expulsion of their Jesuits but had schemes to organise them compulsorily into Congregations independent of the Gesu. On the other hand the governments of most northern and eastern European countries still showed no disposition to consider taking action against Jesuits. The Empress Maria Theresa was particularly adamant. Charles III's chief minister in Naples was despondent. Support for the Jesuits was, he thought, still very strong in many countries and could easily build up a backlash against the anti-Jesuit governments. Half of the Society remained in place, undisturbed. There were Jesuits still living and ministering secretly in France with some connivance from the Government. Louis XV's 'Jesuited' Carmelite daughter was urging on her father a plan to organise these relics of the French Provinces into a new Congregation with a noviciate. In the eyes of the lawyers the Congregation would be separate from the Society: but its members in secret would still be Jesuits subject to the Gesu. Tanucchi suspected that even 'enlightened' rulers had a deep superstitious fear of carrying action against the Society too far.

Clement XIII died in 1769 and a Consistory met to elect his successor. Charles III and the chief ministers of France, Portugal and Naples, Choiseul, Pombal and Tanucchi, used all their considerable powers of persuasion and bribery to secure the election of the Franciscan Cardinal Ganganelli who appeared to be the least 'Jesuited' of the candidates. The anti-Jesuits were now sure that only a total and final legal suppression of the Society by a Pope could prevent it recovering its hold on Europe little by little. Ganganelli was elected as Clement XIV. He immediately became the target of two rival campaigns both of which wielded threats and blandishments in equal proportions. French troops marched into the outlying papal town of Avignon. Threats were made to stop the trade of the Papal States. Clement was told bluntly that if he did not suppress the Society the hostile governments would close monasteries and convents wholesale and cut communications between their national Churches and the Vatican. Simultaneously groups of traditionalist exiled Jesuits supported by numerous 'friends' launched a noisy campaign to shame or frighten the Pope into inaction. Sermons and pamphlets flew about his ears like brickbats. Devout nuns and laywomen directed by Jesuits and already famed for their ecstatic and prophetic pronouncements began to announce doom for the Pope if he dared to take action against the Society. For many months he twisted and turned, making gestures of appeasement towards both sides. He drew up a Brief of suppression but kept it under lock and key. He forbade the General to leave the Gesu or send him any messages. He expelled the Jesuits from the *Romanum*. He ordered the Roman Inquisition to take proceedings against the most eccentric and violent of the 'Jesuited' ecstatics. As the months passed journalists and political commentators thronged Rome gleaning every scrap of news and rumour. Some of them said that the matter had already been decided against the Society but that Clement was anxious to make it appear that the suppression was forced on him. Others, including Tanucchi, believed that he was in the grip of superstitious fear, was terrified of plots by the 'Jesuited' to poison him, and intended to spin out his indecision for the rest of his life. In the end, in 1773, the decision came with the publication of the Brief *Dominus ac Redemptor* which appeared to give the anti-Jesuits almost all they wanted.

The Brief reminded its readers, including the Jesuits, that religious Orders were neither divinely ordained nor immortal. The Pope then outlined the history of papal dealings with the Society and the way in which it had repeatedly, while professing to be 'the Pope's Janissaries', frustrated every papal effort to reform it. Nevertheless Clement did not make the Jesuits' faults of disobedience and arrogance the main justification for their suppression. His case rested mainly on the fact that they were a constant and grave source of dissension within the Church. He forthwith freed all unordained Jesuits from their vows. Priests were to receive pensions. With excessive optimism Clement expected that the proceeds of the sale of Jesuit properties would be made available to him by royal governments to fund these pensions. Simply professed priests were to get individual dispensations from their vows within a year. The Professed, for whom dispensation was still a slow and difficult business, were left in an anomalous position. They must either take service in parishes or, if aged, sick or just timid, continue to live in communities like secular clergy: either way they were under the authority of local bishops and forbidden to keep the Jesuit rules or open schools. The Pope now distributed the Jesuit establishments in Rome and the Papal States among other clerical groups. The Gesu and its great church went to the Capuchins, the church of S. Ignazio to the Minorites, the Roman Penitentiary to the Franciscans and the English College to Italian secular clergy professors. All undispensed ex-Jesuits were ordered to live outside the Papal States. Ricci and the senior staff of the Gesu. already under house-arrest, proved an embarrassment. They were Professed and unlikely to seek dispensations. It was very undesirable that they should live in a community either outside the Papal States or, by special dispensation, in Rome. 'Jesuited' visionaries were still causing much trouble throughout Italy and the General would be the natural focus of any movement to restore the Society. The Pope decided reluctantly that Ricci and thirteen companions must be held indefinitely *incommunicado* in apartments in the papal fortress of Sant' Angelo. Some of them were later released but Ricci died in the fortress a few years later.

'Ganganelli', as he was generally contemptuously called in memoirs and early 19th-century history books, became the subject of many legends. Several liberal ex-Jesuits in northern Italy and Germany preached commendatory sermons on the Brief, praising the Pope's bravery and clear-sightedness, but they were almost his only admirers. 'Jesuited' writers regarded him with horror and contempt tempered only by prudence. Most anti-Jesuit writers before Gioberti and Theiner regarded him with suspicion as a typical double-faced cleric. They accused him of deliberately leaving loopholes in the Brief so that a nucleus of determined ex-Jesuits could keep the Society's traditions alive underground pending the day of its restoration. Until the later years of the 19th century historians took seriously the rumour that Clement died of poison administered by ex-Jesuits or their 'friends'. Unfortunately his private papers vanished after his death so modern historians can cast little new light on his intentions.

The execution of the Brief was an enormous business since

the Provinces which were intact in 1773 contained the bulk of the Society's houses, and the attitudes of the civil and ecclesiastical authorities varied from eager compliance to obstructiveness. In the states of Mainz, Cologne, Tuscany and Belgium the Brief was executed rapidly and even brutally. Ex-Jesuits seeking parochial work were cold-shouldered, communities discouraged and the Professed usually expelled from the states' territories. Elsewhere, for instance in the Austrian Empire proper, Poland, Saxony, Holland and England, all ex-Jesuits were treated with some consideration. They were often allowed to retain their missions, have small communities, and even retain corporate ownership of some houses. In England the Vicars-Apostolic, though the heirs of a bitterly anti-Jesuit tradition, were forced to acquiesce in this sort of settlement for the time being since they had not at their disposal enough secular priests to take over the large number of Jesuit missions. It was convenient to allow the ex-Jesuits as a body to retain legal ownership of their mission properties. If the Vicars-Apostolic had tried to take over the properties they would have met a barrage of obstruction from the ex-Jesuits' 'friends' and benefactors. In any case expropriated ex-Jesuits would have secular priests' rights to maintenance by the Vicars-Apostolic. The same sort of practical considerations caused the rulers of a good many German and east European states to drag their feet in executing the Brief. The main cause was always the fact that the local Catholic clerical establishment depended heavily on ex-Jesuits. In Poland in 1773 the Jesuits had such a strong hold on schools and missions that the Diet hesitated for a long time about allowing the Brief to be promulgated. In Saxony the entire Catholic clerical system from the Vicar-Apostolic downwards was ex-Jesuit. The Colleges were soon made over to imported secular priests but the rest of the system stayed in the hands of ex-Jesuits for years. The Palatinate, Rottweil and the free city of Augsburg were compelled to behave in the same way. The rulers of Liège and Julich-Berg had elastic consciences and even maintained six Colleges with totally ex-Jesuit teaching staffs down to the 1790s.

The survival of communities of ex-Jesuits actively engaged in missions and teaching was most marked in Prussia and the Russian Empire. In 1773 Frederick II of Prussia had over 400 Jesuits bearing the brunt of ministering to his Catholic subjects. Catherine II of Russia had recently annexed a large part of Poland containing over 200. It was vital to both rulers that their Catholic subjects should be kept happy. Neither had any intention of ever allowing the Brief to disturb religious arrangements which were long-standing and fairly satisfactory. On the other hand they were anxious to take advantage of the isolation of their ex-Jesuits to get them firmly under state control. Hence the Brief was not promulgated in either country. The ex-Jesuits were organised into separate Congregations financed by the state, subject to government inspection and bound to maintain their Colleges and missions. The local Catholic bishops were forbidden to interfere with this arrangement. The ex-Jesuits were urged to carry on business as usual and reopen their noviciates and student houses. The two rulers even recruited able ex-Jesuits from Germany. A casual observer of Prussia and Russia in the 1780s could be pardoned for thinking that the Catholics had never heard of the Brief.

The early 19th-century apologists of the restored Society insisted that the suppression was totally illegal and disastrous in its results for Catholicism and civilisation. The Brief, they held, was exacted from Clement XIV by force and fraud. Hence, in countries where it was formally promulgated, the Jesuits owed it 'external obedience' only: in Prussia and Russia where it was not promulgated they owed it no kind of obedience at all. Thus, in this view, the Society was never really suppressed. Dispensations and desertions robbed it of all but some 2,000 of its 23,000 members. But the brave survivors constantly renewed their vows and allegiance to the Society in their hearts and consciences. Hence it had a shadowy underground existence in much of Europe and a perfectly open existence in Prussia and Russian Poland. After the death of Clement XIV, it was held, his successors, the 'Jesuited' Pius VI and the Benedictine Pius VII, steadily, though with great secrecy down to 1801, assumed that the Brief had always been illicit. In 1801 Pius VII made the first of a long series of open admissions of this belief. He encouraged many small groups of the ex-Jesuit 'faithful' to surface. Hence the formal restoration of the Society by the Brief *Sollicitudo* in 1814 was, in spite of its diplomatic and ambiguous wording, no foundation of a new Society but a final ratification of a belief that the old Society had never died.

The apologists' case for regarding the suppression of 1773 as an unmitigated disaster was just as impressive. The Brief, they said, touched off an avalanche of religious 'reforms' by 'enlightened' monarchs. These were designed to make the clergy civil servants and reduce religion to 'practical benevolence' and moralism. Religious houses of all Orders were shut down as anti-social or obsolete. The state dictated 'useful and progressive' syllabuses for seminaries and schools. Papal power was reduced to very little. The Brief also was said to have shattered the Catholic education system of Europe by shutting down its best part, half a dozen universities, as many university faculties, and over 800 flourishing Colleges. The Brief practically destroyed Catholic foreign missions since the Jesuits had been their inspiration. The missions, like the religious Orders, were reduced to a pathetic weakness from which they only recovered a century later. Worst of all, the apologists insisted, the Brief dissolved all Jesuit organisations for defending the faith and the rights of the Church and so opened the floodgates to let in the great tide of godless radicalism which produced the French Revolution of 1789 and the spreading of its principles across Europe by force of arms.

This Jesuit case was a declaration of faith, not a rational inter-pretation of historical facts, and so was invulnerable to criticism of its facts. They were set out in an exaggerated and inaccurate way. To all practical intents and purposes the old Society of Jesus was dead by 1790 and the Society of 1814 was a new foundation. There was a thread of personal and spiritual con-tinuity between the old institution and the new one, but it was exceedingly tenuous.

During the two decades after the Brief of 1773 the external structure of Jesuit life, the hierarchy of command, the flow of orders, the life of the vows, the steady course of Acquaviva's complex of observances all perished. Even in Prussia and Russia the reality of that system ceased to exist: the 'Congregational' life which replaced it was *ad hoc* and borrowed from other sources. Meanwhile, the vast majority of ex-Jesuits abandoned the Society in their minds and consciences. In many cases the process of abandonment was slow and painful. These men were the victims of a Jesuit training which had long tried to combine a military style of obedience, making the mind conform to the will, with 'Probabilist' ideas about liberty of conscience and a minimalistic attitude towards rules and legal obligations. The result, in such a great crisis as the suppression, was mental confusion. Many ex-Jesuits gradually became convinced that they must abandon the Society because they owed an assent in conscience to the Brief even if it seemed unjust and had not been formally promulgated in their countries. Most of the Prussian 'Congregation' soon came to think that 'common knowledge' of the edict was equivalent to promulgation. But, in any case,

Frederick II's peculiar relationship with them was ended by his successor after 1786: the 'Congregation' was broken up, the salaries and subsidies withdrawn, and the Colleges put under the control of imported secular clergy. In Russian Poland most ex-Jesuits came to believe that they ought to combine outward obedience to the empress with an obedience in conscience to the Brief. They dressed and behaved outwardly as if they were still Jesuits but thought of themselves as ordinary secular priests. The strain of keeping up this ambiguous condition often proved more than men could bear. Others, incapable of such scrupulosity, simply came to think that there was no future in a lost cause backed by no positive programme of renewal and reform.

Because of this situation very many drifted away from the groups of 'the faithful' or only remained with them until they could find some other means of subsistence. The Russian Congregation wilted. In 1773 it contained more than 200 men. In 1778 alone fifty-three departed and only seventy-eight were left. By 1780 the Congregation was on the verge of collapse. Meanwhile, financial hardship and the loss of hope played havoc with all ex-Jesuit groups throughout the rest of Europe. At Ferrara in Italy a group had congregated beside the university by 1773. By 1779 its leaders had all departed. Antonio Conca, a Spaniard, then became convinced that the Society was dead for good. He went off to become a writer and pillar of the Italian 'enlightenment'. Raimondo Ximenes, another Spaniard, became a radical Freemason. Alessandro Zorzi from Venice became one of the editors of the Italian *Encyclopaedia.*

The French ex-Jesuits were scattered far and wide across Europe by the expulsions. Some, accompanied by Poles and Italians, drifted back to France under assumed names. Dr. Boscovich arrived in Paris in 1773 where his scientific reputation secured him the post of Director of Optics of the French Navy. He lived as a secular priest and seemed quite agnostic about his relation to the Society. Esteban Arteaga, a Spanish ex-Jesuit, abandoned a group of the 'faithful' in north Italy, became a music critic and by 1783 had moved to Paris where his book, *The Revolution in the Italian Musical Theatre*, was published. Joseph-Ignace Guillotin was a Jesuit professor at the Bordeaux College at the time of the expulsions from France. He accepted a dispensation and became a physician. His Jesuit past was not very evident when he stood up in the French Assembly in 1789 and proposed the use of an ingenious beheading machine for the criminals of all social classes. Voltaire took pity on a penniless ex-Jesuit priest who clearly regarded himself as a secular priest. He was provided with the curé of Voltaire's chapel at Ferney. Pierre-Joseph de Clorivière was professed of the four vows in 1773. After many adventures he emerged in the 1790s as one of the few leaders of the ex-Jesuit 'faithful'. Jean Grou was out of France at Pont à Mousson in Lorraine at the time of the expulsions. He took his final vows there. After the suppression he entered France in disguise and under an assumed name was given a pension and a job as a writer by the 'Jesuited' Archbishop of Paris. In Paris he became a spiritual director of 'Jesuited' ladies, a writer of devotional books and almost a hermit. His preoccupation with contemplative prayer prevented him from becoming a 'faithful' activist like de Clorivière: he took refuge from the dangers and distractions of French life in a hermitage provided by the Weld family at their house at Lulworth in Dorset.

In Poland many of the younger ex-Jesuits refused to live in 'faithful' communities and went to work as secular priests. Naruszewicz, a liberal and a poet, did this and ended his life as a diocesan bishop. Bohololec, another liberal poet, stayed after the suppression as editor of the Warsaw *Monitor* which he transformed from a periodical of Jesuit apologetic to a fashionable secular literary monthly. Kniazin, a liberal Jesuit student nearing ordination in 1773, promptly turned away to lay life as a tutor, journalist and writer of erotic verse.

In Germany many young ex-Jesuit students and priests turned to the secular priesthood, schoolteaching and journalism. Among them were two future bishops, Johannes Sailer of Landshut and Ignatius Sattler of Ingolstadt. Sailer had been a Jesuit student in 1773. He left for a diocesan seminary and became a secular priest and seminary professor. Many years later, when he was Germany's most respected Catholic leader, he commented cryptically on the Society and his Jesuit days. He had made no effort to align himself with the ex-Jesuit 'faithful' in the 1790s or again in 1814. His life as a Jesuit student was, he said, 'paradisal': the early Society was 'divine', but the Jesuits of his days 'human' and the suppression 'devilish'. In Italy the tiny scattered groups of the 'faithful' were vastly outnumbered by those who had departed. These included Italian liberals and large communities of South American radicals, men like Guzman and Poco y Sucre, who poured out a mass of published work extolling their homelands, damning the Spanish Government and calling for radical Church reform.

In England, Liège and Louvain there were bands of English

ex-Jesuit 'faithful'. They included Charles Plowden and Howard whose faith never flagged and Stone who was long a doubter. They were quite outnumbered by colleagues whose attitudes varied widely. A few, like Francis Plowden, plunged straight from the Society into enthusiastic Whiggery. Others, like the Americans, Carroll and Wharton, came round gradually to rejection of the Society and to radical views. Others, like Chamberlain of the Bar convent at York, were piously content to accept the Brief as the puzzling will of God and speculate no further about the future. Yet others, at work in old Jesuit parishes in Liverpool or the countryside or on the staff of the ex-Jesuit Academy transferred for safety from Liège to Stonyhurst in Lancashire, saw themselves as permanently out of the Society and were steadily hostile to the plans of the 'faithful'.

In Belgium and Holland there were much the same differences of opinion. At Brussels de Bye kept his tiny research team of Bollandists together in 1773, relying on the continuance of the Austrian Government's annual grants. These would not have been forthcoming if the Bollandists had been obvious 'faithful'. In any case, like Grou the Bollandists were too deeply involved in their own special vocation to concern themselves greatly with speculation about the future. They survived the withdrawal of the grants in 1789 but succumbed to the invasion of Belgium by the French Revolutionary armies in 1794.

Until 1793 it was outsiders, not ex-Jesuits, who strove to get the Society restored. In 1775 a group of *Zelanti* and 'Jesuited' Cardinals tried to get Pius VI to pledge himself to this: he refused. By the 1780s Kaunitz, the Austrian minister, estimated that really influential lay supporters of the Society were few outside Rome: Prinz von Hohenlohe-Schillingfuerst, Madame Louise of France, a few French bishops and reactionary Polish aristocrats. But the publication of Edmund Burke's *Reflections on the French Revolution* in 1790 was the first symptom of a great wave of conservative reaction against the Revolution and the whole 'enlightenment'. The wave gathered impetus in the following years in most countries. It brought partial or complete changes of heart among rulers, aristocrats and writers who had hitherto tended to be 'enlightened'. Writers like von Gentz, Novalis, Heine and Goethe began to speak of tradition and religion with a new respect. There were startling conversions to Catholicism. Publicists like de Maistre, de Bonald and Chateaubriand began to recommend a return to pre-Revolutionary values including respect for the papacy and religious Orders. By 1800 it was becoming fashionable to say that the Brief of 1773 was a mistake and that the Jesuits, with definite safeguards against their excesses, might well be restored. The German Protestant supporters of the new reaction like Novalis of course would not go as far as this. But he noted with interest that 'the Jesuits' were regaining power. He meant by this expression men like de Maistre, imagining that they were the puppets of immensely clever ex-Jesuits behind the scenes. He was quite wrong. The Catholic reaction was an entirely lay movement of converts from irreligion. Its supporters were tardy in making contact with clergy and practised their new-found Catholicism sketchily. They often combined a heady declaration of absolute loyalty to the Pope with anticlericalism. De Maistre had been a pupil of the Jesuits at Turin in his youth, but then became a radical liberal. It was only after his conversion from liberalism that he developed sentimental feelings about his Jesuit schooling. In 1803 he became the ambassador of the King of Sardinia at the Court of St. Petersburg, discovered the existence of the ex-Jesuit Russian Congregation, was astounded at its timidity, and set about trying to galvanise it with 'proper principles'.

Elsewhere, in Italy, France, Belgium and even England, 'de Maistrist' laity, secular priests and nuns were prodding the younger and more susceptible ex-Jesuits into daring action. In 1782, prodded by the Russian Government, the Russian Congregation had started a noviciate and elected a superior called a Vicar-General. Now the enthusiasts extracted from Pius VI some sort of guarded, verbal approval of the act and persuaded scores of ex-Jesuits to write and secure affiliation to the Russian Congregation. As enthusiasm mounted German, Italian, Dutch and English ex-Jesuits and students travelled to Russian Poland to join it. There was a good deal of coming and going at Polotsk, the Vicar-General's headquarters, but the Congregation's numbers mounted to 200 and then over 400. In Parma one of the affiliated ex-Jesuits, Joseph Pignatelli, summoned thither three of his friends who were at Polotsk and established them in an old Jesuit College which he had persuaded the Duke of Parma to reopen. They began a 'Russian noviciate'. Sent packing from Parma by Napoleon's troops, the four men took refuge in Naples, were expelled from there too and wandered to Sicily. In Louvain a group of young and enthusiastic secular priests started a Congregation on vaguely Jesuit lines. The idea was taken up in France by a militant ex-Jesuit, Pierre-Joseph de Clorivière, whose Congregation consisted of secular priests and students.

In Spoleto an Italian secular priest, Niccolo Paccanari, launched an even more ambitious Congregation. He claimed affiliation with Polotsk and the approval of Rome. His Congregation, ostensibly to avoid the attentions of Napoleon's police, passed under several different names. His charm, dynamism and flamboyance rapidly won him a bigger and bigger following among the 'faithful', ex-Jesuits and others. Pignatelli and de Clorivière came under his spell and associated their Congregations with his. The Belgian Congregation also joined them. The 'Paccanarists', as they were called, charmed permission from Cardinal Fesch, Napoleon's uncle, to found schools and nunneries. Joseph Varin and Louis Barat, their French superiors, founded a teaching Order, the Ladies of the Sacred Heart, under Barat's sister. Paccanarist envoys even found ways to cross the Channel and beard the stolid leaders of the English ex-Jesuits at Stonyhurst. Everywhere among the 'faithful' the feeling grew that Paccanari was the great spiritual leader and refounder of the Society of Jesus they had sought.

But much of this hopefulness and enthusiasm turned sour after 1804. Napoleon's power waxed and seemed unbeatable. His troops occupied Rome and carried Pius VII off into captivity in France. His police expelled the Paccanarists from France. The 'faithful' formed rival factions. 'The Russians' accused the Paccanarists of strangling all that was left of true Jesuitry inside their novel, outlandish Congregation. De Clorivière and Charles Plowden of Stonyhurst detached themselves from the Paccanarists and founded small noviciates under the wing of Polotsk, but these were unsuccessful. The Vicar-General urged them to weed out of their recruits 'the turbulent and talented' taking only 'the quiet' and docile. Some of the 'faithful' became fanatical 'de Maistrists', preaching absolute obedience to Polotsk through blood and suffering as the only road to a purified new Society. De Clorivière joined this group and allied himself to royalist guerilla fighters in France dedicated to sabotage and assassinations. Others of the 'faithful' were far more moderate: some were clinging to romantic liberalism. Others, disgusted by the factions, lost all hope.

The abdication of Napoleon in 1814 led to the release of Pius VII who returned to Rome in triumph. He was alarmed by the wildness of the Paccanarists and impressed by the arguments of the Roman *Zelanti*. They demanded a swift return to the 'normality' of the 1740s and a crusade against liberalism in every shape. In fact their allies, *Sanfedisti* street gangs, were already beating up and assassinating known liberals in the Papal States. The *Zelanti* had become convinced that the Society must be restored firmly on the basis of the Russian Congregation and its 'faithful' allies in the west. Hence the Pope issued a Brief, *Sollicitudo*, giving them what they wanted. In the Brief he maintained that he had, since 1801, cancelled the operation of the Suppression Brief, *Dominus ac Redemptor*, of 1773 in favour of Polotsk, Pignatelli, de Clorivière and Plowden and their followers. He now made over to them the Roman Gesu and Noviciate and all the old Jesuit Colleges in the Papal States. In papal law the Society was fully restored. But Pius pointed out that actual restoration in each of the sovereign states of Europe and America would have to await the signing of Concordats between the Holy See and their governments. Thus, quite unexpectedly, and more as an aspiration than a solid reality, the Society regained legal existence. The Gesu house in Rome had stood damp, unrepaired and emptied of furniture for years, its library long dispersed. The great Gesu church was urgently in need of repair and redecoration: the great silver statue of Ignatius Loyola had been sold by Pius VI. The number of ex-Jesuits, Jesuit novices and others who might rally to the call was quite unknown. In the months that followed the Brief the depressing realities became clear. The Vicar-General, named first General of the restored Society by the Pope, tried hard to conceal his new dignity from the Tsar's Government. The French invasion of Russia in 1812 had unleashed a storm of nationalistic fervour in Russia. The Russian Congregation, mostly consisting of Poles, became deeply suspect. It was made plain to the new General that he must either submit himself and his men utterly to the Tsar's authority or take them all out of the empire, abandoning their Colleges and missions. The General unhappily sat on the fence, using every resource of equivocation allowed by his Probabilist textbooks. But neither he nor his men could leave Russia.

By the end of 1814 the total number of Jesuits was still unknown but certainly very few. On one calculation it amounted to 800, of whom 674 were immured in Russia: another calculation made the number barely 600. In every country a large proportion of the surviving ex-Jesuits refused to join the new Society. Even in Russia three old Fathers refused and left the country. In England of the sixty-nine surviving ex-Jesuits thirty-four declined to accept the invitation. In Ireland there was initially no response at all from the few survivors. It was Peter Kenny, a secular priest enthusiast educated at Stonyhurst and already the founder and head of Clongowes College, who became the first, and for a time the only, Irish member of the new Society. There was a similar split among the Paccanarists. A minority of them, including Joseph Varin, were prompt to become Jesuits: the majority, along with Paccanari himself, refused to do so. His Congregation faded away and he himself ended his life in disgrace and obscurity.

7
The New Society:
Tribulation and Recovery 1814-1963

'Jesuitism is a human institution, born in time and destined to die in time . . . it is dead and cannot be resuscitated . . . The second abolition of the Society is not, I repeat, a mere conjecture, a volition, a hope, but a fact already begun and reached to the middle of its course . . .'

(Vincenzo Gioberti, *Il Gesuita Moderno*, t.2, c.I, 1847)

'Now from their wonderful system, and from their natural and commendable *esprit de corps*, the Jesuits tend (if I may use an undignified metaphor) to swamp the Church . . .'

(John Henry Newman, confidential letter to H. J. Coleridge SJ, April 29th 1869)

Pius VII's Brief *Sollicitudo* of 1814 was a highly rhetorical appeal for help from a depressed Roman Curia: it called the Jesuits 'the glory of the Church', 'the strong and experienced rowers' without whom the ship of Peter could never breast the waves of 19th-century free thought. It said, with pathetic exaggeration, that the restoration was 'demanded with unanimous voice' by 'the Catholic world'. A small minority of ex-Jesuits and 'friends' had hoped ardently for such an appeal up to 1803, and despaired of ever hearing it between 1803 and 1814 as their numbers dwindled and their 'friends' bickered. When the appeal did come, unexpectedly and hurriedly, they were far too few to answer it effectively and most practising Catholics regarded them with cold suspicion.

In France the sixty or seventy priests and hastily collected novices dare not wear the old soutane or publicise the fact that they were Jesuits. Their legal status was in doubt. The restored monarchy regarded them with indifference. Even strongly reactionary aristocrats and bishops had a rooted distrust of them. In the Austrian Empire Francis II, backed by Metternich, barred them from Austria, Bohemia, Hungary, Lombardy and Venetia. The ultra-reactionary Ferdinand VII of Spain admitted them with some hesitation, let them take over a very few old Jesuit premises which had been too small and decrepit to attract buyers, and otherwise showed them no particular favour. They had neither governmental permission nor the numbers to enable them to restart work in the old Provinces of Spanish America. In the United States their old base in Maryland was gone, the ex-Jesuit Bishop of Baltimore, John Carroll, was kind but unhelpful, and the President deeply alarmed at the arrival of a few Jesuits from Europe. They were unwelcome in Portugal, Naples, Sicily, Tuscany, Brescia, Malta and the new state of the Netherlands. The English Tory Government seriously considered whether it should not exclude them by statute from the British Isles and the Vicars-Apostolic almost unanimously excluded them from their Districts and refused to ordain their students if they had taken vows in the Society. In Germany practically all the Catholic states and Prussia, now in occupation of the Catholic Rhineland, refused them entry. The great majority of the tiny Society, including its General, Tadeusz Brzozowski, were immured within the Russian Empire almost under house arrest and unable to communicate with their colleagues in the west.

Inside the Society morale remained low and dissension rife. Stonyhurst was so disorderly that the English noviciate had to be moved well away from it to avoid contagion. Some Jesuits, both old stagers and new recruits, were fiercely illiberal and reactionary. Others in France, Fribourg and the United States, were strongly affected by romantic liberalism and demanded reform of the Society. Others, either 'spirituals' or pragmatists, wished confusion on both houses. Bishop Poynter, the leader of the English episcopal resistance to Jesuit activists, was delighted and surprised to find that he had allies in Rome including influential Cardinals and at least one Italian Jesuit, Grassi. Paul VII was alarmed and disappointed by the Jesuits' weaknesses and quarrels. In 1820 Brzozowski died at Polotsk and all his men were expelled from the Russian Empire. The body of over 600 refugees was received with the utmost reluctance by the Austrian Government and settled temporarily within its empire on conditions which greatly limited the Jesuits' freedom of action. Meanwhile a General Congregation had been assembling in Rome to elect a new General. It proved to be a turbulent affair. There were bitter recriminations about the behaviour of the English and French delegates before 1814 and the validity of their vows was questioned. At one time it seemed possible that the Congregation would become hopelessly deadlocked. The Society's enemies confidently awaited either a papal Brief of suppression or the imposition of a new General and stringent reforming orders by papal commissioners. Pius VII sent two Cardinals to preside over the Congregation. They expelled from it a number of the more unruly delegates and ordered the rest to await the arrival from Austria of the representatives of the 'Russians', who were numerous enough to command a majority and solidly conservative. In fact their arrival and further papal pressure secured the election as General of Aloysius Fortis, a safely conservative Italian and the Pope's private theologian. Numbers of liberal reformers were dismissed from the Society and it was instructed by the Congregation to obey the old Constitutions and Acquaviva's rules to the letter.

Under Fortis the Jesuits inched their way painfully, with many humiliations and setbacks, towards stability without really achieving it by his death in 1829. Numbers crept up to 2,000 but recruitment remained very difficult because of the Jesuits' inability to restart their old system of Colleges and student houses attached to universities. Noviciates were small and in them older men, including secular priests, outnumbered schoolboys. In the Society at large priests much outnumbered students. All religious Orders were then making heavy weather of their struggle to re-establish themselves after the Revolutionary cataclysm in a Europe where they were unpopular, denied the old tax exemptions and refused compensation for their lost properties. But the Capuchins, Franciscans and Redemptorists were doing better than the Jesuits who had the humiliation of ranking as a minor Order. In Rome itself they were pushed towards the back of a queue of religious seeking favours. It took them fifteen years to recover the *Germanicum* and longer to reoccupy the *Romanum*. Apart from that their only acquisition in the city by 1829 was the small, select seminary for aristocratic ordinands, the *Nobile*. By the 1850s the control of these establishments was to play a major part in the recreation of a great system of Jesuit influences in Rome, Italy and Germany. But in 1829 the Society almost wholly lacked the influential connections in the Cardinalate, the Roman Curia and the national episcopates of Italy and Germany to enable it to fill the recovered Colleges with able secular ordinands.

In 1829 also the old Catholic university and faculty system had not been rebuilt: the only existing Catholic faculties were at Tübingen and Munster, neither of which welcomed Jesuits or their pupils. Hence the very few, small Jesuit student houses at

Vals in France, Fribourg in Switzerland, at Turin and Stonyhurst were rustic, inbred communities where stolidly conservative professors and students clashed with ardent, frustrated liberals. The General and the General Congregations of 1820 and 1829 attempted, by disciplinary action and dismissals from the Society, to impose on all feebly eclectic courses of philosophy and theology with a formally scholastic, antiquated bias to satisfy the requirements of the Constitutions. Able professors who attempted, like Ventura in Sicily, Freudenfeld in Fribourg, Manera in Turin and Raymond Brzozowski in Rome, to create new, coherent courses borrowing heavily from Kant, Scheiermacher, Lamennais, or even the ultra-conservative de Maistre were reprimanded. Ventura left the Society for the Theatines. Brzozowski was severely disciplined and sent away from Rome. Manera, the friend of Lamennais, hid behind a smokescreen of professions of obedience while he held private seminars with his students and corresponded secretly with Lamennais.

The rebuilding of the College system proved impossible. The old buildings were now used for secular schools, barracks or governmental offices. The Society was so poor that the General had to give general dispensations from the old rule that tuition in Jesuit schools must be free. Over much of Europe Jesuit community life had to settle into a pattern unknown in the old Society outside the Far East. The Fathers lived with their bags packed, frequently moving house as governments grudgingly relented and allowed them entry on condition they operated modestly and obscurely, and frequent outbursts of radical liberal revolutionary fury forced them to take flight. The circumstances of the times, far more than the traditions of the old Society, drove the Jesuits into cultivating secret apostolates. They offered to take over diocesan seminaries in France and Germany on condition that they were allowed to take in a proportion of lay boys disguised as secular ordinands. In France this plan led to the acquisition of eight *petits seminaires* of which one, at St. Acheul near Amiens, housed almost 500 lay boys for a few years before its closure. Since Colleges were few an effort was made to re-establish networks of Jesuit influences in the other ways dear to the old Society: 'circles' of penitents, pious Congregations and Orders of nuns under Jesuit directors. In France de Clorivière and Varin set about this task with a will.

Some sort of basis for their work existed even in 1814. De Clorivière's Marian Congregation for laymen was said by an excited enemy of the Society in 1826 to have 48,000 members.

Two 'Jesuited' Orders of nuns had survived the Revolutionary upheaval, the Institute of the Blessed Virgin Mary in south Germany out of direct Jesuit control, and the Society of the Sacred Heart, an ex-Paccanarist Order in France. Both Orders had Jesuit rules and ran girls' schools which could be fertile seed-beds of Jesuit influence. Varin helped to found several new Orders including the Faithful Companions of Jesus and the Sisters of Notre Dame of Namur.

By 1829 these networks of influence were still small and very loosely knit. The Marian Congregation had, even before de Clorivière's death, become a violently reactionary, monarchist club from which liberal French Jesuits dissociated themselves. The 'Jesuited' Orders of nuns did act as auxiliaries of the Society but in ways of their own making. For a number of different reasons Jesuit directors rarely exercised much control over them: the nuns' 'Jesuitry' was very homemade. For one thing the General was unwilling to grant wholesale dispensations from the rule which forbade Jesuits to undertake the permanent direction of communities of nuns. Again the Jesuits were, with good reason, afraid of getting a reputation for depending on feminine help. The Institute and the Namur nuns were resident in countries from which Jesuits were excluded by law. Lastly, as the ex-Jesuit 'faithful' had discovered before 1814, their 'friends' very often had minds and wills of their own.

There were plenty of examples in the 1820s of the independent-mindedness of the 'Jesuited' nuns. The Congregation of Jesus and Mary was founded between 1818 and 1820 in Lyon by a local spinster and a very newly ordained secular priest. Neither was directed by Jesuits and the Congregation had no formal connections with the Society whatever before the 1890s. Yet, from its earliest days, it used pirated copies of the Jesuit Constitutions, rules and devotions: every nun bore the name of a Jesuit saint. The Religious of the Cénacle were founded by a secular priest and a breakaway group of sisters from an existing Congregation. They used Jesuit rules and devotions and gave the Spiritual Exercises to laywomen. Yet it was only years later, after the death of their secular priest director that the religious, after some hesitation, asked for formal links with the Society. The Sisters of Notre Dame of Namur owed their foundation to Varin's instructions to a group of Belgian women in France. The community moved to Namur in Belgium and had little or no contact with Jesuits until 1831 when they were allowed into the country and were astonished and embarrassed to be presented by the

Sisters with a ready-equipped and endowed College.

When Aloysius Fortis died in 1829 the General Congregation which met to elect his successor found the Society's prospects very bleak. It was excluded by law from two thirds of Europe. There were clear signs that radical liberal revolutions were likely to occur in France, many Italian States and the Netherlands in the near future. A revolution always meant mob attacks on Jesuits and their expulsion ordered by a new government. Indiscipline and laxity were still rife in the Society. In England the Provincial was still in two minds about closing down Stonyhurst College: for lack of pastoral outlets more than half of his manpower was shut up there, underemployed and bored. The lay boys in Jesuit seminaries in France and Italy were notoriously ill-behaved and many resented a tight religious discipline. Scores of them were expelled every year from St. Acheul and very many of its former pupils had abandoned the practice of their religion. Jesuit student houses were very few, their courses wildly eclectic, and their academic standards depressingly low. Fifteen years after the Society's restoration, it had men in only one of its former foreign mission fields, the United States.

Alarmed by this dismal catalogue of failures, the General Congregation chose as General a man whom the majority of delegates cast in the role of a 'second Acquaviva', Johannes Philip Roothaan. Like people picking up again the threads of their lives after nearly fatal illnesses, the delegates were very conscious of the Society's history and the obvious parallel between its situations in 1580 and 1829. Acquaviva had been a 'second Founder' in troubled times and the main architect of the Society's power in the 17th century. Now both traditionalists and liberal reformers desperately wanted a 'third Founder': Roothaan was the traditionalists' choice. His reactionary views, Germanic thoroughness and military decision made him a rather wooden but effective 19th-century copy of Acquaviva. Like him he was a great believer in the educative power of drill, minute regulation and exact obedience. He had left his native Holland as a boy to be trained by Tadeusz Brzozowski at Polotsk in Russian Poland before 1814. With the rest of his 'Russian' colleagues he had been exiled from Russia in 1820 and was retained by Fortis at the Gesu as an Assistant. He had helped Fortis to rebuild from nothing the Gesu's bureaucracy and had learned much from the Italian's expertise in dealing with the complexities of the still often coldly hostile Roman Curia. Roothaan was young enough to hope for a long Generalate — in fact it lasted to 1853, twenty-five years. He was physically very active and the only General before very modern times to travel widely when in office. He even visited England. Like Acquaviva he set the interests, good name and growth of the Society before everything else, even adherence to the *Zelanti* party in Rome which predominated there during most of his Generalate.

A shower of directives, memoranda and regulations flowed out from the Gesu, surpassing Acquaviva's in minuteness of detail especially on the crucial subjects, training, prayer and studies. Roothaan's training policy was traditional to the point of literalism. The Constitutions now had to be obeyed to the letter. A mass of old, customary mitigations was swept away. This was made easy because aristocratic recruits were now few, Jesuit schools and missions rare and foreign missions with estates and trading interests practically non-existent. The 18th-century tendency to extend greatly the number of solemnly professed Jesuits was sharply reversed and the length of training increased. Students' 'regencies', stints of schoolteaching breaking into the study years, were sharply curtailed. It was thus possible to keep Jesuits permanently under a tight supervision and separate the unordained from the community life of the priests. Even the most trusted Professed Fathers would have spent so many years in the training ring that they would have all the habitual reactions of model schoolboys. The Constitutions, in spite of Ignatius Loyola's extremist remarks recorded by his early biographers, carefully limited the demands which superiors might make on their subjects' obedience. Acquaviva, and still more Roothaan, while paying formal homage to the wording of the Constitutions, directed that in practice all Jesuits must acquire a habit of instant, military obedience and suppression of all critical thoughts. Both Generals believed that only a discipline of this heroic kind could enable the embattled Society to survive and prosper.

Roothaan surpassed Acquaviva in the extent to which he regulated Jesuits' devotions. All must perform discursive meditations from a book of a prescribed type, use prescribed private devotions, adopt prescribed postures in prayer, and use the same compulsory instruments of penance. The strong habits ingrained by these practices before ordination were meant to endure for the rest of a Jesuit's life. The Spiritual Exercises, used before 1773 very intermittently and in mitigated forms, now had to be taken in frequent doses by all and in exactly the forms laid down by Ignatius. Every novice was to be provided with a whip or 'discipline' for use twice each Friday and a barbed wire ring to be clamped round his right thigh on the flesh every morning from rising to the breakfast bell. He was also to receive a spiritual notebook and a set of '*examen* beads'. The beads were a kind of moral abacus to be pinned under a flap of his gown and used for the secret counting on the spot of each sin or omission. The moral score had to be entered up in the notebook twice a day. Acquaviva's rules on demeanour were revived and set out more sharply. For instance when appearing before a superior a Jesuit must lower his head slightly and never look the superior directly in the eye.

It is easy for us today to marvel that such a system was ever accepted. Roothaan created none of it. Loyola and Acquaviva took most of the details automatically from the then current monastic practice. Roothaan added the rest from the rule book of the seminaries run by the strictest of French Congregations of secular priests, the Sulpicians. His only personal contribution was an earthy practicality and fine military precision of a sort usually possessed by drill sergeants. His achievement was secretly admired and imitated by most of the older Orders, including the Dominicans, and practically all the founders of new Congregations. In a real sense therefore most religious in the later 19th century were 'Ignatian' and the system still endured among the Jesuits and some other religious to the 1940s.

Ever since 1820 the Gesu had promised to try to put some uniformity and rational order into the *Ratio* rules for Jesuit studies and school syllabuses. Long before 1773 the old rules were widely disobeyed in the Society: the scholastic form of theology and Aristotelian philosophy were regarded by many professors as totally obsolete and meaningless and an unrelieved diet of Latin grammar and literature as unnecessary cruelty to schoolboys. The General Congregation of 1829 only narrowly defeated a motion to jettison Aristotle. Roothaan's observation that 'everything has been reduced to a mountain of erudition which conceals an abyss of emptiness and vague uncertainties' must, as a diagnosis of the ills afflicting all Catholic schools at that time, have pleased both traditionalists and liberals. But his new edition of the *Ratio* issued in 1838 outraged the liberals and did little to solve the problem for the Society. It left the theology course as a mish-mash of scholasticism, history of doctrine and apologetics, philosophy a mixture of Aristotle and some outdated physics, and the College course still exclusively Latin and the classics but taught through the vernacular. Extra-curricular sessions in speculative theology or modern philosophy and mathematics and, for schoolboys, in history, modern languages, mathematics and science were strongly discouraged.

Acquaviva's great multiplication of regulations was self-defeating and bred lip-service and then wholesale evasion. In the long run Roothaan's even tighter system produced the same results. Soon after his entry into the Society in 1880 the convert George Tyrrell was shocked by the light-hearted attitude of the English Jesuits to rules. In 1905 he wrote to his General that 'disobedience is the Jesuit's distinguishing mark'. But in the short run, at least to the 1870s, Roothaan's drills, though producing a small number of outright defections and a good deal of quiet evasion of the provisions of his *Ratio* by Jesuit intellectuals, was greeted with enthusiastic compliance by the great majority of the Society. It has, at no other time in its history, before or since, displayed such a remarkably high degree of regular observance of rules and of uniformity of practice and policy. Roothaan was, in fact, aided by exceptionally easy conditions. A new, strong wave of romantic religiosity was sweeping over Europe. Even men like Lamennais, Montalembert, Newman, Gioberti and Döllinger, much inclined towards intellectual or political liberalism, ardently sought order, authority, certainty and tradition in religion. For a time at least they were deeply impressed by the new face of the Society and attracted towards it. Undoubtedly it was Roothaan's system, austere and outdated as it was, which, more than any Jesuit expertise in winning 'friends' and influencing people, accounted for the considerable increase in the size and power of the Society between 1840 and 1853. In 1829 Roothaan had only 2,000 subjects: by 1847 he had over 5,000. By then the Jesuits had at last gained entry to the old 'German Assistancy' and were making good headway in Germany, Austria and Belgium. A new and higher degree of stridency in the abuse of Jesuits by French radical liberals and a new attitude of respect for the Society among conservatives and moderate liberals all indicated that it had become a power in Europe at last.

Though the Jesuits were excluded from Prussia and Bavaria until 1848, they now established themselves solidly in the Austrian Empire and the small independent states of south Germany. Their houses were few and small compared with the great array of Colleges they had had in the same areas in 1773. They very rarely regained possession of their old College buildings and fine city churches. But they did gain entry to the university faculties in Vienna and Innsbruck and established a dozen Colleges. Of much more importance was a gradual change of heart among Austrian and German bishops who, lacking seminaries of their own, now consented to send their secular ordinands to the Jesuit Colleges or to the *Germanicum* in Rome. The empty benches at the *Germanicum* filled up at last. After ordination in Germany or Rome the best educated of these secular priests, imbued with respect for the Society and warm friendship for their old teachers, moved on to seminary professorships in Germany: some became diocesan bishops; one or two became Cardinals. Even before the Jesuits gained entry to Bavaria and Prussia 'Jesuited' priests occupied posts in major seminaries and universities there. Two years after Roothaan's death Herbert Vaughan, an extremely 'Jesuited' young English secular priest visited Munich and met Johann Joseph Ignaz von Döllinger at the university. Döllinger, in spite of his possession of a Christian name which indicated some old devotion to the Society in his family, was a largely self-educated secular priest scholar with no Jesuit friends. Vaughan found him sharply critical of the German Jesuits' low academic standards but still sure that the Society was the greatest single force for progress among German Catholics. It had, said Döllinger, 'the education of all Germany', both clerical and lay, in its hands. Another unbiased German witness was Prinz Chlodwig von Hohenlohe-Schillingfuerst. Like Döllinger and most well-educated Catholics he had some slight family connections with Jesuitry but no personal experience of its education. Nevertheless in 1846 he wrote that he had hitherto adhered to the 'Ultramontane' or 'Jesuit' party, accounting it the 'safest' and most progressive force in German Catholicism.

It was much the same story in Belgium and France. The Jesuits were not allowed into Belgium until it gained its national independence in 1830. There they made rapid headway. Their Belgian 'friends', educated mostly in French Jesuit schools, provided College buildings and endowments. The Fathers were soon ensconced in Brussels, Bruges, Namur and Louvain, where they had entry to the revived Catholic university. As in Germany some bishops began to call in Jesuits to train their ordinands. The usual 'circles' of lay 'friends' appeared. Emilie d'Oultremont, Baronne d'Hooghevorst was a fairly typical example of the more extreme of these 'friends'. Her father, the first Belgian ambassador to the Holy See, founded at his own expense the new Jesuit College at Namur. As a young married woman with a large family of small children, Emilie's life was full of fantasies and visions about founding a convent closely linked to the Society and devoted to 'reparation' for the sins of society, especially sexual irregularities. She dismissed a string of Jesuit confessors who urged her to caution and attention to the needs of her children. In the end she found an exiled French Jesuit confessor, Petit, who sympathised with her wishes and was willing to go along with all her extremist notions. He knew little of her family circumstances and accepted her versions of events blindly. The sudden death of her husband enabled her to carry off her children to France away from the protests of her relatives. She placed her children in boarding schools, and, brushing aside the warnings of the French Provincials, founded the Order of Marie Reparatrice with herself as superior and several of her young daughters as novices.

Her confessor, Petit, was fairly representative of the French Jesuit 'spirituals' of his generation. The French Revolution of 1830 began more than a decade of disturbance and change for the French Provinces. At first all French Jesuits were expelled from France and took shelter in Belgium with their novices, students and schoolboys. The Belgian Provincial took full advantage of this windfall of manpower. By 1840 more and more French Jesuits slipped back in disguise into France. Their delicate situation and inability to reopen their old schools in any numbers left a good many of them with time on their hands. The 'spirituals' now had unusual scope for freelance enterprises among 'friends', both men and women, who were often, at that period, unusually susceptible to ideas of 'absolute sacrifice', 'total obedience' and 'a life of reparation'. The rapid spread of Jesuit-directed 'retreats' based on the *Spiritual Exercises* made it easy and natural for these ideas to spread far beyond the groups who had relations with the Society as ex-pupils or penitents. In Paris, from the Jesuit house in the Rue des Postes, given to the Society by a converted cabinet minister, de Ravignan became famous for his large number of famous conversions and his crowded assemblies in the Cathedral of Notre Dame where he answered the contemporary barrage of abuse of the Society in newspapers, novels and plays. But de Ravignan's ideas and methods were moderation itself compared with those of his colleagues, Ginhac, Ramière, Fouillot, Petit and Pomian. With immense enthusiasm, charm and ruthless determination these men founded Congregations of religious men and women under their own absolute authority, directed their penitents into them dictatorially, and interfered, often disastrously, in the internal affairs of dependent Orders. They almost wrecked the Society of the Sacred Heart by trying to impose the Jesuit Constitutions on to it. The Religious of the Cénacle went through two decades of upsets, humiliations and confusion because of the follies of the Jesuit directors, Regnault and Ginhac. The founder of the Order was relegated to the status of a lay sister, her companions ejected and the community filled with 'friends' of the Jesuits headed by a succession of aristocratic widows who played havoc with its finances. It was Ginhac who gave free rein to the pious fancies of Emilie d'Oultremont in the Order of Marie Reparatrice. The result was a regime so extreme and unhealthy that the nuns, including Emilie's two teenaged daughters, died of diseases contracted from lack of sleep and fresh air. It was Pomian whose frantic efforts to turn Bernadette Soubirous into a great mystic and prophetess foundered on the rock of Bernadette's peasant common sense.

In Rome and Italy Roothaan's Generalate saw an equally start-ling extension of Jesuit activity and influence. Here the Revo-lutions of 1830 were turned to the Society's benefit. The Austrian Government, deeply alarmed, and soothed by the evidence of Roothaan's disciplinary procedures and conservatism, admitted the Jesuits to Lombardy and Venetia: Tuscany followed suit. In those parts of the peninsula where liberal revolutions tem-porarily dispersed the Jesuits, their 'travels in plain clothes as exiles often opened up new fields of conquest. The careers of Giuseppe and Vincenzo Pecci illustrate all this well. They were the sons of Count Pecci and were educated in a Jesuit College at Viterbo. Giuseppe left for the Roman noviciate. Years later, as a Jesuit priest, he was caught up in a dangerous revolutionary situation, donned disguise and secured a post as a professor in the municipal University of Perugia. His teaching and studies there made him a scholar of repute and eventually a Cardinal. His brother Vincenzo passed from Viterbo to the Jesuit-directed *Nobile* in Rome, to ordination as a secular priest and service in the Roman Curia, where he joined the increasing number of 'Jesuited' officials. In 1878 he was elected as Pope Leo XIII.

There is plenty of other evidence of the growth of a new net-work of Jesuit influences in Rome and Italy. Round 1843 Gioberti, a secular priest, was a member of a wide circle of friends, priests and students, who were increasingly ardent liberals and nationalists. They were on friendly terms with moderately liberal Jesuits, mostly College professors, who were in quiet revolt against Roothaan's *Ratio* of 1838. Gioberti had visited some of these Jesuits in Louvain and Brugelette, the student house of the exiled French. In Rome the Jesuit *Romanum* had its liberal professors, Liberatore and Passaglia. It was here also that Gioberti had a great Jesuit friend Taparelli d'Azeglio. D'Azeglio, as an aristocrat, had licence to speak freely to Roothaan and urged him fervently to abandon his reactionary principles. By 1843 d'Azeglio planned to get permission to launch a mildly liberal Jesuit periodical to be called *Civilta Cattolica*. He hoped to wring permission out of the General by suggesting that the periodical might win over many Italian liberals, even of the anti-clerical and revolutionary kind, to support the Society. Roothaan's Dutch caution and strong conservatism made him sceptical and the project was confined to the Gesu's pigeon-holes.

Newman, when still an Anglican in his 'monastery' at Littlemore near Oxford, had cherished and used a copy of the *Spiritual Exercises*. After his conversion to Catholicism in 1845 he set out for Rome not only to study Catholic theology but to decide which religious Order or Congregation he and his convert disciples should join. From the start of the journey he was fascinated by the Jesuits. He visited their houses in Paris and Genoa and, on his arrival in Rome, was pleased to find that the College of Propaganda, in which he was housed by protocol, was directed by Jesuits. He took a Jesuit confessor, met Roothaan, made pilgrimages to the tomb of Ignatius, and had long talks with Liberatore and Passaglia. In 1847 he wrote home:

> 'The Jesuits of course are the most wonderful and powerful body amongst the regulars . . . I can never cease to admire them . . . They are a real working body, mixing devotion with work . . . I respect them exceedingly and love individuals of them much . . .'

His decision to enter the Oratory, not the Society, was taken after a great deal of thought and owed something to the influence of a great Oratorian whom he met in Rome, Augustin Theiner. Though by that time Theiner was turning against the Society he also had very nearly joined it earlier in his career. He was a Silesian Prussian who, as a student, had passed from Catholic practice to extreme Catholic liberalism and then to the edge of Protestantism. He became a research historian and travelled widely round European archives, reverting as he did to non-practising Catholic liberalism. Arriving in Rome he became a convert to Catholic conservatism, took the Spiritual Exercises in 1833 and was appointed a professor in the Jesuit-directed

College of Propaganda. Very gradually he parted with the Jesuits, entered the Roman Oratory, and published a history of Clement XIV which was really a very strong manifesto against Jesuitry.

As Newman arrived in Rome Mrs. Cornelia Connelly was quitting it for England. In 1839 she and her Episcopalian clergyman husband, Pierce, had become converts to Catholicism at their home in the United States. Both had Jesuit directors. Pierce's idea that the couple should separate and that he should become a Jesuit and she a nun was strongly encouraged by a wildly pious French-American bishop. They had a number of small children. The couple travelled to Rome where the plan was accepted without much difficulty by the Pope: Roothaan judged it unwise to refuse to accept Pierce into the Jesuit noviciate. Cornelia, who was originally very dubious about the design, was taken into a Roman convent of the 'Jesuited' Society of the Sacred Heart. It was significant that in 1845 Jesuit influence was so strong in the Curia that an anti-Jesuit party there which thought the Connelly plan monstrous dared not make their protest openly. It was typical of the naïve and romantic religious enthusiasm of the period that even the collapse of the plan did not discourage most of its supporters. Pierce soon backed out of the Society, became a secular priest, reverted to Protestantism and went to law in England to recover conjugal rights over his wife. Cornelia disliked the Sacred Heart nuns, but came round to a complete surrender to the idea that she had a religious vocation which took precedence over her marriage and her duty to her children. Originally her attitude towards the Jesuits had been respectful but cool: now she was as resolutely 'Jesuited' as Emilie d'Oultremont. The Pope summarily despatched Cornelia to England to found a teaching Order, a task which, in spite of appalling difficulties and obloquy, she performed with skill and good sense. It is very difficult to believe that she was not constantly directed by Jesuits during her years in England. If she was she and the Jesuits concerned concealed the fact with remarkable success. In her case, as in those of so many other 'Jesuited' nuns in the 19th century, the Society was very unwilling to reveal the extent of its involvement.

In 1846 the Society had good reason to be content with the rule of its General. Its intellectuals found his *Ratio* antiquated and limited. The position of the Society in Rome was still rather insecure. But its discipline and credit in the Church at large were immensely improved. The advent of a new Pope, Pius IX, in 1846 alarmed Roothaan and the Gesu but seemed unlikely to halt the

Society's progress. From the start of his pontificate Pius was cool towards Roothaan and critical about his administration. In 1845 a minor storm had blown up in Italy. Gioberti, hitherto friendly towards liberal Jesuits, published his plan for an Italy united politically under the Pope and added, apparently as an after-thought, an appendix attacking some Jesuits for insincerity and intrigue. The victims reacted strongly and Pellico, a former friend of Gioberti's, was allowed to publish a strong attack on the plan and the appendix. Gioberti was enraged and in 1847 published in Protestant Lausanne a vast attack on the Society in five volumes, *Il Gesuita Moderno*. The book was full of rhetoric and repetition. It raked up again in detail the charges against the Jesuits of 1773. But the main theme was clear and to the point: the Society was justly suppressed in 1773 because it prostituted itself, changing from a real Order into an ecclesiastical power-machine bent on domination of the Church by any and every means. In 1814 the Society was restored in the hope that it would return to its early integrity: in fact history had repeated itself and all the old faults had reappeared. Hence, Gioberti argued, the Society had proved itself incorrigible. The hopes of liberals like himself that it had changed its ways had been dashed. The liberal Jesuits who had associated themselves with Gioberti and his friends had either been cheats or dupes of their own superiors.

The book caused an immense sensation among the Italian reading public. Newman, who was then in Rome, wrote that many Italians had turned against the Society. He was momentarily puzzled:

> 'It is difficult to say what will become of the Jesuits. It is hard to understand how a body with such vitality, so flourishing internally, so increasing in numbers could break up . . .'

Theiner, who was not a friend of the Society, reported rumours that the Pope was complaining the whole affair was due to the Jesuits' uncharitableness, their intrigues and their 'self-consciously contrived attitudes'. He also reported that the Pope meant to suppress the Society. The storm was certainly a warning to the Society that its strength depended ultimately not on numbers and 'friends' but on its general standing in Catholic public opinion and on the favour of the Pope. But Gioberti's book had little effect outside Italy and Pius IX, however surly, never contemplated strong action against the Society. In any case 1848 brought events which gave him and most of Europe other, and much graver, preoccupations.

In January 1848 a new wave of liberal militancy hit the capitals of Europe. Inflammatory journalism, protest meetings, student uproars, strikes, barricades and even street fighting with troops had become familiar hazards for city dwellers since the 1820s. What was startlingly new was the size, determination and extent of the new liberal attack. It struck simultaneously every capital except London, Madrid and St. Petersburg. In some capitals, including Paris and Vienna, the rulers lost their nerve and fled: new liberal provisional governments set up republics. Elsewhere rulers hastily capitulated, repealed repressive laws, dismissed reactionary officials and formed liberal governments. There was widespread rioting, looting and arson by urban mobs. Socialist and Communist clubs surfaced defiantly and *The Communist Manifesto* was published. Like all other groups of Catholic clergy the Jesuits had mixed reactions to these great events. Many of them were too narrowly and professionally concerned about the disturbance of their work to bother about the political issues at stake. The behaviour of many others strongly reminded Newman of that of his High Tory Anglican friends during the violence accompanying the Reform Bill crisis of 1832. 'There is', he wrote of these conservative Jesuits in 1847, 'a deep suspicion of *change*, with a perfect incapacity to create any thing *positive* for the wants of the time.' There were, however, liberal Jesuits who warmly sympathised with the more moderate revolutionaries. In Paris Ravignan was pressingly invited to take a seat in the Revolutionary Assembly called after the fall of the monarchy. The Gesu's two abominations were the Italian priest-philosophers and the ardent liberals, Gioberti and Antonio Rosmini. Both still had supporters in the Society in 1848, Villefort, the French Assistant at the Gesu, Curci and Passaglia on the staff of the *Romanum*, Gautrelet in Paris, Martin at Vals, Gamard at Laval, and Taparelli d'Azeglio in Turin. In 1848 Gioberti became President of the Chamber of Deputies in Turin and Prime Minister of Piedmont: in his cabinet was the Marquis d'Azeglio, son-in-law of the liberal poet Manzoni and elder brother of the liberal Jesuit Taparelli d'Azeglio. Rosmini, an ardent liberal who preferred to remain in Rome to influence the Pope, was the founder of a new Congregation, the Institute of Charity. Due to his close association with French and Italian Jesuits the Constitutions of his Congregation were modelled on those of the Society.

But whatever the private sympathies of these Jesuit liberals they felt themselves bound by the Society's discipline, clericalism and loyalty to their colleagues under attack in cities taken over by revolutionaries. Liberal and conservative Jesuits alike were strongly affected by the other-worldliness of contemporary Catholic revivalism and Roothaan's strictures on worldly, political action. In 1848 and much of 1849 the structure of the Society was badly strained. It was expelled from the Austrian Empire, from Paris and from most Italian capitals. Hundreds of Jesuits, dressed as secular priests or in ill-fitting borrowed lay clothes, had to take to the road with only such luggage as they could carry themselves, feeling hunted from place to place and uncertain of finding shelter and food. The General himself and the Gesu staff were prominent among the victims. From as early as 1846 Pius IX had made large and vague gestures of conciliation towards liberal opinion. But his flat refusal to support military action against Austrian troops still occupying Lombardy and Venetia, the inability of the moderate liberals in Rome to keep out radicals, and his own basic conservatism led to increasing mob violence. Pius coldly instructed Roothaan to withdraw himself and his colleagues from the Papal States since the physical safety of Jesuits could no longer be guaranteed. As they fled across the Neapolitan border to Gaeta a mob broke into and sacked the Gesu. A radical Roman Republic was set up and Pius IX and his entourage also took refuge in Gaeta. There, in the acute discomfort of improvised and crowded lodgings and uncertain how long the Neapolitan Government would tolerate his presence on their soil, Roothaan found himself living cheek-by-jowl with a Pope who disliked him and an 'arch-heretic', Rosmini, whom he himself detested.

During 1849 and the first months of 1850 a dramatic change took place in the political fortunes of Europe. The revolutionary governments collapsed one after another, the exiled conservative rulers returned home at the head of armies and liberal leaders were shot, gaoled or forced to flee to England or the United States in thousands. The process took time and it was only in 1854 that the dust finally cleared sufficiently for the Society to be able to take stock of its losses. It discovered with delight and surprise that it was not only basically intact but much strengthened. The liberal decrees passed in 1848 in Prussia, Bavaria, Holland and Denmark were not repealed so that Society's work in those countries could now either take firmer root or begin. By far the greatest gains were in Germany and France. With the active help of 'friends' already ensconced in positions of influence there, Jesuit Colleges sprang up in Mainz, Cologne, Bonn, Augsburg, Munich and Würzburg. As early as 1855 Döllinger was marvelling at the hold the Jesuits had secured on the education of German secular ordinands and lay boys. That year also the Austrian Government re-admitted the Jesuits to the empire on such terms that their work could now take much wider and firmer root. In France the collapse of 'the Second Republic' and the advent to power of the Emperor Napoleon III brought great advantages to the Jesuits. Like other religious Orders and Congregations they received a kind of official governmental recognition and a good deal of favour and indirect subsidies. The *Loi Falloux* of 1850 gave them a firm and even privileged footing in the French system of secondary education. In a few years the eight small, camouflaged Jesuit private schools grew into, at first twenty-five and then twenty-nine, properly authorised Colleges, all of them fashionable and besieged with applicants for admission. The old Rue des Postes establishment in Paris which Newman had found half-empty and small in 1846 and the Vaugirard College rapidly became France's Eton and Harrow. Similarly the 'Jesuited' women's teaching Orders enjoyed a great expansion of work and *clientèle* among the French upper and middle classes, even among families with a strongly liberal tradition.

In England, which had endured 'the Hungry Forties' but had no 1848 Revolution, the increasing liberalism of the establishment led to a modest flowering of Jesuit activity. Their numbers doubled in the 1850s: there was an influx into the Society of converts from High Anglicanism and, very significantly, of a few able secular priests. More and more bishops admitted Jesuits into their dioceses to take over missions. In 1849 the insistence of Rome forced the London District to admit them and one small Jesuit establishment appeared coyly in a mews in Farm Street in Mayfair. In 1842 Colleges were opened in Liverpool and at Mount St. Mary's near Sheffield, and in 1859 the opening of Glasgow College heralded a second irruption into Catholic secondary education. Everywhere in Europe anti-Jesuit feeling among churchmen and conservative politicians was tempered by a wholly new, if grudging, willingness to ally with the Society and to use it to prop up the crumbling establishment. The traumatic experiences of 1848 had exposed the chronic vulnerability to social and economic change and secularism of the old order of Church and state. Nervous conservative politicians and churchmen decided that they could no longer allow themselves the luxury of anti-Jesuitry. Prinz Hohenlohe was fairly typical of this kind of person. In 1856 he noted that he still had an uncomfortable feeling that the Jesuits might turn out to be bad allies: he feared their rooted tendency towards other-worldly religious fanaticism and that their famed efficiency would turn out to be grossly overrated. On the other hand he assiduously attended Jesuit churches and found their sermons more to his taste than those of other clergy. In London in 1857 on a visit to his relative, Prince Albert, he argued with his host about the Jesuits, maintaining that it was not they but revolutionary secret societies who were 'the root of the trouble' in Europe.

Even the painful expulsion of Jesuits from some states in 1848 did good to the Society. Since 1814 it had taken almost no part in Catholic foreign missions which fell into the hands of newly founded Congregations. The expulsions led Jesuits from Piedmont and Naples across the Atlantic to work in California, New Mexico and the Argentine. Austrian Jesuits, cast out of Vienna and Ingolstadt and homeless, went to work in Brazil and Australia. They were the first of a Jesuit migration which increased by the 1860s as a result of French colonisation in Indochina and the flight of a good many Jesuits, expelled by a revolution in Spain in 1868, to South America. But the real revival of Jesuit foreign missions awaited the growth of European Imperialism in the later decades of the century.

Yet by far the biggest bonus for the Society after 1850 was the acquisition of real influence in Rome. Like most of his conservative contemporaries Pius IX never became 'Jesuited'. Late in life he revealed that, as a youth, he had proposed to enter a Jesuit noviciate, but had, he thought very fortunately, been dissuaded by his tutor and a Jesuit director. To his dying day he was very wary of undue Jesuit influences round him. But his experiences at Gaeta had convinced him that he must make a thorough use of the Society. Roothaan, for his part, was deeply alarmed by this sharp change of front by the Pope. He feared that the Society was to become a tool of papal policies which its enemies would attribute to the Gesu and that uniform obedience to papal directives would destroy that Jesuit flexibility in dealing with local crises which was one of its main strengths. The increasing disposition of Pius to load educational establishments in Rome on to the Society, to promote Jesuits to curial posts and commend their services to bishops whom he wished to influence smacked of bribery to secure Roothaan's acquiescence in a papal take-over of control of the Society. A key issue was the launching of *Civilta Cattolica*. In 1850 Pius ordered this project of d'Azeglio's, long shelved in the Gesu, to be revived and put into execution by an editorial team of Jesuits chosen by himself, Bresciani, d'Azeglio and Curci. Roothaan's excuse that the Society could not afford to finance the enterprise was brushed aside: the Pope provided the funds. There was lavish spending on publicising the launching, with circulars and posters. The articles were to be unsigned, which meant that non-Jesuits or the Pope himself could write some of them. The Pope's practical control of the editors meant that ordinary Jesuit rules of censorship, designed to protect the Society's good name, could be breached. The General therefore had good reason to dread that *Civilta Cattolica* would become a grave embarrassment to the Gesu.

To the Pope's relief Roothaan died in 1853. His successor, a comparatively young, clever and independent-minded Belgian Pierre Jean Beckx, was chosen for his proven ability to get on with Pius IX. But his charm, tact and moderation availed him and the long-term interests of the Society little. He could not recover for it the relative freedom of action it had enjoyed before 1848. His very long Generalate, to 1887, saw the practically inevitable consolidation of the close partnership between the Society, a strongly conservative, dictatorial Papacy, and the forces of rabid reaction in the Church at large. The partnership produced a very rapid expansion of Jesuit numbers, works and influence. During the disturbed, revolutionary years before 1853 Jesuit numbers had stagnated to about 5,000. After 1853 they shot up steadily, reaching 13,000 by 1887. History was repeating itself. As in the early 17th century, so in the 1850s, the Society was settling into a course which assured it of extraordinary prosperity and expansion and the attainment of a dominating position in the Church. As in the later 17th century, so in the 1870s, its excessive power brought down on it increasingly bitter Catholic opposition, both conservative and liberal, and then anti-Jesuit legal action by governments. The Society remained completely excluded from the Russian Empire by a law of 1820 and from the Swiss Confederation by a law of 1847. It was expelled from Spain in 1868 by a revolutionary government whose agents behaved with violence: some Jesuits were murdered. It was expelled by law from the German Empire in 1872. The fall of Napoleon III in 1870 and the brief rule in Paris of the Commune caused the wrecking of Jesuit houses in the city and the murder of some of the inmates. Then in 1880 the Third Republic closed down Jesuit Colleges in France by law. Between 1870 and 1873 the Italian Royal Government closed down most

Jesuit houses, including the Gesu. Some Roman Jesuits took refuge under the German flag in the *Germanicum* but were soon expelled thence by the German ban. Beckx and his staff took refuge in a villa in Fiesole near Florence owned by a lay 'friend'. The business of the Gesu had to be carried on here in a makeshift way until the Italian Government relented in 1893 and allowed a later General to reoccupy the Gesu in Rome.

If these extremely damaging blows had happened in the 18th century they might well have led to the demise of the Society. Now, however, the damage and grave inconvenience did not stunt the Society's growth.

Many factors combined to make it seem indestructible and the greatest single clerical force in the Church. It was sustained by the continuance of its strange *mariage de convenance* with the Papacy. That marriage was never one of sentiment and was punctuated by occasional quarrels which became more frequent under Pius IX's successor in 1878, Leo XIII. But the quarrels had a marital character about them. They were noisy, even vicious, but brief and did not disturb a mutual dependence which had become an ingrained habit. The anti-Jesuits, including Lord Acton, Döllinger and even Newman, tended to think that the Jesuits had some secret hold over the Popes. In fact Pius IX and Leo XIII were very much the masters in their own house. The Society generally got its privileges but never easily or as a matter of course and it was sometimes resoundingly rebuffed. In 1874, relying confidently on local influence and the 'papal connection', the Jesuit superiors in England and the United States claimed virtual independence of episcopal control. To their surprise and Beckx's embarrassment Pius IX refused to take sides in the dispute. It was decided legally in Rome in 1881 in the bishops' favour in spite of pressures by a galaxy of Jesuit and 'Jesuited' Cardinals. The decision hindered the foundation of a few Jesuit Colleges and pleased the Society's enemies but it did nothing to diminish the Society's general prestige and influence in Rome and the Church at large.

A second, and just as considerable, source of that prestige was the close association of Jesuits with the Ultramontane movement. Before 1850 the average practising Catholic, conscious that he belonged to a despised minority, tended to stand on the defensive. He hid, or even jettisoned, features of his religious practice which seemed particularly 'superstitious' to Protestants and secularists. He tended to be absorbed in local Catholic affairs and to regard the Pope as merely the distant and passive centre of Catholic communion and the ultimate arbiter in obscure clerical disputes. The Ultramontane movement, which gained ground ever more widely after 1850, stood for aggression and a heavy stress on Catholic doctrines and practices which were most obnoxious to moderns. Ultramontanes loathed science and rational enquiry in matters of religion: they exalted tradition, insight, instinct and the supernatural. They rejected any idea that Catholics ought to fit into modern society: they condemned that society as false. They thought of the Pope as, by God's appointment, their inspired leader, endowed by virtue of his office with infallible judgement, supernatural insight, absolute spiritual power and great holiness. They revived old theories that the Pope had an 'indirect power' to censure and control governments. To the Ultramontane therefore Catholic loyalty required that bishops and religious superiors should be utterly subject to the Pope, that Roman devotions, liturgical customs, church fittings, and terminology should be copied throughout the Church.

Pius IX was carried away by this tide of feeling. His public condemnations of 'modern errors' became more and more strident. He expected all bishops to visit Rome frequently and refer their lightest decisions to his arbitration. When the Italian Government seized the Papal States he excommunicated those who took part in the seizure, spoke of the Government as an illicit organisation, and solemnly condemned the liberal patriotic opinions of his old friend Gioberti. The Ultramontanes acclaimed the Pope as a hero and martyr. They loudly applauded his *Syllabus of Errors* in which he roundly dismissed 19th-century liberalism as a tissue of heresies. In 1870 Ultramontane enthusiasm reached fever-pitch. Pius assembled a General Council of bishops in Rome. A large majority of those present joined with him in defining Papal Infallibility. The Council was then dispersed by the outbreak of the Franco-Prussian war which speedily brought the drama of the anti-religious Commune in Paris and the seizure of all the city of Rome except the Vatican by Italian troops. To many extreme Ultramontanes these stirring events seemed signs from heaven presaging the 'crucifixion' of the Pope and the Church and their 'resurrection' into a new age of history to be marked by supernatural wonders and the triumph of Catholicism over its enemies.

Jesuits took a prominent part in every side of the Ultramontane movement. Jesuits and the 'Jesuited' acted as vigorous publicists spreading its principles far and wide. In some countries they formed activist groups which secured promotion in the Church hierarchy for Ultramontane clergy and delated to Rome those thought to be dangerously liberal or critical. Between 1854 and 1870 the Holy Office in Rome was deluged with these delations, especially from Germany and Austria. In spite of tough opposition from the Archbishop of Vienna, Cardinal Schwarzenburg, the teaching of Anton Günther, an eminent Austrian philosopher and theologian, was formally condemned in Rome. Earlier in life Günther spent a few years as a Jesuit. Three very able German seminary professors, critics of Ultramontanism, were dismissed from their posts. Gioberti's books, formerly regarded by Pius IX as harmless, were condemned. Döllinger, the most respected priest-professor in Germany and hitherto mildly liberal and friendly towards the Society, was repeatedly delated to Rome. When he visited the Holy Office he was refused a hearing: the Office's Consultors included Kleutgen, a particularly activist Ultramontane Jesuit professor at the *Romanum*. In England Newman and Richard Simpson were constantly in trouble with the Ultramontanes. Newman was critical of their excesses but friendly with some Jesuits there and in Rome. He found that his books were met by a barrage of hostility in Rome and that there seemed to be a conspiracy to brand him as a dangerous liberal disloyal to the Pope. In Italy Rosmini and his Institute of Charity were subjected to constant harassment and delations.

The Syllabus of Errors owed much of its material to drafts supplied to the Pope by professors at the *Romanum*. Its teaching was enthusiastically disseminated by Jesuit periodicals, the *Civilta Cattolica* in Rome, *Stimmen aus Maria Laach* in Germany, *Etudes* in Paris and *The Month* in London.

Throughout Europe the homes of Ultramontanes were distinguished by the display of three large pictures, one of the Sacred Heart of Jesus, one of our Lady of La Salette or Lourdes, and one of Pius IX. The three pictures stood for sets of ideas which were closely interconnected. The Sacred Heart was shown as reigning over the world yet wounded by sin, especially the sins of liberal secularists, French Republican politicians, Italian liberal patriots, and, most of all, false 'so-called Catholics'. The true believer owed a debt of 'reparation'. This consisted of prayers, penances, Holy Communion received on nine successive 'first Fridays' in each month, and action to forward the Ultramontane cause. Every effort was to be made to draw families, Catholic institutions, and even Catholic nations under the rule of the Sacred Heart by a solemn act of 'consecration'. The cult was definitely militantly evangelistic and had clear political implications. The pious young aristocrats who served in the papal Zouaves defending Rome against the assaults of the Italian army nearly all wore badges of the Sacred Heart. Moreover, this was a distinctively Jesuit cult, owing most of its form to a 17th-century 'Jesuited' nun and her Jesuit director. The cult was spread with immense zeal and ingenuity by a French Jesuit team led by Henri Ramière, a converted liberal. He founded militant *Cercles*, organised religious Congregations consecrated to the Sacred Heart, distributed hosts of pictures of it, enrolled three million people into his *Apostolate of Prayer* pledged to promote the cult, and provided countless Catholic families with Sunday reading, *The Messenger of the Sacred Heart*.

The cult of our Lady has always been associated with Catholic crises, disasters and holy wars fought with armies and rosaries and penances. In a sense therefore it was only natural that the Ultramontanes should have been fertile soil for a great new crop of startling and uncompromising apparitions, revelations of doom, and deliverances from unbelief and disease. The apparitions at La Salette in 1846, Lourdes in 1858, Pontmain in 1871 and Knock in 1879 were only the most widely popular of scores of 'sightings' of our Lady. Almost invariably the recipients were peasants, usually children, in remote, poverty-stricken places. The foolishness of the poor, illiterate and backward seemed to confound the wisdom of the world of urban areas, technological progress and scepticism. The worldly-wise, drawn by curiosity to the shrines, faced acute physical discomfort, dirt, disease and crudity of manners. They were faced by revelations that liberalism was heading fast for hell-fire and ruin if it did not submit its proud intellect to faith. But the 19th century, even at La Salette and Lourdes, was not the middle ages or even the 17th century: Ultramontane devotion to the cult was tinged with a modern, commercialistic practicality and lack of taste, a forced pietism, and a frantic credulity. Jesuits were associated with almost every feature of the cult. Among the many priests attracted by the case of Bernadette Soubirous of Lourdes was a Jesuit as her main director. He tried in vain to make her conform to his preconceived idea of a vessel of grace and prophecy. She politely but firmly refused to agree that she had received a message for the world or to make herself a 'victim of reparation': the most she would do was to assure Pius IX that her 'lady' approved of his campaigns. The very active French Jesuit directors, Ginhac and Olivaint, imposed on their subject

Congregations of nuns an iron spirituality derived from the spirit and 'secret' of La Salette, the grimmest and strangest of the apparitions. *The Graces of Prayer*, the classical compendium of all this Ultramontane high mysticism, published in 1901 by another French Jesuit, Augustin Poulain, was based on personal observation. The author had dabbled in the 1870s in the extreme practices of its most fanatical devotees. He and his penitents, the Visitation nuns of Nevers, had practised 'vicarious suffering', taking on oneself the mental and physical agonies of the sick, but had drawn the line at Satanism, belief in an imminent second Pentecost, and immoral 'unions of life'.

Teilhard de Chardin, as a pupil of the Jesuits and their novice in the 1890s, was brought up in the backwash of this intense, claustrophobic spirituality. He wrote in his diaries of those days that his vocation was to 'give back to Mary one of the brightest jewels in her crown', France, and pledged that he would, for the rest of his life, constantly meditate on 'the three feminines, Mary, the Church and the Society'.

Jesuits were also much to the fore during the period of feverish Ultramontane excitement preceding the Vatican Council of 1870. A wildly extremist article on Papal Infallibility in *Civilta Cattolica* deeply upset Newman. Pius IX, he wrote in January, 1870, was 'listening to the flattery of a clique of Jesuits, Redemptorists and converts'. At the Council itself Kleutgen, Franzelin, Schrader and Liberatore of the *Romanum* staff were more active than any other of the theological experts. Henceforward Döllinger, Lord Acton and other liberals firmly believed that the definition of Papal Infallibility had been contrived by Jesuits. Acton thought that, because of the 'papal connection', the apparently enormous new power attributed to the Popes by the definition gave the Society 'the supremacy of the Church'. In April 1869 Newman had already tried to confide to a Jesuit friend, Henry Coleridge, his dread that the Society was tending 'to swamp the Church', a fear which, he wrote, was shared by 'most thinking men'. It was, however, impossible, in the highly explosive clerical atmosphere of those days, for Newman to dispatch the letter. It remained unposted in his files and was marked pathetically: 'to be burned when read'.

A lesser, but real, cause of the growth of the Society's influence was the relative ineffectiveness of governmental measures taken against it. In France the disruption caused by the Franco-Prussian War, enemy occupation, and the Commune in Paris in 1870-1 did not prevent a vigorous upsurge of the Society's works throughout the 1870s. In 1880 came a violent reaction by the radical Republican Government when the Ferry laws were passed closing down all Jesuit houses in France. Their doors were sealed by the police and the novices and students were dispersed to Belgium and England. Unemployed Jesuit priests volunteered for service overseas. But the persecution soon slackened. The much divided Paris Government, most of whose wives were practising Catholics, proved unable to keep up the execution of the laws for long. The local authorities in the *pratiquant* areas were ready to turn a blind eye towards covert Jesuit activity. The 'Jesuited' gave the Society every assistance. Soon many of the fathers slipped back to work in France disguised as secular priests. New schools were opened under a light camouflage: old works were resumed. By 1900 the strength of the French Provinces was so evident that the radical Republicans planned another, better contrived, persecution. Even the long exile of the French Jesuit novices and students had done no more than slow down the steady increase in numbers of the Provinces.

It was the same story in Spain, where the anti-Jesuit laws of 1868 were repealed in 1876. In Italy and Germany governmental resistance was more stubborn but the final results very similar. After 1870 the General and Gesu staff went to ground in Fiesole so successfully camouflaged that the bitterly anti-Jesuit Cardinal Gustav von Hohenlohe imagined that they were in hiding in Paris. The Italian noviciates and student communities were dispersed to foreign Provinces and for some years recruitment sank very low. Unemployed Fathers mostly shared the desolation of Botalla: he ate his heart out in exile, teaching stolid English Jesuit students theology at St. Beuno's in the fastnesses of Wales. But during the 1880s, as von Hohenlohe reported disconsolately, the Italian Provinces covertly took shape again in their own country: almost every member of the Italian cabinet had a Jesuit brother or nephew. By 1893 the Gesu was back openly in Rome in its old house. The *Romanum* and *Germanicum* were also back, even if in new premises, and functioning vigorously. The German Jesuit experience was similar. For a time the Fathers had to face exile of the bitter kind suffered by, for instance, Weninger in the United States, Knabenhauer in a little Jesuit school in southern England, and Strassmeier, an eccentric Assyriologist, tied to parish work at Farm Street in London. But very soon ingenious ways were found of evading the Reichstag's and the provinces' 'May Laws' and a vigorous, if camouflaged and rather stunted, Jesuit activity was resumed under the noses of officials who became increasingly indulgent. Thus the local authorities in Würtemburg never did execute the laws wholeheartedly. In the 1890s the German Chancellor, von Bülow, influenced by the Catholic Centre party and perhaps also by his devoutly Catholic wife, considerably relaxed the laws and allowed foreign Jesuits into the empire.

It is very likely that these anti-Jesuit laws did the Society a positive service. They certainly helped to strengthen the conviction of many Jesuits that they were living in the midst of the Armageddon of world history, the final conflict between the Church and unbelief. By concentrating their fire so heavily and ostentatiously on the Jesuits the hostile governments reinforced the general impression in Europe that the Society was the backbone of real Catholicism. Also the persecution brought healthy new features into Jesuit life. Adaptability became almost as important as the maintenance of tradition. The German element in the Society, so increasingly powerful in the 1860s, declined in importance. The Italian element, already on the wane in 1870, shrank still further. On the other hand the French and foreign mission elements became steadily larger and more influential.

Of course the Society of these years of growth and stress was never as united, single-minded, and efficient as its members and its opponents often imagined it to be. Jesuits did not create Ultramontanism and they were far from being its only publicists. The Society was almost a microcosm of the Church at large and even the Roothaan discipline could not make all its members think and react in exactly the same way. By the 1860s Ultramontanism had permeated the Church so much that most thinking Catholics were influenced by it in some degree: even Newman and Rosmini were. The great quarrel of 1870-1 within the Ultramontane movement was between extremists and moderates. The issues were comparatively narrow: they were family quarrels and for that reason singularly vicious. Veuillot, the editor of the rabidly extremist newspaper, *L'Univers*, was writing of Dupanloup, the Bishop of Orléans, and Montalembert, both exceedingly devout, if very moderately Ultramontane Catholic leaders, in this statement in one of his editorials:

'Liberalism is a disease whose symptoms are a lack of hatred of heresy and a constant kindness towards error . . .'

So also the very moderately liberal Newman asked a friend of Döllinger's to pass on to him in 1873 the message:

'I cannot overcome the sad feeling that he should have felt it right to place himself in such antagonism to men who, though his inferiors in moral worth and unscrupulous in their proceedings, have, as I think, the right on their side.'

Those 'inferiors' were Pius IX, Manning, the Archbishop of Westminster, and a great host of prominent extremist clergy.

As we have seen, the Society had its share of extremist Ultramontanes. They could, man for man, match up to the wildnesses and ferocity of their colleagues in other Orders and the secular clergy. Klemens Schrader, a Hanoverian Jesuit, was another Veuillot. He held that every word of *The Syllabus of Errors* was infallibly defined truth. He showered the Holy Office with delations of the moderates and pursued ex-Jesuits who had left with a particular venom. In 1870 he volunteered to stay on in Rome to encourage the papal Zouaves in their fruitless defence of the city against the Italian army. There were many Jesuits who never showed any particular desire to take sides in the great quarrel but who tried hard to keep themselves and the Society on an even keel and engaged in its ordinary work of evangelism. In the English Province Bernard Vaughan and Eyre were of this type: both factions, most probably unjustifiably, claimed them. Even the General, Beckx, belonged to this peace party. At the Vatican Council of 1870 he chose as his theological adviser a very definite moderate, the Belgian historian de Buck.

The anti-Jesuit moderates like Döllinger, Acton, Chlodwig von Hohenlohe and Newman found it very hard to understand how a Jesuit could possibly be a moderate and stay in the Society. Newman's comment on his Jesuit friend Henry Coleridge was typical:

'. . . now his simple duty is to be obedient — alas, how difficult in the case of sensitive minds, with intellectual and logical perceptions. It is the duty of all members *sentire* what the existing body *sentit* — to believe *because* others believe: how confusing! There are men of hard minds who can do it — but there are those whom it crushes . . .'

Newman wrote as a biased outsider who, in any case, believed passionately that Coleridge ought never to have been a Jesuit. In fact Newman's friend at the Gesu, Robert Whitty, Coleridge, and some nameless English and Italian Jesuit moderates who conveyed discreetly through Coleridge their warm approval of Newman's books were neither 'hard men' nor 'crushed'. If Newman had ever dared to cross-question them about their loyalties, they would undoubtedly have admitted having tough problems but would have insisted that theirs were not essentially different from those of all contemporary Catholic moderates. They would also have pointed out that Beckx had never imposed on the Society belief in extremist Ultramontane views and that, even if he had, Probabilist moral principles allowed them to interpret their duty of obedience in a minimalist way.

The two principal centres of Jesuit influence, Rome and Paris, contained numbers of confirmed moderates. At the *Romanum* the extremist minority of the staff had become fanatical advocates for a complete 'medievalisation' of the syllabus, cutting out all modern authors and using only the pure texts of Aristotle and Thomas Aquinas. These ultra-reactionary views outraged the majority of the staff and confirmed them in generally moderate opinions. Passaglia, by far the ablest *Romanum* theologian of the century, and Curci, a founder-editor of *Civilta Cattolica,* both took the moderate position so passionately that they left the Society, Passaglia voluntarily in 1858 and Curci by expulsion on the orders of Pius IX in 1875. Several of the moderate professors including Quarella worked hard behind the scenes at the Vatican Council to strengthen the hand of the moderate bishops and get the decree on Papal Infallibility toned down. In 1878 Pius IX died and Leo XIII ascended the Papal throne. In theory his reign ought to have produced an official reaction towards moderation and even greater papal favour for the Society. Leo had a reputation for moderate views: he had been educated in a Jesuit College and at the *Romanum* and his brother was a Jesuit. In practice these expectations were only very partially fulfilled. Leo was an aristocrat whose considerable personal charm and diplomatic gifts concealed a sharp authoritarianism. His gestures included opening up the Vatican archives to scholars, limited approaches to the Italian and French governments, an exchange of courtesies with Bismarck, and the award of a Cardinal's hat to Newman in his old age. These liberal gestures were accompanied by a determined assault on Catholic academic freedoms particularly at the *Romanum*. Neo-Thomism became papal orthodoxy. All the *Romanum* and *Germanicum* professors who refused to toe the line were removed from their posts. Extremist Jesuit professors received key posts in all the Society's main study houses.

Leo XIII's attitude towards the Society reflected the fact that he was both thoroughly 'Jesuited' and yet also quite capable of viewing the behaviour of Jesuits objectively and very critically. On the one hand his constant, unthinking references to Jesuit terms, saints and devotions charmed the Gesu. They revelled in the steady increase of the Jesuit presence in the Cardinalate, Congregations and rapidly multiplying Roman Commissions and Institutes. On the other hand the Gesu was deeply disturbed by Leo's alarming tendency to expect automatic and total Jesuit support for every project he launched. When that support fell short of his expectations he could be terrifyingly angry with the Society, even in his public pronouncements.

His two main complaints concerned dogged and very wide-spread Jesuit resistance to two of his favourite projects: Neo-Thomism and the 'rallying' of French Catholics to support of the Third Republic. Apart from a small band of Jesuit professors headed by Cardinal Mazella, most of the Society studiously ignored the Pope's call for a return to the thought of Aquinas. For the most part this attitude stemmed from hidebound conservatism and merely reflected the views of the average Catholic priest. Most seminaries and Jesuit study houses had, for the last half century, settled down into a comfortable, if intellectually debased, compromise. Their courses were a strange mixture of antique scholastic forms and 'modern' ideas, borrowed rather indiscriminately from thinkers as diverse as Descartes, de Maistre, Kant, Hegel, Schleiermacher, Günther and even Newman. The highly refined intellectual purism of the Neo-Thomists was as offensive to most priests, Jesuits included, as the artistic purism of Dom Guéranger and the French Benedictines who wanted to revive 12th-century plainchant and ban all 'modern' music in churches. Yet this intellectualist Pope backed both the Neo-Thomists and Guéranger. Moreover, there were young Jesuit professors who kept alive the Society's tradition of 'dissidence' and liberalism. They could stomach neither the Neo-Thomists' 'medievalism' nor the established academic compromises. They were turning with increasing enthusiasm towards the new, evolutionist philosophy of a lay Catholic professor, Maurice Blondel in a French state university. Leo XIII was infuriated by all this Jesuit incomprehension and dissidence.

Meanwhile French society was convulsed by the Dreyfus Affair. The trial for espionage of a Jewish staff officer, Alfred Dreyfus, in 1894 became the unlikely occasion of the biggest politico-religious storm in France since 1871. The Catholic right wing, monarchist, stiffly Ultramontane and violently anti-Semitic, treated Dreyfus as an outrageous example of the spiritual and moral degeneration of Republican France, dominated by Jews, Freemasons, Socialists and atheists. The radical Republican left wing saw the attack as the prelude to a seizure of power by Catholic army officers and the proscription of all unbelievers. Leo XIII's plan for a Catholic *Ralliement* was shattered. He noted sourly that very many Jesuits, including the editors of *Etudes* and *Civilta Cattolica* enthusiastically condemned Dreyfus. He failed to notice that many others remained so silent that two of the most fanatically 'anti-Dreyfusard' Jesuits left the Society in disgust.

* * *

When Leo XIII died in 1903 the inevitable left wing backlash in France had just occurred. The radical Republicans imposed by law much severer restrictions on the Catholic clergy and Orders than those of 1880. The last vestiges of the state establishment of the Catholic Church were swept away. State salaries for the clergy were ended, Church property nationalised, and the more right wing Orders, headed by the Jesuits, bundled neck and crop out of France. The Government took note of the failure of the expulsion laws of 1880: this time the Jesuits found it impossible to slip back into France in disguise and resume work in covert ways. Yet the Gesu was not disheartened by the blow. In its eyes the 'dispersion' of the French and German Provinces bulked small beside the great advances the Society was making in many other countries. Thanks mainly to contemporary European imperialism and a strong tide of right wing political reaction in Latin America the Society's Provinces and infrastructure outside Europe were multiplying fast. Even the Russian Empire, forbidden ground since 1820, now seemed open to Jesuit evangelism. For many years Jesuits had worked among Polish and Orthodox Russian expatriates in France and Italy. Gagarin, the first editor of the Paris *Etudes*, was a convert from Russian Orthodoxy. The Russian College in Rome was under Jesuit direction from its inauguration. Now in 1903 the Tsar ended the legal ban on conversions from Orthodoxy which were soon said to number 300,000.

The Society's numbers had topped 16,000 and it had become the Church's largest Order. This fact and the continuing stagnation of recruitment to the other Orders and the secular clergy made it abundantly clear that the Society was the only clerical body with men to spare for new and crucial enterprises. Leo XIII's successor, Pius X, was not 'Jesuited' and very anxious to find advisers and assistants from outside the charmed circle of 'Jesuitry'. Few could be found: the Society did really seem to be indispensable. Most bishops owed their promotion to the Jesuits. In 1903 Rome had the right to appoint to a third of the sees in the Church. In most cases the priests chosen were trained in the Jesuit-directed Gregorian University in Rome or in one of its satellite Colleges. It was acknowledged that 'Gregorians' were possessors of a perfect 'Roman spirit'. Incidentally, of course, most of them had a deep respect for the Society. The other two thirds of the sees were filled with priests appointed by Catholic governments. The successful candidates were almost invariably priests who had been trained in diocesan or Congregational seminaries. The great majority of these seminaries used 'Ignatian' rules and forms of devotion and invited Jesuits to give ordination retreats. The future John XXIII was a typical candidate of this type. He was never properly 'Jesuited', but his whole attitude to life had been determined by a seminary education which could hardly have been more 'Ignatian'. His first seminary, in Bergamo, his native place, was riddled with Jesuit influences. As he himself explained later in his career, Bergamo provided most of the men who revived the Italian Province of the Society in 1814. The seminary used the old Jesuit rules and Sodality of 1773. John XXIII kept those rules all his life and tried to model himself on three favourite Jesuit saints. He finished his training in a Redemptorist seminary in Rome. There his director criticised Jesuit spirituality but simultaneously insisted that his Order stood foursquare on Jesuit foundations.

The ramifications of the underground tap-roots of 'Jesuitry' and 'Ignatianism' seemed endless in 1903. At least half of the curial officials were 'Jesuited Gregorians': the rest were mostly 'Ignatian' by training. All the modern Congregations in the Church, even the strongly anti-Jesuit Rosminians, were definitely 'Ignatian' in character. Quite two thirds of the very numerous Orders and Congregations of women were 'Jesuited': the rest, with very few exceptions, were more or less 'Ignatian'. By 1903 the older religious Orders of men contained leaders who were trying hard to cut through the thick web of 'Ignatianism' and revive the older monastic spirit and ways of their Orders. They found the task hard and frustrating.

If Jesuit influence, consciously or unconsciously accepted, was stronger than ever before among secular priests, male and female religious and laywomen educated in convents, it remained thin among laymen. There were many reasons for this. The Jesuit connection with thrones and governments was a very pale shadow of what it had been in the 17th century. Now it only included a few very superannuated German princelings, some princesses, and a thin sprinkling of cabinet ministers and senior civil servants. The decision of the Catholic convert Marquis of Ripon to take his Jesuit chaplain with him to Delhi when he was appointed Viceroy of India struck contemporary Catholics as a crazy anachronism. The Jesuits had never acquired much of a connection with Europe's great landed aristocracy. The Gesu repined because parents of this class now sent their sons to secular priest tutors or to Benedictine and Oratorian schools. As in the 17th and 18th centuries the *clientèle* of Jesuit schools was drawn mainly from the professional and commercial middle class. In the last decades of the 19th century the Society's most inveterate enemies professed to be deeply alarmed about the extent of the hold it had gained on this class. In the 1870s Chlodwig von Hohenlohe imagined that it had penetrated deeply into the upper echelons of the German Government and even into the cabinet and Court. In the 1880s, while on a visit to Paris, he and the Portuguese ambassador to France compared notes and counted up the major French businesses which, they thought, were 'in the hands of the Jesuits': these included the Parisian fancy goods trade and the whole of the French import of Chilean guano fertiliser. In the 1890s, at the height of the Dreyfus Affair, radical Republican publicists reckoned that since the 1870s Jesuit schoolmasters had achieved practical control of the French armed forces and civil services. It was calculated that, by cramming able boys in Jesuit Colleges, the masters had gained a phenomenal number of entries into St. Cyr, the *Polytechnique*, the *Navale*, and establishments for training future administrators. Published statistics seemed to demonstrate that, for instance, in 1898 a quarter of the students at St. Cyr were 'Jesuited' and so many of the General Staff that one Jesuit confessor, du Lac, could control army policy. It was also freely asserted that a very effective Jesuit 'Old Boy' network operated in the forces to place 'Jesuited' officers in crucial posts. The career of Ferdinand Foch certainly appeared to bear out these allegations. He and his brother Germain were the sons of a plodding civil servant. After special courses at the Jesuit Colleges at St. Etienne and Metz Ferdinand won a place in the *Polytechnique*: his brother became a Jesuit. Ferdinand did brilliantly in the army, soon rising to be deputy head of the *Ecole Supérieure de la Guerre*. From that exalted position he helped the careers of able 'Jesuited' officers. In the great political storm of 1898-1901 he was accused of conspiracy, dismissed from his post in the *Ecole* and sent back to regimental duty.

In recent years Jesuit apologists have given some substance to these theories by listing the famous men who were educated by the Society in the years before 1914. The list is certainly impressive. It includes, among Frenchmen, Foch and his Chief of Staff, de Castelnau, Charles de Gaulle, de Lattre, de Tassigny, Leclerc de Hauteclocque, Admiral Darlan, Georges Bernanos, Cardinal Gerlier, Henri Brémond, Charles de Foucauld, Marcel Prévost, Pierre Teilhard de Chardin, General de Grandmaison and his Jesuit brother Léonce, and Georges Bidault. Among Germans there were Martin Heidegger, Cardinal von Galen, Berthold Brecht, Kurt Schuschnigg, Artur Seyss Inquart and Karl and Hugo Rahner; among Belgians Léon Degrelle leader of the Rexists. Among Englishmen there were Arthur Conan Doyle, Charles Laughton, Lord Devlin and Alfred Hitchcock, and among Irishmen James Joyce and Eamon de Valera. The Latin countries of the south contributed Gabriele d'Annunzio, Pius XI, Pius XII, Luigi Sturzo, Ramon Perez de Ayala and Rafael Alberti.

But in reality by 1903 the Jesuit stake in the education of lay boys was very much smaller than it had been in the 17th and 18th centuries. Large Jesuit Colleges concentrating on intensive study of the Latin classics were a thing of the past. The Society now had to struggle to maintain any sort of presence in an educational system dominated in almost every country by dictatorial ministries of education, state universities and schools, and parents demanding a syllabus geared to the entry requirements of the universities and professions. In this changing and difficult environment Jesuit teachers had to adopt methods never envisaged by Loyola or Acquaviva. Increasingly they had to accept teaching posts in Gymnasiums, Institutes and universities they did not control or try, as chaplains and tutors, to make some impact on lay private schools and youth organisations. Even before 1903 the Gregorian University in Rome had made history by admitting as an unofficial, extra-mural theology student a young Englishwoman, Maude Petre, a member of a highly modern French lay Congregation.

For these reasons and because of the disarray of the French and German Provinces few of the men listed as distinguished ex-pupils of the Society had ever been subjected to the distinctly old-fashioned Jesuit College routine described by James Joyce in his *Portrait of the Artist as a Young Man*. His revulsion from it was shared by Conan Doyle, Laughton, Hitchcock, Ayala, Alberti (who was expelled from College for truancy at the age of fourteen) and even Pierre Teilhard de Chardin. De Chardin and his brothers happened to be of school age in France during the halcyon years for Jesuit schools there between the expulsions of 1880-5 and 1901. The small Jesuit private school they attended at Notre Dame de Mongré gave them large doses of antique piety and a very slight academic education. Very much later in life Pierre commented to a close friend that he never wanted to set eyes on his old school again. He wrote:

> 'It leaves me with a feeling of revulsion . . . a vague sense of somehow (with the best of intentions) having been played upon and misled by my educators . . .'

Henri Brémond and his brothers became Jesuits. But they were of school age in the later 1870s and the 1880s and so had very little formal education from the Society. Its influence on them during their years in state schools came from Jesuit friends of the family. Charles de Foucauld revolted against the school system of the Jesuit College in the Rue des Postes in Paris in the 1870s. After barely two years of it he was expelled for insolence, womanising and loudly proclaiming that he had lost his religious faith. After he had had narrowly escaped expulsion from St. Cyr and had been forced to resign his commission in the *Chasseurs d'Afrique* he returned to the practice of his religion through the influence of a woman cousin. He was persuaded to undergo a course of the Spiritual Exercises but sheered away from the Society, first to the Cistercians, and then into the life of a hermit in the Sahara desert.

There was nothing distinctively 'Jesuited' about the strange, violent and wayward careers of d'Annunzio and Bidault. Both were rescued from state schools by pious relations and despatched to narrowly Jesuit private schools, d'Annunzio to Prato and Bidault to Turin. Both men soon reacted strongly away from the influence of this schooling but retained for life a sneaking affection for Jesuits and, perhaps, a trace of the crusading fervour of their schoolmasters. Heidegger, Brecht, Sturzo, von Galen and Baron Friedrich von Hügel all shared the same experience in varying ways. Heidegger and Brecht attended state Gymnasiums, Heidegger in Konstanz and Freiburg, Brecht in Augsburg, during the years between 1894 and 1917 when the German Government came round to tolerating a very limited amount of teaching and pastoral work by Jesuits provided they lived singly in the dress of secular clergy. Both men seem to have been taught a few classes by disguised Jesuits: both had contacts with Jesuits outside school. Heidegger was persuaded by the Fathers to undertake training for the secular priesthood in Freiburg but he soon abandoned the practice of his religion. Brecht, whose family was part-Protestant, part-Catholic, left school with no religious faith but a fairly accurate knowledge of the Protestant Bible and Jesuit ways. Von Galen and Sturzo had no Jesuit school education but were brought up in an atmosphere of 'Ignatianism': both attended lectures at the Gregorian University in Rome and retained for life Jesuit acquaintances and a kind of critical respect for the Society. Von Hügel's very mixed education included no formal instruction from Jesuits. His friends presumed that the spiritual influences on his early life were a Dutch Dominican and a French secular priest director. They were very surprised when he wrote, late in life, that though he would never advise any young man to enter the Society he felt that he himself owed the preservation of his faith in adolescence to Jesuits.

The one group of distinguished ex-pupils of the Society which appeared really 'Jesuited' was entirely French. Its older generation, Foch, de Castelnau and the de Grandmaisons had an orthodox Jesuit College education before 1880. They were what Republicans called 'Jesuits' or 'field-booted Capuchins'. The mainspring of their lives was not so much religious faith as a grim asceticism and a very passionately patriotic conservatism. Some Jesuits shared these attitudes: an increasing number did not. The younger generation of French ex-pupils caught the attitudes in a modified form not directly from Jesuits but from one celebrated 'Jesuited' laymaster, Henri de Gaulle. He began his teaching life as a lay assistant in a Jesuit College in Lille. After 1880 and the expulsion of the Fathers he ran it single-handed until 1890 when the Paris Provincial offered him the 'front' headship of the College in the Rue de Vaugirard in Paris. History repeated itself. The Fathers were expelled again in 1901. De Gaulle then, without their help, succeeded to their 'educational goodwill' and ran a succession of small proprietary schools in Paris until 1914. 'Jesuited' laymen like de Gaulle and Foch were, as Pierre Teilhard de Chardin said of his own married brothers, Joseph and Gabriel, 'true Jesuits', much more 'Jesuitical' than any of the Fathers. Charles de Gaulle and his Gaullist soldier-colleagues, de Lattre and Leclerc, owed most of their education to Henri de Gaulle. They were 'Jesuited' in a curiously 'lay', old-fashioned way. The odd circumstances of their schooling gave them a theoretical respect for the episcopate,

priesthood and Society as institutions combined with a sharply
critical, even cynical, attitude towards prelates, priests and
Jesuits in the flesh.

Thus in 1903 the power and influence of the Society appeared
inescapable to most clerics and nuns. But their ecclesiastical
firmament was narrower than ever after almost half a century
of Ultramontane reaction and Roman centralisation. Even inside
that firmament, now as in 1773, an 'Ignatian', or even a 'Jesuited',
cleric could often show a critical detachment from the Society
and its works. In 1903 as in 1773 great Jesuit activity and influence
did not automatically win the Society affection and security.
Meanwhile it had little positive influence in the secular world.
Its public image, part legend and part truth, was still strong
enough to keep it excluded by law from the German and Russian
empires, France, Switzerland, Scandinavia and some Latin
American countries. Its train of 'Jesuited' nuns and convent-
bred women for the most part merely serviced the existing
network of Jesuit influences. The case of Maude Petre was to
show that well-educated 'Jesuited' women could be as strongly
critical of the Society as their clerical counterparts. The Society's
train of male ex-pupils was small, its casualty rate considerable,
and its men of real mark in the secular world few: even if
'Jesuited' they were not always kindly disposed towards all
Jesuits. As Pierre Teilhard de Chardin was to discover, in the
early 20th century world very many regarded Jesuits with deep
mistrust, many more with sheer indifference, and the most
friendly non-Catholics with that kind of curious interest usually
reserved for rare, exotic animals.

*   *   *

While the western world was heading towards the catastrophe
of August·1914, Catholic ecclesiastics were deeply absorbed in
a noisy and, to the outsider, highly obscure, family quarrel
known as 'the Modernist Affair'. Since the mid-19th century the
Ultramontane conservatives had tried to build up an effective
clerical penal system to replace the antique one, with its Inquisitions and ecclesiastical prisons, swept away by the tide of
political liberalism after 1789. By 1903 the Ultramontanes were
deeply alarmed. Their new disciplinary system, based on strait
Roman authority over bishops, considerable legal and financial
control of bishops over secular priests, and a tight control of
religious by Roman Congregations and major religious superiors

based in Rome, seemed to be breaking down. During the long reign of Leo XIII the best educated and most active clergy had shown a disturbing independence of mind. New clerical academic Institutes, research groups, publishing houses, editorial committees producing learned periodicals, and experimental teams working among students and the urban masses had sprung up all over Europe. There were Catholic political parties, Catholic trades unions and even Catholic Socialists. A steadily increasing number of clerical professors, lecturers and students worked in state universities, research Institutes and Gymnasiums. Others were deeply involved full-time in politics, trades unionism, youth work and social work. Many were religious who had escaped from the narrow confines of their Orders' houses. Others were secular priests, seconded indefinitely from diocesan work or even ordained 'to the title of their patrimony' and so only minimally subjected to episcopal authority. Most of these secular clergy had state salaries, private incomes or other sources of financial support which rendered them independent of episcopal subsidies. All these clerical academics and activists enjoyed an almost inebriating feeling of freedom. They felt they had escaped from the stifling atmosphere of Ultramontane school discipline and pietistic conformism. They felt mentally liberated and able to profit from exciting new developments in non-Catholic thought. The long Ultramontane winter was surely over: 'reformism' was in the air. Inevitably these stirrings affected diocesan seminaries and the Orders' study houses where an increasing number of professors and students yearned to join in the new enterprises.

An Ultramonte reaction against these developments grew up well before 1903. It was greatly increased in that year by the election of Pius X, a rigid conservative and disciplinarian, and the publication, by chance, of a number of particularly daring 'reformist' works of Biblical exegesis, philosophy and apologetics. The Pope initiated a fierce drive against any and every kind of 'modernism'. The affair rumbled on with the usual barrage of strongly worded papal pronouncements, regulations, official censures on books and individuals and delations to Rome. At first the drive aroused little alarm among the 'reformists'. They felt that their movement was far too-well-established to be suppressed. They were accustomed to periodical Ultramontane attacks, usually directed against the clergy of countries thought to be particularly libertarian and godless. There had recently been a noisy but abortive effort to secure a papal condemnation of 'Americanism' and threats to condemn 'Englishism'. But the anti-Modernist drive grew into a real 'reign of terror'. By 1907 events came to a head. A number of leading 'reformists' were formally excommunicated. 'Reformist' organisations were disbanded by orders from Rome. Seminary professors were dismissed from their posts, especially in Italy. A papal encyclical, *Pascendi Gregis*, formally defined and condemned 'Modernism' as a heresy. According to the Pope this was an importation of liberal Protestant ideas into Catholicism reducing Catholic belief to a vague humanism, rejecting the doctrinal and disciplinary authority of the Church and the validity of Scripture, and so directly threatening the Church's life. Modernism was said to be a creeping cancer which had already gained a great hold on seminaries and establishments of clerical higher education. Diocesan boards of censors, acting as secret 'vigilance committees', were to be set up to keep a close watch on clergy and ordinands and delate all suspects to the Holy Office. All Catholic teachers, clerical and lay, were to subscribe under oath to a 16th-century formula of Catholic faith: if they refused they were to lose their posts. An especially powerful central 'vigilance committee', the *Sodalitium Pianum*, was set up in Rome and subsidised by Pius X. It was managed by his Secretary of State, Cardinal Merry del Val, and a certain Monsignor Benigni. The committee built up a network of correspondents and informers and so amassed dossiers on practically every clerical and lay academic and activist in the Church. Benigni was required to provide the Pope with a daily report on the committee's findings.

Learned periodicals and other clerical publications became so censored and painfully orthodox that they were unreadable. Biblical exegesis and historical research practically ground to a halt. The average standard of Catholic writing degenerated back to the low level of conformism and Ultramontane pietism current in the 1870s. Learned societies went out of existence. Catholic academics began to avoid colleagues suspected of informing and to write their letters in code. Unrepentant 'reformists' met secretly and published articles in non-Catholic periodicals under assumed names. One French seminary professor, Turmel, is said to have used seventy pseudonyms between 1907 and 1914. The *Sodalitium Pianum*, more convinced than ever that it had to deal with a massive, dishonest and well-organised conspiracy, employed handwriting experts, code-breakers and ingenious tests to detect covert Modernism. In 1910 a special and very long anti-Modernist oath was issued for imposition on all ordinands and teachers. The fact that only forty priests in all Europe and America refused to take the oath left the *Sodalitium* unmoved. Its members were convinced, with good reason, that many were evading the oath or taking it with mental reservations. In France state law prevented the imposition of any doctrinal test on teachers in public institutions. In Germany the many priests teaching in state universities successfully went on strike against taking the oath, protesting that it would be a breach of their right to academic freedom.

The anti-Modernist drive was part of a considerable revival of militant Ultramontanism in the pre-war years. The movement had stagnated under Leo XIII, whom most pious conservatives regarded as a weak-kneed dilettante. They now rallied enthusiastically behind Pius X who, they felt, was reviving the old, true Catholic crusading spirit of Pius IX. *Pascendi Gregis* was a worthy successor to the *Syllabus of Errors*. The deep preoccupation of the Pope and Merry del Val with frequent Holy Communion, the Sacred Heart, pilgrimages to Marian shrines and reparation convinced the Ultramontanes that they were living saints. In France the revival launched *Action Française*, yet another typically French politico-religious movement designed to give the nation back its soul and sweep away the godless Third Republic. Pius X openly supported the movement, deliberately turning a blind eye to its excesses, its sinister connections with the army, its urban guerillas, the *Camelots du Roi*, and the doctrinal vagaries of its founder, Charles Maurras, an avowed agnostic. The Ultramontane movement also brought a campaign throughout Europe against the 'contraceptive mentality', regarded as the vilest and most suicidal feature of a godless civilisation fast heading towards disaster. The campaigners were particularly incensed with the generality of bishops, confessors and moralists who still, as throughout the 19th century, refused to combat contraception openly while asserting that they had no right to enquire into marital intimacies and that anyway those practising Catholics who used contraceptive methods could never be persuaded that they were sinning. By 1914 persistent angry lobbying by Ultramontanes had driven the bishops of Belgium and Germany into issuing strong declarations against contraception.

The Jesuits were inevitably much affected by all these stirring events. The General in 1903 was a Spaniard, Ludovico Martin. Ensconsed in his new curial headquarters in the Borgo Sancto Spirito directly opposite the papal residence in the Vatican he was the first General for nearly forty years to have a home that he could call his own and a proper governmental centre. In the 1880s Martin had been posted to the side of his predecessor as his secretary and general factotum. At that time the Generalate, long ago expelled from Rome by the Italian Government, lived a hand to mouth existence at Fiesole near Florence on the charity of 'Jesuited' supporters. The General Congregation which elected Martin General in 1892 had to be held in the discomforts of Loyola in Spain. During the first three years of his Generalate he had wandered, mostly dressed as a secular priest, round Jesuit establishments, open or concealed, in England, Ireland, France, Belgium, Germany and Austria. In 1895 the Italian Government relented and allowed him to take up residence in Rome discreetly, though not in the battered remains of the old Gesu. By 1903 he had at last reconstituted his Curia. In the process of these labours he fell gravely ill and in 1905 suffered the amputation of one arm.

His first preoccupation was to clear the Society of all imputations of Modernism. In one way this was easy. Martin himself was above suspicion: he was no intellectual and all his instincts were solidly conservative. Ultramontane conservatism of the most hidebound kind was very widespread in the Society. In Rome *Civilta Cattolica*, long sheltered in the Vatican, and its Italian Jesuit writers constituted a Pontifical College, dutifully thundered against Modernism. At the Gregorian Louis Billot, soon to be a Cardinal, headed a group of professors who were rabidly anxious to define and refute Modernism and support *Action Française*. In Paris the police tactfully averted their eyes from the distinctive figures of Georges de Pascal, very fat and redfaced, and Augustin Poulain, thin and ascetic, heading through the streets to lecture to appreciative audiences of *Action Française* members, de Pascal on the *Syllabus* and Poulain on La Salette and its divine message of retribution stored up for the godless. The Jesuit editors of *Etudes*, exiled to Belgium, and *Stimmen der Zeit*, exiled to Holland, steadily attacked Modernism. In Belgian Jesuit Colleges the professors besieged the newsagents' shops for the latest numbers of *Action Française* and *La Croix*, and read the more stirring articles to their classes. In the English Province the temperature was lower but Francis Woodlock preached inflammatory sermons against Modernism at Farm Street and Mother Forbes of the 'Jesuited' Sacred Heart Order secured the assistance of Fathers with Roman connections as she busily composed biographies of Pius X and Merry del Val.

In Austria in 1902 Jerome Noldin, a leading Jesuit moralist, published a textbook which delighted the Ultramontanes. He insisted that, in areas where contraception was widely practised, it was the solemn duty of all confessors to cross-question their married penitents on the subject. In 1905 Arthur Vermeersch, the most celebrated Belgian Jesuit moralist, took a leading part in Ultramontane lobbying of the bishops to secure strong action against contraception.

On the other hand liberal, even 'Blondelian', ideas were very current in Jesuit study houses in England and Belgium and among German professors working in their homeland. The French Jesuit theologate exiled to Hastings on the south coast of England was crammed with the best brains in the French Provinces. Their reactions to the Modernist Affair varied. Pierre Rousselot, hitherto a mildly liberal Neo-Thomist, now persuaded himself that it was his duty to join *Action Française* while retaining his private interest in modern philosophy. The strain on his feelings and his conscience was great. His philosophical teaching was eventually condemned in Rome while his new-found intense patriotism led him into the war and to his death in action. Pierre Charles, a definite Blondelian, took refuge in cynicism and satire of the anti-Modernists. Auguste and Albert Valensin were brothers and both deeply pious in an Ultramontane way. Auguste had been attracted by modern philosophy. He now went through agonies of conscience. As he wrote in his diary, he tried frantically 'to see the word of Jesus Christ in the word of the Pope' and 'to stifle bit by bit, the Modernist me . . . exhaust it, starve it, kill it . . .' The strain drove him to a nervous breakdown. His brother Albert accepted what came from Rome without apparent misgivings. Joseph Huby, whose speciality was Scriptural exegesis, a particularly dangerous subject in those days, rapidly became practised in holding his tongue about his real convictions. Meanwhile Pierre Teilhard de Chardin and his fellow student Felix Pelletier watched their young professors' reactions with sympathy, read Bergson, studied science and dug up fossils, secure in the knowledge that their ordination and taking anti-Modernist tests lay some years ahead of them. When Teilhard was ordained at Hastings in 1911 he persuaded himself that the anti-Modernist oath was simply a disciplinary measure and that he was not bound to give an interior assent to all its propositions. He regarded the philosophical and theological framework of the oath as primeval, but comforted himself with the reflection that the Pope must have some good reason for wanting to shelter ordinary Catholics for a few more years from the great adaptations of official Catholic thought which must come soon.

Meanwhile in Belgium Henri Brémond was intensely unhappy in his post on the editorial staff of *Etudes*. His attitude of mind was liberal and he was much influenced by a close reading of Newman's books. The editors were allowed, as exiles and as a matter of prudence, to publish articles under assumed names. Brémond supplied *Etudes* with a string of innocuous articles on literary subjects. In his spare time he wrote, mostly under assumed names, and put into the hands of discreet publishers, a book on Newman and a number of mildly 'reformist' articles. He wanted to quit the Society. Indeed he yearned for an escape from clerical life into marriage. But he had two Jesuit brothers who would be deeply distressed by any such action. He knew that Rome would almost certainly refuse to grant him a laicisation with a right to marry. He knew also that if he left the Society he would face a great wall of ostracism in France and lose most of his old friends. He took the plunge in 1904, left the Society 'by mutual agreement', acquired a small country house far from Paris and a private income from his family, and settled down to a very lonely but respectable existence as a self-employed secular priest historian. He became a model of discretion. His published historical work, read out of the context of his life and times, seems simply historical narrative and comment. But when read closely in that context we can detect, permeating every volume but put obliquely, a Christian humanism utterly at variance with Pius X's orthodoxy along with sharp criticisms of the Church and the Jesuits. Brémond even later explained away the force of the words he used during his one and only overt act of rebellion against ecclesiastical authority, his funeral oration over the grave of his Modernist friend, George Tyrrell:

> 'We know that for him the Roman Catholic Church as a fact stood for the oldest and widest body of corporate Christian experience, for the closest approximation so far attained to the still far distant ideal of a Catholic Church . . .'

In Belgium old Charles de Smedt, who had rescued the Jesuit team of Bollandist historians from Ultramontane pieties and taught them critical standards, soldiered on grimly through the anti-Modernist drive. He was utterly out of sympathy with it and confided to his friend Friedrich von Hügel that in his opinion now only the Protestants had intellectual freedom. A distin-

guished German Jesuit exile teaching Scriptural exegesis at
St. Beuno's, the English theologate, was regarded with suspicion
by the General and, on his orders, packed off to Bombay to teach
English to schoolboys.

Thus by 1904 the General could report to Pius X that the whole
Society, with the exception of one man, George Tyrrell, had conformed to the anti-Modernist line. Tyrrell had been silenced,
the General said, and he was of little importance being a sick
eccentric who had caused trouble throughout his years in the
Society. Pius X retorted angrily that, on the contrary, Tyrrell
was the most dangerous of all the avowed Modernists, a great
source of infection inside the Society and far outside it, especially
in that area which touched the Pope closely, northern Italy. The
General wrote to Tyrrell that the Pope 'said things about you and
other Jesuits which were so strong that I dare not commit them
to paper'.

Who was this remarkable heresiarch, the Society's only open
rebel? Tyrrell was an Irish convert from High Anglicanism who
entered the English Province noviciate in 1880. Until 1896 his
superiors noticed nothing about his demeanour to suggest he
would be a heresiarch. As a novice, student and young priest he
appeared to be an uncompromisingly zealous Ultramontane,
so incapacitated by partial deafness, migraines and ill-health
that he was unlikely to make old age. He was devoted to absolute
obedience and very impatient with the English pragmatism and
common sense that made his colleagues seem to treat rules
light-heartedly. He was the only one in the Province who rigidly
obeyed Leo XIII's directives on Neo-Thomism. His philosophy
teaching at Stonyhurst was so uncompromisingly Thomist that
his students rebelled and he was removed to Farm Street. He
regarded the Society's Probabilism in matters of morality as a
shameful desertion of basic Christian imperatives. Then to all
outward appearances his outlook changed with startling rapidity
in 1896 and 1897 at Farm Street. No doubt reading and reflection
had begun to crack the hard shell of his Ultramontanism before
he left Stonyhurst. But the life into which he was plunged in
London completed the change. It quickly became evident that he
had very exceptional gifts as a director, retreat-giver and writer
for audiences of intelligent, sensitive lay people who, with the
best will in the world, could no longer accept the narrow version
of Catholicism in which they had been brought up. His relations
with penitents, retreatants and the many who got in touch with
him after reading his books blew away the last vestiges of his

own Ultramontanism and made him a 'reformist'.

Simultaneously he became friendly with Friedrich von Hügel who acted as his mentor, introducing him to modern works of philosophy, theology and exegesis written by 'reformist' Catholics and liberal Protestants. Through von Hügel Tyrrell made the acquaintance of numbers of prominent foreign 'reformists'. He began to read their literature and contribute, under assumed names, to their periodicals. Soon he was writing to Henri Brémond that the Church was in the painful process of sloughing off its old skin, like a moulting snake. Inside the Society, he wrote, small numbers of 'irrepressible men' were trying to ensure that it would share in the general 'resurrection' of Catholicism. The Jesuits must emerge as that free association of devoted, adaptable men which Ignatius Loyola had half-intended to found, but which his own military mind and the force of circumstances had perverted into the highly regimented and institutionalised Society of history.

It was during the early years at Farm Street that Tyrrell formed his very close friendship with Maude Petre. At the time she was a 'lay nun' and religious superior, a member of a very 'Jesuited' French Congregation, a forerunner of modern Secular Institutes. She was a highly intelligent woman who had had a theological training under Jesuit auspices in Rome. Tyrrell helped her to complete her emergence from Ultramontanism into 'reformism', a process which she had begun before she met him. In return she fell in love with him, served him devotedly the rest of his life through all his tribulations, and was, as he said, the only true 'confessor' he ever had.

Very soon, and some years before the start of the anti-Modernist drive, his new 'reformism' brought him into sharp collision with Roman authority. In 1898 he was at odds with the General about his final profession in the Society. Like all Jesuits he was vowed to accept whatever grade of membership the General might choose to assign to him. He was ordered to become a Professed Father, one of the small Jesuit elite devoted to preventing all major change. He tried to satisfy his conscience by making the required profession with private, written reservations.

In 1900 the General formally 'silenced him'. His increasing volume of published work, all passed by the Provincial censors and widely appreciated by Catholics, stirred some unknown conservatives to delate him to Rome. There was a brisk passage of arms between the English Provincial and the General. The result could not be in doubt. The Provincial was removed from his post. Tyrrell was ordered to print a retraction, publish no more books, and confine himself to writing pious and innocuous articles for *The Month*. He was removed from his post in London and banished to the most remote of all English Jesuit country missions, Richmond in north Yorkshire. The blow concentrated his mind wonderfully and aroused his combative instincts. For the next six years he resided in the presbytery at Richmond, walking the presbytery dog, saying Mass for the nuns at the local convent, and writing incessantly. His view of what was wrong with the Society and the Church became much clarified. He wrestled with ways of expressing fundamental Catholic doctrine so that it could be meaningful to the host of worried, educated Catholic lay people with whom he now completely identified himself. Drafts of books and articles accumulated on the tables and the floor of his room. Maude Petre came to live in lodgings in Richmond and to spend time with him every day discussing his ideas, criticising his drafts and posting his letters. Suitably innocuous articles went off to the editor of *The Month*. Much more forthright ones were posted, under assumed names, to circulate among the foreign 'reformists' to whom von Hügel had introduced him. Occasionally he consented to their publication for very restricted audiences, mostly in Italy. Behaviour of this kind, when the *Sodalitium Pianum* was swinging into action, was asking for trouble. But, as Tyrrell remarked, the Society had always been ruled by hidebound conservatives whose 'Acquavivaism' positively encouraged underground action by Jesuit liberals. Tyrrell was doing nothing which had not been done many times before by eminent Jesuits, by Mariana, Ricci, Passaglia, Curci and Ravignan. The English Province was then an island of relative tolerance in the Society: in it private letters did not have to be submitted unsealed to superiors, and articles could be printed for private circulation without being submitted to the censors. It was ironic that the quiet little town of Richmond figured twice in the major affairs of the Society in the 19th and early 20th centuries. In the 1870s, at the height of the first Ultramontane movement, an English Provincial, with the General's approval, had planned to make the town the seat of a Pontifical University as far away as possible from the heresies of the universities of Oxford, Cambridge and London. Now between 1900 and 1906 the Society's one Modernist rebel communicated through Richmond's tiny post office with the General and with 'reformist' leaders like von Hügel, Loisy, Le Roy,

Murri, Semeria, Laberthonnière and Buonaiuti.

By 1905 Tyrrell could see that his days in the Society were numbered. He forwarded to the General a request for release from his vows, enclosing what must surely be the fullest and most thorough indictment of Jesuit conservatism ever composed by a serving member of the Society. The document concluded with a prophecy that the Society would wither away, killed by its inability to fit into a changing world, and that its *coup de grâce* would be delivered by women, hitherto its most faithful supporters. The General and the Roman Curia now wanted to be rid of him as soon as possible. It was hard to get legal proof that he was a heretic or disobedient. Once they had that proof they could drum him out of the Society, suspend him from the priesthood or even sever him from the Church by formal excommunication. Failing proof they could only accede to his request and free him from his vows honourably if some bishop were prepared to take him as a diocesan secular priest. But no such bishop could be found. Before the end of 1906 a chance event provided the authorities with a way out of their dilemma. Some Italian 'reformists' printed one of Tyrrell's articles over his name without his permission or that of the English Provincial. Rome made this doubtful ground its basis for a formal dishonourable dismissal from the Society and suspension from the priesthood.

Tyrrell withdrew sadly from Richmond, setting aside the idea of retiring to a cottage in Wensleydale at Bainbridge or Askrigg. Friends provided him with an annuity and house-room at Storrington in Sussex. He was now a semi-invalid, increasingly incapacitated by Parkinson's disease. Maude Petre, dismissed by her Congregation because of her association with him, came to live in Storrington to nurse him and prepare his manuscripts for the printers. He was now in a desperate hurry to present his full case for 'reformism' to the world before he became too ill to think or write. In the three years left to him he published four books. They, like all the Modernist literature of the time, are full of flashes of insight, harbingers of developments of thought in Catholicism which would only mature in the 1960s and 1970s. But neither he nor any of his 'reformist' friends had time or opportunities for the immense amount of reading, research and discussion required to bring their seminal thoughts to maturity. Jesuit orthodoxy dismissed his criticisms of the Society and his provocative new ideas out of hand as the work of a man whose 'apostasy' automatically made him untrustworthy and even dishonest. The Jesuit Cardinal, Steinhuber, in Rome and the editors of *Stimmen der Zeit, Civilta Cattolica* and *Etudes* attacked him bitterly. The English Jesuits were deeply embarrassed but for the most part kindly disposed toward him personally for old acquaintance sake. As he said wryly, the English Province was an island of relative tolerance in the Society. He regretted the fact that his conscience had made him 'their Jonah'.

The dismissal of Tyrrell was one of the last official acts of Ludovico Martin's life. His successor as General, Franz Xavier Wernz, was known only to the clerical world as the author of a standard canon law textbook of the most conventionally Roman type. Yet in spite of his stolid conservatism he soon became convinced that close association with Pius X and the *Sodalitium Pianum* was unhealthy for the Society. Cynics suggested that he had an eye on the Pope's failing health and the distinct possibility that his successor might come from the ranks of the moderate conservatives who regarded the activities of the *Sodalitium* with growing distaste. There was truth in the charge. But Wernz was finding it increasingly hard to keep the peace between anti-modernist fanatics like Steinhuber, Billot, Vermeersch and Matiussi and moderate liberals like Léonce de Grandmaison, Rousselot, Huby and Charles. He was also frightened that the fanatics might destroy the growing *détente* between the Society and the French and German governments. Hence, with Wernz' rather hesitant encouragement moderate liberals took over the management of *Etudes* and *Stimmen der Zeit* and used them to criticise the more absurd and brutal actions of the *Sodalitium Pianum*. Pius X became increasingly angry with Wernz.

None of these curious developments saved Tyrrell from the sentence of excommunication, which was imposed on him in 1907. When he died in Storrington in 1909 the diocesan bishop refused him Catholic burial, sentenced Brémond to suspension for conducting an informal funeral service, and banned Maude Petre from receiving the Sacraments in the diocese. Tyrrell left behind him an unpublished memorandum. It repeated the charge he had made at the start of his course as a 'reformist':

> 'The most liberalising Order ever conceived has become the one block in the way of the Church's expansion . . .'

Manifestly he could not get the Society out of his system: he died still, like a trained Jesuit, automatically seeking to make everything an occasion for evangelism.

By the spring of 1914 Pius X's animus against Wernz came to a head and he planned to summon a General Congregation of the Society and order it to depose him and elect General Matiussi, an arch-conservative, in his place. A rapid deterioration in the Pope's health prevented the execution of the plan. He and Wernz died on the same day in mid-August 1914.

*   *   *

The 1914-8 war dislocated the structure of the Society greatly. Nationalism had always been a threat to its unity. The Franco-Prussian War of 1870-1 had seen the deaths of a number of Jesuits in action on both sides and had poisoned relations between the German and French Provinces for a time. Yet on the whole 19th-century Europe had been extraordinarily peaceful and the sudden and violent tensions in the Society caused by the 1914-8 war came as a great shock to men who had long grown unused to such upsets. In most of the warring countries young, or even middle-aged, Jesuit priests and students were conscripted into the armed forces: noviciates were emptied and often shut up until 1919. Over 6,000 men, a third of the Society, saw action at the fronts, the majority of them as combatants, and casualties were high. In 1916 nearly 2,000 were serving in the German armies and over 1,000 in the French. Jesuit missionary communities were quite often split by fierce quarrels about the war and Germans and Austrians interned as enemy aliens by the Allied authorities. The general dislocation was exacerbated by the markedly pro-German sympathies of the Roman Curia and the Jesuit headquarters in the Borgo Sancto Spirito. The new Pope, Benedict XV, was distressed by this situation but incapable of making much headway against a Roman ecclesiastical establishment stuffed with Germans, Austrians and men promoted by Pius X to high office. The war prevented the assembly of a Jesuit General Congregation until February 1915. The sympathies of the majority of the delegates present were clearly indicated by their choice for the Generalate of the German Assistant, Vladimir Ledochowski. He was a Galician Pole of Austrian nationality, an aristocrat brought up as a page at the Imperial Court in Vienna. He saw a German victory as right, inevitable, and the only way in which the Russian hordes could be driven out of Polish territories and the Poles restored to some kind of nationhood. But in May 1915 the Italian Government declared war on Austria and Germany. Many of the pro-German curial officials took refuge in papal property and were thus sheltered from internment by the Italian laws guaranteeing the

Pope's status as a sovereign ruler. Ledochowski was either unable or unwilling to take advantage of this expedient: he decided to leave Italy and take refuge in neutral Switzerland. By a Federal law of 1847 Jesuits were totally excluded from that country. But before and during the war its Government was willing to give shelter to political refugees of every kind including Russian Bolsheviks and Mensheviks. It granted Ledochowski a temporary residence permit. He settled in Zizers near Chur and the Austrian border, probably because he was intensely preoccupied with the affairs of his native Austrian Galicia and Russian Poland, both just 'liberated' from Russian occupation. It was practically impossible for him to administer the Society from Swiss soil, but he was eventually allowed to summon a few of his Assistants from Rome to live with him in Zizers.

However, the war did bring the Society some modest benefits. The stresses of wartime did not produce a religious revival in Europe. Willy Doyle, the very devout Jesuit chaplain of Irish regiments in France, found his men very responsive. But Teilhard de Chardin's experiences as a medical orderly and unofficial chaplain to a very mixed French regiment were much more typical. The rank and file and most of the officers rejected his overtures. On the other hand the uninhibited patriotism of Catholic priests and ordinands produced a very general diminution of anti-clericalism throughout Europe and the Society profited from this situation. In 1917 the German Government and Reichstag repealed the anti-Jesuit Falk laws. By the end of the war the German Jesuits, depleted in numbers, had established a Vice-Provincial organisation in their homeland. The French Jesuits shared in the benefits accruing to Catholics from increasing Republican tolerance. The anti-Jesuit Combes laws remained on the statute book until the 1940s, but the Government raised no objection to the reconstitution of the French Provinces in 1921. The occupation of the Baltic States and Russian Poland by German forces led, with the encouragement of Ledochowski, to the establishment of a makeshift 'Slav Province' of the Jesuits in those areas.

The war did not kill anti-Modernism but the *Sodalitium Pianum* lost contact with most of its informers, stagnated, and had died a natural death by 1921. The Society's ultra-conservatives and liberal intellectuals broke off their bickering for the duration of the fighting. The Russian Revolution of 1917 diverted the attention of the ultra-conservatives from European atheism and Socialism to 'the Red menace'. The apparitions at Fatima in

Portugal that year roused much 'ultra' enthusiasm among Portuguese and French Jesuits: the left wing Government of Portugal dismissed the affair sourly as 'a jesuitical farce'. For their part the Jesuit liberals enjoyed a wartime respite from Roman harassment. Teilhard de Chardin found time in his rest billets at the front to compose the first sketches of his new cosmic philosophy and to despatch copies to his Jesuit friends and superiors. He was due to make his solemn profession in the spring of 1918. His Provincial was very uneasy about his novel ideas. If it had been peacetime the General would undoubtedly have 'silenced' Teilhard or dismissed him from the Society outright. The Provincial, left by the war with the responsibility for a decision, at first favoured the idea of dismissal, and then shrugged his shoulders and let the profession go ahead without imposing any conditions. No doubt he reflected that the Germans' March offensive was threatening Paris, that Teilhard had to return to the front, and that the expectation of life there for men of his age and devotion to duty was sadly short.

* * *

The inter-war years, at any rate from 1925, saw a further remarkable increase in the Society's numbers, activity and influence. When Ledochowski returned to the Borgo Sancto Spirito from Switzerland in the last days of 1918 such a development seemed unthinkable. The Society was sorely battered, its numbers, especially of young men, much reduced and Europe chronically unstable and disillusioned. Communist revolution seemed imminent in Germany, Hungary and Italy. Poland was threatened with invasion by the Bolshevik Red Army. It took all of Ledochowski's formidable energy and the Society's discipline, resilience and powers of improvisation to get it back on an even keel by 1925 and its numbers restored to their pre-war level. Any greater achievement seemed out of reach. Anyway by 1929 the European outlook became appallingly bleak. From the autumn of that year the great world economic depression brought mass bankruptcy and unemployment. In country after country appeared Fascist dictators and totalitarian regimes. Then came the Spanish Civil War and the threat of the second world war. Yet these storms were the background to an extraordinary time of prosperity for the Society.

Its numbers increased very greatly, from barely 15,000 in 1925 to 28,000 in 1939. Yet again its levels of recruitment completely outclassed those of the other Orders and the secular clergy. At long last, by 1935, it had outgrown the old Society of the 1750s. From 1922, under Benedict XV's successor, Pius XI, it became more prominent and influential in Rome than ever before in history. The new Pope was conventionally 'Jesuited'. His devotional habits were thoroughly 'Ignatian'. His theological education had been gained at the feet of the great Jesuit Neo-Thomist, Liberatore. His advancement in the curial service owed much, at every step, to the help of Ledochowski and Franz Ehrle, the Jesuit head of the Vatican Library until 1914. The new Pope made both of these benefactors his privileged advisers. He made much more intensive use of Jesuit experts than any of his predecessors, even Pius IX. The crucial secret negotiations with Mussolini which led to the Lateran Treaty of 1929 and the foundation of the Vatican State were conducted by a Jesuit, Tacchi Venturi, an ardent admirer of Fascism and hitherto known only as a historian of the Society. He was assisted by a number of editors of *Civilta Cattolica*. Whenever in later years there was friction between the Italian State and the Church Tacchi Venturi was called in to have conversations with the Duce. The negotiations with Hitler which produced the German Concordat of 1933 were conducted by the Cardinal Secretary of State, Pacelli. He was a very thoroughly 'Jesuited' official most of whose closest advisers were German Jesuits. He had served as papal nuncio in Berlin after 1918 and acquired his train of advisers there.

The drafting of Pius XI's major encyclical on marriage and contraception, *Casti Connubii*, was almost entirely the work of two Jesuit professors at the Gregorian, Arthur Vermeersch, the 'hammer of contraception', and his assistant, Hürth. The Pope's encyclical on capital, labour and Marxism, *Quadragesimo Anno*, was drafted by a team of German and Austrian Jesuits imported by Ledochowski from Munich and Feldkirch. The Jesuit Cardinals Ehrle and Billot advised the Pope on matters concerning academic theology, while Billot was resident adviser on French affairs and *Action Française* of which he was an ardent supporter. For some years the principal adviser on Russian affairs was Michel d'Herbigny, a largely self-appointed Jesuit expert on all Slav concerns. His massive verve had made him rector of the Oriental Institute, head of the Pontifical Commission *Pro Russia*, founder of the *Russicum* College, Bishop for the East, and leader in disguise of several 'cloak and dagger' expeditions into Soviet territory in the 1920s.

It seemed impossible to turn a stone anywhere in Rome without starting a Jesuit. Jesuits were expert consultors to most curial Congregations. They dominated the Roman academic work from the Gregorian and the new Academies. They ran *Civilta Cattolica* and, almost as a matter of course, took over the Vatican radio station when it was founded in 1923. Jesuits directed the Biblical Institute and the Vatican Observatory. No one could claim to be surprised when Pius XI issued an encyclical in 1929 to commend the *Spiritual Exercises* or when he canonised such Jesuit heroes as Peter Canisius, Robert Bellarmine, the Canadian martyrs and Andrew Bobola.

Most of the Jesuit Provinces showed a similar access of zeal and energy in the years after 1925. The old staple works, educational, pastoral and spiritual, continued to occupy the time and attention of most Jesuits. But a well-publicised minority turned away from these stereotyped activities to specialise in new enterprises of a distinctly modern kind. The keyword for these was a new French idea: *Laïcité* or evangelism by indirect influence, to evangelise a secularised and scientifically-minded society by penetrating it, becoming highly expert at its techniques and using them to influence and convert laymen. They could then be formed, inside their professions, into evangelistic societies. Young Jesuits were trained for this work as journalists, scientists, archeologists, historians, psychologists, economists and sociologists in state universities or technical Institutes. Later, wherever possible, Jesuit universities and faculties set up their own training institutes in these disciplines. Once qualified the Jesuits joined teams infiltrating the learned professions, trades unions and youth organisations. The conversation of these experts became peppered with technical jargon and the mysterious-sounding initials of the names of the organisations they infiltrated or founded: in France it was the *ACJF, AC, FNC, AP, ALP, JOC, CE* and *Scoutisme*; in Germany it was the *VKANO, VV* and *BKHSN*; and in Spain the famous *ACNP* from which eventually grew *Opus Dei*. The cult of planning and new techniques for evangelism spread, at second hand, to Jesuit city parishes. By the 1930s these often had, alongside their traditional confraternities, Catholic Working Mens' Clubs with their own dance halls, cinemas, savings banks, benefit clubs, labour exchanges and night schools.

Modern planning techniques were applied to the giving of the *Exercises*. The result was the appearance of a multiplicity of special retreat houses gathering in a clientèle of the 'non-Jesuited' and unbelievers. Much more energy and ingenuity now went into the Jesuit 'apostolate of the Press'. Provincials acquired a financial stake in publishing houses, established editorial teams and greatly variegated and modernised the output of literature. Thus the Madrid Jesuits founded a daily newspaper: the Louvain scholasticate house staff ran a publishing house, the *Musée Lessianum*. The rising generation in the Society became fascinated by technology and especially by statistics. It mattered intensely now that in 1936 Jesuits gave 18,940 retreats to 701,790 exercitants all round the world, that in 1939 the Society had 851 periodicals, 26 of them of a generally cultural kind, 152 devoted to technical theology, 77 to foreign missions, and 596 to matters spiritual and ascetical: these sold 13,340,000 copies. Between 1936 and 1947 the backward Mexican Provinces, only very recently rebuilt from the ruin caused by the revolution of 1917, produced no less than 3,626,403 books, 22,296,906 magazines, 130,509,684 small, and 9,144,717 large, religious tracts. It seemed to be very reassuring that in 1932, in the Far East alone, the Jesuits had 3 universities, 7 university Colleges, 22 seminaries, 125 High Schools, 351 Middle Schools, 100 trade schools, 3,180 adult schools and 6,867 schools for catechumens.

However, this impressive Jesuit expansion had its limitations. The great numerical growth of the Society was more quantitative than qualitative and oddly lopsided. Recruitment was relatively thin in Germany, Austria, Belgium, Holland, France and northern Italy, the most progressive and intellectually distinguished of the Provinces. There the traditional sources of recruitment, Colleges, seminaries and alumnates, were scarce. There was a distinct shortage of manpower to staff the new enterprises in which these Provinces specialised. Meanwhile recruitment of Asian and African Jesuits remained small because of the rooted conservatism of the General and the missionaries. The really remarkable expansion of the Society's numbers took place in the more backward and intellectually undistinguished white areas, southern Europe and the Americas. Here the traditional sources of recruitment still offered the greatest potential for boosting numbers and the increased manpower was promptly ploughed back into expanding them. The American and Canadian Provinces doubled in size. The Portuguese Province, a broken and exiled remnant in the 1920s, was back home and rebuilt larger than ever by 1935. The five Spanish Provinces were shattered and their numbers decimated by the Civil War which ended in 1936: yet by 1945 recovery was so complete that a sixth Province was in process of formation.

The Jesuit presence in Rome was impressive but much thinner on the ground and less influential than it appeared at first sight. The teams of experts were small and contained few of the Society's best minds: its real talent was suspect of liberalism or retained at home in France and Germany to man the new enterprises. The main command structure of the Roman Curia was firmly in the hands of a cabal of conservative Italian Cardinals, 'Ignatian' to a man, but disposed to hold Jesuits at arm's length. Pius XI was a great autocrat and no tool of the Society. He liked Ledochowski but kept his confidences for a Franciscan from his native Milan. The Pope treated his Jesuit aides severely. In 1927 Billot, the most subservient of them all and over eighty years of age, was stripped of his Cardinalate and banished out of Rome to spend his last days in a noviciate house. His crime was communicating with Charles Maurras at a time when *Action Française* lay under a papal ban. D'Herbigny's brashness earned him a similar eclipse in 1935. Tacchi Venturi lived under threats of dismissal and his ablest assistant, Enrico Rosa, was removed by the Pope from the staff of *Civilta Cattolica*. Pius also tolerated the strange activities of Reginald Garrigou-Lagrange, a French Dominican professor in Rome, a fantastically rigid Thomist, the self-appointed successor of the *Sodalitium Pianum*, and a bitter enemy of all Jesuits. Pius even let pass unrebuked Garrigou-Lagrange's suggestion that Ledochowski was a favourer of Modernists and should be deposed from the Generalate.

The Society certainly had its fair share of the available clerical talent. In this field it outshone all its Catholic rivals except perhaps the Dominicans. The Jesuit strength lay not so much in scholars of the calibre of Delehaye, Peeters, Grosjean, Jungmann, Huby and de la Taille but in its array of very able publicists, for instance de Lubac, Daniélou, Teilhard de Chardin, Pierre Charles, d'Ouince, Doncoeur, Pribilla, the Rahner brothers, Maréchal, Martindale, Darcy, R.H.J. Steuart, and, in Latin America, Hurtado, Pradel and Aguirre. Yet in this sphere also the Jesuit achievement of the 1930s was distinctly limited.

Like all contemporary Catholic clerical intellectuals these talented men were gravely handicapped by the continuance of the long Ultramontane 'state of siege' of the Church. There was no real tradition of Jesuit creative scholarship. In spite of the slowly increasing number of contacts with non-Catholic academic institutions and scholars, talented Jesuits were trained, and worked for the most part, in a Catholic 'purdah'. It was all too easy for standards of scholarship to be low, and intellectual reputations artificially high, in such a tightly enclosed mental world. Ledochowski's outlook on doctrine and learning were in perfect accord with those prevailing in the 1930s among most rank and file Jesuits. He agreed, up to a point, that the Society must move with the times. He actually installed telephones in the Borgo Sancto Spirito house and rebuilt much of it in the 1920s in an ugly, Germanic, modernistic style. But because of his rooted conservatism and his panic fear that Jesuit intellectuals would get out of control and damage the painfully built-up credit of the Society in Rome he exercised a severely paternalistic rule over all scholars, writers and workers in the new enterprises. Theologians and philosophers had to reproduce to the letter the doctrine authorised by Rome: all deviation from that, speculation and experiment with new ideas were deeply suspect. The talented were closely supervised by superiors and Visitors sent from Rome. They were directed away from dangerous fields of study and writing. So, for instance, de Lubac, Mersch, Lippert and the Rahners were steered away from theology to the apparently innocuous areas of Church history and patristics. Maréchal, Doncoeur, Charles and the Valensins were steered away from modern philosophy into devotional writing, missiology and literary criticism. D'Ouince was gradually weaned from *Etudes* and turned into an administrator. 'Tamed' intellectuals, like Charles and de la Taille, were rewarded with professorships at the Gregorian. Ledochowski clearly regarded the Jesuit new enterprises as necessary safety valves for unquiet spirits. Teilhard de Chardin's case was an unusual one because of his chosen field of study and his character. Few Jesuits showed any ability for scientific research. Teilhard had that rare ability and, even worse, chose paleontology as his field. This was, in the 1930s, an even more dangerous ground for Catholics than philosophy. Paleontologists had to take for granted that theory of evolution which was still rejected violently by all Catholic traditionalists. Teilhard was also an immense enthusiast, almost totally lacking in discretion, and a great charmer: students and women flocked to hear him lecture. Delations of his articles and lectures piled up in Rome to such an extent that Ledochowski reacted with unusual ferocity. In 1923 Teilhard was forced to write out a humiliating retraction, forbidden to publish any more books or articles, and banished from France to China. There he remained, in spite of all his anguished appeals to Rome, until 1946.

Jesuit history repeated itself. The intellectuals were driven to adopt the traditional practices of Jesuit 'dissenters'. They formed private societies round which circulated mimeographed articles which would never pass the official censors. Teilhard de Chardin, and perhaps some of his friends, published articles under assumed names in non-Catholic periodicals. The libraries of some Jesuit houses mysteriously acquired copies of non-Catholic philosophical, theological and scientific works quite against Ledochowski's regulations. When Visitors from Rome appeared, the books vanished: when they had gone, the books reappeared on the shelves. Here and there, in Germany and France, daringly original texts could very occasionally slip by the Jesuit censors. Such books were invariably camouflaged as works of apologetics, history or even devotion, sprinkled piously with references to papal encyclicals and unimpeachably orthodox writers, and vetted very carefully by informal committees of sympathetic colleagues. In this way Alfred Delp of the editorial team of *Stimmen der Zeit* secured publication of his study of Heidegger's existentialism, *Tragische Existenz*, in 1935, and in 1938 Hugo Rahner of the Innsbruck Faculty his study of Protestant 'kerygmatic' theology, *Theologie der Verkündigung*, and Henri de Lubac of Lyon-Fourvière his interpretation of the thought of Blondel and Bergson, *Catholicisme*. Meanwhile Teilhard de Chardin's *Le Milieu Divin* and Joseph Huby's studies of Protestant Biblical 'form criticism' remained in manuscript unpublished because their authors were unwilling to disguise what they had to say.

The Jesuit intellectuals were busy and even happy as long as they could reside in 'advanced' houses. The moment they were parted from their friends and put into ordinary Jesuit communities they complained bitterly that they had run into a blank wall of incomprehension and outright hostility. If we are to believe Teilhard de Chardin the blank wall faced him everywhere he went away from Paris and Lyon-Fourvière: in Toulouse, Versailles, Lille, Bordeaux, at Enghien in Belgium, in Jersey and London, in New York, Chicago and Fordham, in Shanghai and Tientsin. Reactionary conservatism prevailed everywhere in the Society and the Church at large. In France there was widespread Jesuit applause for Charles Maurras's attacks on liberalism, parliamentary democracy, socialism, freemasonry, the Jews and the English and for his open admiration for Fascist regimes. In Germany strongly right wing conservatism was very common among Jesuits. Even in 1939 such men deplored the Nazis' assaults on Catholic organisations and the Society's establishments while insisting that National Socialism was the only possible bulwark against the Bolshevik tide. They saw Nazism as a fallen angel of light who had somehow to be restored to a state of grace: meanwhile it must not be provoked by imprudent enthusiasts. The tiny minority of German Jesuits who spoke out boldly against Nazism, including Rupert Mayer, Max Pribilla and Friedrich Muckermann, were unpopular with most of their colleagues. Yet Mayer, a very brave man who was in the Oranienburg concentration camp in 1939, and Muckermann, who 'emigrated' to Oldenzaal in Holland in 1934 to launch his strongly anti-Nazi periodical *Der Deutsche Weg*, were fundamentally as stiffly conservative and nationalistic as their colleagues. Muckermann had published several strongly militant attacks on Soviet Communism.

In the 1930s and 1940s one of the most widely admired books among Portuguese, Spanish, French and Italian Jesuits was *The Miracle of Fatima*. Its author, Gonzaga da Fonseca, was a professor of exegesis at the Pontifical Biblical Institute in Rome. For him the sun whirling in the sky over Fatima in 1917 was a prophecy of the greater Marian miracles, the defeat of Bolshevism in Portugal and Spain and, one day very soon, in Russia itself. The positive side to the miracles was the establishment of strongly disciplined, right wing Catholic, totalitarian governments closely allied to the Church. All this was naturally achieved by dedicated military force, the saying of the rosary, and the consecration of homes and nations to the Immaculate Heart of Mary.

Practically every feature of the old, reactionary Ultramontanism enjoyed a new lease of life in the 1930s. There was a spate of heavenly apparitions, at Beauraing, Banneux and elsewhere. Mariology was born as a theological science and pledged to secure a papal definition of the Assumption and Mary's mediation of all graces as necessary parts of the Catholic faith. Pius XI made a resolute effort, with considerable success, to reinvigorate the old devotion to the Sacred Heart with its attendant cults of rigid asceticism, reparation and redemptive suffering. The 'personality cult' of the Popes reached new heights: Pius X was canonised, Pius XI treated as a living saint, and his numerous encyclicals widely regarded as infallible pronouncements. The campaign against contraception went from strength to strength. A phalanx of moral theologians demonstrated conclusively that the practice destroyed the moral fibre of nations and wrecked family life. They damned the Ogino-

Knaus or 'rhythm' method of birth control, founded societies to glorify large families, lobbied governments to get the sale of contraceptives banned, and exhorted wives to resist 'onanistic' husbands as they would rapists. All these Ultramontane movements were closely interrelated: only devotion to papal authority, our Lady and the Sacred Heart could enable contraception to be defeated and families to expand; only a tight Catholic discipline, our Lady and the Sacred Heart could enable the Christian West to destroy Soviet Communism. Jesuits were well to the fore in all the movements under the leadership of the Gregorian and its patriarch, Arthur Vermeersch. He was the life and soul of the campaign against contraception, along with his pupils Hürth and Creusen: he wrote books on our Lady and on the Sacred Heart.

The thinking and writing of the Jesuit intellectuals was gravely hampered by this claustrophobic atmosphere and by their own inhibitions. They found it practically impossible to break out of the closed mental world in which they had passed their formative years. Some, like Charles, de la Taille, Mersch, de Lubac and Daniélou, ultimately gave up the struggle. Others, like Huby and Hugo Rahner, fought on but without hope. Others again, including the arch-radical Teilhard de Chardin, always fought tenaciously and hopefully but without realising the extent to which Ultramontanism retained its hold on their minds and affections. No one could have been more critical than Teilhard: he attacked narrow apologetics and evangelism, adulation of Rome, 'the Lourdes-Fatima contagion', the 'subhuman atmosphere' of a Society in which, he wrote, 'I have stifled for fifty years', and the absurd crusades against 'modern errors'. Yet for him science was sterile unless it was of the Church and evangelistic. For him Rome, the French nation and the Society were the living heart of the creation. His room in China contained, flanking a crucifix, engravings of Galileo and the Sacred Heart. His breviary markers were Sacred Heart and Marian prayer cards of the lushest kind. In private he sketched out Mariological speculations which far surpassed those of the *Marianum* in Rome. His views on women, celibacy and marriage always remained narrowly clerical, even Victorian. Late in life he suggested that, as mankind evolved, it would increasingly sublimate its desire for sexual intercourse so that contraception would automatically fall into disuse. He and his fellow liberals made a real contribution to the coming Catholic *aggiornamento* of the 1960s and 1970s, but their vision of religious truth and the Church's future was blurred by the Catholic fog of the 1930s.

*   *   *

By the early 1960s solidly conservative Jesuits could be pardoned
for thinking that the Society positively thrived on the world's
disasters. Two world wars, with all their train of death, upset
and unsettlement, had signally failed to check the Society's
steady progress or alter its strongly conservative character. The
Catholic reference books of the 1950s and 1960s seemed to give
ample proof of the truth of this judgement. Their statistics were
impressive. The 26,000 Jesuits of 1939 had become 28,000 in
1946, 30,000 in 1950, 34,000 in 1958 and over 36,000 in 1962. It
had thus doubled in size since 1920 and become by far the largest,
best organised and most expert clerical body in the Church. The
reference books described, in the statistical language normally
reserved for company reports, how Jesuit manpower was
deployed. The great majority worked in three main fields, communications, higher education and lay organisations. The communications field had over 1,000 newspapers and periodicals
and an unspecified number of private radio stations and
scheduled programmes on television networks. The higher
education field had 771 establishments of which sixty were
Jesuit universities or faculties and the rest Institutes or hostels
attached to universities. Thus, for instance, in 1953 the Society
controlled eight establishments granting academic degrees in
Spain together with a variety of Institutes of science, engineering,
economics and sociology. It controlled five universities and
faculties in Germany and Austria, four in Britain and Ireland,
three in France, and two each in Belgium, Holland and Poland.
In France it also had a technical school, two engineering schools,
a cramming establishment for entry into the best technical
Institutes, and Jesuit lecturers in a number of Catholic faculties
in state universities. The field of lay organisations was wide and
variegated. It included traditional Jesuit enterprises like retreat-
giving, directing convents, and administering Marian Congregations along with more modern efforts like *Action Populaire*
in France, the Cana Movement in the United States, *ACNP* in
Spain, and the Better World Movement in Italy.

The main targets of this evangelistic activity were the most
influential classes in the society of the 1960s: the ablest ordinands
and student members of other Orders, and the technocrats
manning the board rooms of great companies, the upper echelons

of government, and the staffs of universities and research Institutes. The reference books tried to indicate very sketchily the scale of the impact the Jesuits were making on these classes. In the higher education field some 12,000 Jesuits assisted by 25,000 lay teachers dealt with a quarter of a million students. In Rome the Gregorian and its satellite establishments had 2,500 students from sixty nations. Its former students made up 27.6 per cent of the College of Cardinals and 30 per cent of the whole Catholic episcopate. The Society had a hand in the education of most of the Latin American secular clergy and a large minority of the native clergy in the Far East. It was said to have a particularly strong influence among Spanish technocrats through its universities and *ACNP* organisation for former pupils.

In the 1960s the Society appeared to be a large and integral part of the strongly conservative Catholic establishment. It seemed to have a more intimate connection with the Papacy than ever. Since 1939 two major threats, wartime disruption and post-war dissidence, had been warded off remarkably successfully.

Pius XI died early in 1939. His successor from 1939 to 1958, was perhaps the most 'Jesuited' Pope on record. He left routine administration to the curial officials while he worked out his policies in secret with a small group of intimate advisers. These were almost entirely Jesuits, in the main Germans resident at the Gregorian. Bea was the Pope's confessor and Leiber his private secretary who wrote all his many speeches. Hentrich provided all his reading matter, helpfully marking the more important passages. Hürth advised him on 'family morality' while Gundlach and Lombardi were the experts on social questions. The Pope's housekeeper, a German nun, belonged to a 'Jesuited' Order. All the members of this extraordinary entourage behaved with exemplary discretion, but it was hardly surprising that ecclesiastical journalists later imagined that the Pope's apartments during those years had the atmosphere of a Jesuit house: they certainly attributed most of his policies to his Jesuit advisers.

Although World War II was more widely and heavily destructive than the first, its impact on the Society was probably somewhat less damaging. Part of the reason for this was that by 1939 a very large part of the Jesuits' manpower and resources and their main growth areas were sheltered from war operations in the Americas and Spain. Also the losses in manpower and infrastructure in the war-torn areas of Europe and the Far East were surprisingly limited. There was certainly no repetition of the holocaust of Jesuit combatants and chaplains of 1914-8. With some very notable exceptions in Germany, eastern Europe and northern France the Society came through the war relatively intact. On the other hand it suffered more during the second war from political dissension within Provinces and communities. In both wars rampant nationalism caused conflicts and some Jesuits again accused the Borgo Sancto Spirito of pro-German sympathies. But in the second war there was a new factor, bad blood between 'collaborators' and supporters of the 'Resistance'. In some Jesuit communities in Germany, France and eastern Europe this hostility continued to poison the atmosphere for years after the war. It will be a very long time before the detailed wartime history of those Provinces can be written.

Ledochowski fell gravely ill in 1938 and until his death in 1942 the routine work of the Generalate was carried on by a Vicar-General. It then proved impossible to assemble a General Congregation until the end of 1946 and a skeleton administration was headed by a succession of Vicars-General apparently chosen with an eye on the war in Italy and the nationality of the candidates: the first was an Italian, the second a Frenchman with both Vichy and Free French credentials, and the third an American. From 1939 to 1943 Pius XII and his German Jesuit entourage were intermittently and very secretly engaged in acting as diplomatic intermediaries between German Resistance groups and the British Government. The Catholic *Abwehr* officer who was the groups' agent also represented a number of clerics in Germany who smuggled details of the Nazi persecution of the Church to the Vatican in his luggage. Roman Jesuits, mostly German, played a lively part in this affair and, for a time, they introduced the officer into the Gregorian. The details of the persecution were broadcast from the Jesuit-controlled Vatican Radio and published in Britain. Ledochowski got wind of all this on his sick-bed. He was outraged that Jesuits should involve themselves in such dangerous matters without his consent. The General had good reason to believe that the Gestapo would find out what had happened and take its revenge on the Jesuits in Germany. But the conspirators were under the Pope's protection. All that Ledochowski could do was to insist that the secret meetings should take place outside Rome, that details of the persecution of the German Jesuits should be kept secret, and that one of the principal conspirators should be despatched out of harm's way to a mission in the Congo. From 1942 to 1945 the

Vicars-General at the Borgo Sancto Spirito spent most of their time urging Jesuits to keep out of politics and doing their best to silence or hide those whose national or political connections might make them a danger to the Society's interests.

In Germany the superiors were in a very difficult position. Although their Provinces were relatively thinly manned they suffered from an unemployment problem because the Nazis gradually closed down many of their establishments and it was no longer possible to continue the pre-war practice of sending professors and students abroad in difficult times. The superiors, like many of their subjects, had considerable reservations about the Nazi regime, but found it hard not to enthuse over the German victories in 1939-41 and the assault on Soviet Russia. They found the idea of fomenting resistance to the Government repugnant especially after 1943 when Germany was threatened with a Russian invasion. Yet from 1940 the Jesuits were constantly reminded that they were marked men, classed by the Gestapo and the SS with Communists, Jews and gypsies. Their identity cards had to bear the official stamp: 'Jesuit: unworthy of military service'. The superiors lived in fear that Jesuit hotheads would draw attention to the Society by joining Resistance groups. Few Jesuits ever had a chance to do so and most of these shrank from close involvement. Some two dozen ended the war in gaol because of outspoken attacks on Nazi paganism: these included Rupert Mayer of Munich and von Nell-Breuning, the author of the encyclical *Quadragesimo Anno*. Wehrle, a Jesuit chaplain to the forces, was executed because he had been consulted by one of Colonel von Stauffenberg's associates about the ethics of tyrannicide. Four of five Jesuits actually attended meetings of Resistance groups in 1944. Two of them, Delp and Rosch, were arrested: Delp was executed and Rosch's life saved by the ending of the war.

In France the Jesuits endured many discomforts and some painfully sharp dissensions between the supporters and the critics of the Vichy administration. Otherwise there were few dramatic developments and the Provinces managed to keep their numbers up to the pre-war level. A very few militants left for England. Henri de Lubac spent the last part of the war in Switzerland writing against the Nazis. Other militants, including Teilhard de Chardin's friends Fessard, Chaillet and de Montcheuil, played a very modest part in Christian Resistance groups. De Montcheuil was killed in action serving as an impromptu chaplain to the Maquis. A small number of militants were confined in German concentration camps. But the great majority of their colleagues tried to steer clear of politics and immerse themselves in the limited wartime opportunities for evangelism. Many served in Vichy organisations like the *Chantiers de Jeunesse* and *Service de Travail Obligatoire*. A few, including Henri Perrin, a recent recruit from the secular clergy, volunteered to join the French 'slave workers' in Germany, evading the German ban on Jesuits. Others helped to run *Construire, Témoignage Chrétien* and other short-lived, and sometimes clandestine, religious periodicals.

Meanwhile in eastern Europe, in the Baltic States, Poland, Czechoslovakia and Romania, the Polish and Slav Provinces were shattered. In 1946 the Borgo Sancto Spirito was genuinely surprised to discover that they had retained a small-scale, underground existence.

The new General in 1946, Jean-Baptiste Janssens, a Belgian canonist, was a punctiliously conservative and timid man. He was obsessed with the necessity for re-establishing the Society's pre-war standing and character. He lacked Ledochowski's aristocratic verve and ability to get on with Popes and curial potentates. Hence during his Generalate he all too often seemed a well-meaning but weak man constantly frightened into action by the Pope, the curial Congregations, and a band of very astute and determined Roman Jesuit conservatives. These included such hammers of heresy as Charles Boyer and Sebastian Tromp of the Gregorian, Bigador, the secretary of the Holy Office, Norbert de Boynes and other 'Old Guard' Frenchmen, and a cohort of intensely reactionary, McCarthyite Americans. The post-war years therefore saw a vigorous upsurge of Jesuit liberalism and an even more vigorous effort by authority to squash it.

Teilhard de Chardin returned to France from China in 1946. He was staggered by the warmth of his reception in Paris and felt 'a prophetic sense of new beginnings'. Roman authority seemed asleep, *Action Française* and Ultramontanism discredited, and many of the old enmities in the French Church laid to rest. The *Mission de France, Mission de Paris* and 'worker-priest' movement had been launched. *Témoignage Chrétien* and the Resistance had generated a host of lively new lay groups with contacts far outside traditional Catholicism. The old, clericalised Catholic Action organisations shared in the new spirit of adventure. Jesuit chaplains were to be found far outside the Society's normal gambits, cooperating self-consciously, with Dominicans, free-thinkers, trade union militants and Communists. Henri Perrin, for instance, was based in the offices of an established Jesuit lay organisation in Paris turned distinctly left wing, *Action Populaire*. He was dressed in dungarees and working in a Paris factory. Into his spare time he crammed work with the *JOCF*, active membership of the Left Wing Workers' International, and efforts to infiltrate the hitherto distinctly secularist Youth Hostels Association. Everyone wanted to discuss the ideas of Teilhard, Marcel, Blondel, Sartre, Heidegger, Kierkegaard and Karl Marx. The same post-war ferment appeared among Jesuits in Innsbruck, Cologne, Louvain, Lyon-Fourvière. There were even distant reverberations in the United States and Latin America.

The expected counter-attack by Pius XII and Janssens was not long in coming. It reached its peak in the 1950s with vigorous Roman efforts to resurrect the Ultramontane spirit. Pius XII had already declared his ardent support for the Marian movement and Fatima: he consecrated the world to the Immaculate Heart of Mary in 1942. He declared 1950 a Holy Year with mass pilgrimages to Rome and a papal definition of the Assumption as a doctrine of faith. He also issued a new *Syllabus of Errors*, the encyclical *Humani Generis*. A Marian Year was declared for 1954 for pilgrimages to Fatima, Lourdes, La Salette, Beauraing and Knock. Janssens gave Teilhard a stark choice: confinement under strict surveillance in a rustic retreat-house, or exile to America. After a depressing and futile visit to the Borgo Sancto Spirito and the General, he set sail for the United States, a sick and desperate man. All his friends at Lyon-Fourvière were deprived of their teaching posts and dispersed far from each other and students. Liberally-minded Jesuit professors and students everywhere were shifted round to break up cabals and were expressly forbidden to publish work on dangerous subjects. The blows fell on the Rahner brothers, Jungmann and Fransen in Germany, Lombardi, Lyonnet and Zerwick in Rome, Courtney Murray, LaFarge, Ford, Kelly and Callanan in the United States, and Vekemans and Arroyo in Latin America. As the storm clouds gathered over the *Mission de Paris* and the French worker-priest movement the tiny group of Jesuits involved in them was hastily deployed in more orthodox works. All over France Jesuit chaplains were withdrawn from the new, informal lay groups and Catholic Action organisations. A few left the Church: some, like Henri Perrin, quit the Society for the secular priesthood.

Janssens was deeply alarmed by this Jesuit dissidence and clear evidence that Roman curial reactionaries were making it an occasion for an all-out attack on the Society. Both he and the reactionaries had some reason for alarm. On the one hand the great liberal ferment was much stronger outside the Society than in it. The great majority of the leading thinkers and publicists of the movements, men like Mounier, Dirks, Thils, Suhard, Congar, Chenu, Godin, Daniel, Comblin, Cerfaux and Heinrich Böll were not Jesuits. Hans Urs von Balthasar, who had been the ablest liberal Jesuit, left the Society. On the other hand the ferment among Jesuits was now so strong that Janssens' repressive measures proved largely ineffective. The liberal leaders' articles continued to circulate in manuscript and find publication so fast, and in such varied and novel ways, that the Borgo, the censors, and the Holy Office could not keep pace with the flood. Once out of the Society von Balthasar had founded a publishing house, the Johannes-Verlag at Einsiedeln. In 1953 he published the cautiously phrased but resoundingly liberal manifesto, *Das Frei Wort in der Kirche*, written by Karl Rahner. When the liberal leaders were exiled, their able disciples generally succeeded to their teaching posts. Even the 'Old Guard's' academic citadel, the Gregorian, was infected with the liberal virus. Hans Küng arrived there from his native Switzerland in 1948, the year that Janssens' offensive began in earnest. The formal scholastic orthodoxy of the professors and their course work was not in doubt. The students were put through the *Spiritual Exercises* more often and more intensively than any Jesuit. But quite inadvertently the professors encouraged the liberal tendencies of their ablest students. It was considered vitally important that Küng and others should make a study in depth of modern errors, particularly the works of Sartre, Marx and Karl Barth. They were trained in the critical methods of modern scholarship and encouraged to seek teaching posts in state universities. Meanwhile their Jesuit directors dealt with their crises of faith by instructing them in the Society's way of combining instant outward obedience to orders with a very minimalistic interpretation of the substance of the orders. Küng later attributed much of his theological radicalism to his training at the Gregorian. A few years later, when he published his first radical work at the Einsiedeln press, his old Jesuit teachers sprang to his defence. They naïvely supposed that no student trained in their system could possibly be a real radical.

The curial reactionaries became convinced that the Society was untrustworthy and out of control. They therefore decided to wean the Pope from his dependence on it and persuade him to reduce its influence. They had plans to create a new Roman university, the Lateran, as a kind of papal Ministry of Education exercising a dictatorial control over all Roman academic institutions including the Gregorian and its satellite Institutes. In spite of feeble protests by Janssens the Holy Office dismissed the Jesuits Lyonnet and Zerwick from the Pontifical Biblical Institute as a first step towards incorporating the Institute in the Lateran. The reactionaries also favoured the rise of 'Secular Institutes'. These were new lay Congregations of a strictly orthodox kind, very closely associated with the Curia and strained free of Jesuit influences. Their mushroom growth proved a mortal threat to some large, Jesuit-controlled lay organisations from which they began to poach members. In Spain the Priestly Society of the Holy Cross (commonly known as *Opus Dei*) was founded in 1928 under the wing of the very powerful Jesuit National Catholic Association of Propagandists (the *ACNP*). By the 1950s, with increasingly practical support from Rome, *Opus Dei* was beginning to overshadow *ACNP* and steal its thunder. Janssens was so frightened by these developments that he ventured to encourage Jesuits to attack *Opus Dei*.

The death of Pius XII in 1958 and the accession of John XXIII gave the General no comfort. Although the new Pope was quite as 'Jesuited' in outlook as his predecessor, he was no friend of the Society. He politely dismissed Pius XII's strange Jesuit entourage, approved of the plans to found the Lateran, and favoured the rise of *Opus Dei*. When he announced his intention of holding a General Council in 1962 Janssens and the 'Old Guard' were puzzled and apprehensive. Though the Pope was solidly conservative about doctrine and devotion he was genuinely anxious that the Council should give the Church a new image, positive, unrepressive, frank and open. The preparations for the Council were a disconcerting mixture of traditionalism and liberality. On the one hand curial Cardinals and conservative theologians were given control of the agenda, the drafting of ready-made Conciliar decrees and the steering of Conciliar debates. On the other hand the world's press and Protestant observers were invited to be present. Most of the Church's liberal theologians were allowed to come as official advisers of bishops. Janssens was dismayed. Jesuit representation on the official steering bodies and among the advisers was distinctly thin and embarrassingly mixed. The steering bodies contained Bigador and Boyer, both stiff 'Old Guard' conservatives. The Jesuit advisers consisted of de Lubac, Daniélou, Karl Rahner, Jungmann, Weigel, Lyonnet and

Courtney Murray, all notorious liberals repeatedly delated by Boyer and Bigador and recently disciplined by the General. The Council's press lobbies had an equally mixed Jesuit representation. The reporters from *Civilta Cattolica*, Vatican Radio and *Razon y Fe* would take a conservative line. The editors of *Etudes, Revue d'Action Populaire, America, Stimmen der Zeit, Orientierung* and *The Month* were expected to take the liberal side: they had all recently felt the weight of the General's displeasure.

Janssens' anxieties were a part of his character. It is very unlikely that either he or any other Jesuit seriously thought that the Council would upset the Society violently and confront it with its greatest crisis since 1773.

8
The Modern Jesuit Dilemma

'All attempts to change the functions of this Order must be rejected . . . we have the right and the duty to maintain the law under which we entered . . . There are certain characteristics peculiar to our Order which, if they are resolutely lived out, contain also a promise for the future.'

(Karl Rahner SJ, Conference to Jesuits at Olpe, September, 1970)

Janssens died in 1964 before the closure of the second Vatican Council. But he and his 'Old Guard' associates must have regarded it as a nightmare. Liberalism gained the centre of the Council floor amid a blaze of publicity. The liberal advisers conducted seminars for sympathetic bishops, Protestant observers and reporters. The Pope, his successor Paul VI, the official steering bodies and a good many conservative bishops were forced into a humiliating retreat. Janssens' policy of repression lay in ruins. From his point of view the Council had been a disaster for the Society, discrediting it in public. Its experts, apart from Karl Rahner, de Lubac and Courtney Murray, had taken a back seat and Jesuits had openly and violently disagreed with each other.

In 1965 a General Congregation assembled in Rome to elect a new General and take steps to bring the Society into line with the Council's directions for the reform of the religious Orders. The new General, Pedro Arrupe, was relatively young. He had served in a wide variety of Provinces in Europe, America and the Far East and was not associated with the Borgo bureaucrats. His first action was to move almost all of Janssens' 'Old Guard' into honourable retirement. Then he and the Congregation, in one short session, 'reformed' the Society. A Jesuit official spokesman commented in *Civilta Cattolica* that the Congregation assumed the Society was 'essentially sound' and only needed 'structural repairs' and certain small adjustments of its young men's studies, living conditions and work. The Congregation certainly pinned its hopes on its young General by giving him even greater powers than his predecessors. He had a reputation for liberalism and firmness. They expected him to charm and push the liberals and their student followers into moderation and compliance and to rebuild the bridge between the Borgo and the Vatican broken down in Janssens' time. By 1967 conservative Jesuits were feeling hopeful, even complacent. The Pope was carrying out the Council's reforms in a way which left the old order of things basically intact. The Society's numbers were still increasing. A very distinguished English Jesuit told a reporter: 'Success breeds success . . . we fill most of the Church's shop-window': some Provincials bought larger premises to house future big noviciates. The General engaged business efficiency experts to plan a rationalisation of the Society's world-wide operation. But in other quarters in the Society, among both liberals and 'middle of the road' seniors, there was an increasing feeling of unease and foreboding.

From 1968 the general Catholic crisis set in very sharply and Jesuit complacency vanished. During the next decade the Society's overall numbers declined by a third: the decline seems to have been slightly greater than that suffered by the rest of the Catholic clergy and nuns. According to the official Vatican statistics the numbers of Jesuit establishments and priests remained stable while the tally of novices and students declined catastrophically from 16,000 to 3,000. The decline was clearly due to both a sharp fall in recruitment and a considerable increase in the number of departures from the Society. But the relative sizes of these two factors cannot be gauged. Statistics of dispensations from vows are very rarely published and many Jesuits remain in simple vows for many years and so can depart by private arrangements with a minimum of formality. Large noviciate and student houses were sold off or converted to other uses. Colleges were closed or kept going by recruiting ever larger numbers of lay staff. Provinces and communities were hit by a great wave of uncertainty, unrest and dissension between traditionalists and liberals. All these troubles were felt most acutely in the United States, Latin America, Spain and Holland which had hitherto been the Society's fastest growing and most conventionally conservative areas. In earlier times such developments would have been covered with a veil of domestic secrecy. Even today the Jesuit veil remains in place but occasionally a corner of it is raised as a matter of official policy or because of the persistence of that new breed, the investigative clerical journalists.

In the United States Jesuit theological faculties, which had hitherto been placid backwaters of conformism, became quarrelsome and full of radicalism. They had been especially renowned for their stolid defence of the ban on contraception: now they headed the attack on it. Daniel Berrigan, an ardent young Jesuit radical, became the hero of clerical and lay students in Jesuit universities. His left wing views and his campaigns for liturgical experiments, the marriage of priests, the ordination of women and the end of the ban on contraception convulsed the American Provinces for some years. Janssens and Cardinal Spellman exiled him several times: Boyer delated him to the Holy Office. Fordham students picketed Spellman's house on his behalf and senior Jesuits insisted that he should be allowed his say. While one Jesuit held a seat in Congress to support conservative measures and another lived in Watergate and occupied the post of special adviser to President Nixon, Berrigan went to gaol with 'the Catonville Nine' for burning army draft cards. Some of his colleagues were disciplined or exiled for supporting Martin Luther King and 'freedom marches' in the Deep South. In California progressive Jesuits tussled with the rigidly conservative Cardinal McIntyre and, advised from afar by Karl Rahner, helped most of the American Province of the very 'Jesuited' Immaculate Heart of Mary Order of nuns to quit their convents and formal religious life.

The Canadian Province, for decades a quiet backwater of conventional traditionalism, now produced a lively centre of radicalism, the Montreal Faculty, and the Society's most influential liberal theologian, Bernard Lonergan. In Latin America tough reactionary Jesuits vigorously supported right wing military governments while their liberal colleagues came out in support of left wing freedom fighters and trade union militancy. In Uruguay the Jesuit theologian Juan Segundo helped to develop a very Socialist 'liberation theology' which was promptly delated as heresy to the Holy Office by reactionary colleagues. In Chile a group of Jesuits headed by Gonzalo Arroyo warmly supported Allende's very left wing Government. After its fall Arroyo fled to Europe to rally support for his radical organisation, *Christians for Socialism*. He did not always get house-room from his new colleagues. In Argentina, under a barrage of ecclesiastical delations and police harassment, left wing Jesuits directed a periodical, *El Criterio*, and a militant organisation, *Priests for the*

Third World. In Mexico, to the horror of old-fashioned colleagues and patrons, the Provincial supported the radical *Priests for the People* and closed down the Jesuit town Colleges. Things went much the same way in Nicaragua, Colombia, Venezuela, Guyana and Honduras. The Latin American Jesuit radicals were a small foreign body in Provinces which remained heavily conservative and conventionalist. Their use of Marxist slogans, the 'liberation theology' and political militancy were second-hand, caught from a rapidly-growing movement sweeping through the Orders and secular clergy of the continent.

In Spain reactionary Francoism and Ultramontane traditionalism remained strong in the Provinces. Jesuits continued to act as chaplains to Francoist parties and head traditionalist pressure groups and to incite the police to raid Protestant establishments. Some of them planned to form a totally traditionalist Jesuit Province, an island of true Ignatianism in a Society falling away into heresy and degeneration. Meanwhile more and more ardent Jesuit spirits, influenced by foreign periodicals and a strong trend among the Spanish clergy against the Franco regime, became converts to theological liberalism and Socialism. Liberalism gained a hold on Jesuit faculties and city houses. There was a lively group of Jesuit Socialists led by Llanos and Diez-Alegria. Alegria, who came from a strongly Francoist establishment family, embraced very extreme ideas of Church reform and utterly refused to comply with any form of censorship. His Provincial knew well that the traditional methods of repression would be useless even in Spain. The General, landed with the case, pointed out to Alegria that the Society was now the freest clerical group in the Church. In accordance with Arrupe's new censorship rules an author could reject a ban by the ordinary censors and demand the appointment of non-Jesuit referees. When Alegria remained recalcitrant Arrupe resorted to what was now his ultimate sanction in such cases. He ordered the rebel to go away on holiday for two years to consider whether he wanted to be a Jesuit or leave the Society.

In Holland respectable lay Catholics ostentatiously quitted the congregations of certain Jesuit city churches, protesting that heresy was preached there. In universities the Jesuit chaplains became particulary 'emancipated'. They wore long hair and lay clothes and led their students in noisy demonstrations against curial dictatorship, clerical celibacy and the ban on contraception. This clerical radicalism was not a Jesuit invention: Dominicans, Franciscans and secular priests carried it much further. But

Jesuit radicalism was particularly shocking to conservatives because they had always been able to assume, even if they disliked the Society, that it was one of the main bulwarks of Catholic tradition. One of the most eminent Jesuit theologians, Schoenmaeckers, strongly attacked his radical colleagues, calling them 'Modernists'. They were defended very stoutly and with the utmost publicity by the greatest Dutch Jesuit theologian, Piet Schoenenberg.

In Belgium, France, Germany, England and Ireland the same tensions and upsets existed. But here, for a wide variety of historical reasons, they were mostly confined within the walls of Jesuit houses or the covers of learned and abstruse periodicals with a small circulation. There was a muffled collision in Brussels between a Provincial and radicals. In England the protagonists were often treated half-tolerantly and dismissively as representatives of one or other of two familiar English breeds, the eccentric and the Tory radical. When the most distinguished English Jesuit, Archbishop Thomas Roberts, launched out on public campaigns against Roman curial bureaucracy and the papal ban on contraception it was easy to dismiss him as an eccentric without authority. It was noted that he was a retired archbishop and, as such, seconded from the Society. Almost to a man the English Province's theologians came down definitely on the liberal side. Their utterances were concealed in technical language in learned journals. The Province had two periodicals, *The Month*, devoted to popular theology and culture, and *The Way*, devoted to spiritual renewal in the post-Vatican II Church. The editors and contributors were constantly decimated by departures from the Society. The survivors generally took the liberal side but their articles had little impact since their circulation was small and select. An English Jesuit university chaplain defended contraception and announced his intention of communicating Protestants at his altar. A Jesuit student published a fiercely radical letter attacking the stolid traditionalism of the Province's most eminent historians. It was easy to dismiss the chaplain as unusually naïve: in fact his superiors removed him from his post and sent him off on a foreign holiday. The student was a nobody immured in the dangerous atmosphere of a French Jesuit study house. The Irish Jesuit Province was small, provincial, anti-intellectual, defensive, and without a gift for publicity. It certainly felt the weight of the Jesuit crisis. During the bad decade its numbers declined twice as fast as those of other Orders and the secular clergy. But its upsets and wounds were nursed in private. English Catholics unfamiliar with the Irish situation were always startled when they encountered a visiting Jesuit radical: his long hair, jeans and liberated conversation seemed somehow alien, American or continental, not Irish.

In Rome itself, as fundamentally illiberal as ever in spite of its superficially Vatican II appearance, Jesuit radicalism could only survive if it were disguised as either ordinary clerical cynicism or a pastoral tactic. The General was struggling to hold the Society together in some sort of decent order by a rather piecemeal policy of minor reforms, liberal gestures and lectures on tradition. He was only very moderately successful and had lost the confidence of Paul VI who showered him with strong complaints about Jesuit indiscipline. The Society's politicians began to speculate about the identity of Arrupe's successor. Most of them seem to have favoured Carlo Martini, the rector of the Biblical Institute and a man respected by liberals and by the Pope. As the General grew less and less sure of his ground in the Vatican he increasingly made use of Martini as his link with the Pope. The General could hardly ignore the Jesuit 'Old Guard' in Rome. It still existed and now had an embarrassing independence of the Borgo Sancto Spirito. Its old stagers were Boyer and Bigador, its new recruits de Lubac, Daniélou, Bertrams, Tucci and Galot. Bigador and Bertrams were canonists heavily involved in important papal commissions. De Lubac and Daniélou were Paul VI's theological experts: their odd combination of liberal terminology and fearful conservatism fitted in well with his own inclinations. Tucci was the director of Vatican Radio and Galot a theologian at the Gregorian and Boyer's successor as a Grand Inquisitor and 'hammer of heretics'.

In 1974 the General summoned an extraordinary General Congregation. It was held partly at the insistence of the Pope and partly to comply with a decree of Vatican II on the renewal of religious life. Paul VI made it clear that he expected the Congregation to call the Society to order and obedience: the radicals must be brought to heel or dismissed from the Society. The decree of Vatican II had ordered all religious to submit themselves to an arduous process of study, self-criticism, and spiritual renewal. The authors of the decree hoped that all this would put an end to the Orders' excessive institutionalism, legalism and subjection to obsolete rules and customs and thus generate a new community spirit, a real democracy, and a genuine unity of mind and purpose. Hence almost every Order spent the decade after

1965 attending meetings, joining study groups, and endlessly discussing 'renewal'. Vatican II expected that each Order would round off the process with a solemn General Congregation. Arrupe had done his best to involve Jesuits in all this activity. The German and American Provinces had held endless seminars. Karl Rahner had been in great demand as a speaker. In the United States an Institute had been founded to research into the mind and intentions of Ignatius Loyola. The Provinces of California and Oregon employed a nun trained as a sociologist to help them carry out an intensive 'self study'. The report on the completed study was published in 1970. Its conclusions were depressing. The editor noted that:

> 'The basic problems we are currently experiencing in the Society stem from lack of agreement regarding the fundamental beliefs and rationales . . . underlying our . . . values, attitudes and practices relating to religious life . . .'

He concluded that the Society could not survive unless a real consensus were reached, and that this could only come as the result of a long and painful process of rethinking Jesuit life.

The General Congregation of 1974-5 was, like its predecessor of 1964-5, a failure. The Jesuits were still much too divided to be able to agree on any thoroughly effective new common line. One relatively small but influential minority was traditionalist, wanted no change at all and severe disciplinary action against liberalism. Another group wanted the Society to close its large and expensive Institutes, withdraw its men from salaried, professional posts in secular institutions, make its houses more monastic and its apostolate a purely spiritual one. Yet another group, strong in the Americas and with surprisingly large support in Europe, wanted to cut out academic pretensions and 'bourgeois occupations' and concentrate the Society on the fight for social justice and the gospel of Christian 'liberation' of the toiling masses. On the other hand the Society's intellectuals, headed by Bernard Lonergan and Karl Rahner, inclined to think that the Society, like the Church at large, must simply accept a 'life in the catacombs' in an era when life and religion must seem meaningless because of the death of the old European culture and the delayed birth of a new one to replace it. Rahner grimly envisaged the Society of the twenty first century as a group of tiny communes content merely to be Christian. Faced with this division of opinion the General Congregation eventually hammered out a modest list of reforms which was acceptable to all groups except the die-hard traditionalists. Paul VI then intervened angrily, forbidding almost any change in the Constitutions and rules. The traditionalists rejoiced at his intransigence: the General, the Congregation Fathers and the other Jesuit groups were deeply embarrassed and depressed.

Since the closure of the Congregation in 1975 the question of Jesuit reform and renewal has hung in the air unanswered. Some members of the Society have daringly suggested that there can be no answer so long as the Catholic Church remains dominated by a dictatorial Pope and Roman Curia and the Society tied hand and foot to their service. This seems to be a vain hope. In 1980 Rome and the close Jesuit connection with it remain virtually unchanged after two recent papal conclaves. The present Pope has more than once rebuked the Society for its liberals, its indiscipline and its departures from ancient norms in terms very reminiscent of Paul VI. Meanwhile, like Mr. Micawber, most Jesuits soldier on, hoping that something will turn up to get them off the horns of their dilemma.

A curious outsider who had tried to study their odd and tangled history is bound to feel a mixture of sympathy and puzzlement. Modern sociologists classify the Society as a 'Utopian organisation' and regard it as undoubtedly the most thorough-going, influential and impressive of its class. The successes and failures of large 'Utopian organisations' inevitably tend to be larger than life. They attempt great enterprises, even the apparently impossible, and sometimes achieve staggering successes. On the other hand they are very prone to fanaticism, 'double-think', over-institutionalism and violent internal dissensions. They take political revolutions, persecution and minor social changes in their stride, but find major intellectual and structural change impossible. Their domestic crises are often dramatic and sometimes squalid. The Society has all these characteristics in abundance. We can appreciate and share in the strong feelings of, say, Newman and von Hügel. They criticised it very sharply, held themselves aloof from it, but genuinely admired its good qualities and could not conceive of a Catholicism without it.

But an outsider is also bound to feel puzzled. The sociologists observe that all 'Utopian organisations' rely on myths and images to mould their members to a common outlook and discipline and to make a deep impact on the world outside. Some do this more intensively and self-consciously than others. The oldest religious Orders have had a much longer experience than the Jesuits. They have endured change, adversity, division and dissension repeatedly over the course of a good many centuries. Traditionalism and ancient myths and images die hard among them. But, on the whole, they have learned to live with their difficulties, to be agnostic about many of their traditional images, and pragmatic in their outlook. Hence they have tended to 'muddle through' periods of change, confusion of mind and decline fairly successfully. The Society, however, and all those many modern Orders and Congregations which have, consciously or unconsciously, grown up under its wing, seem much more straitly tied to one very particular and dated set of myths and images. As we have seen the Jesuits have always bred their own critics and dissidents. The great periods of growth for the Society and its survival through difficult times have been at least as much due to the originality and pragmatism of its grass roots as to its Generals, Jesuit discipline and the power of the Jesuit myth. In practice the Society has often 'muddled through' like ordinary mortals. But it has become so identified with its totalitarian myth and structure that the most emancipated of Jesuits cannot imagine how it could survive without these props.

Bibliography

A. GENERAL SOURCES

1. *Reference Books*

The most useful were: *Annuario Pontificio*, Rome (annual); *Dictionnaire de Droit Canonique* (Paris, 1935 ff.); *Dictionnaire d'Histoire et de Géographie Ecclésiastiques* (Paris, 1912 ff.); *Dictionnaire de Spiritualité Ascétique et Mystique* (Paris, 1937 ff.); *Dictionnaire de Théologie Catholique* (Paris, 1923 ff.); *Enciclopedia Cattolica* (Rome, 1929 ff.); *Enciclopedia Italiana* (Rome, 1921 ff.); *Lexicon für Theologie und Kirche* (Freiburg, 1957 ff.).

2. *Periodicals*

Archivum Historicum Societatis Jesu (Rome); *Catholic Historical Review; Church History, Concilium; Etudes; Herder Correspondence, Journal of Ecclesiastical History; The Month; Revue d'Ascétique et Mystique* (from 1972 *Revue d'Histoire de la Spiritualité*); *Revue d'Histoire de l'Eglise de France; Recusant History; The Tablet; Theological Studies; The Way* (supplements 3, 19, 20, 29, 30); *Woodstock Letters.*

3. *Published Collections of Documents*

Record Series (Catholic Record Society); *Constitutiones Societatis Jesu*, 1558 (and other documents; pirated Protestant edition, London, 1838); *Constitutions of the Society of Jesus*, ed. G. Ganss S.J. (St. Louis, 1970); *Records of the English Province S.J.*, ed. H. Foley S.J. (London, 1877-82); J. F. Gilmont S.J., *Les Ecrits Spirituels des Premiers Jésuites* (Rome, 1961: catalogue and synopses); *Gli Scritti di Ignazio de Loyola*, ed. M. Gioia S.J. (Turin, 1977); *Institutum Societatis Jesu* (Florence, 1893); *Jesuit Religious Life Today*, ed. G. Ganss S.J. (St. Louis, 1977); *Jesuit Relations in New France, 1610-1791*, ed. R. G. Thwaites (Cleveland, 1896 ff.); *Catalogo dei Gesuiti d'Italia, 1540-1565*, ed. M. Scaduto S.J. (Rome, 1968).

4. *General Histories of the Society*

H. Becher S.J., *Die Jesuiten: Gestalt und Geschichte des Ordens*

(München, 1951); H. Boehmer, *The Jesuits* (E. T., New York, 1975; sympathetic Lutheran view); J. Brodrick S.J., *The Origin of the Jesuits* (London, 1940) and *The Progress of the Jesuits* (London, 1946): only go to 1579; J. Crétineau-Joly, *Histoire Religieuse, Politique et Littéraire de la Compagnie de Jésus* (Paris, 1859, 6 volumes; very full and apologetic); R. Fulop Miller, *The Power and Secret of the Jesuits* (London, 1957); A. Guillermou, *Les Jésuites* (Paris, 1963).

5. *Histories of Jesuit Provinces*

Are numerous but almost all official, apologetic, antiquarian. I have used: B. Basset S.J., *The English Jesuits* (London, 1967); B. Duhr S.J., *Geschichte der Jesuiten in den Ländern Deutscher Zunge* (Munchen, 1907-28: goes to 1773); H. Fouqueray S.J., *Histoire de la Compagnie de Jésus en France, 1528-1762* (Paris, 1910-24); J. Burnichon S.J., *La Compagnie de Jésus en France, 1814-1914* (Paris, 1914-22); A. Poncelet S.J., *Histoire de la Compagnie . . . dans les Anciens Pays Bas* (Bruxelles, 1927: to 1773); P. Tacchi Venturi S.J., *Storia della Compagnia . . . in Italia* (Rome-Milan, 1931-51, only to 1556) continued by M. Scaduto S.J., *L'Epoca di Giacomo Lainez, 1556-65* (Rome, 1964); T. Hughes S.J., *History of the Society of Jesus in North America* (New York, 1907-17); G. Garraghan S.J., *The Jesuits of the Middle United States* (New York, 1938).

6. *Accounts by ex-Jesuits*

M. D. Petre, *Autobiography of George Tyrrell* (London, 1912) and *George Tyrrell's Letters* (London, 1929); H. von Hoensbroech, *Vierzehn Jahre Jesuit* (Leipzig, 1910); E. Boyd Barrett, *The Jesuit Enigma* (London, 1928); D. Meadows, *Obedient Men* (London, 1956).

B. SPECIALIST WORKS

1. *Ignatius Loyola*

J. Brodrick S.J., *St. Ignatius of Loyola: the Pilgrim Years, 1491-1538* (London, 1956); H. Boehmer, *Ignatius von Loyola* (Stuttgart, 1951); A. Guillermou, *St. Ignace de Loyola et la Compagnie de Jésus* (Paris, 1958), *Ignatius of Loyola: his Personality and Spiritual Heritage, 1556-1956*, ed. F. Wulf S.J. (E. T., St. Louis, 1978); J. Osuna S.J., *Friends in the Lord* (E. T., *The Way*, supplement 3, 1974); D. Knowles, *From Pachomius to Ignatius:*

the Constitutional History of the Religious Orders (New York, 1969).

2. *The Spiritual Exercises*

Annotated texts of the *Exercises* in English by Rickaby S.J., J. Morris S.J., and recently by T. Corbishley S.J. (Wheathampstead, 1963); S. Axters, *The Spirituality of the old Low Countries* (E. T., London, 1954); L. Cognet, *Introduction aux Mystiques Rheno-Flamands* (Paris, 1968) and *De la Devotion Moderne à la Spiritualité Française* (Paris, 1958); J. de Guibert S.J., *La Spiritualité de la Compagnie de Jésus* (Rome, 1953); H. O. Evennett, *The Spirit of the Counter-Reformation* (Cambridge, 1968); D. Fenlon, *Heresy and Obedience in Tridentine Italy* (Cambridge, 1972); F. von Hügel, *The Mystical Element in Religion as studied in St. Catherine of Genoa and her Friends* (London, 1909); A. Hyma, *The Christian Renaissance: a History of the Devotio Moderna* (Hamden, Connecticut, 1965); E. F. Jacob, *Brethren of the Common Life* in *Essays in the Conciliar Epoch* (Manchester, 1953); R. W. Southern, *Western Society and the Church in the Middle Ages* (London, 1970); J. Leclercq, *The Spirituality of St. Ignatius Loyola* (E. T., London, 1953); H. Rahner S.J., *St. Ignace de Loyola et la Génèse des Exercices* (Toulouse, 1948); H. Watrigant S.J., *La Méditation Methodique et l'Ecole des Frères de la Vie Commune* (*Revue d'Ascétique et Mystique* III, 1922, pp. 134 ff.), *La Méditation Methodique et Jean Mauburnus* (ibid., IV, 1923, pp. 13 ff.) and *La Génèse des Exercices de S. Ignace* (*Etudes*, LXXI, pp. 506 ff., LXXII, pp. 195 ff., LXXIII, pp. 199 ff.); J. Toussaert, *Le Sentiment Religieux en Flandre à la Fin du Moyen Age* (Paris, 1965); *The Pursuit of Holiness in Late Medieval and Renaissance Religion*, ed. C. Trinkhaus and H. A. Oberman (London, 1974); *The Works of St. John of the Cross*, ed. E. Allison Peers (London, 1934).

3. *Jesuit Education*

A. P. Farrell S.J., *The Jesuit Code of Liberal Education* (Milwaukee, 1938); *Monumenta Paedagogica Societatis Jesu*, ed. L. Lukacs S.J. (Rome, 1965-74). Philosophical and theological education: L. Willaert S.J., *Après le Concile de Trente, Histoire de l'Eglise, XVIII* (ed. A. Fliche and H. Martin, Paris, 1960); E. Hocedez S.J., *Histoire de la Théologie au XIXe. Siècle*. Jesuit seminaries for secular clergy: H. Watrigant S.J., *Les Exercices Spirituels et la Naissance des Seminaires* (Paris, 1912); P. Delattre S.J., *Les Etablissements des Jésuites en France depuis Quatre*

Siècles (Enghien, 1949-57) and *Les Jésuites et les Seminaires* (*Revue d'Ascétique et Mystique*, XX, 1953); M. E. Williams, *The Venerable English College, Rome: a History* (London, 1979). Jesuit Colleges: F. de Dainville S.J., *La Naissance de l'Humanisme Moderne* (Paris, 1940) and *L'education des Jésuites au XVIe. et XVIIe. Siècles* (Paris, 1978); G. Dupont-Ferrier, *Du Collège de Clermont au Lycée Louis-le Grand* (Paris, 1921-5); H. Chadwick S.J., *St. Omers to Stonyhurst* (London, 1962); P. Ariès, *L'Enfant et la Vie Familiale sous l'Ancien Régime* (Paris, 1973); J. W. Padberg S.J., *Colleges in Controversy: the Jesuit Schools in France from Revival to Suppression, 1815-80* (Harvard, 1969).

4. *Jesuit Casuistry and Confessional Practice*

L. Braekmans, *Confession et Communion au Moyen Age et au Concile de Trente* (Gembloux, 1971); T. N. Tentler, *Sin and Confession on the Eve of the Reformation* (Princeton, 1977); J. Bossy, *The Social History of Confession in the Age of the Reformation* (*Transactions of the Royal Historical Society*, 5th series, vol. 25, 1975); *The Counter-Reformation and the People of Catholic Europe* (*Past and Present*, 47, May 1970) and *Holiness and Society* (ibid., 75, May 1977); *Dictionnaire de Théologie Catholique* cit., articles: *Penitence du IVe. Concile du Latran à nos Jours, Laxisme, Péché, Probabilisme, Prudence, Satisfaction, Théologie*; B. Häring, *La Loi du Christ*, vol. I (Paris, 1960); J. T. Noonan, *Contraception* (New York, 1967); G. Guitton, *Le Père de la Chaize* (Paris, 1959).

5. *Jesuit dangerous missions*

In general: S. Delacroix, *Histoire Universelle des Missions Catholiques* (Paris, 1956-7); K. Latourette, *History of the Expansion of Christianity* (London, 1939); S. Neill, *History of Christian Missions* (London, 1977); C. R. Boxer, *The Church Militant and Iberian Expansion 1440-1770* (Baltimore, 1978). On the Portuguese sphere; J. Hemming, *Red Gold: the Conquest of the Brazilian Indians* (London, 1978); H. Dominian, *The Life of P. Jose Anchieta* (New York, 1958); C. R. Boxer, *The Golden Age of Brazil, 1695-1750* (Berkeley, 1967) and *A Great Luso-Brazilian Figure: Padre Vieira S.J.* (London, 1957); R. Chantal, *Prophétisme et Messianisme dans l'Oeuvre d'Antonio Vieira* (Paris, 1959); K. R. Maxwell, *Conflicts and Conspiracies in Brazil and Portugal, 1750-1808* (Cambridge, 1978); J. Brodrick S.J., *St. Francis Xavier* (London, 1952); C. R. Boxer, *The*

Christian Century in Japan, 1549-1600 (Berkeley, 1967); J. F. Schutte S.J., *Valignanos Missions grundsätze für Japan* (Rome, 1951-8); C. R. Boxer, *South China in the 16th Century* (London, 1953); G. H. Dunne S.J., *Generation of Giants: the First Jesuits in China* (London, 1962); R. Attwater, *Adam Schall: a Jesuit at the Court of China* (London, 1963); E. Maclagan, *The Jesuits and the Great Mogul* (London, 1932); V. Cronin, *A Pearl to India: the Life of Roberto de Nobili* (London, 1959); C. Wessels, *Early Jesuit Travellers in Central Asia, 1603-1721* (The Hague, 1924). On the Spanish sphere: P. Chaunu, *Conquête et Exploitation des Nouveaux Mondes* (Paris, 1969); R. Ricard, *The Spiritual Conquest of Mexico* (E. T., Berkeley, 1966); J. I. Israel, *Race, Class and Politics in Colonial Mexico, 1610-70* (Oxford, 1975); F. Chevalier, *La Formation des Grands Domaines au Mexique: Terre et Société aux XVIe. et XVIIe. Siècles* (Paris, 1952); F. C. Turner, *Catholicism and Political Development in Latin America* (Chapel Hill, 1971); H. F. Bolton, *A Padre on Horseback* (Chicago, 1963). On North America: M. Trudel, *The Beginnings of New France, 1524-1663* (E. T., Toronto, 1973); G. de Bonnault, *Histoire du Canada Française* (Paris, 1950); B. Capps, *The Great Chiefs* (Alexandria, Virginia, 1977). On northern and eastern Europe: O. Garstein, *Rome and the Counter-Reformation in Scandinavia* (Copenhagen, 1963); O. Halecki, *From Florence to Brest, 1439-1596* (Rome, 1958); A. Berga, *Pierre Skarga S.J.* (Paris, 1916); *Cambridge History of Poland*, ed. W. F. Reddaway (Cambridge, 1941-50); J. Brodrick S.J., *St. Peter Canisius* (London, 1935); J. B. Neveux, *Vie Spirituelle et Vie Sociale entre Rhin et Baltique au XVIIe. Siècle* (Paris, 1967). On the English Mission: H. More S.J., *Historia Missionis Anglicanae Societatis Jesu* (St. Omer, 1660); A. O. Meyer, *England and the Catholic Church under Queen Elizabeth* (E. T., London, 1967); *Letters and Memorials of . . . Robert Persons to 1588*, ed. L. Hicks S.J. (Catholic Record Society, vol. 39, 1942); H. J. Pollen S.J., *The Politics of English Catholics*, in *The Month* (March, 1902); A. J. Loomie S.J., *The Spanish Elizabethans* (Cambridge, Mass., 1965); J. Bossy, *The English Catholic Community, 1570-1850* (London, 1975) and *The Character of Elizabethan Catholicism* in *Crisis in Europe, 1560-1660*, ed. T. Ashton (London, 1965) and *The English Catholic Community, 1603-25* in *The Reign of . . . James I*, ed. A. G. R. Smith (London, 1963); T. H. Clancy S.J., *The Jesuits and the Independents, 1647* (*Archivum Historicum Soc. Jesu*, XL, 1971); P. Caraman S.J., *John Gerard* (London, 1956); *William Weston* (London,

1953); *Henry Morse* (London, 1966) and *Henry Garnet* (London, 1964); R. Simpson, *Edmund Campion* (London, 1867); C. Devlin S.J., *Robert Southwell* (London, 1956); *The Letter Book of Lewis Sabran S.J.*, ed. G. Holt S.J. (Catholic Record Society, vol. 62, 1970).

6. The Spanish Jesuit Dissidents

L. von Pastor, *History of the Popes* (E. T., London, 1928 ff.); G. Levy, *The Struggle for Constitutional Government in the Early Years of the Society of Jesus* (*Church History*, XXIX, 1960); A. Castro, *The Structure of Spanish History* (Princeton, 1954); R. Pike, *Aristocrats and Traders: Sevillian Society in the 16th Century* (Ithaca, 1972); R. L. Pridmore, *Cervantes* (London, 1973); H. Kamen, *The Spanish Inquisition* (London, 1965); J. H. Elliott, *Europe Divided, 1559-1598* (London, 1968) and *Imperial Spain, 1469-1716* (London, 1963).

7. The Jesuits and the Thirty Years War

H. Kamen, *The Iron Century* (London, 1971); *The Courts of Europe: Politics, Patronage and Royalty, 1400-1800*, ed. A. G. Dickens (London, 1977); H. F. Schwarz, *The Imperial Privy Council in the 17th Century* (Cambridge, Mass., 1943); C. V. Wedgwood, *The Thirty Years War* (London, 1950); J. F. N. Bradley, *Czechoslovakia: a Short History* (Edinburgh, 1971); G. Mann, *Wallenstein: His Life* (E. T., London, 1976); G. Benecke, *Society and Politics in Germany, 1500-1750* (London, 1974); E. Sagarra, *A Social History of Germany, 1648-1914* (London, 1977); L. Kolakowski, *Chrétiens sans Englise: la Conscience Religieuse et le Lien Confessionel au XVIIe. Siècle* (Paris, 1969).

8. The Jesuits in 17th Century France

R. Mandrou, *Introduction à la France Moderne, 1500-1640* (Paris, 1961); P. Broutin, *La Réforme Pastorale en France au XVIIe. Siècle* (Paris, 1956); H. Brémond, *Histoire Littéraire du Sentiment Religieux en France* (Paris, 1967); ed. J. Delumeau, *Histoire de la Diocèse de Rennes* (Paris, 1979); A. Latreille, *Histoire du Catholicisme en France* (Paris, 1960-2); R. Mousnier, *L'assassinat d'Henri IV* (Paris, 1964); A. L. Martin, *Henry III and the Jesuit Politicians* (Geneva, 1973); V. Kerns, *St. Margaret Mary: her Autobiography* (Westminster, Maryland, 1961); J. Delumeau, *Catholicism between Luther and Voltaire* (E. T., London, 1977);

J. Orcibal, *Le Cardinal de Bérulle: Evolution d'une Spiritualité* (Paris, 1965); J. Steinmann, *Pascal* (E. T., London, 1962); H. Lefebvre, *Pascal* (Paris, 1949-54); L. Cognet, *Le Jansénisme* (Paris, 1961); F. Coucel, *La Vie et les Oeuvres du P. Lallemant* (Paris, 1959); A. Huxley, *The Devils of Loudun* (London, 1952).

9. Jesuit Architecture and Theatre

F. Haskell, *Patrons and Painters: A Study in the Relations between Italian Art and Society in the Age of the Baroque* (London, 1963); E. Hempel, *Baroque Art and Architecture in Central Europe* (London, 1965); R. Wittkower and I. B. Jaffe, *Baroque Art: the Jesuit Contribution* (New York, 1972); J. Muller, *Das Jesuitendrama in den Ländern Deutscher Zunge vom Anfang (1555) bis zum Hochbarock (1660)* (Augsburg, 1930); J-M. Valentin, *Le Théâtre des Jésuites dans les Pays de Langue Allemande (1554-1680): Salut des Ames et Ordre des Cités* (Bern, 1978).

10. 18th Century Jesuits and the Suppression

M. Vovelle, *Pieté Baroque et Dechristianisation en Provence au XVIIIe. Siècle* (Paris, 1973); E. Preclin and E. Jarry, *Les Luttes Politiques et Doctinales aux XVIIe. et XVIIIe. Siècles* (*Histoire de l'Eglise*, ed. A. Fliche, vols. 19, 20, Paris, 1955-7); R. R. Palmer, *Catholics and Unbelievers in 18th Century France* (Princeton, 1939); F. Venturi, *Italy and the Enlightenment* (E. T., London, 1972); M. Picon-Salas, *A Cultural History of Spanish America* (E. T., Berkeley, 1963); A. Desautels S.J., *Les Mémoires de Trévoux et le Mouvement des Idées au XVIIIe. Siècle* (Rome, 1956); T. Besterman, *Voltaire* (Oxford, 1976); R. Hayman, *de Sade, a Critical Biography* (London, 1978); *The Expulsion of the Jesuits from Latin America*, ed. M. Morner (New York, 1965); P. Gay, *The Enlightenment: an Interpretation* (London, 1970); R. Shackleton, *Montesquieu: a Critical Biography* (Oxford, 1961); S. Smith S.J., *The Suppression of the Society of Jesus* (*The Month*, XCIX-CII, 1902-3).

11. The 19th Century Restored Society

C. J. Ligthart S.J., *The Return of the Jesuits* (New York, 1980); *The Christian Centuries, V, the Church in a Secularised Society*, ed. R. Aubert (E. T., London, 1978); R. Aubert, *Vatican I* (Paris, 1964); C. S. Phillips, *The Church in France, 1789-1848* (New York, 1966); J. McManners, *Church and State in France, 1870-1914* (London, 1972); A. Dansette, *Histoire Religieuse de la*

France Contemporaine (Paris, 1965); M. Larkin, *Church and State after the Dreyfus Affair* (London, 1974); R. Griffiths, *The Reactionary Revolution: the Catholic Revival in French Literature, 1870-1914* (London, 1966). On Italy: H. L. Hughes, *The Catholic Revival in Italy, 1815-1915* (London, 1935); C. R. Letham, *Luigi Gentili* (London, 1965); V. Gioberti, *Il Gesuita Moderno* (Lausanne, 1846); Quirinus, *Letters from Rome on the Council* (London, 1870); R. Aubert, *Le Pontificat de Pie IX* (Paris, 1963); E. Soderini, *The Pontificate of Leo XIII* (E. T., London, 1934-5). On Germany: A. Dru, *The Contribution of German Catholicism* (New York, 1963); *Memoirs of Prince Chlodwig of Hohenlohe Schillingfuerst*, ed. F. Curtius (E. T., London, 1906); O. Chadwick, *Catholicism and History* (Cambridge, 1978). On England: M. Trevor, *Prophets and Guardians: Renewal and Tradition in the Church* (London, 1969); J. G. Snead Cox, *Life of Cardinal Herbert Vaughan* (London, 1911); V. A. McClelland, *Cardinal Manning* (London, 1962); J. H. Newman, *Letters and Diaries*, ed. C. S. Dessain (London, 1961 ff.); *Newman the Oratorian: His unpublished Oratory Papers*, ed. P. Murray O.S.B. (Dublin, 1969); *Bishops and Writers: Aspects of the Evolution of Modern English Catholicism*, ed. A. Hastings (Wheathampstead, 1977); Lord Acton, *The History of Freedom and Other Essays* (London, 1907); *The Letters of Lord Acton to Mary Gladstone*, ed. H. Paul (London, 1904); R. L. Schuettinger, *Lord Acton: Historian of Liberty* (La Salle, 1976); A. Thomas S.J., *Hopkins the Jesuit* (London, 1969). L. Hocedez S.J., *Histoire de la Théologie au au XIXe. Siècle* (Paris, 1947-8); M. Trouncer, *Charles de Foucauld* (London, 1937); J. Marshall-Cornwall, *Foch as a Military Commander* (London, 1972); T. B. Macaulay, *Historical Essays contributed to the Edinburgh Review* (Oxford, 1936); A. Hamon S.J., *Histoire de la Devotion au Sacré-Coeur* (Paris, 1930-2); A. Poulain S.J., *Des Graces d'Oraison* (Paris, 1919); H. Delehaye S.J., *L'Oeuvre des Bollandistes à travers Trois Siècles* (Louvain, 1959).

12. *Jesuit 'friends' and connections*

On Sodalities and Congregations: R. Mendizabel, *Liber Congregationum Aggregatarum, 1587-1829* (Rome, 1957); E. Villaret S.J., *Les Congregations Mariales* (Paris, 1947); articles *Congregations Mariales* and *Congregations Secrétes* in *Dictionnaire de Spiritualité Ascétique et Mystique*; J. Duhr, *La Confrérie dans la Vie de l'Eglise* (*Revue d'Histoire Ecclesiastique*, 1939, pp. 437 ff.).

On Jesuit influences on women religious: H. Rahner S.J., *St. Ignatius' Letters to Women* (E. T., New York, 1958); P. Guilday, *English Catholic Refugees on the Continent, 1558-1795* (London, 1914); M. C. E. Chambers, *Life of Mary Ward* (London, 1882); L. Hicks S.J., *Mary Ward's Great Enterprise* (*The Month*, CLI, CLII, 1928-9); J. Grisar S.J., *Die Ersten Anklegen in Rom gegen das Institut Maria Wards* (Rome, 1959); J. B. Richter, *Currents of Spirituality in 18th Century France: Nuns, Sisters and Philosophes* (Univ. of Wisconsin Ph.D. thesis, 1972); A. Rayez S.J., *Clorivière et ses Fondations* (*Revue d'Histoire de l'Eglise de France*, LIV, 1968); Anon., *Emilie d'Outremont, Baroness d'Hooghevorst* (London, 1932); Anon., *Life and Work of Mother Mary St. Ignatius, Foundress of the Congregation of Jesus and Mary* (London, 1955); Anon., *Life of Cornelia Connelly, Foundress of the Society of the Holy Child Jesus* (London, 1922); J. Wadham, *The Case of Cornelia Connelly* (London, 1956); R. Laurentin, *Thérèse de Lisieux: Mythes et Realité* (Paris, 1972); H. Thurston S.J., *Beauraing and Other Apparitions* (London, 1934); C. R. Boxer, *Mary and Misogyny: Women in Iberian Expansion Overseas, 1415-1815* (London, 1975); G. L. Sheil, *Mother F. A. Forbes: Religious of the Sacred Heart* (London, 1946); *The Medical Missionaries of Mary*, ed. M. Martin (Dublin, 1962).

13. *The Modernist Crisis*

J. Ratte, *Three Modernists: Loisy, Tyrrell, Sullivan* (London, 1968); M. Ranchetti, *The Catholic Modernists, 1864-1907* (E. T., London, 1969); H. Barmann S.J., *Baron von Hügel and the Modernist Crisis in England* (Cambridge, 1971); G. Tyrrell, *Medievalism* (London, 1908); T. M. Loome, *Liberal Catholicism — Reform Catholicism — Modernism* (Grunewald, 1979); M. Petre, *My Way of Faith* (London, 1936).

14. *Jesuits, 1914-1945*

C. Falconi, *The Popes in the 20th Century* (E. T., London, 1967); A. Rhodes, *The Vatican in the Age of the Dictators, 1922-45* (London, 1973); P. Nichols, *The Politics of the Vatican* (London, 1968); J. R. Glorney Bolton, *Roman Century, 1870-1970* (London, 1970); M. and E. Lukas, *Teilhard: a Biography* (London, 1977); R. Speaight, *Georges Bernanos* (London, 1971); *Teilhard de Chardin: Letters to Leontine Zanta*, ed. R. Gaine and H. de Lubac S.J., (E. T., London, 1967); *Teilhard de Chardin: Letters to Two Friends, 1926-52* (E. T., London, 1970); H. de Lubac S.J., *The*

Religion of Teilhard de Chardin (E. T., London, 1967) and *The Eternal Feminine* (E. T., London, 1971); H. de Lubac S.J., *Catholicisme* (Paris, 1938); J-R. Tournoux, *Sons of France: Petain and de Gaulle* (E. T., New York, 1964); E. Weber, *Action Française, Royalism and Reaction in 20th Century France* (Stanford, 1962); A. Dansette, *Le Destin du Catholicisme Française, 1926-56* (Paris, 1957); H. R. Kedward, *Resistance in Vichy France* (Oxford, 1978); H. Michel, *Histoire de la Résistance en France* (Paris, 1972); J. Lebreton, *Le Père Léonce de Grand-maison* (Parison, 1932); A. Valensin S.J., *Textes et Documents Inédits* (Paris, 1961); Henri Perrin, *Priest and Worker* (E. T., London, 1965). E. R. Tannenbaum, *The Fascist Experience: Italian Society and Culture, 1922-45* (New York, 1972); R. A. Webster, *The Cross and the Fasces* (Stanford, 1960); Pope John XXIII, *Journal of a Soul* (E. T., London, 1965). G. Levy, *The Catholic Church and Nazi Germany* (New York, 1964); G. C. Zahn, *German Catholics and Hitler's Wars* (London, 1963); P. Hoffmann, *History of the German Resistance, 1933-45* (E. T., London, 1977); H. C. Deutsch, *The Conspiracy against Hitler in the Twilight War* (Minneapolis, 1968); V. Conzemius, *L'Eglise Chrétienne et Totalitarianisme National Socialiste* (*Revue d'Histoire Ecclesiastique* LXIII, 1968, 2/3); *The Persecution of the Catholic Church in the Third Reich* (E. T., London, 1942). J. Devlin, *Spanish Anticlericalism: A Study in Modern Alienation* (New York, 1966); B. Welles, *Spain: a Gentle Anarchy* (London, 1965); *Spain in Crisis: the Evolution and Decline of the Franco Regime*, ed. P. Preston (Hassocks, 1976). *The Two Voices: Spiritual Conferences of R. H. J. Steuart*, ed. C. C. Martindale S.J. (London, 1952); T. O'Rahilly, *Life of Father Willie Doyle S.J.* (Dublin, 1922).

15. *Jesuits, 1945-80*

E. Poulat, *La Naissance des Prêtres Ouvriers* (Paris, 1965); K. Rahner S.J., *Free Speech in the Church* (E. T., New York, 1959) and *Opportunities for Faith* (E. T., London, 1974); T. Roberts S.J., *Black Popes: Authority, its Use and Abuse* (London, 1954) and *Contraception and Holiness* (with others, New York, 1964); J. L. Segundo S.J., *A Theology for Artisans of a New Humanity* (New York, 1973); D. Berrigan S.J., *No Bars to Manhood* (New York, 1970); H. Rondet S.J., *Gratia Christi* (Paris, 1948); H. de Lubac S.J., *L'Eglise dans la Crise Actuelle* (Paris, 1969); X. Rynne, *Letters from Vatican City* (London, 1963-6); W. Bosworth, *Catholicism and Crisis in Modern France*

(Princeton, 1962); F. du P. Gray, *Divine Disobedience: Profiles in Catholic Radicalism* (London, 1970); H. Küng, *Infallible?* (E. T., London, 1971); *Hans Küng: His Work and his Way*, ed. H. Häring and K. J. Kuschel (E. T., London, 1979); *Introducing the Thoughts of Bernard Lonergan*, ed. P. McShane (London, 1973); B. Lonergan S.J., *A Second Collection* (London, 1974); *The Way*, Supplements 29, 30, *The 32nd General Congregation, 1974-5*; M. Turk, *The Buried Life: a Nun's Journey* (London, 1972); C. Hollis, *The Seven Ages* (London, 1974); G. Reimer, *The New Jesuits* (Boston, 1971); M. Martin, *The Encounter: Religions in Crisis* (London, 1970); G. W. Hughes S.J., *In Search of a Way* (Rome, 1978); H. R. F. Ebaugh, *Out of the Cloister: a Study of Organisational Dilemmas* (Austin, Texas, 1977); *Changing Perspectives in the Scientific Study of Religion*, ed. H. W. Eister (New York, 1974); T. Franck, *The Exploding Church* (London, 1968); P. Hebblethwaite, *The Runaway Church* (London, 1975), *The Year of Three Popes* (London, 1978) and *The New Inquisition* (London, 1980); A. M. Greeley, *The Making of the Popes* (London, 1979).

16. Jesuits in Literature

In general: C. Sommervogel, *Bibliothèque des Ecrivains de la Compagnie de Jésus* (Paris-Bruxelles, 1890 ff.); J-L. Prévost, *Le Prêtre, ce Heros de Roman* (Paris, 1952); A. Blanchet, *Le Prêtre dans le Roman d'aujourd'hui* (Paris, 1955); P. Bert, *Le Clericalisme* (Paris, 1900); M. Tillet, *Stendhal: the Background to the Novels* (London, 1971); H. J. Hunt, *Balzac's Comédie Humaine* (London, 1959); N. Atkinson, *Eugéne Sue et le Roman Feuilleton* (Paris, 1929); R. Carr, *Anarchism in France: the Case of Octave Mirbeau* (Manchester, 1977); R. A. Levine, *Benjamin Disraeli* (New York, 1968); F. W. J. Hemmings, *Emile Zola* (Oxford, 1966); J. Cornuz, *Jules Michelet* (Geneva, 1955); K. Mochulsky, *Dostoevsky: his Life and Work* (Princeton, 1967); M. Maison, *Search your Soul, Eustace: Victorian Religious Novels* (London, 1961); R. L. Wolff, *Gains and Losses: Novels of Faith and Doubt in Victorian England* (London, 1977); *Aubrey's Brief Lives*, ed. O. L. Dick (London, 1949); Duc de Saint-Simon, *Historical Memoirs* (E. T., London, 1967); Denis Diderot, *Encyclopédie*, ed. J. Lough (Paris, 1976); F. M. Brodie, The *Devil Drives: life of Sir Richard Burton* (London, 1971); *Charles Kingsley: His Letters and Memories of his Life*, ed. by his wife (London, 1878); E. Longford, *A Pilgrimage of Passion: life of Wilfrid Scawen Blunt* (London, 1979); T. L. Conolly, *Francis*

Thompson (Milwaukee, 1946); P. Julian, *Oscar Wilde* (E. T., London, 1969); M. J. Benkowitz, *Frederick Rolfe, Baron Corvo* (London, 1977); R. Gittings, *Young Thomas Hardy* (London, 1978); W. H. Gardner, *Gerard Manley Hopkins* (London, 1961); Antonia White, *The Hound and the Falcon* (London, 1969); M. Esslin, *Brecht: a Choice of Evils* (London, 1959); C. Sykes, *Evelyn Waugh* (London, 1975); *Letters of James Joyce*, ed. R. Ellmann (London, 1968); R. J. North, *Le Catholicisme dans l'oeuvre de François Mauriac* (Paris, 1950).

Novels, short stories and plays featuring Jesuits: Kingsley Amis, *The Alteration* (1978); Charlotte Bronte, *Villette* (1853); John Buchan, *Castle Gay* (1920); Anthony Burgess, *Earthly Powers* (1980); W. Blatty, *The Exorcist* (1972); Berthold Brecht, *Galileo* (1938); Paul Claudel, *Le Soulier de Satin* (1923); John Donne, *Pseudo-Martyr* (1610) and *Ignatius His Conclave* (1610); Denis Diderot, *The Nun* (1766); Charles Dickens, *Pictures from Italy* (1853); B. Disraeli, *Henrietta Temple* (1837) and *Lothair* (1870); Ferdinand Fabre, *Lucifer* (1870); Thomas Hardy, *The Laodicean* (1881); Aldous Huxley, *After Many a Summer* (1924) and *The Devils of Loudun* (1952); Jack Higgins, *Day of Judgement* (1976); Mrs. Elizabeth Inchbald, *A Simple Story* (1791); James Joyce, *A Portrait of the Artist as a Young Man* (1916); Charles Kingsley, *Westward Ho* (1855); J. Michelet, *Les Jésuites* (lectures, Paris, 1844); Prosper Merimée, *Les Faux Demétrius* (1852); Octave Mirbeau, *Sebastien Roch* (1890); Thomas Mann, *Der Zauberberg* (1924); Mary McCarthy, *Memories of a Catholic Girlhood* (1957); François Mauriac, *Le Noeud de Viperes* (1933), *Le Feu sur la Terre* (1951), and *Paroles Catholiques* (1954); Somerset Maugham, *Don Fernando* (1950); J. H. Newman, *Loss and Gain* (1874); Blaise Pascal, *Les Provinciales* (1658), and *Pensées* (1966); Marcel Prévost, *Le Scorpion* (1887); Roger Peyrefitte, *Les Clés de Saint Pierre* (1954); Frederick Rolfe, *Hadrian VII* (1904) and *The Stories Toto Told me* (1901); Marquis de Sade, *La Philosophie dans le Boudoir* (1794); Stendhal (Henri Beyle), *La Chartreuse de Palme* (1839); Eugene Sue, *Le Juif Errant* (1845); J. Shorthouse, *John Inglesant* (1885); R. L. Stevenson, *Across the Plains* (1894); Muriel Spark, *The Abbess of Crewe* (1974); W. M. Thackeray, *The History of Henry Esmond* (1850); Voltaire, *Candide* (1759), *Le Jésuite Berthier* (1759), and *L'Ingénu* (1767); Mrs. Humphrey Ward, *Helbeck of Bannisdale* (1898); Evelyn Waugh, *Vile Bodies* (1930) and *Edmund Campion* (1935); Antonia White, *Frost in May* (1933); Emile Zola, *Lourdes* (1894) and *Rome* (1896); John Gallahue, *The Jesuit* (1973).

Index

Blatty, William, 48
Blondel, Maurice, 325, 337, 360
Bobadilla, Nicholas, Jesuit, 31,
  61, 121, 124, 125, 131, 163
Bobola, Andrew, Jesuit Saint,
  348
Boehmer, Heinrich, 17, 189
Bohololec, Franz, ex-Jesuit, 290
Bollandists, 269–70, 291, 338
Bordeaux, 216, 246
Borgia, Francis, Jesuit General
  and Saint, 63, 92, 111–2,
  116–8, 121, 123–4, 127ff.,
  131–3, 137, 195, 222
Borromeo, Carlo, Archbishop,
  129, 131, 135, 203, 232
Boscovich, Giuseppe Ruggiero,
  ex-Jesuit, 268, 289
Bossuet, Jacques Bénigne,
  bishop, 259
Boyer, Charles, Jesuit, 359, 362,
  366, 369
Boynes, Norbert de, Jesuit, 359
Brecht, Berthold, 24, 45–6, 189,
  329–31
Brémond, Henri, ex-Jesuit, 31,
  189–90, 329–30, 338, 340,
  343
Bresciani, Antonio, Jesuit, 28–9,
  315
Brodrick, James, Jesuit, 32
Bröet, Pasquier, Jesuit, 104, 121
Brooke, Adam, Jesuit, 159
Brzozowski, Raymond, Jesuit,
  299
Brzozowski, Tadeusz, Jesuit
  General, 297ff., 301ff.
Buck, Charles de, Jesuit, 323
Buffon, Georges-Louis, Comte
  de, 259
Bülow, Bernhard von, 322
Burton, Sir Richard, 145, 189

Bye, Father de, ex-Jesuit, 291

Caceres, Lope de, 76
Calderon, Pedro de la Barca, 47
Camara, Luis, Gonçalves da,
  Jesuit, 196
Campanella, Tomas, Dominican,
  237
Campion, Edmund, Jesuit Saint,
  135, 148, 155–6
Campion Hall, Oxford, 1, 4, 14
Cano, Melchior, Dominican, 107
Capuchin Order, 136, 177, 207,
  224, 230–1, 235, 243, 285,
  298
Caroll, John, ex-Jesuit, bishop,
  271, 291, 297
Castelnau, General de, 329, 331
Catherine II, Empress of Russia,
  274, 286
Caussin, Nicholas, Jesuit, 226,
  244
Cenacle, Religious of the, 300,
  307
Centurioni, Aloysius, Jesuit
  General, 277
Cervantes Saavedra, Miguel de,
  141
Chaillet, Pierre, Jesuit, 358
Champion, Pierre, Jesuit, 248
Charles, Pierre, Jesuit, 337–5,
  343, 350–1, 354
Charles II of England, 251
Charles III of Spain, 258, 281ff.
Chateaubriand, François René
  de, 291
Cheminot, Didier, Jesuit, 237,
  244
Choiseul, Etienne-François, Duc
  de, 259, 283
Christina, Queen of Sweden,
  261

Jesuits *(continued)*
301, 314–5, 349, 357, 365–7;
Mariology, Jesuit, 353–4;
Modernism, 332ff.; Mussolini
and Fascism, 347ff.; Name
'Jesuit', origins of, 20;
Obedience, religious, 119ff.;
Oblates, 234; *Opus Dei*, 348,
362; Politics, 160–1, 228ff.,
236ffff.; Poverty religious,
117ff., 130, 220; 'Reductions'
in Central America, 275ff.;
Restoration Brief (1814), 287,
294, 296; Scientists, Jesuit,
180–1, 188; Secular Institutes,
362; Spirituality, Jesuit, 81ff.,
246ff., 306ff.; 'Spirituals',
Jesuit, 132, 246–7, 306ff.;
Statistics of the Society,
(1556–1580) 106–7, 126ff.,
134, (1615) 198, 222, (1681)
250; (1681–1773) 256, 282,
289, (1814) 294, (1829) 298,
(1847) 304, (1853–87) 315,
(1903) 326, (1925–39) 346–7,
349, (1939–62) 355, (1970s)
365; Theatre, Jesuit, 29–30,
215; Theologians, Jesuit, 143,
202ff, 320, 324–5, 337–8,
362–3; World War I, 344ff.;
World War II, 356ff.;
Witchcraft, 227; Vatican I,
320; Vatican II, 362–3; Words,
Jesuit, 18ff.; Women, Nuns,
Sisters and the Society, 66f.,
234–5, 236, 284, 300, 305–7,
313, 320, 327, 332
John XXIII, Pope, 327, 362
John Casimir, King of Poland,
ex-Jesuit, 225
John of the Cross, Saint, 87, 93,
141
Joyce, James, 18, 22, 44–5, 329

Jungmann, Josef Andreas, Jesuit,
350–1, 360, 362

Kanis (Canisius), Pieter, Jesuit,
58, 62, 105, 107, 115, 130–1,
133–4, 137, 141, 148–9,
153–4, 202, 348
Kennedy, Grace, 44
Kenny, Peter, Jesuit, 294–5
Kepler, Johannes, 158, 246
Kino, Eusebio, Jesuit, 262
Kircher, Athanasius, Jesuit, 161,
170, 180, 189
Klau (Clavius), Christopher,
Jesuit, 58, 143, 152, 180–1,
188, 199, 212, 216
Kleutgen, Josef, Jesuits, 318, 320
Knabenhauer, Josef, Jesuit, 321
Kniaznin, F.D., ex-Jesuit, 321
Knowles, David, Benedictine, 15
Kostka, Stanislas, Jesuit saint, 55
Küng, Hans, 361

Labadie, Jean, ex-Jesuit, 248
La Chaise, François d'Aix de,
Jesuit, 251
Lallement, Louis, Jesuit, 189–90,
246–8
Lamartine, Alphonse-Marie-
Louis, 24
Lamennais, Felicité de, 299, 304
Lamormaini, Wilhelm, Jesuit,
226ff., 228, 235, 237, 245
Langdale, Thomas, ex-Jesuit,
157
La Rochefoucauld, Duc de, 259
La Salette, 56, 319–20, 360
Lattre de Tassigny, de, General,
329, 331–2
Laughton, Charles, 329–30